Royal Flying Corps 1915–1916

Uniform with this volume

Royal Air Force

Communiques 1918

ROYAL FLYING CORPS COMMUNIQUES 1915 - 1916

Edited by
Christopher Cole

TOM DONOVAN
LONDON

ISBN: 1–871085–03–9

PUBLISHED BY
TOM DONOVAN PUBLISHING LTD
52 WILLOW ROAD
HAMPSTEAD
LONDON NW3 1TP

PRINTED BY BOOKCRAFT (BATH) LTD

Contents

Illustrations

Acknowledgements

The Royal Air Force Communiques are Crown Copyright, and thanks are due to the Controller of Her Britannic Majesty's Stationery Office for permission to publish extracts in this form.

Thanks are also due to Mr Leonard Bridgman for the wash drawings of R.A.F. aircraft. For help in providing photographic material acknowledgement is gratefully made to The Ministry of Defence, Mr Frank Cheesman, The Imperial War Museum, the *Musée de l'Air*, and the J. M. Bruce/G. S. Leslie Collection.

Introduction

This book is not intended to be a history of the Royal Flying Corps nor of the first war in the air. Those subjects have already been covered by various authors.

It is, rather, a complementary reference to such works, presenting for the first time what might be termed some of the raw material, the day by day activities of the British aircrews and squadrons operating in the major theatre of the First World War, as originally recorded by the R.F.C. Headquarters staff.

Any rapidly expanding organisation sooner or later reaches a point where its component units become out of touch with the overall aims and achievements. Enthusiasm, efficiency and morale can obviously be raised if this situation is remedied. By the summer of 1915 the Royal Flying Corps had substantially expanded from the handful of reconnaissance squadrons which flew to war the previous year, and Headquarters therefore decided to produce for internal consumption regular communiqués covering the main activities. Based on squadron combat reports and other operational returns, the communiqués presented each day's situation as understood at the time. They were produced quickly, without the benefit of any detailed news from the enemy side, and for this reason some of the information given should clearly be regarded as an assessment rather than established fact. This applies in particular to reports of enemy aircraft losses in combat and bomb damage to enemy installations.

The communiqués relate only to R.F.C. operations on the Western Front, and do not cover activities in other theatres or the work of the Royal Naval Air Service.

The war had been in progress for nearly a year when the first communiqué was issued, and a brief outline of the earlier R.F.C. period may therefore be useful to some readers.

British military aeronautics began in 1878, with War Office sponsorship for ballooning experiments at Woolwich. In 1906 the Government financed research into heavier-than-air machines, but because of the high cost withdrew their support three years later—just before Blériot's cross-channel flight of 1909 underlined the military potential of the aeroplane. Official interest was revived in 1910, when privately-owned aeroplanes took part in Army manoeuvres, and in 1911 the various military activities were concentrated into the Air Battalion of the Royal Engineers. On May 13, 1912, the operational value of aircraft was recognised by the establishment of the Royal Flying Corps.

The carefully selected officers and men of the R.F.C. viewed with enthusiasm the wide spectrum presented by the new medium of warfare. They instituted a research programme into the many aspects of war in the air and conducted trials with machine-gun installations, wireless telegraphy, bombing and night flying. The R.F.C's awareness of the possibilities is evident in this passage from a training manual produced a few months before the outbreak of war:

> It is probable that one phase of the struggle for the command of the air will resolve itself into a series of combats between individual aeroplanes or pairs of aeroplanes. If the pilots of one side can succeed in obtaining victory in a succession of such combats, they will establish a moral ascendancy over the surviving pilots of the enemy, and be left free to carry out their duties of reconnaissance. The actual tactics adopted must depend on the types of the aeroplanes engaged, the object of the pilot being to obtain for his passenger the free use of his own weapon while denying to the enemy the use of his. To disable the pilot of the opposing aeroplane will be the first object. In the case of fast reconnaissance aeroplanes it will often be advisable to avoid fighting . . .

Yet not one aircraft in the four squadrons which flew to France in August 1914 was equipped for air fighting. No individuals or organisation can fairly be blamed for this state of affairs, and the main reason was simply the impossibility of working miracles in a short time. If the best products of the infant aircraft industry—plus the best designs of the Government Royal Aircraft Factory, Farnborough—could have been put into rapid production, if every good idea and suggested technical advance had been immediately accepted by officials gifted with foresight bordering on genius and if unlimited money had been available, things would have been very different. But at that stage of aviation development it is idle to pretend that events could have proceeded in such a fashion. Fortunately the German air organisation—although larger—was no better equipped.

Other factors contributed to the military shortcomings. Despite the enlightened pre-war experimental work of the R.F.C. the essential function of the military aeroplane was still regarded as reconnaissance, with all other applications assuming a lesser importance. This resulted in a natural tendency to concentrate on developing a good, all-round and reliable aeroplane that flew well. It was generally assumed that the aircraft must be a two-seater, and the Royal Aircraft Factory B.E.2 series met these requirements admirably. The Farnborough designers placed great stress on stability, and the superbly stable B.E.2c development of May, 1914, was selected for large-scale production. In later service the

B.E.2c's stability was a disadvantage in combat and the inadequate provision for armament rendered it very vulnerable. The heavy losses stimulated violent criticism of the whole Farnborough organisation, and many of the critics chose to ignore other excellent Farnborough designs which helped to give the R.F.C. a definite superiority as they appeared.

For fighting duties the Factory had developed a pusher design, with the engine and propeller placed behind the crew nacelle to give the observer-air gunner at the front a wide field of fire. Orders were also placed for a Vickers machine of similar layout, the F.B.5 Gunbus.

Two highly promising single-seaters had emanated from Farnborough—the S.E.2 and the S.E.4, capable of 92 and 130 m.p.h. respectively—but these aircraft were not considered as potential fighters because there was no adequate means of fitting a machine-gun to be used by the pilot. Such aircraft were regarded as scouts, for high-speed reconnaissance work.

All the Farnborough designs were known by initial letters according to their category. B.E. indicated Blériot Experimental, meaning an aircraft of the tractor type with engine and propeller at the front, as favoured by the famous French pioneer. S.E. originally stood for Santos Experimental, meaning a 'canard' or tail-first type—as designed by the Brazilian, Santos Dumont—but was later used for the Scouting Experimental series. The F.E., or Farman Experimental, class followed the pusher layout, popularised by the French Farman products. The R.E. designation was self-explanatory, meaning Reconnaissance Experimental.

Most of the 63 aeroplanes flown to France in August 1914 were two-seaters—B.E.2s, B.E.8s, Blériots, Farmans and Avros—capable of speeds between 60 and 80 m.p.h. There were four Sopwith Tabloid single-seat scouts, which had a top speed of 92 m.p.h., and none of the machines was armed.

Brigadier-General Sir David Henderson took command of the R.F.C. in France, and the first reconnaissance flights were made on August 19. During the retreat from Mons, the battles of the Marne, the Aisne and Ypres, aircraft performed valuable services in this role. First attempts at photographic reconnaissance with makeshift equipment in September were promising, and by March 1915 a specially designed air camera was in use. Wireless telegraphy was fitted to a few aircraft from the early weeks of the war, but for some months most of the signalling from observation machines to the artillery was by Very lights and electric lamps. An efficient lightweight wireless-transmitting set was in general use by the autumn of 1915.

Organised bombing sorties by the R.F.C. began in March 1915, with the object of delaying enemy reinforcements for the battle of Neuve Chapelle. The first Victoria Cross for air operations was posthumously awarded to Lieutenant W. B. Rhodes-Moorhouse, for gallantry during a bombing attack on April 26.

The R.F.C. communiqués were predominantly devoted to air combat, and it is therefore necessary to trace in more detail the development of the aeroplane as a fighting machine.

Neither of the pusher fighters—the Farnborough-designed F.C.2 and the Vickers F.B.5 Gunbus—was ready for delivery at the outbreak of war. In September 1914 machine-guns were fitted to a few of No. 4 Squadron's Farmans, but these aircraft were far too slow to be of real value. Observers in the reconnaissance two-seaters optimistically carried rifles and the pilots their revolvers. The fast single-seaters, although not used for their intended 'scouting' duties and despite their lack of armament, proved a useful deterrent to enemy aerial incursions. The Sopwith Tabloids were joined by other aircraft of the scout category—Martinsydes, Bristols, French Morane-Saulniers and the solitary S.E.2.

Squadrons were quick to appreciate that the scout's value could be enhanced by the addition of some form of armament, and various expedients were adopted. The most common was the fitting of a Lewis machine-gun to the fuselage side, angled to fire forwards clear of the propeller. This made aiming very difficult. Rifles were sometimes mounted in this way, and the S.E.2 had the additional refinement of a fitted revolver holster. In various ways a few aircraft on both sides were forced down.

The first of the Vickers Gunbus two-seaters arrived at the Front in February 1915, and the larger, more powerful F.E.2a in May, but like the single-seater scouts, these were distributed among the existing squadrons for escort work.

The initial struggle for air superiority began in the autumn of 1915 and was won by Germany, which produced the first effective fighting aeroplane. By this time it was accepted that the tractor aircraft generally possessed better performance than pusher types, and there was a strong school of thought which believed—rightly as it proved—that best results could be achieved by aiming the aircraft, fitted with a fixed forward gun, at its target rather than by using a free gun. A French attempt to produce an aircraft which could fight in this way employed a crude system of steel plates fitted to the propeller to deflect any stray bullets which would have otherwise damaged the blades. Working on a captured specimen, the German Fokker company rapidly developed a mechanical interrupter gear which stopped the gun from firing when a propeller blade passed in front of the gun muzzle. The Fokker EI monoplane armed in this way, which entered service in July 1915, possessed no particular merit as an aircraft, but its highly effective armament gave it a tremendous advantage.

In mid-1915 the most widely used general-purpose aircraft in the R.F.C. was the tractor B.E.2c, in which the observer occupied the forward cockpit. Gun brackets were mounted at various points, but the field of fire was severely limited and the man-handling of the gun from one mount to another presented further difficulties. Fixed guns to fire forwards at an angle were sometimes fitted as well, but generally the B.E.2c stood little chance against a determined Fokker pilot. At about the same time some of the British scouts were improved by mounting the gun on the top wing, to fire above the propeller.

On the German side, where most of the flying units were originally placed under control of the Army's railway and transport organisation, evolution had been broadly similar to that in the R.F.C. The early B-type reconnaissance biplanes and Taube monoplanes were mostly unarmed, but the C-series which followed usually had the observer-air gunner's cockpit more sensibly located behind the pilot. The basic German air unit was the *Feldflieger Abteilung* (Field Flying Section) with the role of reconnaissance. The first Fokkers were attached to these units in ones and twos, but as production increased local German commanders unofficially grouped them into fighter 'commandos' and they began to take heavy toll of British and French aircraft. Boelcke and Immelmann, two of the earliest German 'aces', were originally with Fl Abt 62, and later served together in one of these fighter commandos.

Allied losses steadily increased and in January 1916 R.F.C. Headquarters instructed that every reconnaissance aircraft must be escorted by at least three others. It was now apparent that without an adequate fighter force no other daylight activities of the air arm could be effectively mounted. Early in 1916 the first full squadrons of F.E.2bs and D.H.2 fighting scouts arrived at the Front and the position began to improve. No British interrupter gear was available and the D.H.2 was therefore a pusher design. The French introduced the tractor Nieuport, with a gun mounted on the top wing, and a few specimens of this excellent machine were supplied to the R.F.C. All these aircraft could out-perform the Fokker, and as more squadrons went into action the 'Fokker scourge' was eliminated by the spring.

Other good new aircraft types followed—the Martinsyde Elephant scout and the Sopwith 1½-Strutter two-seater—and in due course the various single-seaters attached to the general-purpose squadrons were withdrawn to form new homogeneous fighter units. When the Somme battle opened on July 1, 1916, the R.F.C. had regained a clear air superiority. Unfortunately this was not to last for long, and again it was an advance in fighter design which swung the battle in the enemy's favour.

Realising that the Fokker monoplanes were outdated, the designers of the German Fokker, Halberstadt and Albatros firms produced more powerful fighters, with greater speeds and higher rates of climb. By the end of the year large numbers were in service and many of them were equipped with two synchronised machine-guns. The Albatros, introduced in August, was an outstanding machine which may be regarded as one of the great aircraft of World War I. With the introduction of these new fighters, completely outclassing the R.F.C. pushers, came major changes in the German air organisation. Most significant was the formation of specialist fighter squadrons, or Jagstadffeln. The first two were established in August and others quickly followed. On October 8 the whole of the German air organisation was placed under centralised control.

To help restore the balance a Royal Naval Air Service squadron was deployed to the Western Front. This was equipped with the Sopwith Pup—unquestionably the best contemporary British fighting scout—which possessed excellent manoeuvrability and could outfly the Albatros at high altitudes. It was, however, often unable to fully exploit this advantage, possessing only a single synchronised machine-gun.

Brigadier-General H. M. Trenchard, who had taken command of the R.F.C. in August 1915, was fully aware of the dangerous situation facing the British squadrons at the end of 1916, and had repeatedly urged the War Office to expedite supplies of new aircraft. In all the combatant nations the search for better performance was being vigorously pursued in the aircraft and engine design offices. The air commanders knew that whoever possessed the best aircraft would hold the initiative. Although Britain had for the second time fallen behind the enemy, promising new fighter and bomber prototypes were under test and the outlook was not one of unrelieved gloom.

The first of the great fighter 'aces' emerged during the period of these communiqués. The early successes of Albert Ball and the first combat victory of James McCudden were reported in the summer of 1916. The two leading Germans, Boelcke and Immelmann, were killed during the year, but the pilot who was to amass the highest victory score on either side—von Richthofen—was as yet unknown to the world.

25 – 27 July, 1915

This first communiqué, produced to circulate within the Royal Flying Corps items of general interest and value, was a modest document, type-written and rolled off on an office duplicating machine. Nearly three years later, when the R.F.C. and the Royal Naval Air Service were amalgamated to form the Royal Air Force, the communiqués had grown ten-fold in size and were produced in printed form. Communiqué No. 1 mentions five squadrons. In 1918 the activities of more than fifty were frequently reported.

Fittingly the first communiqué opened with an account of a combat for which Capt L. G. Hawker, 6 Sqn, was awarded the Victoria Cross. It was later established that he had shot down two enemy aircraft, and not only one as the first account suggested. His aircraft was armed with a single Lewis machine-gun fitted above the top wing. Hawker's V.C. was the first awarded for air fighting.

On the same day the arrival at the Front of the first real fighting squadron was reported. This was 11 Sqn, completely equipped with the Vickers FB 5 Gunbus.

COMMUNIQUÉ NO. 1

Combats in the air

On the 25th July, Capt Hawker in a Bristol Scout attacked two hostile machines; one at Passchendaele at 6 p.m. and one over Houthulst Forest at 6.20 p.m. Both machines dived to escape. Capt Hawker then climbed to 11,000 feet and at 7 p.m. saw a hostile machine being fired at by anti-aircraft guns at about 10,000 feet over Hooge. Approaching down-sun Capt Hawker opened fire at about 100 yards range. The hostile machine burst into flames and turned upside down, the observer falling out. The machine and pilot crashed to earth south-east of Zillebeke in our lines.

In front of the IIIrd Army area a machine of 4 Sqn, proceeding on reconnaissance, met and pursued a hostile machine. The latter met another machine of 4 Sqn piloted by Lt Weir, observer Lt Hankin, who opened fire on it. At the same time a second German machine came up and joined in the fight. Eventually both German machines dived, apparently undamaged, in order to escape.

On the 26th, Capt Carthew, D.S.O., and Capt Milne (2 Sqn), on a B.E.2c, and Lt Yule, and 2 Lt James (7 Sqn), on a Voisin had encounters with hostile machines, both of which were driven off.

Bomb dropping

On the 26th inst., Capt Hubbard (3 Sqn), on a Morane, obtained a direct hit with a 20-pound Hale's bomb from a height of 7,000 feet on a house at *T.30.b.*=7, Sheet 36. Capt Hubbard was using a Blackburn bomb sight.

Arrivals

On the 25th instant, 10 machines (B.E.2cs) of 10 Sqn and two complete flights (Vickers Fighters) of 11 Sqn arrived at G.H.Q.

One pilot started from Netheravon for Folkestone and was fired at by anti-aircraft guns at Southend-on-Thames. He turned north and is reported to have landed and broken his propellor at Felixstowe.

Zeppelins

At 10.30 a.m. on the 27th, the officer commanding the Flying School at Le Crotoy reported a Zeppelin 5 miles west of Le Crotoy flying in a northerly direction. Machines varying from a Maurice Farman to a Bristol Scout were despatched to intercept the raider. No further reports have been received.

Artillery co-operation

On the 26th instant, Capt Barratt and Lt Summers (3 Sqn), located a hostile anti-aircraft gun firing at them. This anti-aircraft gun was engaged by the 10th Siege Battery and several direct hits were recorded on its position.

On the same date, Lts Hanlon and Nichols located, engaged and silenced two anti-aircraft guns. Most of the shots are recorded as having fallen within a radius of 10 yards from the anti-aircraft guns.

General

It is proposed to issue a communiqué of all items of interest in connection with the Royal Flying Corps twice weekly. If brief details of items of interest are included in the daily summaries of work rendered by Wing Commanders, it will considerably assist in making this communiqué of interest and value.

26–31 July, 1915

During the early part of the war the German Air Force operated a few unarmed Fokker M5 monoplanes on reconnaissance and scouting duties, but this communiqué made what was obviously the first reference to the new EI model fitted with interrupter gear enabling a machine-gun to be fired forward between the propeller blades.

The first Fokker EI was demonstrated to German squadrons in May, and about a dozen were in use by mid-July.

The De Havilland scout mentioned on 29 July was presumably the prototype of the D.H.2, sent to the Front for evaluation trials. It was to enter service in 1916 and played an important part in the defeat of the Fokkers.

Various versions of the Voisin pushers were used by the French air force throughout the war, but the R.F.C. operated a few only during the first year of hostilities.

The exchange of messages dropped from the air, seeking and offering news of casualties, was common practice in the early years of World War I. It illustrates the bond which existed between the aviators of all nations, regardless of hostilities.

COMMUNIQUÉ NO. 2

Combats in the air

On the 26th July, near Roulers, Lt Bell Irving, 1 Sqn, on a Bristol Scout was attacked by a German machine, which had the appearance of a very small L.V.G. It was armed with a machine-gun.

On the 27th July, Lt D. L. Allen and 2 Lt Peck, 7 Sqn. on a Voisin encountered a small hostile tractor somewhat resembling a Bristol Scout —light brown colour.

The black crosses on the top of his planes were painted within a white ring. The German followed up the Voisin firing a signal of silvery stars, apparently to anti-aircraft guns. When challenged the German declined battle and sheered off into a cloud.

On the 28th July, Capt Strange and Capt Braddyll, 6 Sqn, on a F.E. while getting height observed a hostile machine, an Aviatik, in the act of attacking a B.E.2c.

The F.E. got as close as possible under the German and opened fire, chasing him as far as Passchendaele, when owing to engine trouble the chase had to be abandoned. The Aviatik dived and disappeared towards Roulers.

On the 29th July, 2 Lts Strugnell and Anderson, 1 Sqn, encountered four hostile machines south-east of Lille.

Three of the machines were of the Scout type—with planes similar to the Bristol Scout.

On the 29th July, Capt Smith and Lt Davis, 2 Sqn, on a B.E.2c when on a photographic reconnaissance observed Capt Hearson engaged with a Fokker over Seclin.

Capt Smith attacked the monoplane which dived and was lost to view.

Capt Hearson and Lt Marshall on a B.E.2c on July 29th attacked a Fokker armed with a machine-gun, over Seclin.

The German was driven off, Capt Smith joining in the pursuit. During this reconnaissance (photographic) two other Fokker monoplanes were attacked and driven down by Capt Hearson.

On 29th July, Capt Strange and Lt Braddyll, on an F.E. at 10,000 feet observed an Albatros at 8,000 feet over Hooge.

Capt Strange dived to attack and the Albatros dived, followed by the F.E. firing, and was last seen about 2,000 feet near Staden. On climbing to 8,000 feet an Aviatik was seen at about 11,000 feet over Boesinghe. The F.E. met and attacked it returning over Vlamertinghe. 300 rounds were fired at it from almost vertically underneath, but without apparent damage. Owing to lack of petrol the F.E. could not follow. Capt Strange advances the following theory:

> From the above narrative, it appears quite possible that the Albatros came up with the sole object of drawing the F.E. down to enable the Aviatik to carry out its reconnaissence.
>
> If this is so, it achieved a double purpose, for the Aviatik was able to do its reconnaissance and the F.E. was drawn down and over the anti-aircraft guns. The reason for the above supposition being that the weather conditions had been unfavourable in the early morning, owing to the fog, and were at the time becoming so again, owing to clouds. Consequently the Aviatik had to do its reconnaisance at that time or not at all, and it would appear quite probable that the Albatros was sent out first to attract the attention of our fighting machines.

On the 29th July, Capt Pike on a De Havilland Scout attacked a very large Aviatik—probably the new big machine, with a gun mounted for firing over the pilot's head. He reported as follows:

> I saw a German machine about 3 miles away and rapidly overhauled him. He had no idea of the speed of my machine, and attempted to evade me by climbing. I caught him up and fired a drum at him from about 100 to 80 yards.
>
> I then turned to reload and found the clip on the drum had stuck. I lost sight of the German while struggling with the drum, but heard his machine-gun going until his belt had finished.

On July 29th, Capt Reese and Capt Kennedy, 4 Sqn, in a Vickers fighter attacked a Fokker, which was at the time following a B.S. When attacked the German made a steep spiral descent, firing at the Vickers when vertically underneath it. He eventually descended at the Cambrai aerodrome. The Vickers was hit in the lower plane—the bullet passing through both main spars, cutting two bracing wires and breaking one rib.

On the 29th July, 2 Lt Mitchell, 4 Sqn, met a large tractor biplane rather similar to an R.E. with extensions on the top planes, small tail plane, wings either swept back a little or a slight dihedral. This machine out-climbed the Scout and made off in the direction of Cambrai without being engaged.

On July 29th, Capt Vaughan and 2 Lt Lawes, 4 Sqn, on a B.E.2c were followed and attacked by a tractor biplane with square tipped wings and mounting a machine-gun. The hostile machine was eventually driven off without suffering damage.

Hostile machines

The machine brought down by Capt Hawker on the 25th inst. was a large Albatros. It struck the ground upside down and burnt for a quarter of an hour. Only the wing tips, undercarriage, engine, and tail plane were recognisable. It could not be ascertained if wireless had been fitted.

The frame of the tail plane, elevators, rudder, fin, and back half of the longerons were steel. Span of tail plane about 12 feet. Main spar and ribs of the wings were wood with steel struts.

Undercarriage usual 'V' type, with a heavy axle fitted with a brake in the middle.

The engine was badly damaged by contact with the ground, and by fire. The stroke seemed exceptionally long. The engine is thought to be a 150 horsepower Mercedes. It had two carburettors and two magnetos. A pair of Zeiss glasses, magnifying power 8, were found on the pilot; also a map showing the position of three hostile heavy batteries, and a copy of the *Kolnische Zeitung* of the 25th inst.

Artillery co-operation

2 Lt Reid with Lt Russell, 2 Sqn, obtained a direct hit in a gun emplacement when registering for the 10th Battery.

Capt Collins and Lt Sweet registering for 3rd Bde, obtained two direct hits on and set on fire a portion of the enemy's works.

On the 28th July, a machine of 1 Sqn directed battery fire on an ammunition column. A direct hit blew up the depot.

Miscellaneous

On July 28th at 11.30 p.m. a hostile aeroplane dropped eight bombs on St. Omer. The machine flew very low, about 900 feet. Three civilians were killed, otherwise the damage was negligible. Before dropping bombs the German fired a light blue light, and a white light breaking into small white stars when he had dropped all his bombs. His engine was particularly noisy.

On the 30th July, a hostile aeroplane flew over St. Omer at 7.0 a.m. and dropped two bombs. One fell in the Rue Carnoy. There was no loss of life.

A German aeroplane dropped the following message in the Belgian lines, on the 29th July:

> *For the English Royal Flying Corps.*
>
> *The officer you asked for (13th) was dead wenn coming down. The bombes are the answer for last night, in which we had much pleasure. Were the German officers dead who came down the 25th near Hooge.*

The first part of the message probably refers to Capt James, 6 Sqn. The latter refers to the two brought down by Capt Hawker.

31 July – 4 August, 1915

This communiqué describes another action which won the Victoria Cross. Capt U. A. Liddell, 7 Sqn, was awarded the V.C. for bringing back his badly damaged R.E.5 after the combat of 31 July. He was seriously wounded and died a month later.

The Avro 504 is best remembered as a trainer aircraft and only a few were employed operationally. The entry on 31 July suggests that 1 Sqn had recently adopted a new armament installation. Further armament progress is indicated by the reference to a 6 Sqn F.E. fitted with two Lewis guns.

COMMUNIQUÉ NO. 3

Combats in the air

On the 31st July, 2 Lt Learmount, and 2 Lt Watkins of 7 Sqn, on a Voisin on two occasions encountered a German tractor biplane with covered in fuselage, armed with a machine-gun firing to the rear. The German showed little fight.

On the 31st July, Lts Mansfield and Braddyl, 6 Sqn, on a F.E. were attacked by a large fast Albatros, which retreated shortly after fire was opened from the F.E.

On the 31st July, Capt Hawker of 6 Sqn, on a Bristol Scout attacked a large Albatros near Houthulst Forest. The Scout rapidly overhauled the German and got above him. Owing to the Lewis gun jamming, the chase had to be abandoned.

On the 31st July, Capt Spratt, 7 Sqn, on a Bristol Scout met and attacked a hostile tractor biplane with covered in fuselage, straight wings with modified type ailerons, slight extensions to upper planes, and usual German empanage. The German declined battle and dived to his aerodrome, firing at the Scout from behind and shooting away the right rear centre strut.

On the 31st July, 2 Lt Filley and Lt Jacks, 1 Sqn, on an Avro encountered two Aviatiks, driving both off. 2 Lt Filley reports that the fixed Lewis gun proved extremely satisfactory.

On the 1st August, Capt Rees and Lt Lane, 11 Sqn, in a Vickers fighter twice attempted to attack a hostile biplane. The enemy declined fight on both occasions.

On July 31st, Capt Liddell, and 2 Lt Peck, 7 Sqn, on a R.E.5 were attacked by a tractor biplane, with covered-in fuselage, similar to a Bristol Scout but at least twice as large, with crosses on both lower planes. It was armed with a machine-gun and had a speed of about 90 m.p.h. Shortly after leaving Ostend during the morning reconnaissance the R.E.5 sighted the hostile machine when crossing the lines some miles away to the south-east. The R.E.5 was flying at about 5,000 feet and the German machine was several thousand feet higher. The reconnaissance was continued with and the hostile machine was finally lost sight of. When near Bruges the R.E.5 was heavily fired on from above but the occupants could obtain no view of the enemy. A little later they were able to get a glimpse of him and the observer was able to fire one drum of ammunition at him which caused him to withdraw. 2 Lt Peck had just reloaded when his machine nose dived and then turned completely over when all the remaining ammunition fell out. The pilot had apparently momentarily lost consciousness, but regained control of the machine after dropping 3,000 feet. Capt Liddell then handed the observer a message stating that his leg was broken and that he proposed landing on the sands west of Nieuport as he could not steer sufficiently to land in enclosed country. Lt Peck then pointed out the aerodrome near Furnes and the pilot, working the rudder control with his hand by holding the cable, was able to land. He was unable to throttle his engine down owing to the throttle control being shot away, but switched off shortly before reaching the ground.

On the 1st August, Capt Barratt and Lt Cleaver, 3 Sqn, in a Morane-Saulnier Parasol, chased and drove off an Aviatik. When over the trenches this machine fired a white light which broke into stars. The machine was faster than the Morane. On the same day these two officers were attacked by a Fokker monoplane and drove it off.

On August 2nd a hostile machine was sighted at 6.30 a.m. and 2 Lts Gay and Hardie of 16 Sqn, left the ground in pursuit on a B.E.2c. They were attacked when over the Bois de Biez and the hostile machine was engaged at close range. He retired towards Lille losing height. The observer appeared to be using an automatic rifle. Iron crosses were painted on the top planes in a white or light blue circle.

Capt Hawker and Lt Payze, 6 Sqn, on a F.E. armed with two Lewis guns encountered two German machines of the Albatros type ranging with Very's lights at about 7,000 feet. The F.E. dived at the nearest and fired 2½ drums at about 150 to 200 yards range. No. 1 dived steeply and the F.E. attacked and fired at No. 2 who dived home firing two red Very's lights. Later an Aviatik appeared but on being fired at vanished in the clouds.

From other information received it seems probable that one of these machines was brought down in close proximity to the German trenches near Wolverghem.

Miscellaneous

Extract from reconnaissance report of 1st August

Major Richey and Major Smith report that while over Peronne a series of rockets were sent up apparently from four holders. The height of these rockets shewed a gradual increase, possibly an attempt at ranging anti-aircraft guns on the machine, as anti-aircraft fire was fairly intense at the time. The rockets were white and ended in a white star.

2–12 August, 1915

Little is recorded about the disposition of the early Halberstadt single-seater scouts used by the German air force, and many authorities date their introduction later in 1915 or early 1916. During the air fighting of 1915 fairly frequent mention is made of enemy biplane scouts, but descriptions are too vague to attempt any reliable identification.

COMMUNIQUÉ NO. 4

Combats in the air

On the 2nd August, whilst photographing a portion of the Hooge district, 2 Lt Cooper-King and 2 Lt Leggatt on a B.E.2c were attacked by a German machine of the Albatros type carrying one machine-gun. The enemy was driven off in the direction of Houthulst Forest.

Capt Hawker on the same date in a Bristol Scout, armed with a Lewis gun, attacked and drove off one machine over Langemarck which was thought to be a Halberstadt Scout. He then approached a second machine coming towards Hooge which either decided to give battle or did not observe the Bristol Scout which obtained a favourable position at a range of about 100 yards. Unfortunately the machine-gun jammed and the German opened fire. The Bristol turned for home pursued by the German which proved to be a scout, so the Bristol nose dived through the clouds. After getting the gun in working order again, Capt Hawker resumed the attack and finally, after two further indecisive attacks he remained patrolling over Ypres owing to lack of ammunition, until the German went home.

On the 9th August, Lt Grey Edwards and Lt Leggatt on a F.E. sighted and engaged a German machine resembling a Fokker and drove the enemy off.

Airships

The Zeppelin which attacked Dover on the night of the 9th/10th appears to have been completely wrecked.

A signal was received by the R.N.A.S. at 8.15 a.m. on the morning of the 10th to the effect that a damaged Zeppelin was being towed towards Ostend. Flt Cmdr Smyth-Pygott on a B.E.2c proceeded towards Ostend and observed a Zeppelin just above water three miles out to sea and apparently in the process of being hauled down. He glided to 500 feet and dropped two 20-pound bombs, then retreated into the clouds and prepared for a second attack. Turning, and coming down to 500 feet again, he noticed the rear compartment but one to be broken, apparently not due to a direct hit, but from the concussion of one of the 20-pound bombs, the mark of which was observed on the water alongside. The Zeppelin was surrounded by four T.B.D.s which opened heavy machine-gun fire.

Later, Flt Sub-Lt Besson left on a Bristol Scout for Ostend and saw the Zeppelin being towed between the harbour piers. From a height of 1,500 feet he attacked with four 20-pound bombs and observed the first bomb to fall about 30 yards on the west side of the objective. The Zeppelin appeared to be badly crushed in the rear half.

Flt Lt Bettington then proceeded on a Bristol Scout, approaching Ostend at 2,000 feet in clouds and came out nearly over the Zeppelin. He saw kites about his level, apparently endeavouring to foul him. He dropped six grenades, two 20-pound bombs and then six more grenades, apparently straddling the target, though, on turning away, the Zeppelin appeared in the same position as before.

Flt Sub-Lt Leslie in a Henry Farman flew over Ostend at a height of 9,000 feet, obtaining a good view of the Zeppelin which was half on the pier and half in the water. He dropped seven 20-pound bombs at a height of 8,000 feet. There was a crowd of workmen surrounding the wreck but on the appearance of the hostile machine they disappeared. Owing to the thickness of the black smoke from anti-aircraft shells, observation was carried out with the greatest difficulty.

Later, the Zeppelin was observed to be hauled up on the quay. Her back was broken and the rear half appeared to be pointing into the air. Groups of workmen were on the quay by the side of the airship. Flt Sub-Lt Buss on an Avro dropped four bombs on the target, and when next observed, the Zeppelin was apparently in the water again.

Towards evening, Flt Sub-Lt Besson, when flying over Ostend in a Nieuport, observed that the Zeppelin had the rear half in the water and the remainder was covered by the smoke of a big oil flare burning by the side.

On the morning of the 11th the remains of the Zeppelin had been dismantled and taken away.

Artillery work

On August 9th, an aeroplane of 5 Sqn engaged a train in Langemarck station with two heavy batteries. The train was cut in half, the engine and some coaches escaped, but there was a big explosion in one of the remaining trucks and some of them were set on fire.

During the attack on Hooge on August 9th four German batteries were silenced as a result of observations from one machine of 6 Sqn.

11–19 August, 1915

Despite the official assessment, it is doubtful whether the Fokker monoplane attacked by Capt Hawker and Lt Clifton, 7 Sqn, was in fact damaged. The Fokker was very manoeuvrable, and could be dived steeply with great confidence.

COMMUNIQUÉ NO. 5

Combats in the air

On the 11th instant, Capt Hawker and Lt Clifton on an F.E. had a series of combats. They first attacked and drove off an Albatros over Houthem, and then were confronted by two Halberstadt Scouts and an Albatros over Polygon Wood which kept them engaged for 20 minutes. At the end of this time the three hostile machines retired. They then attacked an Aviatik over Houthem and left it in a nose dive. Between Lille and Roubaix at 9,000 feet, they were attacked by a very fast Scout monoplane which tried to get behind their machine. However, Capt Hawker turned sharply and the Scout crossed about 50 feet in front and then made a vertical nose dive. From reports received it appears that it was hit.

Capt Moore and 2 Lt Peck on a R.E. whilst returning from reconnaissance in clouds on the 14th instant, suddenly heard the report of a machine-gun firing and on looking up observed a German machine about 1,000 feet above them. A forced landing had to be made at Houteavesnes owing to the induction pipe being pierced. 2 Lt Cooper King and 2 Lt Leggatt sighted and attacked a hostile aeroplane over Hooge, driving off the enemy in the direction of Coucou.

Capt Collins and Lt Davis (2 Sqn), on the 12th August engaged and silenced an anti-aircraft gun. Lt Hanlon with 19th Siege and 35th Heavy Batteries directed fire on to four battery positions, silencing one.

2 Lt Mond and Lt Hyde on the 13th of August observed a large white cross laid out on the ground at Beaucoups. On passing over, the cross was replaced by an arrow head pointing in the direction in which their machine was going. The first signal is apparently an indication to German aeroplanes that all is clear and the second, an indication of the direction of the hostile machine.

On the night of the 17th three Zeppelins were reported over various parts of the East Coast of England.

18–25 August, 1915

In the early days of the Fokker monoplane it was not infrequently confused with the Morane Bullet, though there were many detailed differences. Graham Gilmour, who encountered a Fokker on 18 August, was a well-known pre-war pilot, who had learned to fly in 1910.

The 'Parasol Fokker' referred to could have been one of the AI type artillery spotters—which was of shoulder wing configuration rather than parasol—or a Pfalz AI or EIII. The latter types were very similar to a pre-war Morane design.

COMMUNIQUÉ NO. 6

Combats in the air

On the 18th August, 1915, 2 Lt Grey and 1 AM Nicholls on a Vickers Fighter when near Boesinghe at a height of 11,000 feet, saw an Albatros going South from Houthulst Forest, about 9,000 feet high. By diving, Lt Grey got within 300 yards of the German and then fired one drum of ammunition. The German dived and opened fire on the Vickers but the chase had to be given up as the hostile machine got too low. The machine was hit in several places by fire from the enemy's guns.

On the 19th August, 2 Lt Kelway Bamber and 2 Lt E. W. Leggatt on a B.E.2c whilst over Lille at 8,000 feet met and engaged a hostile aeroplane. They fired most of their ammunition off and drove it away, when a second appeared, but being short of ammunition they decided to return home.

On the 22nd August, Capt Read on a Bristol Scout came up to a machine ('Aviatik') over Boesinghe and although noticing that it had a red, white, and blue rudder he decided to get nearer as he did not recognise the type. He did not realise that it was a hostile machine until he was fired on. The Aviatik retired over Houthulst Forest.

On the same date, Lt. Graham Gilmour and 1 AM Buckerfield, when flying over Ypres on a Vickers, met a German monoplane (Fokker) flying westward. At first the observer mistaking the machine for a Morane did not fire but later he got an opportunity and fired half a drum of ammunition when a jam occurred. The Fokker dived almost vertically, flattened out and dived again but was apparently undamaged.

Again on the 22nd, Lt Cooper King, in response to a wireless call, went up on a Bristol Scout and when over Boesinghe observed a hostile machine and gave chase. The German then turned and made off in the direction of Houthem, but after a few minutes a second hostile machine appeared and they both came back towards Ypres. The Scout had reloaded and when about 150 yards from the enemy, dived at him but the gun jammed and it was impossible to put it into working order in the air. The Scout being defenceless, returned to the aerodrome.

On this same day Lt Leather and Lt Davis, on a B.E.2c while photographing between Seclin and Lille encountered a Parasol-Fokker. The machine-gun was hit almost immediately and consequently jammed but they managed to complete their work. From the damage done to the machine it would appear that steel-cored bullets were used.

On the 23rd, 2 Lt Scholefield, on instructions received from the IIIrd Wing, left the aerodrome on a Bristol Scout to intercept a hostile machine reported near Albert going north. He came across the machine about 2 miles north of the town mentioned and gave chase opening on the enemy with the Lewis gun; then the machines manoeuvred and fired at one another for several minutes. 2 Lt Scholefield found he was being drawn to the vicinity of Peronne and as his height was now about 3,000 feet he turned towards Albert. When near that place he saw the hostile machine coming north. He waited for it, emptied his last drum and returned home.

Artillery Observation

Lt Gower and Lt Inglis when doing observation for a French battery on the 22nd, engaged and silenced a hostile A.A. gun.

25–29 August, 1915

No definite claim was made for the sinking of the enemy submarine attacked by Sqn Cdr A. W. Bigsworth with 65-pound bombs on 26 August.

The combat fought by Captain Lombridge and Lt Greenwood in a B.E.2c on the same date illustrates virtue being made out of necessity. The B.E. had no forward gun, and the observer, standing in front of the pilot, did his best by switching his gun to various mounting brackets.

The Martinsyde flown by Lt Cooper-King was an S1 single-seater scout. Usually armed with a Lewis gun firing over the top wing, the S1 had been in use since the end of 1914, had an indifferent performance and was by this time obsolescent.

COMMUNIQUÉ NO. 7

August 25th

Lt Cooper-King and 2 Lt E. W. Leggatt set out on a F.E. armed with two machine-guns. When over Polygon Wood at a height of 11,400 feet, the pilot saw a hostile biplane over Hooge and dived to 7,200 feet, getting within 100 yards of the enemy. Both machine-guns were fired simultaneously and the German aeroplane was seen to dive, turning in the direction of Menin. A small puff of blue smoke was observed in the hostile machine and from this and other indications it was apparently hit.

Capt P. H. L. Playfair and Lt J. Semlyn Jones on a Vickers, armed with a Lewis gun, when patrolling near Bertrancourt, sighted a German crossing the lines at Sailly-au-Bois. The observer opened fire at 300 yards and the enemy replied by firing long continuous groups. Our machine was struck, the right rear main bottom spar being shot through and the cylinder damaged.

August 26th

Sqn Cdr Bigsworth in a Henri Farman proceeded at 6,000 feet over Nieuport heading seaward, and when about 4 miles out to sea he sighted a submarine and made towards it. When over the target he made a spiral descent coming down to 500 feet. During this time the submarine, having first fired two rockets which appeared to be a signal to the shore batteries to open fire on the aeroplane, as shells were observed pitching into the sea, commenced zigzagging in all directions. The pilot dropped three bombs over the target which was temporarily hidden from view by flames and smoke. For a moment the machine was partly out of control due to the concussion of the exploding bombs but the pilot managed to right it and then turned to observe the effect. All that remained was a small portion of what appeared to be the bow of the submarine pointing straight out of the water. Sqn Cmdr Bigsworth was then attacked by a big sea-plane, but being unarmed he was forced to return.

Lt Greenwood and Capt Lombridge in a B.E.2c, whilst engaged in taking photographs over Haubourdin were attacked by a German machine which approached from behind and dived underneath them opening fire with a machine-gun from below. It then circled round and behind, evidently to fit a new drum to the machine-gun. As the hostile machine returned the observer opened fire from the stern mounting. The German returned to the fight and passed across the left bow, evidently thinking that our gun could only be fired from the rear mounting, but the observer had in the meantime changed the gun to the front mounting and so was able to keep the hostile machine under fire until it flew away.

August 27th

2 Lt Shield and Lt Leeson, while over Lille, observed a small Scout machine coming towards them. They gave chase to the enemy and after having expended one drum of ammunition succeeded in driving the German machine away.

2 Lt Collis and Lt G. A. Parker on a B.E.2c when flying over Ypres attacked and chased an Aviatik which, upon being fired at, dived and appeared to land. A second machine, a German Scout, attacked them near Hooge and, hitting the wireless set, succeeded in breaking it. After a good deal of ammunition had been expended the German machine flew away towards Roulers.

Lt Cooper-King on a Martinsyde, seeing a German machine in the direction of Houthulst, gave chase and opened fire at about 200 yards distance, the enemy replying with his machine-gun. After discharging one drum of ammunition the Martinsyde turned away to change it and tried at the same time to get higher. In the meantime the enemy also climbed higher at a slightly greater rate, and a further encounter took place at about 9,200 feet up. When the Martinsyde ran out of ammunition it returned to the aerodrome, the enemy being last seen flying towards home.

August 28th

Lt Neale and Lt Lane, on a Vickers Fighter while on patrol near Hebuterne, observed a Fokker monoplane over the lines and gave chase whereupon the enemy's aeroplane beat a hasty retreat.

1—B.E.2C—90 H.P. RAF 1A ENGINE

Descended from the original B.E.1 produced by the Royal Aircraft Factory in 1911 and from the early B.E.2's which accompanied the British Expeditionary Force to France in 1914, the B.E.2c was first used in France early in 1915. The first squadron to be completely equipped with the B.E.2c was No. 8 which went overseas on April 15, 1915. The B.E.2c was largely used for reconnaissance and corps work but owing to its poor defence it was one of the principal victims of the Fokker 'scourge' in 1915–16. Twelve B.E.2c squadrons took part in the Battle of the Somme in 1916.

Lt Collier and 2 Lt Summers, on a Morane whilst out on photographic duties, met a hostile aeroplane over Givenchy and for about 20 minutes were engaged in active combat. At the end of this time the enemy retired and the observer finished taking the photographs required.

2 Lt Harrison-Mitchell and Lt Minchin chased an Aviatik from the east of Peronne towards Cambrai and fired a drum of ammunition at the machine. The observer was able to take steady aim and probably hit some part of the hostile machine as it descended slowly towards the ground.

2 Lt Ridley and 2 Lt Cleaver in a Morane Parasol saw an Aviatik near La Bassee and gave chase. For 20 minutes it circled over the enemy's 'Archie' and then made off towards Lille, where, owing to it being faster than our machine, it was lost sight of. They were then attacked by two large fighting bi-planes about 1,000 feet above them, fired 1½ drums of ammunition away and, as it was getting dark, the pilot turned for home, the enemy aeroplane following as far as the trenches.

28 August – 5 September, 1915

Apart from several inconclusive air combats, this was a week of little activity.

COMMUNIQUÉ NO. 8

August 28th

2 Lt Collis and Lt Parker when on a B.E.2c carrying out artillery registration near Hooge, saw a hostile machine coming to attack them from the direction of Roulers. Turning to meet it, they fired fifty rounds and then manoeuvred round again to get into a more favourable position. Having expended most of their ammunition, a wireless message was sent for a Scout to come out, but on firing the last few rounds, the German machine dived steeply.

The observer then signalled to say that the German had gone.

The registration was continued, and was interrupted twice by hostile machines which, however, when approached shewed no fight.

August 31st

2 Lt Fairbairn and 2 Lt James, when near Douai, while carrying out a distant reconnaissance on a B.E.2c, saw a German machine below them, and diving, came within 100 yards of the enemy.

The observer fired one drum, and seeing the German observer fall away from his gun, presumed him to be hit. The chase was given up at 5,500 feet, as the engine was missing badly.

Capt Rees and Flt Sgt Hargreaves on a Vickers came across an L.V.G. at a height of 7,000 feet between Bucquoy and Bapaume when patrolling. The hostile machine was much faster than the Vickers, but throttled down and allowed the Vickers to approach to 200 yards, when the enemy observer fired a few rounds with an automatic rifle and then accelerated. This occurred five or six times. The Vickers having expended four drums, returned to the aerodrome for more ammunition. It then went back to look for the hostile aeroplane, and found it near the same place. It was 1,000 feet lower than the Vickers, which dived at it and fired one drum. The hostile machine dived into the clouds. The engine of the Vickers cut out owing to the steep angle of glide, causing the petrol to run into the top of the tank. This second encounter was seen by 2 Lt Cooper (pilot) and 2 Lt Insall (observer), who were patrolling near

Achiet-le-Petit. They report that the German machine came down in spirals and irregular 'S' turns, apparently badly hit, but owing to thick clouds they could not see it come to earth.

September 1st

Capt Playfair (pilot) and 2 Lt Murray (observer), when patrolling between Coigneux and Dernancourt in a Vickers, engaged a hostile aeroplane of the L.V.G. type, with slight extensions on top planes. This machine was faster than the Vickers and went away after a few rounds had been exchanged at 200 yards. The patrol was continued, and when over Hebuterne another hostile machine was sighted and intercepted over Pusieux-au-Mont. This machine was 500 feet below the Vickers, and when engaged, turned away and fired backwards. The chase was given up owing to Lewis gun jamming.

September 4th

At 9.30 a.m. two German machines appeared over the lines. They were chased by Capt Thomson in a Bristol Scout and Lt Shield in a B.E.2c and were finally lost sight of in the clouds beyond La Bassee.

2 Lt Cooper and 2 Lt Insall when patrolling near Douchy-les-Ayet in a Vickers, chased and engaged a L.V.G. After drawing the L.V.G. across our lines, the Vickers turned sharply and dived, getting within 200 yards behind it. One drum was fired from the Lewis gun, and the hostile machine was driven down behind the German lines.

The Kite Balloon of 6 Section was shelled by the enemy at 1.15. Flt Sub-Lt Geddes observed the flashes after the third shot, and reported to 109th Battery. The battery opened fire, ranged from the balloon, and the hostile gun was silenced.

5–8 September, 1915

The *ad hoc* state of aircraft armament prevailing in the R.F.C. is shown by the 3 Sq operations on 5 September, when one Morane Parasol was armed with only the observer's rifle, and by the incident on the 7th, when the observer of a 1 Sq aircraft of similar type, defenceless from the rear, used a telescope to simulate a gun.

The reference to 'spangles' thrown from a German aircraft is puzzling; it may be the pilot's description of some form of signal cartridge.

COMMUNIQUÉ NO. 9

September 5th

2 Lt Ridley (pilot) and 2 Lt Cleaver (observer), 3 Sq, on a Morane with Lewis gun, when on patrol attacked two Aviatiks over Lille at about 5.30 a.m.

One of the hostile machines fought, the other remained out of range. Lt Cleaver fired one drum and a few rounds of a second drum, when the Lewis gun jammed. The combat was then broken off and the Morane was chased about a mile over our lines.

Cap Barratt (pilot) and 2 Lt Finnerty (observer), 3 Sq, on a Morane armed with rifle, saw a German aeroplane being shelled over our lines. It was a small tractor biplane with the passenger's seat slightly in front of main planes, and was armed with a machine-gun. The hostile machine was about 800 feet below the Morane, which dived at it. After some shots from rifle, the German machine made for home, throwing out spangles over its own lines. Half an hour later another German machine was sighted, when an inconclusive fight followed. This hostile machine was a good deal faster then the Morane.

2 Lt Cooper (pilot) and 2 Lt Insall (observer), 11 Sq, in a Vickers Fighter when patrolling near Gommecourt, sighted an L.V.G. at 7,500 feet, they themselves being at 9,000 feet. The Vickers intercepted the L.V.G., and got in front of it, and above it. The hostile aeroplane then came straight at the Vickers and passed underneath, opening fire with a machine-gun. The L.V.G. then turned so as to get the Vickers on his broadside and dived past it. During this manoeuvre, he was fired on and then assumed a steeper angle (80°). When last seen, smoke and bright yellow flames were coming from his exhaust pipe above the

engine. The Vickers could not follow owing to engine failing to pick up. Reports of eyewitnesses of this encounter indicate that the German machine struck the ground while still in a nose dive.

Capt Adamson (pilot) and Lt Braddyll (observer), No 6 Sq, in a F.E.2a. were seen by one of our A.A. batteries to engage and drive off in succession three hostile aeroplanes in front of the Vth Corps at about 5 p.m. While successfully fighting these three German machines, they themselves were under heavy and accurate fire from the enemy's A.A. guns. At about 5.20 p.m. the British machine was brought down by A.A. gun fire and seen to fall in the enemy's lines. The pilot and observer are unofficially reported to have been killed.

September 7th

Capt Playfair (pilot) and 2 Lt Murray (observer), 11 Sq, in a Vickers engaged an L.V.G. between Albert and Bois D'Aveluy. The German circled once above the Vickers, coming to within about 100 yards, when he opened fire with long groups. After getting into a good position, about three drums were fired at him from the Lewis gun, when the German suddenly dived and made for home.

Capt Darley (pilot) and 2 Lt Robinson (observer), 11 Sq, in a Vickers engaged an Aviatik biplane which carried an observer and machine-gun for which there were two mountings. The observer fired from either side to the rear. After firing away five drums the Lewis gun jammed. The Aviatik went down towards its own lines.

Capt Hawker, V.C., D.S.O., 6 Sq, in a Bristol Scout armed with Lewis gun engaged a German scout (a short single-seater biplane) when over Bixhoete at a height of 9,000 feet. The Bristol approached unobserved from above and to the right and opened fire at about 50 yards. The German fell in a nose dive and was observed by eyewitnesses to be still travelling vertically when last seen at about 200 feet from the ground. With reference to the fight the following telegram was received by 6 Sq:

6th Squadron, R.F.C.

C.C. 269. Seventh.

Congratulations and thanks from all units of the 18th Infantry Brigade for your prompt and most successful action against the German aeroplane this morning.

18th I.B.

2 Lt Gay (pilot) and Lt Leeson (observer), 16 Sq, in a B.E.2.c when near the Bois de Biez, encountered an Aviatik which turned and attacked. The two machines were on the same level and going the same way, the Aviatik leading. It suddenly turned to the right, the B.E.2c following suit, thus bringing the hostile machine directly behind and exceedingly close. Lt Leeson opened fire with the Lewis gun over the

tail of the B.E.2c and after about 30 rounds the German machine suddenly nose dived and went straight down towards the ground. It did not come up again.

2 Lt Balcombe Brown (pilot) and Lt Hughes (observer), 1 Sq, in a Morane was overtaken and pursued by four Albatros machines between Ypres and Courtrai. The Lewis gun of the Morane was on a fixed mounting pointing forward and could not be brought to bear on the German machines. It was fired in the air while the observer pointed his telescope at the Germans, range about 250 yards. The Albatroses sheered off at once and kept further off.

8 – 15 September, 1915

The aircraft sighted by a 16 Sq crew is something of a mystery. The description fits no contemporary German type and is more indicative of the French Caudron G4—perhaps a captured example.

The report on the combat with a Fokker monoplane on 13 September shows that the R.F.C. still believed the aircraft to feature a deflector propeller rather than a mechanical interrupter gear.

An Albatros CI reconnaissance biplane was shot down in the British lines by a 16 Sq B.E.2c.

COMMUNIQUÉ NO. 10

September 8th

2 Lt Cooper (pilot) and 2 Lt Insall (observer) of 11 Sq, on a Vickers, chased an L.V.G. near Hebuterne. The German machine avoided action and tried to draw the Vickers over his own A.A. guns.

Capt Playfair (pilot) and 2 Lt Insall (observer), 11 Sq, in a Vickers, had a similar experience in the afternoon with an Aviatik, which was faster than the Vickers.

Lt Hanlon and Lt Peel, 3 Sq, registered a French battery on a house with a hostile battery in it. The house was well hit, a heavy explosion occurring.

When Fl Cmdr Haskins and Lt Dalbiac, R.N.A.S., were ranging a ship bombarding Ostend, two of the shells of a German battery which was firing accurately at the ships passed close to the aeroplane at 7,000 feet and were clearly visible to both pilot and observer till they fell close to one of the ships.

September 9th

Capt Playfair (pilot) and 2 Lt Insall (observer), 11 Sq, in a Vickers, with Lewis gun, while engaged on patrol and photography, observed an Aviatik over Boyelles at 8,000 feet. The Vickers headed off the Aviatik and dived at it, firing two drums. The chase had to be abandoned owing to the superior speed of the enemy.

September 10th

2 Lt Hobbs (pilot) and 2 Lt Goldie (observer), 8 Sqn, in a B.E.2c with Lewis gun, when on a reconnaissance, sighted a German biplane of

brownish colour near Gommecourt, which got behind the B.E.2c. On a few rounds being fired from the back mounting the enemy machine went away. Later on, when near St Quentin, another hostile machine approached—a few rounds were exchanged with no apparent result to either side.

2 Lt Pattinson (pilot) and 2 Lt Findlay (observer), 11 Sqn, in a Vickers with Lewis gun, whilst patrolling near Gommecourt sighted three hostile machines, two were flying at 9,000 feet and one at 6,000 feet. On chasing the latter, an L.V.G., it dived steeply, the German observer firing over the tail put a bullet through a centre section strut of the Vickers. Three drums were fired at the L.V.G. without apparent result. The pursuit was discontinued when the L.V.G. was down to 2,000 feet. During the encounter the Vickers was subjected to heavy and accurate A.A. gun fire.

Capt Morgan, 6 Sqn, in a Bristol Scout, engaged a German machine (Albatros) over Wieltse. By diving from 9,500 feet, Capt Morgan got about 150 yards behind and above the hostile aeroplane, and fired at it. The Albatros went down.

Lt Archer (pilot) and Lt G. A. Parker (observer), 6 Sqn, in a B.E.2c while observing artillery fire near Ypres drove off an Albatros after firing one drum at about 150 yards.

Capt Carthew and Lt Russell, 2 Sqn, working with the Canadian Heavy Battery, silenced two anti-aircraft guns, obtaining direct hits on both guns.

Aeroplanes of the IInd Wing, in conjunction with the artillery of the IInd Army, attacked German kite balloons. At a pre-arranged time field artillery opened fire on known anti-aircraft guns while the aeroplanes attacked the balloons.

When they were hauled down, heavy artillery shelled the balloons on the ground, being ranged by wireless from aeroplanes. One balloon was destroyed and the other definitely shifted, probably damaged.

September 11th

Capt Halahan (pilot) and Lt Evans (observer), 4 Sqn, in a B.E.2c with Lewis gun and rifle, when on a reconnaissance north of Bapaume were attacked by a hostile machine, probably an Aviatik, which bore down on left rear of B.E.2c firing from a distance of ½ mile. It was this premature opening of fire which attracted the attention of Capt Halahan, who put his observer on the alert. About half a drum was fired at the Aviatik, which then sheered off and flew round the B.E.2c being much faster: during this the observers were firing at one another. After a short time the German threw overboard two silver balls which burst into a shower of white puffs. Thinking this was a sign to the A.A. guns giving the height of his machine, Capt Halahan dived 200 feet when 7 shells burst just above and all round his machine. After further shooting between the aeroplanes, the German dived and went quickly to ground in a long circular glide, landing in a field 3 miles south of Bapaume.

2 Lt Gay (pilot) and Lt Leeson (observer), 16 Sqn, in a B.E.2c with Lewis gun, when patrolling Ypres sighted a machine like a large Wright biplane, open fuselage, monoplane tail and no elevator, with two petrol tanks (probably engines also) showing between the planes on either side of the nacelle. It had two propellors. Lt Gay attacked it, Lt Leeson opening fire at 200 yards, but was unable to close with it. The German did not reply to the fire, but fired a Very light (white), whereupon the A.A. guns became very active, under course of which the German machine went towards Menin.

Lt Cooper King (pilot) and 2 Lt Howey (observer), 5 Sqn, in an F.E. with rifle and machine-gun, while patrolling over Polygon Wood drove off a German machine after firing two drums at it. Another hostile aeroplane seen in the same region later was driven off by rifle fire, the Lewis gun being dismounted at the moment. Soon afterwards a third Aviatik was seen and followed but declined combat.

September 12th

2 Lt Douglas (pilot) and 2 Lt Orde (observer), 8 Sqn, in a B.E.2c with Lewis gun, while ranging artillery near Adinfer, encountered a German machine, which opened fire, forward, from a machine-gun at 200 yards range. After a few rounds, the German put his nose down steeply and glided down behind his own lines. Lewis gun jammed but was got going again.

Capt Darley (pilot) and Lt Robinson (observer), 11 Sqn, in a Vickers with Lewis gun when patrolling near Albert, attacked an Aviatik at 6,800 feet. The enemy went down before being fired on. Shortly afterwards another Aviatik was engaged at about 350 yards. After half a drum had been fired at him, the German ceased fire and nose dived, landing in a field. It is probable that the German observer was hit as well as the engine.

Capt Barratt (pilot) and Lt Lewis (observer), of 3 Sqn, in a Morane with Lewis gun, attacked and endeavoured to head off Aviatik near Locon. The Aviatik was faster than the Morane, which was unable to close with it. After firing at one another the Aviatik broke off the fight by going down near La Bassee.

Lt Cooper King (pilot) and 2 Lt Thomas (observer), 6 Sqn, in an F.E. with Lewis gun, made for an Aviatik seen over West Roosebeke at 9,000 feet. While approaching to within 300 yards of the Aviatik, the observer continued ranging our artillery by wireless. The Aviatik headed straight for a point 150 yards to the right of the F.E. fired twenty rounds, dived and circled right. The F.E. turned, dived and followed, firing one drum at 100 yards. The German was then heading at right-angles across the front of the F.E. The observer aimed two lengths in front, but seeing momentarily the sun glint on the stream of the bullets, he reduced this to half a length. The Aviatik dived steeply, but switched on again about 300 feet over Oukene.

Lt Cleaver, 3 Sqn, ranged the 35th Battery on to an anti-aircraft gun, obtaining five direct hits.

Lt Simpson and Lt Elliott, 16 Sqn, located a hostile anti-aircraft battery and successfully ranged 28th Siege Battery on to it.

September 13th

Lt Grenfell, 1 Sqn, alone in a Morane, with Lewis gun, when patrolling at 14,700 feet at 7.40 a.m. observed an Albatros below him trying to cross the line. Lt Grenfell waited for some 20 minutes for him to cross so as to engage him on our side of the trenches, but the German turned back five times when shelled by our A.A. guns so Lt Grenfell dived at him when he was approaching Wytschaete. The German did not observe the approach of the Morane, which got to within 140 feet before Lt Grenfell opened fire. The enemy dived straight down after turning towards Menin. Some 42 rounds were fired at him when the Lewis gun jammed. A quarter of an hour later, Lt Grenfell observed another Albatros 2,500 feet below him over Gaapard, which went down after three rounds at long range and escaped.

2 Lt Quinnell (pilot) and Lt Sugden-Wilson (observer), 10 Sqn, in a B.E.2c with Lewis gun, when on reconnaissance over Lamain, were attacked by a Fokker, with machine-gun and deflector propellor. The hostile aeroplane dived at the B.E.2c from behind, opening a heavy fire which hit the B.E.2c repeatedly, and among other injuries pierced its lower petrol tank, and shot through one engine bearer. Lt Sugden-Wilson fired one drum at the Fokker, which then turned away and glided down towards Tournai. Owing to shortage of petrol the B.E.2c was unable to pursue.

2 Lt Shield (pilot) and Cpl Bennett (observer) in a B.E.2c with Lewis gun, when patrolling over the Bois Ce Biez at 10,000 feet attacked an Albatros (small type) which was crossing over our lines towards Armentieres. While the Albatros was circling to re-cross the line, Cpl Bennett fired two drums into it from the first mounting. The engine was hit and the hostile machine brought down. The pilot, Lt Suwelack, 24th Flieger Abteilung attached to XIXth (Saxon) Corps, and the observer, Lt Oskar Teuchmann, 2nd Photographic Section, were both killed by bullets. The machine which was undamaged except by bullets, was a new

Albatros of the small type with 160 horse power Mercedes engine, its number was *C 60/5*, maker's number *853*. There was a machine-gun unit on a good type mounting, admitting of all-round fire. Three cameras were found in the aeroplane.

Miscellaneous

The following officers who have been missing since the dates noted are unofficially reported to be prisoners of war in Germany: August 22nd: 2 Lt Drury, pilot, 8 Sqn, and 2 Lt McLean, observer, 8 Sqn. September 1st: Capt F. J. C. Wilson, 8 Sqn (observer), and 2 Lt Scholefield, pilot, 8 Sqn.

18 – 25 September, 1915

Preliminary operations in connection with the Battle of Loos, which opened on 25 September, resulted in increased air activity.

During the week various new and unfamiliar enemy aircraft were reported and tentative identifications can be made from the descriptions supplied.

The large twin-engined pusher biplane encountered by a 5 Sqn crew is likely to have been a Rumpler GI, powered by two 150 hp Benz or 160 hp Mercedes engines. It had a wing span of over 63 feet. The twin-engined tractor aircraft reported by 7 Sqn on 19 and 21 September was almost certainly an A.E.G. GI or GII, used for bombing and fighting duties.

The double-fuselaged aircraft met by 7 Sqn was clearly one of the unorthodox A.G.O. CI or CII two-seaters, with a single pusher engine and twin-boom tail, employed for reconnaissance. The similar aircraft reported by 11 Sqn was probably an A.G.O., wrongly credited with two engines.

A surprising disclosure in this communique was that the old Maurice Farman—armed with a rifle—was still employed for artillery observation.

COMMUNIQUÉ NO. 11

September 18th

Capt Thomson, 16 Sqn, in a Bristol Scout with Lewis gun mounted on rear spar of top plane saw an Aviatik near Gheluvelt at 7.55 a.m. The German machine dived to avoid combat. One and a half hours later when near Souchez he encountered an Albatros Scout which was being fired at by our own anti-aircraft guns. He dived directly beneath the German machine and fired one drum at it from about 300 feet. The German turned away to the left firing. Capt Thomson got beneath him again and fired another drum at 500 feet. The German stopped firing and went back over his own lines and at the same moment another German machine of the same type appeared.

Capt Thomson got behind and slightly beneath him and fired one drum at 200 yards whereupon the German machine went away towards Douai.

September 19th

Lt Powell (pilot) and 1 AM Shaw (observer), 5 Sqn, in a Vickers with a Lewis gun, when patrolling east of Polygon Wood at 6.0 a.m. and at a height of 9,000 feet saw an L.V.G. at a height of 6,000 feet. The Vickers dived at the German who also dived firing upwards over his tail. The Vickers followed firing until he had dived so low that it was impossible to follow him further. He was last seen flying very low towards Menin. Immediately afterwards Lt Powell looked round and saw a large machine (German) of unknown type coming up behind him. The machine was a three-seater with two engines, single fuselage, propellers behind main plane, two machine-guns. The machine was very much larger than a F.E.2. Lt Powell turned to engage it when he was about 100 yards away coming straight on and some 30 feet above the Vickers. The German was firing both his machine guns. When he was about 50 feet away 1 AM Shaw emptied a drum into him and he dived straight down just over the tail of the Vickers. One of his engines had stopped and a cloud of smoke was seen coming from the other engine.

Another machine was seen flying westward along the River Lys. When the Vickers turned towards him this machine went away.

While regaining height over Ypres Lt Powell observed an Albatros east of Poelcapelle. The last two drums of the Lewis gun were fired at him at a range of 200 yards. The German replied with his machine-gun but continued to fly eastwards. Having no more ammunition Lt Powell gave up the pursuit.

2 Lt Medlicott (pilot) and 2 Lt Gilbert (observer), 2 Sqn, in a B.E.2c, while doing artillery observation at a height of 9,800 feet near Lens, attacked an Albatros, getting within 150 yards of it and 100 yards above it. At that point the German opened fire. On closing to 100 yards, Lt Gilbert opened fire from the front left-hand machine-gun mounting. After one drum was fired the German nose dived and caught fire. Lt Medlicott switched off his engine and followed him down, enabling his observer to fire another drum. The German was last seen on fire and diving steeply 4 miles north-east of Vitry.

Lt Sommervail (pilot) and Lt Ryan (observer), 6 Sqn, when doing artillery registration near Zillebeke at 10.50 a.m. attacked a large double tractor biplane which was travelling in a southerly direction at Hooge at a height of about 8,000 feet. When the machines met the German was higher and opened fire from a machine-gun of which he had two. Lt Sommervail turned sharply to the left and then turned about to face the German. The machines then flew straight past each other firing with machine-guns forward, passing each other at about 75 yards distance. The German seemed 200 feet higher. This was repeated three times. In all 150 rounds of ammunition were fired at the German who had the advantage of being able to fire backwards from another machine-gun. The hostile machine then flew away in a south-westerly direction. On re-crossing the lines near Hill 60 a drum of ammunition was fired at an Albatros over Sanctuary Wood. It turned away immediately and disappeared towards Gheluvelt. The German machine first engaged was a double-engine tractor biplane with large nacelle between the wings, mounted with machine-guns fore and aft, and with lifting tail of the unstable type. The upper plane had laid-back extensions.

Information has been received that on the 19th instant a German aeroplane fell at Lawe, pilot and observer both being killed, and that another fell at Bisseghem on the same day; the pilot and observer were badly hurt. It is probable that the former machine was brought down by Lt Powell and 1 AM Shaw, and that the latter was brought down by Lt Sommervail and Lt Ryan.

Capt Mansfield (pilot) and Capt Holt (observer), 7 Sqn, in a B.E.2c with Lewis gun, rifle and pistol, while on reconnaissance engaged a German machine which was seen to come up from the aerodrome at Roulers. It was a double fuselaged machine with the observer in front and one machine-gun. After a brief exchange of shots at 150 yards the hostile machine dived towards the ground apparently under control. The combat could not be continued as the sump of the B.E.2c was shot through and it was only possible to cross the lines at 1,800 feet.

September 20th

2 Lt Medlicott (pilot) and 2 Lt Rice (observer) in a B.E.2c with Lewis gun while on a practice reconnaissance attacked two German machines 1½ miles from Lens. These were lost in the haze. Shortly afterwards near Douai two Albatroses were observed, each of them 200 feet below the B.E.2c and about 200 yards on either side. The machine to the left threw out some green lights and the one on the right some gold lights. The latter attempted to get under the B.E.2c which dived and turned bringing both hostile machines on its left. The Lewis gun jammed after one round when a third hostile machine joined the other two. It was a Fokker with machine-gun firing through the propellor which engaged at a distance of 50 yards and closed to 20 feet behind the B.E.2c. Machine-gun being still out of action, Lt Medlicott pointed his pistol which was not loaded at the observer in the Fokker. The hostile machine then went off towards Douai followed by the B.E.2c.

September 21st

Capt Rees (pilot) and Flt Sgt Hargreaves (observer) of 11 Sqn, in a Vickers Fighter with Lewis gun and pistol when photographing at 11 a.m. between Dompiere and Flaucourt observed a German machine 2,000 feet below them. It was a two-engined, twin-fuselaged tractor biplane, armed with two machine-guns. Its tactics consisted in getting the British machine broadside and then firing bursts of 50 rounds from both guns. The Vickers dived at the German machine and engaged it when at a height of 7,000 feet. His engine was apparently hit as he gave a quick turn and glided down towards Peronne followed by the Vickers which put two more drums into him on the way down. Smoke was coming out of one engine.

Capt Thomson, 16 Sqn, in a Maurice Farman armed with rifle, when observing for artillery in front of 1st Army at 10.15 a.m., saw a hostile aeroplane (Albatros) approaching from the direction of Erquinghem, crossing our line at about 8,500 feet. Capt Thomson opened fire on the enemy with his rifle. The hostile machine went back behind its own lines, Capt Thomson following. Capt Thomson pursued him as far as Wytschaete and fired about 45 rounds at him. During this fight Capt Thomson was subjected to very heavy gun and rifle fire, his machine being much hit about.

Capt Kinnear (pilot) and Lt Morgan (observer), 6 Sqn, in a F.E. with Lewis gun when doing artillery observation near Hooge at 8.25 a.m. sighted a German machine over Houthulst. It had two engines and a single fuselage; a very handy machine and a very good climber, and was armed with a machine-gun. Capt Kinnear and the German machine fought one another for about 35 minutes. Each time the German swerved to the left when about 80 yards away. On the fifth occasion he did not do so soon enough, and Capt Kinnear was able to dive beneath him getting about 50 feet from him. Unfortunately at that moment the Lewis gun jammed. This large machine was attended by a Mercedes Scout which manoeuvred very skilfully over the F.E. and kept firing vertically downwards at it. When over Staden the two hostile aeroplanes went off towards Roulers. The F.E. only had half a drum left when a third German machine came up and fired about 50 rounds and then went off towards Ypres. When this third aeroplane was over Poperinghe Capt Kinnear got to about 400 yards from him but could not close as the German was faster. The German machine then went back over his lines. The artillery observation was then continued.

With reference to this fight a telegram was sent to 6 Sqn by the 10th A.A. Section as follows:

> A British F.E. remained over the German lines for ¾ hours and succeeded in driving off four German patrolling planes one of which was a twin engine tractor, after a stiff fight.

2 Lt Glen (pilot) and 2 Lt Drenon (observer) of 8 Sqn, in a B.E.2c with Lewis gun and rifle, while carrying out a wireless reconnaissance south of Arras at 6.30 a.m., attacked an Aviatik which was trying to

cross our lines. During this fight 1½ drums of ammunition were fired at the German after which he went back, escaping owing to superior speed. The same two officers at 7.15 a.m. between Hebuterne and Rausart attacked another German machine which was trying to cross the lines. During this fight all the ammunition for the Lewis gun was fired and the German was then engaged with a rifle. The hostile machine came down; from the evidence of soldiers in the trenches, it is probable that it fell about ¾ mile behind the German lines.

Capt Rees (pilot) and Flt Sgt Hargreaves (observer), 11 Sqn, in a Vickers with a Lewis gun, rifle, and pistol, while patrolling south east of Albert at 5.30 p.m. engaged an Albatros. The German machine went down at a very steep angle of descent with his engine running full on which must have been doing 150 miles per hour. He was then 2,000 feet above Le Sars.

The artillery observation by machines of the 1st Wing for the 1st Army trench bombardment was successfully carried out. The Siege Group congratulated 3 Sqn on the excellent work done. 10th Siege Battery, ranged by 10 Sqn destroyed one target and partly destroyed another by 12.55 p.m. Lt Murray, 2 Sqn, turned the Canadian Heavy Battery on to a German battery and silenced it. Capt Hearne, 2 Sqn, with 13th Siege Battery, got a direct hit and five 'Y's on an A.A. gun.

September 22nd

The bombardment proceeded satisfactorily on the 1st Army front, ranged by machines of 1st Wing. 10th Canadian Battery, ranged by 3 Sqn, destroyed four targets.

Artillery of IInd Army, ranged by machines of IInd Wing, obtained hits on a big gun at Houthulst with the fifth, sixth, eighth and tenth rounds fired.

September 23rd

2 Lt Chamberlain (pilot) and Capt Lane (observer), 11 Sqn, in a Vickers with a Lewis gun when near Ham doing reconnaissance were attacked by a Fokker at 1.25 p.m. The Vickers turned in a cloud and dived on to the Fokker firing two drums on the hostile machine when broadside on. The German machine appeared to be hit as the machine nose dived for a long distance, side-slipped and came to earth. These same two officers at 3.10 p.m. near Peronne when on reconnaissance engaged a doubled fuselaged biplane. The Vickers turned suddenly and fired one drum into this machine when broadside on. The hostile machine went away in the direction of Peronne. It was much faster than the Vickers.

2 Lt Hobbs (pilot) and 2 Lt Orde (observer), 8 Sqn, in a B.E.2c with Lewis gun, when doing artillery reconnaissance south-west of Bapaume at 8.30 a.m., sighted two hostile machines about 1 mile to the south

2—MORANE-SAULNIER PARASOL TYPE L—80 H.P. LE RHÔNE ENGINE
The Type L was the earliest version of the French Morane Parasol. It had warping-wing lateral control and its only defence was that provided by revolver, rifle or hand-held machine-gun. It was succeeded by the Type LA which was powered by the 110 h.p. Le Rhône engine, had aileron control, was generally cleaned-up and provided with a more sophisticated armament. Both types were used for reconnaissance, artillery spotting and contact patrol by Nos. 1 and 3 Squadrons in 1915–16.

flying north-west about 500 feet above them. One of these hostile aeroplanes threw out a white light whereupon the German A.A. guns opened heavy fire. One German machine then turned and attacked the B.E.2c from behind. After 35 rounds were fired at him the German turned away and went down. The other followed the B.E.2c and engaged it. After some 60 rounds were fired at it the German machine turned and went off.

German artillery still in action on 1st Army front.

Canadian Heavy Battery ranged by Lt Medlicott, 2 Sqn, got several direct hits on a hostile battery and silenced it.

Wire cutting by heavy batteries ranged by machines of 2 Sqn was apparently successful. The Meerut artillery ranged by Lt Henderson, 10 Sqn, completely destroyed a house.

Miscellaneous

It is reported on good authority that Capt T. W. M. Morgan, 6 Sqn, missing on 13th September, was injured near Courtrai, through his machine striking a tree. He is said to be a prisoner of war.

23 September – 4 October, 1915

This communiqué reported some of the bombing operations mainly against railway targets—in support of the Loos battle. Despite poor weather considerable damage was caused. B.E.2cs undertook most of the bombing and some were armed with two Lewis guns for escort duties.

Between 23 and 28 September, R.F.C. aircraft in the Loos battle flew 1,131 hours. Ninety-two bombing sorties were flown and 5½ tons of bombs were dropped. Seven members of aircrews were missing and four wounded.

COMMUNIQUÉ NO. 12

September 23rd
The line Douai-Valenciennes was bombed by the IIIrd Wing. One of the bombs (100 pounds) was dropped by Capt Brock of 4 Sqn, from a height of 200 feet on the centre of a goods train; this part of the train was wrecked, but the front portion steamed away. One 100-pound bomb fell on several trucks at a junction.

The line Lille-Valenciennes was bombed by the IInd Wing and 1 Sqn. One 100-pound bomb dropped by Capt Moore of 7 Sqn, from a height of 550 feet, just missed a moving train but hit a signal box and wrecked it.

September 25th
Lt Evans and Lt Saunders of 3 Sqn, flew for an hour at a height of 4,000 feet ranging the 8th Siege battery on a bridge over the Haute Duele Canal. They were exposed to heavy fire throughout and were also attacked for 20 minutes by an hostile machine armed with a machine-gun, but which they kept off with a pistol. The pilot and observer were both hit, but not seriously hurt. They succeeded in getting two shots within 10 yards of the bridge.

The line Douai-Valenciennes was bombed by the IIIrd Wing. A truck on the railway was hit from a height of 500 feet by a bomb dropped by Lt Horsfall of 4 Sqn and the line was damaged in several places. A junction was hit by one 100-pound bomb and four 20-pound bombs dropped from a height of 150 feet by Lt Nicholls, the rails and turn-table were probably damaged.

The lines Lille-Douai and Lille-Don were bombed by machines of 12 Sqn. On the former line a bomb dropped by 2 Lt Lees hit track in front of a moving train which stopped and turned back; this pilot dropped his bombs from a height of 400 feet. A bridge over a main line carrying a light railway was hit from a height of 150 feet, by a 100-pound bomb dropped by Lt Douglas. The bomb fell on the main line, probably causing complete temporary stoppage.

Lt Horsfall of 4 Sqn, got a direct hit on a stationary train which was on a main line, blowing one truck to pieces with a 100-pound bomb dropped from a height of 500 feet.

September 26th

Capt Lawrence, pilot, and Lt McArthur, observer, 12 Sqn, in a B.E.2c with two Lewis guns, when guarding bomb dropping machines, south-west of Lille, at 4.15 p.m., were attacked by an Albatros with a machine-gun firing behind the main plane. Several bullets hit the B.E.2c Lt McArthur fired one drum over the tail. The German then came up closer on the left and opened fire again. Capt Lawrence then turned towards him and fired one drum from his fixed gun. The hostile machine then turned away north and went down towards Lille.*

2 Lt Learmount, of 7 Sqn, in a B.E.2c armed with two Lewis guns mounted to fire above and forward when bomb dropping near Seclin at 1 p.m. was attacked by an L.V.G. which was below and behind him. On the German machine opening fire, 2 Lt Learmount, who was alone, turned towards him and dived at him firing one drum. The German dived and disappeared below the clouds.

Capt Spratt, and 2 Lt Bell Irving in an R.E.5 with Lewis gun when on reconnaissance near Roulers at 1.30 p.m. were attacked by a Fokker which approached from the rear firing continuously from long to close range. When half a drum had been fired at it the Fokker went down, gliding steeply.

The lines Cambrai-Douai and Cambrai-Roisel were bombed by IIIrd Wing, the line Lille-Valenciennes by IInd Wing and the lines Lille-Don and Lille-Seclin-Douai by 12 Sqn. On the Lille-Valenciennes line Lieut. Symington, of 7 Sqn, from a height of 500 feet got a direct hit well forward on a moving troop train, the forepart of which was completely wrecked. Shortly afterwards, 2 Lt Learmount found this train standing where it had been bombed by Lt Symington, and hit a coach in the centre of the train with 100-pound bomb. The railway lines attacked were hit in several places.

September 27th

2 Lt Gay, pilot, and Lt Leeson, observer, of 16 Sqn, in a B.E.2c when

* See also under 'Bombing', page 54.

on a reconnaissance over Couriere at 6.30 a.m. encountered an Albatros which approached to about 250 yards when it turned round presenting its tail presumably in order to fire from a back mounting. When one drum had been fired at it the Albatros dived almost vertically and was followed down to a height of 1,800 feet by the B.E.2c which continued firing at it. The German then fired a white Very's light. On this, machine-guns and rifles were fired from the ground at the British machine and the chase was given up. Lt Gay and Lt Leeson then attacked a sausage balloon firing 2½ drums into the envelope and car. The balloon was hauled down.

September 28th

2 Lt H. S. Shields, pilot, and Cpl Bennett, observer, of 16 Sqn, in a B.E.2c with Lewis gun, when on a reconnaissance north-east of Wavrin at 7.5 a.m. observed a small Albatros with machine-gun in back seat approaching from Lille. Lt Shields turned to meet this machine. The two aeroplanes passed each other at point blank range, so close that the faces of the German pilot and observer could be distinguished. Some rounds were fired at this range, after which the hostile machine dived almost vertically and continuing machine-gun fire until out of range. When at a very low altitude clouds of smoke came from the engine, but the machine recovered sufficiently to fly back to Lille.

A machine of 8 Sqn sent to attack the rolling-stock damaged the line Bapaume-Achiet-le-Grand. One pilot reports that at a point on this line he observed some 500 yards of debris, which might have been a wrecked train or timber. He was doubtful whether a train could get along it.

During the bombing operations recorded above, the main lines are known to have been damaged in sixteen different places, and five or six trains partially wrecked.

September 30th

Capt Rees, pilot, and Flt Sgt Hargreaves, observer, of 11 Sqn, in a Vickers attacked an Albatros biplane, near Gommecourt. After firing one drum of ammunition the hostile machine dived through a cloud. Flt Sgt Hargreaves then fired off another drum when the enemy started to spiral and nose dived. At the same time he was apparently hit by anti-aircraft shell, as his right wing fell off when at about 5,000 feet. Subsequent investigations showed that the hostile pilot had a hit through the head with a machine-gun bullet.

October 3rd

Lt Summers of 3 Sqn, with 111th Battery registered point at *B.14.b.2.5.* A train was seen approaching, which stopped in a small wood and shut off steam. Two direct hits were observed on the spot where the train was last seen, and the train was not seen to move on again.

2–10 October, 1915

News of several recent British casualties—at least one a Fokker victim—was reported from various sources.

The 'Albatros' encountered by 2 Sqn on 7 October was, from the description given, clearly one of the A.G.O. two-seaters.

COMMUNIQUÉ NO. 13

October 2nd

Lt Kemp and Capt Lane of 11 Sqn, in a Vickers when patrolling north of Arras at 9.45 a.m. at a height of 10,000 feet, observed a hostile aeroplane crossing the line 3 miles away. Lt Kemp succeeded in heading off the enemy's aeroplane which then turned towards the Vickers, and the two machines approached each other end on. Capt Lane opened fire at 80 yards range. The hostile machine immediately dived almost under the Vickers and a drum was emptied into it while diving. The Vickers then dived down after the hostile aeroplane firing three more drums into it at close range. The hostile aeroplane which was an Albatros, crossed the line diving to earth at a very low altitude.

Lt Miles (pilot) and Capt Prickett (observer), 1 Sqn, in an Avro with Lewis gun, at 7.30 a.m., when on reconnaissance west of Lille at a height of 7,500 feet, were attacked by three hostile aeroplanes at the same time from above and behind. They were two Albatroses and an L.V.G.

The first Albatros came within 50 yards on the left of the Avro and opened fire but without much result. On being fired on with the Lewis gun, this Albatros turned and withdrew in the direction of Lille, as did the other hostile aeroplanes.

October 3rd

Lt Powell (pilot) and 1 AM Shaw (observer), of 5 Sqn, in a Vickers with Lewis gun when patrolling south-west of Passchendaele and Becelaere at 5.50 a.m. attacked an L.V.G. which dived, pursued by the Vickers. An Albatros then appeared on the scene and opened machine-gun fire at about 300 yards range and then turned away. The Vickers followed the Albatros down to about 2,000 feet.

Lt Turton (pilot) and Lt Stammers (observer), of 2 Sqn, in a B.E.2c with Lewis gun, at 5.15 a.m. when doing artillery patrol over Wingles, engaged a Fokker with deflector propeller. The hostile machine went off towards Douai and was shortly joined by two Aviatiks. After 20 rounds had been fired at the first Aviatik it turned away sharply, throwing out four white lights whereupon anti-aircraft gun fire was opened on the B.E.2c. The hostile machines were lost to sight in the direction of Douai.

Kite balloons were in the air 22 hours 30 minutes making 11 ascents and 19 observers being taken up. Ten targets were successfully ranged on.

October 6th

A B.E.2c, pilot, Lt Awcock, observer, 2 Lt Brown, when on artillery registration was hit when over Hulluch and was forced to descend. The machine was found to be on fire over the lines and came down near Vaudricourt. The machine was in flames and was totally destroyed. Neither pilot nor observer were hurt.

October 7th

Capt Carthew (pilot) and Lt Gilbert (observer) of 2 Sqn, in a B.E.2c with Lewis gun, when on artillery patrol at 11.30 a.m. near Pont-a-Vendin encountered a hostile machine flying at 10,000 feet; the B.E.2c was 500 feet lower. The enemy aeroplane was a large Albatros with single engine and propellor and two nacelles, one on either side of the engine. It carried two machine-guns. The hostile machine opened fire with both guns and, upon being replied to, headed for Carvin followed by the B.E., which fired three drums at it. The German dived steeply making for Carvin and at this moment the Lewis gun jammed. The German was apparently trying to draw the B.E.2c over anti-aircraft guns which were firing at every opportunity.

October 8th

Capt Babington and Lt Davies, 2 Sqn, located a hostile battery of five howitzers which was engaged by the 19th Siege Battery, and the 21st Heavy Battery and silenced. Another hostile battery was then located and engaged and silenced by the 21st Heavy Battery.

Artillery patrols of 3 Sqn located fourteen hostile batteries in action in the afternoon.

Capt Barratt of 3 Sqn, with the 25th Siege Battery obtained eight hits on communication trenches.

Bombing

A report has been received that on the morning of the 26th September, a train passed through Lille with four trucks completely destroyed and traces of blood in many carriages. It was probably the train bombed by Capt Lawrence, 12 Sqn, at 12.45 p.m. on the 25th September. He then reported that three trucks appeared to be wrecked. (*See Page 50.* *Capt Lawrence is not mentioned.*)

Casualties

The German wireless stated on the 29th September that two British machines had been shot down and that the occupants were made prisoners. It is probable that one of these reports may refer to Capt Spratt (pilot) and 2 Lt Stubbs (observer), 7 Sqn, missing on the 28th September. It is not possible to say whom the other report refers.

With reference to Capt Morgan, 6 Sqn, reported missing on the 13th September, a report has been received that at 5.15 a.m. that day an Allied aeroplane had to make a forced landing near Oygem on the River Lys, when the tail of the machine hit the tops of some trees. The pilot was badly cut on the forehead and was taken to Courtrai hospital by the Germans.

Miscellaneous

A balloon of 8 Kite Balloon Section broke away at about 12.50 p.m., 4th October, owing to the cable being cut by high tension wires. The balloon was landed safely near Houchin by Flt Lt Ogilvie Davis and Sgt Borard.

A French machine landed at 11 Sqn's aerodrome and reported that a German machine, which the French had captured a few days ago to the south, had on board a Lewis gun, which the German pilot said had been taken from Lt Washington's machine, a B.E.2c. Lt Washington was apparently wounded in a fight in the air. 2 Lt Washington, and 2 Lt Greenhow, of 8 Sqn, were missing on the 25th September while engaged in bomb-dropping on the Douai-Valenciennes railway. In the German wireless news of the 26th it was stated that one of their fighting aeroplanes had shot down an English machine west of Cambrai. This probably referred to the B.E.2c with the above-mentioned pilot and observer.

The total time flown, by the R.F.C. in the field, during the period July, August, September, is as follows:

July	2,102 hours 10 minutes
August	2,674 hours 3 minutes
September	4,740 hours 50 minutes

10–16 October, 1915

Indication of the coming 'Fokker scourge' reported in this communiqué. Six crews encountered the new enemy scouts, which do not appear to have pressed home their attacks with great determination. At this stage their role was purely defensive, and the enemy was anxious to avoid any risk of the secret armament installation falling into Allied hands.

Some categories of German aircraft were no more advanced than those of the R.F.C., and the artillery observation Albatros BII forced down on 11 October was not armed in any way.

This communiqué makes first mention of the R.E.7, a large single-engined biplane with a 57-foot wing span intended for reconnaissance. The German scout reported by 12 Sqn on 10 October remains a mystery. The description generally applies to the A.G.O. DVIII, but this type is not believed to have entered production.

Capt Gordon Bell, mentioned on 13 October, was a noted pre-war civilian pilot.

COMMUNIQUÉ NO. 14

October 10th

Capt Babington, and Lt Chadwick of 2 Sqn, in a B.E.2c with Lewis gun and automatic pistol; when doing artillery observation at about 3.15 p.m. sighted a small hostile monoplane approaching from straight ahead. Capt Babington sheered off slightly to give his observer a good opportunity to fire, and then both machines opened fire. The hostile monoplane passed on the left of the B.E.2c slightly above it and then turned quickly and attempted to come up behind. Capt Babington then dived and turned when some more shots were fired by both aeroplanes. The monoplane then sheered off but attacked again a little later diving steeply in an attempt to get under the tail of the B.E.2c. Capt Babington met this attack by diving and turning towards the hostile monoplane, on which fire was opened. The hostile machine then sheered off dived steeply and then went away.

2 Lt Medlicott and 2 Lt Rice of 2 Sqn, in a B.E.2c with two machine-guns whilst engaged on strategical reconnaissance near La Bassee were attacked by a Fokker at 2 p.m. After five rounds had been fired at the Fokker at close range it dived and went off in the direction of Lille. At

2.50 p.m. when near Wavrin an Albatros was observed 300 yards away and slightly higher than the B.E.2c. 2 Lt Rice fired one drum at the Albatros at this range whereupon the hostile aeroplane glided down in the direction of Douai.

Lt Ward and 1 AM Digby of 16 Sqn, in a B.E.2c with Lewis gun when photographing in the neighbourhood of Lille sighted an Albatros slightly below them at which one drum was fired from the front mounting. After following this Albatros down to 3,000 feet it was abandoned. Soon after 3 p.m. two Albatroses were sighted, probably the one already mentioned and another. After half a drum had been fired the Lewis gun jammed and the encounter was broken off.

Lt Eastwood and 2 Lt Hardy of 16 Sqn, in a Maurice Farman when doing artillery observation at 12.45 p.m. saw an L.V.G. engaging an R.E. On being attacked by the Maurice Farman the L.V.G. dived towards Lille and escaped through superior speed.

2 Lt Williams and 2 Lt Henderson of 10 Sqn, in a B.E2c with Lewis gun while taking photographs of the Lille defences at 4.30 p.m. were attacked by an Albatros which opened fire at them from behind. About 25 rounds were fired from the Lewis gun at the hostile aeroplane at a range of 20 yards. The Albatros appeared to manoeuvre more quickly and engaged the B.E.2c twice whilst the shooting of the German observer appeared to improve. One petrol tank, propellor, and parts of the fuselage of the B.E.2c were hit, which damage necessitated the return to a landing ground as soon as possible, so the action was broken off, and the B.E.2c returned to our lines.

2 Lt Fairbairn and 2 Lt Allan of 10 Sqn, in a B.E.2c with Lewis gun when doing artillery registration at 2 p.m. were attacked by a Fokker mounting a machine-gun. The hostile machine attacked from behind opening fire, on which the B.E.2c dived and then came up again in a position to return the enemy's fire. After about 30 rounds the German machine turned away, and got out of range, dived about 2,000 feet and went away.

Capt Parker and Lt French of 5 Sqn, in a B.E.2c with Lewis gun when on a reconnaissance over Houthulst Forest at 3.30 p.m. attacked an Albatros and engaged it after about 20 minutes pursuit. The hostile machine then withdrew in the direction of Roulers.

Capt Lawrence and Lt Birch of 12 Sqn, in a R.E.7 with two Lewis guns when returning from long-distance reconnaissance were attacked by a single-seater Scout which approached from the left rear firing. The hostile Scout passed across the rear of the R.E. firing in long bursts at a distance of about 100 yards. Lt Birch fired one drum from the rear mounting and then Capt Lawrence turned the R.E. towards the Scout firing one drum from the fixed mounting. The German machine turned away and made for his own lines quickly. The encounter took place near Armentieres. The German Scout is reported to have a tail like a Martinsyde and front like a Nieuport though the planes were probably the same size. It appeared to be 10 to 15 miles faster than the R.E.7.

2 Lt Medlicot of 2 Sqn, in a Bristol Scout, when on patrol over Lens at a height of 11,000 feet, observed an Albatros half a mile to the east. The Scout climbed until it was 500 feet above the German and then dived at it opening fire at a range of 200 yards decreasing to 75 yards. He observed black smoke coming up from the engine of the Albatros which dived steeply about 2 miles east of Lens. He did not see the hostile machine reach the ground as his attention was just then diverted to another hostile machine.

2 Lt Johnson and Cpl Roberts of 3 Sqn, in a Morane armed with rifle, when doing photography over Hulluch at 2.15 p.m. were attacked by a hostile aeroplane which approached close behind them unseen and fired about 20 rounds from a machine-gun hitting Cpl Roberts in three places. The Morane then returned to our lines.

October 11th

2 Lt Sanday and 2 Lt Ellison, 2 Sqn, in a B.E.2c with Lewis gun, when doing artillery observation over Cite St. Elie at 8.45 a.m. encountered an Albatros between 7,500 and 8,000 feet. They engaged the Albatros and forced it towards Noeux-les-Mines, where another drum was fired at it as it started to spiral down. The German pilot seemed quite bewildered and turned northwards, closely pursued by 2 Lt Sanday and 2 Lt Ellison, who fired two more drums at it. Capt Barratt and Lt Cleaver, 3 Sqn, in a Morane with Lewis gun who had been doing artillery observation over Cuinchy then attacked the Albatros, opening fire on it at about 40 yards range and continued to engage it closely until their Lewis gun jammed. The Albatros was then headed by Lt Clark and Lt Stammers, 2 Sqn, in a B.E.2c with a Lewis gun who were observing artillery fire. This B.E.2c intercepted the Albatros as it was trying to get back to its own lines, one drum being fired at it at very close range. The Albatros then turned again and flew towards Noyelles-les-Vermelles. Capt Barratt and Lt Cleaver, having got their gun into action again closed once more and opened fire at 30 to 40 yards range. The Albatros then landed and the German pilot and observer were taken prisoners. The German machine is one of the newest type of Albatros with 130 horsepower Mercedes engine, and was equipped with the latest pattern of wireless. It had no machine-gun on board. According to the pilot the speed was 130 kilometres per hour, and it could climb to 3,000 metres in 20 minutes. The pilot, George Emil Reiman, is an aspirant officer; the observer Arthur Reinhardt, was a lieutenant in the Foot Artillery. They

stated that the machine belonged to the 202nd Feldflieger Abteilung, near Valenciennes. The captured aeroplane is in perfect condition; it appears to have been untouched except by two shrapnel bullets in the fuselage.

Capt Mansfield and Capt Holt, 7 Sqn, in a B.E.2c when doing reconnaissance west of Roulers at 9.30 a.m. were engaged by three Albatroses which followed them at a distance of 800 yards firing with machine-guns. At Poelcapelle the three Albatroses gave up the pursuit and a Fokker attacked the B.E. from the left rear. After one burst of fire the Fokker passed on in a northerly direction.

Capt Loraine and Cpl Fineran of 5 Sqn in a Vickers with two Lewis guns, when patrolling north-east of Vormozelle at 10.50 a.m. saw a Fokker diving at a B.E.2c. Capt Loraine flying towards the Fokker opened fire at it while about 1,000 feet below it. The hostile machine passed directly over the Vickers and tried to get behind it. By turning sharply this was prevented. The Fokker then turned north-east and disappeared in the direction of Polygon Wood.

2 Lt Medlicot and Lt Russell, 2 Sqn, in a B.E.2c with two Lewis guns, while doing artillery registration at 3 p.m. observed an Albatros with two nacelles east of Lens. When attacked and engaged at 600 yards the German machine made off in the direction of Douai and landed there without replying to the fire of the B.E.2c. On continuing artillery registration a hostile machine was observed over Vermelles under A.A. fire and with four British machines in pursuit of it. The B.E.2c with Capt Mitchell and Lt Shepherd, 10 Sqn, met the hostile aeroplane near La Bassee and fired two drums at it, but had to relinquish the pursuit when over the Bois de Biez as two of their flying wires were shot through, one rudder wire was out, and the other had been damaged by bullets. Lt Medlicot and Lt Russell joined in the pursuit and succeeded in getting in front of the hostile aeroplane and underneath it. This enabled them to bring the front machine-gun bracket into action firing over the propellor when some 200 feet below the German machine. Three drums were fired into it from that position when the Lewis gun jammed. 2 Lt Medlicot then passed the second Lewis gun to Lt Russell who got it into action on the right side bracket and the German aeroplane was engaged again, the other machines having given up the chase. When over Haubourdin Lt Russell fired two more drums at it as it dived under the B.E.2c; smoke was seen coming from the engine which then stopped. By diving on the eastern side of the German machine Lt Medlicot succeeded in driving it over our lines south-west of Armentieres at a height of 3,000 feet. The second Lewis gun then jammed. The German landed down-wind near Sailly-sur-Lys and turned over. The observer was found to have been hit in the left leg, both he and the pilot were taken prisoners. (*See also page 62.*)

2 Lt Medlicot and Sgt Craven, 2 Sqn, in a B.E.2c with Lewis gun when testing the aeroplane at 10 a.m. observed a hostile machine over La Bassee and engaged it. After 14 rounds from an automatic pistol had been fired at 130 yards range the hostile machine went off in an easterly direction.

2 Lt Medlicot, 2 Sqn, in a Bristol Scout when patrolling between Lens and Arras observed four hostile machines doing wireless between these two places. He dived at each machine in turn, firing at them, and drove them back over the lines.

One hostile aeroplane landed at the aerodrome at Vitry whilst another came down in a field on the south side of Rouvroy. Having finished all his ammunition Lt Medlicot returned to his aerodrome. The hostile machines were all of the Aviatik type.

Lt Powell and 1 AM Shaw, 5 Sqn, in a Vickers with Lewis gun, when patrolling near Hooge at 10 a.m., observed a German machine flying at a height of about 5,000 feet apparently ranging. The German avoided action by flying eastward. As he was getting further away owing to his superior speed fire was opened on him at a range of about 300 yards. The pursuit had then to be broken off as a shell from an anti-aircraft gun burst not more than 3 feet to the left of the nacelle hitting 1 AM Shaw in the leg and knocking three holes in the petrol tank just behind the pilot.

October 12th

Capt Lawrence and Lt Gordon Burge of 12 Sqn, in a R.E.7 with two Lewis guns when engaged in guarding Capt Christie, who was employed on a special mission engaged an Albatros 3 miles south of Lille. Simultaneously another machine appeared and drew in on the left rear of the R.E.7. Both these hostile machines seemed to be slower than the R.E.7. Lt Burge engaged the Albatros which was the nearest of the two and when just west of Tournai it threw out two white lights. No anti-aircraft gun fire followed this. In a few seconds two more lights were thrown out, again without effect. Both of these hostile machines fired a good deal at the R.E.7. When near Mouscron two more hostile machines appeared from above and coming from the south. The first, an Albatros, began to draw up on the left rear firing very accurately. The R.E.7 was struck thirty or more times. When he was at between 50 to 80 yards range Lt Burge fired and this Albatros drew away. He came up again and after firing at it again went away. This occurred a third time when near Gheluvelt and the German machine went away to the south. Meanwhile another machine, an L.V.G., had remained further off and above the R.E.7 firing a good deal. The two machines originally encountered were gradually left behind.

While taking photographs over Pont-a-Vendin in a B.E.2c 2 Lt Bransby Williams and Lt H. B. Davey, were attacked by an Albatros which repeatedly fired at them at a range of 100–300 yards over a period of half an hour. The British machine replied and was able to fire 20 consecutive rounds at a distance of 75 yards. After this the German dived and did not again come within range. The B.E.2c was hit in the engine, propellor, and aileron.

October 13th

Capt Gordon Bell, in a Bristol Scout with Le Rhone engine, whilst on patrol encountered an Albatros west of Lens about 3 p.m. After he had fired threequarters of a drum the German machine side-slipped, turned completely over, and disappeared in the clouds. At that moment the Bristol Scout was attacked by a large L.V.G. After an indecisive fight the L.V.G. broke off the combat at about 3,000 feet and landed east of Lille.

2 Lt Quinnel and 2 Lt Goodson, 10 Sqn, in a B.E.2c whilst on patrol about 3.30 p.m. saw an Aviatik over our lines. The B.E. chased it back to its own lines; the B.E.'s propellor being hit.

Capt Gould and 2 Lt Vaucour, 10 Sqn, in a B.E.2c whilst on reconnaissance over Douai, about 4 p.m. were attacked by an Albatros biplane with gun shooting over the tail. One drum was fired from the Lewis gun, and the hostile machine then disappeared.

2 Lt Glen and Cpl Jones, of 8 Sqn, in a B.E.2c about 4.30 p.m. when over Douai escorting some bombing aeroplanes attacked a Fokker that was making for one of the bombing machines. The hostile aeroplane was armed with a machine-gun mounted in the fore position on the left side. The Fokker passed over the B.E. six times at a height of about 30 feet and then circled twice round the B.E. at a very high speed. The hostile pilot was apparently very skilful. It then made off in an easterly direction and was not seen again.

On the Ist Army front, hostile guns in seventeen different places were silenced, at any rate temporarily, with the aid of aeroplane observation.

October 14th

Capt Mitchell and Capt Bruce, whilst on reconnaissance duty in a B.E.2c at 4 p.m. over Valenciennes were attacked from above by an Aviatik which dived and reappeared in front of the British machine which fired a total of two drums using both forward and back mountings. The Lewis gun jammed and the B.E.2c was followed by the German machine as far as Douai.

Miscellaneous

Capt Lawrence, when going out on reconnaissance on September 30th had his machine hit by the burst of an A.A. shell. He completed his duty and on return it was found that the machine had been hit in 300 different places.

The German Albatros brought down on the 11th October is a brand new machine of the latest type. It is fitted with a 120 horsepower Mercedes engine and an A.E.G. wireless set.

The account as given by the hostile pilot differs in certain details from that recorded by his opponents. His story is as follows:

> I started from Valenciennes to take out an observer for artillery work. After crossing the lines I was attacked by a Bristol biplane. While dealing with this machine, three others attacked me from behind. My observer lost his head and seeing that it was hopeless to expect him to fight I decided to turn for home. At this moment four other British aeroplanes came up from the ground and attacked me.
>
> Wherever I turned I met a British machine and was unable to break through them. Bullets kept whizzing past me, one took off my goggles, and another grazed my back. Then a large shell burst just underneath one of my wings; this put my machine quite out of control, it fluttered downwards and I was forced to land.

While the Albatros was being tested by the Officer Commanding 2 Sqn, after erection, the patches that had been put over the black crosses unfortunately blew off. The machine being sighted by a junior officer of the same squadron was at once pursued. The Albatros beat a rapid retreat and the pilot succeeded in making a safe landing on his own aerodrome.

19–22 October, 1915

This communiqué reported little operational activity, but underlined the indifferent state of aircraft recognition training—with British anti-aircraft gunners firing on a Bristol Scout. There were also two instances of British aircraft being attacked by enemy machines which our crews did not recognise. These could have been new types of which descriptions had not then been circulated. The information in the communiqué is insufficient to attempt any positive identification.

COMMUNIQUÉ NO. 15

October 19th

2 Lt Edwards, 6 Sqn, in a B.E.2c, when doing photography in the neighbourhood of Verlorenhoek was attacked from behind by a hostile tractor machine, type not recognised. For a few seconds Lt Edwards was unable to locate the hostile machine but eventually sighted it above him and a little to the right rear. He turned sharply to the left in the hopes of being able to engage the enemy machine. He failed to improve his fighting position, and as his machine was badly damaged in the encounter, Lt Edwards dived for home, the German eventually breaking off the engagement.

2 Lt Symington and 2 Lt Welch, 7 Sqn, in a B.E.2c during a reconnaissance near Zarren were attacked by a double-engined biplane carrying apparently one machine-gun. The hostile machine overhauled the B.E.2c and attacked from behind. 2 Lt Welch fired half a drum at the hostile machine which broke off the engagement and descended towards Roulers.

2 Lt Kitchener and 2 Lt Haines, 7 Sqn, in a B.E.2c when on reconnaissance over Lille were attacked by an Albatros from above and behind. After firing one drum the hostile machine turned and retired towards Lille apparently undamaged.

2 Lt Impey and Lt Orde, 6 Sqn, in a F.E. while crossing the lines near Langemarck saw a German machine (apparently an Albatros) and attacked him. After some manoeuvring the F.E. opened fire from above, the hostile machine replying with a machine-gun. When the F.E. had fired a second drum the hostile machine suddenly dived very steeply with a slight lurch and was lost to sight.

Capt Kinnear, 8 Sqn, in a Bristol Scout encountered a single-seater tractor machine with small extensions, wings slightly swept back, small dihedral, fin, fish tail shaped empanage and square wing tips. Capt Kinnear fired three times at ranges between 100 and 150 yards, after which the hostile machine made off towards Roulers, probably short of ammunition as he fired considerably more at the Bristol Scout than the latter fired at him.

October 20th

Capt Grenfell, 1 Sqn, in a Bristol Scout during patrol saw an Aviatik 1,000 feet above him in the vicinity of Hollebeke. The Scout quickly climbed to the level of the hostile machine and getting above fired a drum at him. The hostile machine dived, followed by the Scout fixing another drum. Capt Grenfell now experienced some difficulty in getting the Scout out of a nose dive but eventually righted her after diving some 1,500 feet. Believing that a wire had snapped Capt Grenfell refrained from further forcing the German by diving too steeply and left him still going down between Wervicq and Menin at about 3,000 feet.

Another German machine went down to Lille aerodrome on the approach of the Scout which, however, did not fire a shot, Capt Grenfell watched the hostile machine land and saw it turn very sharply to the left having apparently damaged a wheel for it was lying on its right wing with its left up in the air.

October 21st

Capt Playfair and 2 Lt Findlay of 11 Sqn, Vickers F.B. machine, during army reconnaissance in the neighbourhood of St. Quentin were overtaken and attacked by a Fokker monoplane. The Vickers turned and opened fire at about 30 yards range. The Fokker dived steeply and disappeared.

When over Buire an L.V.G. was sighted about 300 feet above. He opened fire. After firing a drum and a half the Lewis gun jammed. It took from 5 to 10 minutes to put the gun into working order again during which time the L.V.G. kept up a running fight sometimes coming as close as 30 yards. Eventually the L.V.G. came up from behind within about 50 yards. The Vickers then turned sharply towards him and fired a drum and a half at close range. A puff of smoke was seen to come from the hostile machine which immediately turned and dived down.

Miscellaneous

Last week the pilot of a Bristol Scout returning to his aerodrome saw some of our anti-aircraft shells bursting several hundred feet above him. Thinking that there must have been a hostile machine about, he climbed up to where the shells had been bursting. The fire was continued, then gathering that our guns were firing at him, he continued his way home. Shortly after landing some gunners dashed up in a car to seize souvenirs off the German machine they claimed to have brought down.

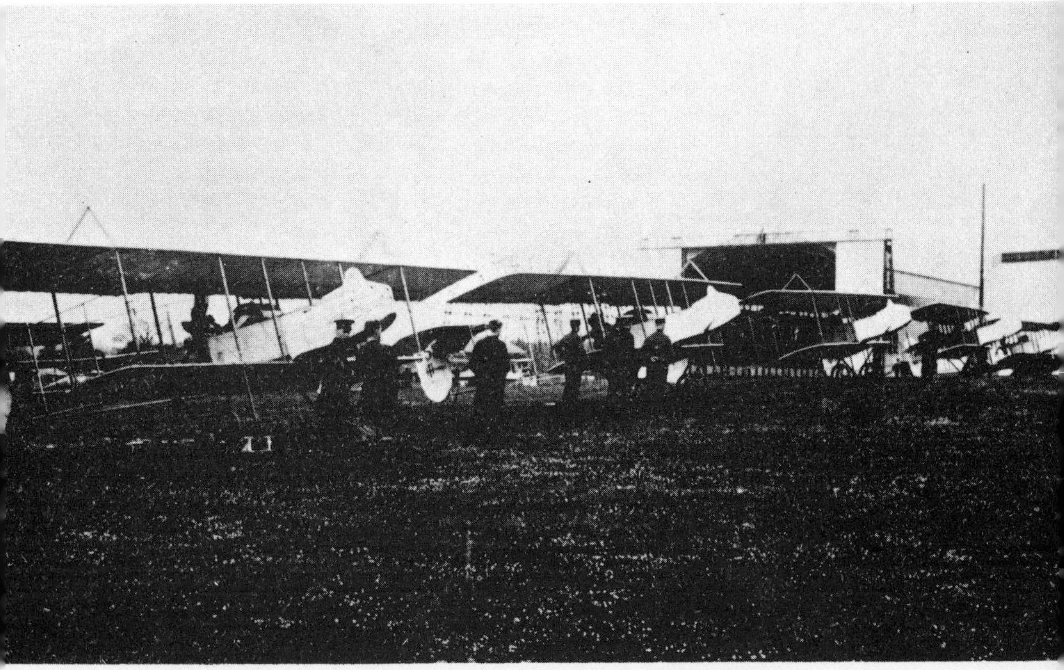

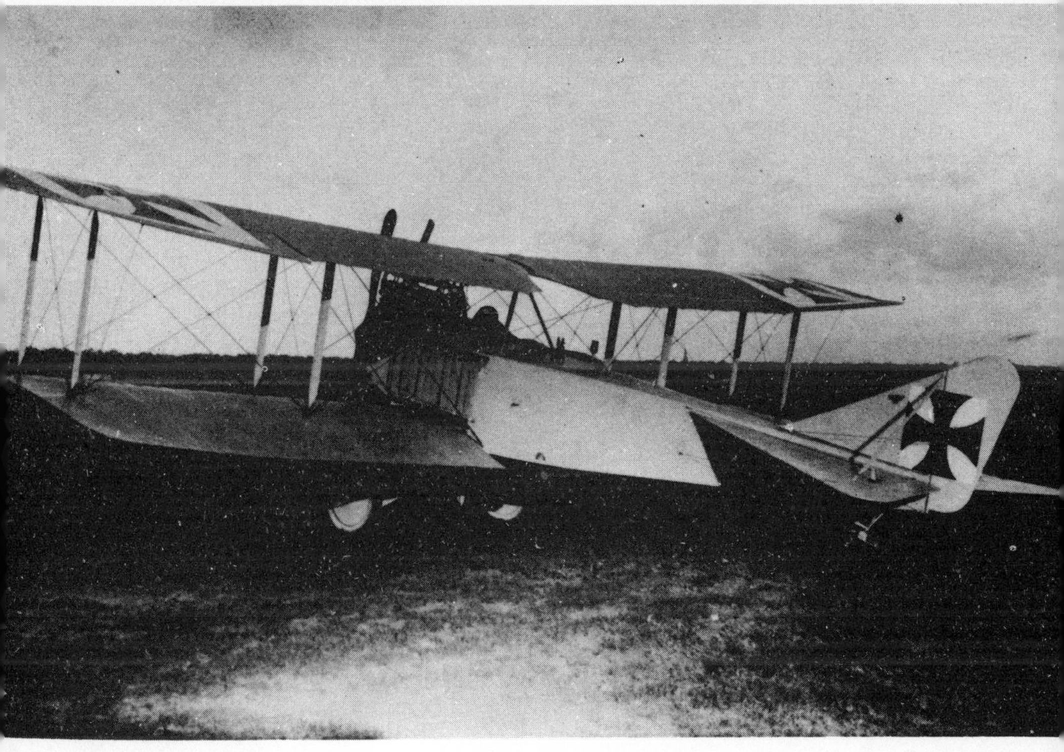

Above: Henri Farman
Below: Albatros C I

Above: L.V.G. C II
Below: B.E. 2a

21–28 October, 1915

Two Fokker monoplanes operating together were reported for the first time—with a reasonable indication that one may have been shot down.

Operations for 26 October included one of the first recorded examples of skill and gallantry by an observer in bringing back his aircraft with a wounded and unconscious pilot. In this instance the observer's task was particularly difficult, since he himself was hit in the hand and was seated in the front cockpit.

After more than a year of war some R.F.C. aircraft were still operating with the observer's rifle as the only armament.

'Flechettes' were small steel darts, dropped in clusters, as a primitive anti-personnel weapon.

An Albatros reconnaissance biplane shot down by 5 Sqn on 26 October was flown by a corporal pilot, with an officer observer. This was currently quite a normal practice in the German air force.

COMMUNIQUÉ NO. 16

October 21st

Sgt Courtney and Sgt Thornton, 3 Sqn, in a Morane, when dropping hand grenades and flechettes on La Bassee were attacked by a Fokker monoplane with deflector propellor. Sgt Thornton was hit in the hand and had his face grazed. When getting out his rifle he was hit in the other hand and the pilot dived towards our lines followed by the Fokker. The pilot was then hit through the leg and a bullet put the engine out of action. On the approach of a B.E.2c the hostile machine abandoned the chase.

October 22nd

2 Lt Glen and Cpl Jones, 8 Sqn, in a B.E.2c when escorting the distant reconnaissance machine to Le Cateau saw a hostile machine at about 5,000 feet. They followed him but lost him in a cloud and also lost touch with the machine they were escorting. They then turned for home and near Cambrai were attacked by two Fokker monoplanes which dived at them from about 11,000 feet. The hostile machines then kept behind them and both fired at the B.E.2c through their propellors. By this time Cpl Jones had mounted his gun in the rear mounting and fired about half a drum from this position. The leading Fokker seemed to tail-glide for a fraction of a second and then went to earth in a vertical nose dive.

The pilot watched the machine go down in this way for several thousand feet. The observer saw the machine fall among some trees and then noticed what appeared to be a cloud of dust rise. The second Fokker machine discontinued the fight and disappeared.

Capt Rees and Lt Skeate (Vickers F.B. 11 Sqn) during patrol sighted an Albatros about 2,000 feet below them. After firing one drum at it the Albatros dived for its own lines. The Vickers followed it and as it turned fired another drum at it and saw a map or piece of fabric about two feet square blow off the hostile machine. The pilot and observer report that they were able to see their bullets, most of which seemed to go to the right of the enemy's nacelle.

Capt Fiennes and Lt Paterson (B.E.2c 4 Sqn) during a IIIrd Army reconnaissance were attacked from below and in rear by a two-seater tractor biplane of the Fokker type. The B.E.2c manoeuvred so as to place the hostile machine behind it and in this position fired half a drum from the rear mounting. After this the hostile machine shewed little fight and the reconnaissance was completed unmolested.

Capt Rees and Lt Slade (Vickers F.B. 11 Sqn) ascended at 10 a.m. to chase an L.V.G. which had passed over the aerodrome. At 5,500 feet they saw an enemy double-fuselage biplane about 2,000 feet above them. He was throttled down and apparently did not see them. His attention was called to them by the anti-aircraft gun firing and he then circled over them. When about 500 feet above them the hostile machine opened fire, the Vickers reserving fire, hoping for a more favourable opportunity, but the hostile machine made off without being fired at. On returning to our lines Capt Rees encountered another hostile machine which made off without being engaged.

Lt Greenwood and Cpl Bennett, 16 Sqn, in a B.E.2c encountered an Albatros in the vicinity of Don. The German fired a white light upon which the anti-aircraft gun fire ceased and the hostile machine then opened fire with his machine-gun. Lt Greenwood turned to meet the German and returned his fire. The enemy at once dived steeply making off eastwards. On recrossing the lines near Bois Grenier Lt Greenwood's machine was hit by a shell, the observer being wounded in the elbow.

Capt Carthew and 2 Lt Chapman, 2 Sqn, in a B.E.2c, engaged and drove an Albatros in the vicinity of La Bassee. The German showed little fight and Capt Carthew completed his artillery registration without further interruption.

2 Lt Neale and Lt Skeate, 11 Sqn, in a Vickers F.B. during patrol sighted and chased an Aviatik. The German made off in the direction of Amiens and was pursued and engaged near Abbeville at a range of about 300 yards. Eventually the enemy was driven over to his own side of the lines.

October 26th

Lt Swart and Capt Simpson, 5 Sqn, in a B.E.2c on a short reconnaissance and counter-battery work, saw and engaged a Fokker, firing about a dozen rounds at him at 100 yards range as he approached. The B.E.2c then made a sharp turn and dived under him opening fire again. The Fokker nose dived steeply followed by the B.E.2c firing the remainder of the drum. While reloading, Lt Swart was attacked by an Aviatik which was well above them. The Aviatik having been driven off, an Albatros approached from behind and above, coming down in a slow spiral and firing all the time. Two French Maurice Farmans approached from the west and the Albatros drew off.

Capt Loraine and Lt Lubbock, 5 Sqn, in a Vickers Fighter on patrol near Houthem observed two German machines approaching from the east. The first was attacked and half a drum fired at him at a range of 15 yards. The German dived almost vertically, followed by the Vickers whose pilot fired the remaining half-drum whilst the observer emptied nearly another drum at him. The German machine, an Albatros was seen to crash to earth and turned completely over at *Square U.13.a.5.6*m *Sheet 28* within our lines. Capt Loraine then found himself at 700 feet and climbed to attack the second German. At 6,000 feet the engine of the Vickers stopped and Capt Loraine was forced to land. The pilot of the German machine was shot by machine-gun fire and the observer was wounded and was made prisoner. (*See also page 69*, '*Miscellaneous*'.)

Lt Russell and 2 Lt Brown, 2 Sqn, in a B.E.2c during artillery observation over the Hohenzollern Redoubt attacked an Albatros which they had observed over Vermelles going in an easterly direction and about 700 feet above them. After the first few rounds from the B.E.2c the enemy machine wavered, recovered and opened fire. After three drums of ammunition had been expended the enemy machine drew out of range.

Capt Porter and Cpl Welch, 2 Sqn, in a B.E.2c whilst engaged in artillery observation over Vermelles, attacked an Albatros which, at the time, was about 200 feet above them and a quarter-of-a-mile away on their left front. A running fight was kept up as far as Arras where Capt Porter, having used up his ammunition and running short of petrol, broke off the fight and returned to his aerodrome.

2 Lt Merton and 2 AM Milne, 16 Sqn, in a B.E.2c when taking photographs in the vicinity of Lille were attacked on three occasions by hostile machines, type not recognised. On each occasion the hostile machine sheered off after a few rounds had been fired at him and eventually disappeared without apparent damage.

2 Lt McEwan and 2 Lt Catherall, 16 Sqn, in a B.E.2c returning from a patrol over Lille sighted an L.V.G. at a height of approximately 12,000

feet. Climbing to 10,000 feet the B.E.2c opened fire on the German at a range of 2,000 feet and pursued him over the lines when the chase was abandoned.

2 Lt Lillywhite and 2 Lt Fielding Johnston, 3 Sqn, in a Morane Parasol on escort duty to photographic reconnaissance, when flying at 10,000 feet saw an Aviatik 500 feet below them and dived towards it opening fire. The Aviatik turned towards its own lines. The Morane was now attacked from behind by two more Aviatiks which both opened fire at about 150 yards. On fire being returned both the hostile machines dived in opposite directions apparently undamaged. A fourth Aviatik now opened fire from above and glided past the Morane into the German lines with its propellor stopped. As Lt Lillywhite was returning to the aerodrome he met yet another Aviatik which he chased for about 15 minutes over the lines, the German eventually turning and going down into its own lines.

Lt Pattinson and 2 Lt Findlay (Vickers F.B. 11 Sqn) while proceeding on a patrol to St Quentin saw an L.V.G. circling round near the trenches. On the approach of the Vickers the enemy sheered off and the patrol was continued. Later the L.V.G. opened fire at a range of 400 yards, the Vickers replying with about 3½ drums of ammunition. The L.V.G. again drew out of range. Five minutes later he again attacked and at a range of 500 yards deliberate fire was opened from the Vickers with a rifle. L.V.G. gradually drew out of range and disappeared, apparently undamaged.

Lt Williams and Lt Hallam, 10 Sqn, in a B.E.2c when doing photography near Lille were attacked by a Fokker with deflector propellor at about 7,000 feet. While manipulating the gun Lt Hallam was hit in the left hand which prevented him from again using this weapon. A certain amount of manoeuvring then took place after which the pilot was hit in the arm and shoulder and lost consciousness. The B.E.2c then started spinning and Lt Hallam, seeing that the pilot was hit, climbed over between the two back struts and caught hold of the control lever. He moved this about but nothing happened. He then tried to close the throttle. This did no good, the wire apparently having been broken. He then turned off the petrol and getting the machine under control managed to land it just behind the French reserve trenches in *Square M.25, Sheet 36*. The machine turned over and Lt Williams was thrown out. Lt Hallam climbed out and assisted Lt Williams who lost a lot of blood. Eventually they were assisted and Lt Williams' wounds attended by men of the French Red Cross.

2 Lt Gilbert, an observer of 2 Sqn, who was at the time arranging an artillery programme with a battery close to the scene, managed to get to the machine under fire and salvage the Lewis gun and instrument board. (*See also last paragraph, page 77.*)

Special mission

The following is a report received from 2 Lt Woodhouse of his experiences in attempting a special mission on the 18th October:

I started at 3.35 p.m. and climbed to 7,000 feet crossing the lines at 4.5 p.m. over Maricourt. There was a very strong north-east wind blowing and thick clouds between 3,000 and 5,000 feet. North of Peronne I was chased by a German machine but having no time to spare I evaded it in the clouds and headed east by compass. At 4.45 p.m. I came down through the clouds to 1,500 feet and tried to locate my position. I followed different roads and tried to find the Cambrai–Roisel railway line, but at 5.5 p.m. was absolutely lost and turned for home. I was fired at several times by rifles. The engine which had been misfiring got worse. At 2,000 feet I was in the clouds so steered west by compass. At 5.45 I decided to land as it was dark but while flattening out changed my mind and went up again as I saw men on the ground. I crossed the trenches a few moments later at 500 feet and was fired at, the machine being hit by rifle fire. I was unable to keep the machine any longer in the air so landed coming to rest on the parapet of a French second line trench outside Conchy, south-east of Montdidier at 5.55 p.m. French reserves helped me to pull the machine under cover of a wood out of danger of German fire.

Miscellaneous

The late Capt G. W. Mapplebeck, D.S.O., the first time he flew over Lille after his escape from that town dropped a message for Prince Rupprecht of Bavaria, Commanding the VIth Army, apologising for his apparent rudeness in not coming to pay his respects to him in person and pleading as an excuse, his hurried departure from Lille.

It has now been ascertained that this message was picked up and duly delivered to Prince Rupprecht but the informant was unable to say what remarks the Prince made when he received it.

The machine brought down by Capt Loraine on the 26th October was an Albatros. The pilot, a corporal was killed by rifle fire. The observer, 2 Lt Buchholz was wounded in the head and is in hospital. He was only 17 years old and had won the Iron Cross when serving as an infantry officer in the IXth Corps. They belonged to the 33rd Flying Squadron attached to the XXVIIth Reserve Corps. The 33rd Sqn is at Moorseele and consists of six Albatros machines, housed in wooden sheds.

There are six pilots and six observers in the squadron. Casualties are replaced from Germany.

Attempts to salve the machine which fell very near the trench line, were unsuccessful and during the attempt the Canadian lost two killed and two wounded.

The machine was fitted with a 6-cylinder Mercedes engine. The following have been rescued from it:

Camera with trigger release for actuating the shutter.
A pair of prismatic binoculars, 18-power, very clear definition.
A Mauser carbine, not automatic.
A Colt machine-gun. This was recognised by the Canadians as one which they had lost last May.
About 100 rounds of Mark VII, 303, S.A.A.
An ordinary aeroplane compass mounted in gymbals.

The machine was not fitted with a revolving machine-gun mounting. A document found on the observer gave a summary of reconnaissances made during the past few weeks. The following are extracts:

30th September:	Hostile batteries located at *W.48.f.*, *W.47.h.*, *V.47.g.*, *V.47.1.*, *V.47.r.*, *V.47.* (These positions are all between Zillebeke Pond, and the Ypres–Menin road.)
19th October:	Saw a hostile aeroplane, which flew off in a north-easterly direction when fired at; we could not pursue as our M.G. jammed.
22nd October:	A Farman aeroplane attacked us but we could not accept fight as our M.G. jammed.

The following W.T. signals are used when working with artillery, each signal being repeated three times:

K = Short.	R = Right.
W = Over.	L = Left.
G = Range.	T = Target.

The following tests are apparently set for pilots and observers:

(1) Flights over the enemy's lines as pilot or observer.
(2) Practice in bomb dropping.
(3) Skill in photography.
(4) Knowledge of wireless.
(5) Skill in using automatic rifle or machine-gun.

26–30 October, 1915

This communiqué was mainly devoted to the interrogation report on Lt Buchholz, observer of the Albatros shot down on 26 October.

COMMUNIQUÉ NO. 17

Captured German Observer

Examination of Lt Buchholz, taken prisoner, 26th October, 1915, in U.1.d.

The above-named prisoner is 17 years of age and started his military career as an Infantry Officer in the IXth Army Corps, where he won the Iron Cross, 2nd Class.

On re-cross-examination he gave information that the IXth Army Corps had been recently withdrawn from its position in the 1st German Army area, and had been replaced by some other Corps of which he could give no information.

He volunteered for the Flying Corps last May and was sent to the chief aeronautical school in Berlin for special training as an observer; all the observers of the German Flying Corps being officers. He remained in this school during the months of June and July and having successfully passed the necessary tests, he was ordered to join the 33rd Feldfliegerabteilung at Moorseele. Here he went through further instruction in flights over enemy's lines, practice in bomb dropping, skill in photography, knowledge of wireless and skill in the use of automatic rifles and machine-guns.

The 33rd Feldfliegerabteilung is attached to the XXVIIth Reserve Corps under command of Hauptmann Spranger, with Headquarters at Moorseele.

The Feldfliegerabteilung consists of six aeroplanes, all of the Albatros type, but he states that this number cannot be regarded as definite, as some abteilungen have as many as ten to fifteen aeroplanes. It is curious to note that three out of the six aeroplanes in his abteilung were mounted with Colt machine-guns, which the prisoner states are called Canadian machine-guns.

The prisoner stated that he had never used an automatic rifle in any of the aeroplanes attached to his unit, but the only information he gave was about a very light air-cooled machine-gun, somewhat similar to the

Colt gun. He said that the special points about this new German gun was that it was very much lighter and easier to handle and did not jam as frequently as the Colt.

The prisoner has been mainly reconnoitring the country around Ypres and during the last reconnaissance of Vlamertinghe and vicinity, he was fired at by anti-aircraft guns somewhere bear Ouderdom. He states his engine immediately started to misfire, the engine having apparently been hit by bursting shrapnel. One of the planes, also, of the machine suffered, and as he could not fly against the strong east wind, he had to set his course, instead of due east, to the south-east. He had no idea where he was landing, and the first thing he did was to secure information as to his bearings. The pilot, Unteroffizier Gereld was severely wounded in the groin by Capt Loraine of the 5th Squadron, attached to the VIth Corps, who pursued the aeroplane until it was brought to earth.

The prisoner was further cross-examined on the basis of a series of special questions compiled by G.H.Q. Owing to the inexperience of this observer a great number of these questions could not be answered. The prisoner was very willing to answer any questions put to him to the best of his ability. He further stated:

(1) All orders and instructions were issued to his Feldfliegerabteilung by Hauptmann Spranger.

(2) Staff officers are not sent up on reconnaissance, this duty always being performed by trained observers.

(3) Observers are obtained from volunteers. They are generally trained at an aeronautical school in Berlin. The training consists in flying observation, use of machine-gun, bomb-dropping, photography, wireless telegraphy, and a special course of shooting in the air on hostile aircraft. All observers have to pass a standard test before they are sent up on reconnaissance. The prisoner could give no definite information as to the nature of this test.

(4) There is no shortage of pilots. Officers are keen and frequently volunteer to become pilots.

(5) The prisoner could give no information regarding the Feldfliegerabteilungen who make use of the various aerodromes in the areas occupied by the German Armies.

(6) Buchholz had flown in no other type of aeroplane than the Albatros. He could give no information as to new types of German machines. If a machine is damaged the pilot and observer are immediately supplied with a new aeroplane.

(7) He stated that squadrons are not told off specially for fighting in the air. He could give no information as to whether German aeroplanes were much damaged as the result of combats in the air.

(8) Asked as to why their pilots so often broke off their combats and dived straight towards their own lines he replied that he was of opinion that the German aviators dived either on account of lack of ammunition or jams in machine-gun.

(9) The prisoner stated that our anti-aircraft guns did very poor registering and their pilots were not often hit by them.

(10) He knew of no sights being used in bomb dropping and could give no information as to types of bombs or special squadrons provided for bomb dropping.

(11) Much use was made of photography, orders for which are apparently issued by the Staff.

(12) The majority of machines are fitted with wireless apparatus, which according to the prisoner is used only for the purpose of artillery registration.

(13) Night flying is very seldom undertaken and apparently only for bomb dropping.

(14) Asked why pilots seldom reconnoitre very far over our lines, the prisoner stated that aeroplanes go on far reconnaissances when specially required to do so for the Staff.

(15) The prisoner had never been on the Russian front and consequently knew nothing of aeronautical matters on that front.

(16) As far as he knew no recognition signals were used in his unit, but he did know that any signals which were being used for other purposes were being constantly changed.

(17) No special signals are used to mark their aerodromes.

(18) There is no shortage in the supply of petrol. Buchholz stated that they could always obtain as much petrol as they needed.

(19) The Albatros type of aeroplane could carry enough petrol to last for six hours. Generally the rate of speed which could be obtained from this type of machine was 130 kilometres per hour, and in order to climb to 3,000 metres it generally took somewhere in the neighbourhood of an hour.

The Albatros aeroplane brought down in our lines was equipped with a Benz 6-cylinder engine. Very little space is required to land. No armour plate has been used on any machine seen by the prisoner and when questioned as to recent experiments which have been made regarding the protection of petrol tanks he said that in his unit this had not been tried.

The camera salvaged from the wrecked aeroplane is of the pistol type fitted with a very powerful Zeiss-Tessar lens. The size of the photograph taken with this camera is 3½ inches by 5 inches, but a new camera is being introduced which would enable them to make photographs

12 inches by 12 inches. These later cameras being much heavier than the present type would in some way be fixed to the plane. Photographs are usually taken at a height of 3,000 metres, and these only under very favourable circumstances.

The prisoner was very thoroughly examined as to the numbering and lettering of the squares of the maps captured. He stated that each squadron numbered and lettered the squares to suit their own requirements, the artillery in each corps having a duplicated map.

When shewn the map captured on a previous occasion from a German aeroplane, he at once volunteered the information that there was no standard in the Flying Corps regarding the marking and numbering of squares.

In his case the squares are lettered horizontally and numbered vertically.

The wireless signals found in his note book are not to be taken as being reliable and are not used in his Corps. These signals, K=short, W=over, G=range, R=right, L=left, and T=target, all of which were to be repeated three times, were used for instructional purposes only.

German Casualties

The following is a summary of casualties from all causes in the German Flying Corps taken from the German official returns. They refer to aeroplane squadrons only.

The months are those in which the casualties are reported and it is probable that the casualties actually took place in the previous month.

	Killed	*Wounded*	*Missing*	*Total*
June	16	21	16	53
July	17	16	10	43
August	39	21	29	89
September	47	26	6	79

31 October – 6 November, 1915

The inference that the Fokker monoplane shot down by 6 Sqn on 4 November was one of the new E-series scouts should be treated with reserve.

This aircraft was reported as having a crew of two, whereas the Fokker monoplanes operated as single-seaters. Nor are there any other historical references to a specimen of the aircraft currently of prime interest to British intelligence coming down in the Allied lines at this time. Several other aircraft were involved in the initial stages of this combat, and it may have been one of these which crashed.

COMMUNIQUÉ NO. 18

October 31st

Capt Rees and Flt Sgt Raymond, 11 Sqn, in a Vickers F.B., during patrol at 7,000 feet in the neighbourhood of Bapaume sighted a hostile machine (L.V.G.) approaching them. They turned to meet it and at a range of about 400 yards opened fire as the hostile machine turned away from them. The L.V.G. then dived towards Pys the Vickers following slightly gaining. Eventually Capt Rees found himself at a height of only 800 feet, the hostile machine about 300 feet below him. At this height either the fabric of the hostile machine was torn or two maps were thrown out. The German machine flattened out and went away leaving the Vickers immediately over an anti-aircraft battery, and under fire of machine-guns from Pys and Irnes. The hostile machine was now out of range and Capt Rees abandoned the pursuit and returned over the lines with some damage to his machine from rifle fire.

November 4th

2 Lt Bright and Capt Ryan, 6 Sqn, in a B.E.2c during an artillery observation flight were attacked by a large hostile pusher machine, closely followed by three tractors. The first, after receiving one drum, flew off followed by two of the remainder. While the B.E.2c manoeuvred for position the remaining hostile machine pursued and dived underneath the B.E.2c. Capt Ryan was twice wounded in the right arm and the petrol tank was pierced.

Lt Kelway Bamber and Lt Payne (F.E. 6 Sqn), while on patrol in the neighbourhood of Zillebeke saw the above B.E.2c closely pursued by a Fokker monoplane. Lt Bamber dived steeply to attack the German who turned and flew directly beneath the F.E. passing at about 30 yards. As the German approached half a drum was fired at him. The Fokker described three circles round the F.E., both machines losing height rapidly. The German then dived towards his lines followed by the F.E. at about 80 yards firing the remainder of the drum. The German was now seen to turn right-handed with a steep bank, turned on his back, and plunge to earth just inside our lines near Zillebeke. The pilot and observer were killed. The Germans heavily shelled the machine setting it on fire. Up to date all that has been salved from this machine is a much battered machine gun.

Lt Powell and Lt Lubbock, 5 Sqn, in a Vickers F.B. while taking photographs observed a hostile machine approaching them. They flew to attack him, the pilot and observer firing one drum each at him. This was at a range of about 600 yards with the German machine 1,000 feet above them. Another hostile machine was now approaching them from the direction of St Eloi. Lt Powell turned to engage him but after firing 35 rounds the Lewis gun jammed owing to the empty cartridge case bag being too full. In the meantime the observer fired about 60 rounds at a range of 500 yards. As the German turned to the west another machine approached from the direction of Ypres flying west. Lt Powell attempted to head off his machine but never succeeded in getting closer than 400 yards and having exhausted all his ammunition returned home.

Lt McConnochie and Lt Perri, 5 Sqn, in a B.E.2c during a reconnaissance encountered an Aviatik flying about 300 feet above them. This machine passed over the B.E.2c firing and at the same time a Fokker attacked from the opposite direction and about 100 feet above them. Lt McConnochie now turned and attacked the Aviatik which went away towards the south. He then again attacked the Fokker which banked vertically, side-slipped, and then disappeared from sight.

2 Lt Kemp and Cpl Monks (Vickers F.B., 11 Sqn) when crossing the lines in the vicinity of Nestle observed an Albatros to the south-west flying north and climbing rapidly. The Vickers had the advantage in height and turned to attack the hostile machine. Apparently the German did not observe the Vickers till it got within 300 yards. The hostile machine turned sharply and dived followed by the Vickers firing 1½ drums into it at a range of 300 yards. The Lewis gun then jammed. The German machine went down and landed 5 miles north of Nestle.

Lt Danby and 2 Lt Howey, 6 Sqn, in a B.E.2c during a reconnaissance on the IInd Army front encountered an Albatros which passed in front of the B.E.2c at a range of about 200 yards. Firing was then heard behind the British machine which turned sharply to the right and discovered another Albatros. At the same time a Fokker monoplane passed to the right of the B.E.2c firing its machine-gun. Lt Danby replied with one drum at the Fokker which immediately made off. The two Albatroses manoeuvred round and fired on the B.E.2c for nearly 20 minutes and then disappeared, apparently undamaged. The British machine was not hit.

November 5th

Capt Gossage and Lt O'Brien, 6 Sqn, in a F.E. on artillery observation in the vicinity of Ypres saw an Aviatik about 1,000 to 1,500 feet above them flying towards his own lines. Capt Gossage turned towards him and followed with his observer firing. The German appeared to have no difficulty in keeping well in front and of outclimbing the F.E., and when last seen, he was about 11,500 feet high, about 2,500 feet above Capt Gossage's machine.

Miscellaneous

Report on an attack on a German observation balloon by machines from the IIIrd Wing, 30th October:

About midday Lt Glen attacked an observation balloon flying near the Bois de Logeast. The balloon was at about 2,500 feet just below the clouds. Lt Glen approached it under cover of the clouds, and eventually attacked from 400 yards, passing over it at about 180 feet. He dropped five incendiary bombs, but unfortunately missed his mark, the balloon being hauled down immediately. Soon afterwards the balloon went up again, and at about 3 p.m. Lt Glen on a Bristol Scout with incendiary bombs, and Capt Allen and Lt Herring on B.E.2cs, each with a 112-pound bomb went out to attack at about 3,000 feet under a heavy A.A. gun fire. The balloon was found to be flying at about 1,000 feet and on Lt Glen's approach was hauled down. Capt Allen dropped his bomb just as the balloon reached the ground. A few minutes afterwards it rose to about 400 feet, and on Lt Herring's approach was not hauled down again. Lt Herring's bomb fell close to the probable position of the winch. The balloon remained at about 400 feet and the supposition is that the winch party had retired to cover.

The B.E.2c of 10 Sqn, reported on the 26th instant as having been brought down near Aix Noulette was found to be lying about 500 yards behind the French front line trench, with the engine the only part worth saving. On the 28th instant, after dark, Capt Gordon Bell with four men, assisted by two French guides, got the engine into a dug-out near at hand where it was dismantled and brought in next day. The party was under shell- and rifle-fire during the operation but incurred no casualties.

6–9 November, 1915

Lt G. S. M. Insall, 11 Sqn, was awarded the Victoria Cross for courage and determination during his air combat on 7 November.

References to Fokker biplanes by the 11 Sqn crew on 6 November are typical of the confusion which existed regarding the various contemporary enemy reconnaissance two-seaters. No Fokker two-seat biplane is recorded as in service at this time, and those of other makes—A.E.G., Albatros, Aviatik, D.F.W., L.V.G. and Rumpler—were very similar in general appearance and were frequently confused. The most frequently employed designation was Aviatik.

During this period intensive bombing operations were attempted but weather caused some interference.

The remarkable aircraft reported by anti-aircraft gunners on 4 November and illustrated in the appendix can be identified as the unorthodox Gotha Ursinus GUH GI, which first flew in July 1915. From a distance of 7,000 yards the description inevitably contains errors, but the position of the crew, and the rudder shape, plus the comment that the aircraft may have had a single fuselage—instead of the boom form illustrated—are enough to identify the machine. Used only in small numbers, the Gotha G.I was powered by two 150 horsepower Benz engines and had a wing span of about 66½ feet. Speed was just over 80 m.p.h. An unusual feature of the design was the low positioning of the biplane wings. (Another sketch of this aircraft is in Communiqué No. 24.)

COMMUNIQUÉ NO. 19

November 6th

2 Lt Hughes Chamberlain and 2 Lt Robinson (Vickers F.B. 11 Sqn), during a reconnaissance in the IIIrd Army area encountered four hostile machines.

When north of Peronne they were attacked suddenly by a Fokker biplane with passenger and machine-gun. Unperceived till within 150 yards, the Fokker dived from 200 feet above them and opened fire at 100 yards. By the time fire was opened on it the enemy machine crossed in front of the Vickers at 50 yards range and in this position 25 rounds were fired at it. The Fokker then circled left passing the Vickers at 150 yards firing from the side in bursts of 15–12 rounds. The remainder of the first drum was fired into it and by the time a new drum had been fitted the range was reduced to 25 yards. The Vickers was head on and at this range half a drum was fired into the Fokker which continued a rapid fire. The enemy then circled round for position to cross the Vickers front but anticipating it, the Vickers fired one drum at the passenger and pilot at 50 feet. The enemy machine dived steeply followed by the Vickers with full engine and in this position another drum was got off. The Fokker disappeared in a belt of clouds at 3,000 feet above Aizecourt. 2 Lt Hughes-Chamberlain and 2 Lt Robinson are convinced that the observer of this machine was put out of action and other serious damage was done.

When over Driencourt a hostile machine was detected climbing from north of Roisel about 1,000 feet below. The observer of the Vickers, as an experiment fired 10 rounds with the rifle. The German machine then gave up climbing and disappeared in a belt of clouds.

When one mile west of St Quentin a Fokker biplane came up unnoticed behind the Vickers to within 200 yards and on the same level. The Vickers turned to engage it, the enemy also turning and firing over his tail with a machine-gun. In this position one drum was fired by the Vickers when the Fokker dived steeply for 300 feet and went away. The Fokker then climbed rapidly and the Vickers closing in on it, fired half a drum when the Lewis gun jammed. The jam was cleared in two minutes but during that time the enemy circled closely firing rapidly. When the Vickers re-opened fire the enemy dived down and disappeared in the direction of St Quentin.

Continuing the reconnaissance a few minutes later another Fokker biplane which had climbed unnoticed, opened fire on the Vickers at about 180 yards and at a slightly higher elevation. The Vickers turned for position and opened fire with the Lewis gun expending 1½ drums and driving the hostile machine away in the direction of Happencourt. The fire from the hostile machine severely damaged the propellor of the Vickers which was forced to return to our lines. In addition to a damaged propellor the Vickers was shot in many places, among them three shots through the nacelle between the passenger and the pilot.

Attempts were made by machines of the IIIrd Wing to bomb the huts at Achiet-le-Grand. The intention was for 13 Sqn to attack as soon after daybreak as possible, 8 Sqn to follow about dinner-time and 4 to continue in the late afternoon. Each group of machines was to be escorted by a Scout of the same squadron, and 11 Sqn was to patrol the areas north-east and south-east of Achiet-le-Grand during the second and third attacks with two machines to prevent interference by hostile aeroplanes. The day broke very clear and 13 started off between 6.15 and 6.30 a.m. A bank of mist was, however, found over the German lines, making observation very difficult and the results of the attack consequently small. As the day went on weather conditions became worse and the continuous low mists blew down from the north-east; the midday attack was therefore abandoned. At about 2.30 p.m. the weather cleared and fourteen aeroplanes from 4, 8, and 13 went out to attack. The objective however was hidden by clouds and the attack failed. The results are disappointing, the difficulties of observation making it almost impossible to accurately determine the results. As far as can be ascertained, Capt Halahan hit some huts with both of his 100-pound bombs. Lt Powell's 112-pound bomb exploded near the huts and appeared to him to cause damage. Capt Metford and Lt Medhurst dropped 112-pound bombs on the railway, damaging the line in both instances. Lt Herring having lost his way, he saw about twenty M.T. wagons in a farm and put three of his 20-pound bombs into the buildings and three into the yard; three missed. The remaining pilots either lost their way, or did not observe the results of their bombs, and in some cases did not release them. A heavy mist came down from the north-east about 3.30 p.m. which rendered the return of the afternoon attack to the squadron landing places very difficult. Five officers were forced to land away from their squadrons on account of fog and approaching darkness; only one aeroplane was damaged however.

November 7th

2 Lt Medlicott (Bristol Scout, 2 Sqn) when on patrol near Lens observed a L.V.G. some 500 feet above him. Lt Medlicott climbed to get above the German machine. It took him three-quarters of an hour to do this, the hostile machine only firing once during that time. Eventually from 500 feet above, the Bristol Scout dived towards the German and opened fire at it at 150 yards. After diving three times and firing two drums into the L.V.G. Lt Medlicott manoeuvred under the tail of the German machine and fired about half a drum at 100 feet. Turning to attack again, Lt Medlicott saw the hostile machine in a spinning nose dive. It disappeared into the heavy ground mist uncontrolled.

Capt Gordon Bell (Bristol Scout, 10 Sqn) reports as follows:

> I accompanied Lt Le Bas and Capt Adams who were in a B.E.2c *1715* doing long reconnaissance. At about 2.45 p.m. over Douai a Fokker and an Aviatik were seen. I was about 2,000 feet higher than the B.E.2c and about the same height as the German machines. I engaged the Fokker and got off about 1 drum at him; he dived as if hit. I then turned to the Aviatik and got off ¾ of a drum when it dived and broke off the fight. I now went to have a look for the B.E.2c and saw it doing a steep left-handed spiral, with the Fokker circling down round it. The B.E.2c apparently hit the ground nose first near Quiery. The fuselage appeared to be broken. The two hostile machines then landed close beside it. My engine was only giving 900 revs., and I was at 4,000 feet so made for home, crossing the trenches at about 1,000 feet and landed near Verguigneuil, the machine turning over on its back in the plough.

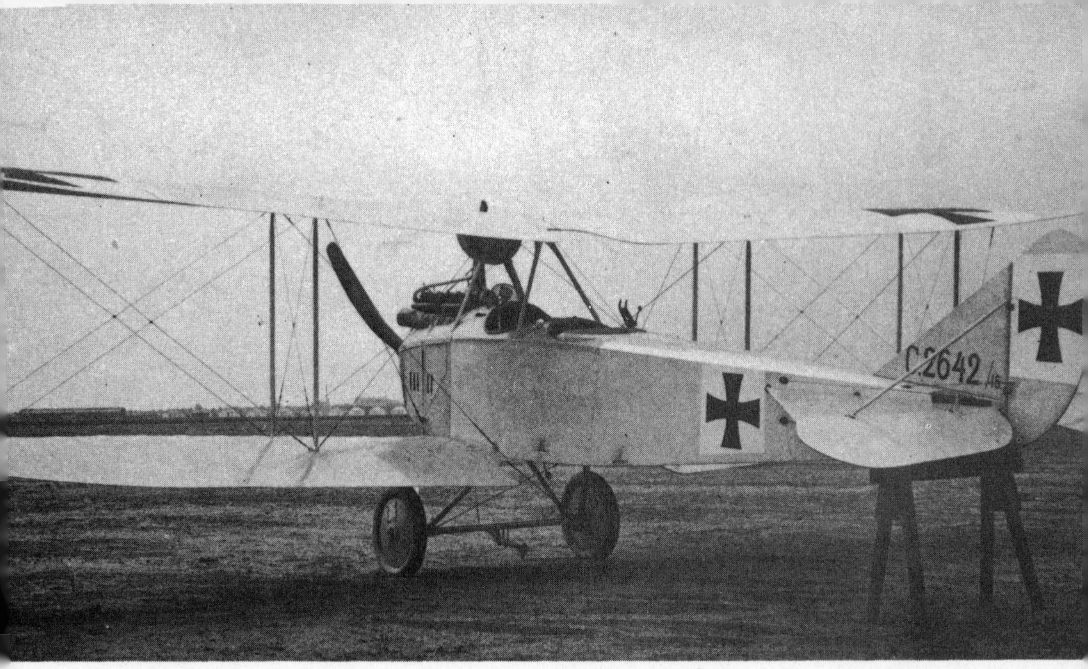

Above: Rumpler C I
Below: Maurice Farman

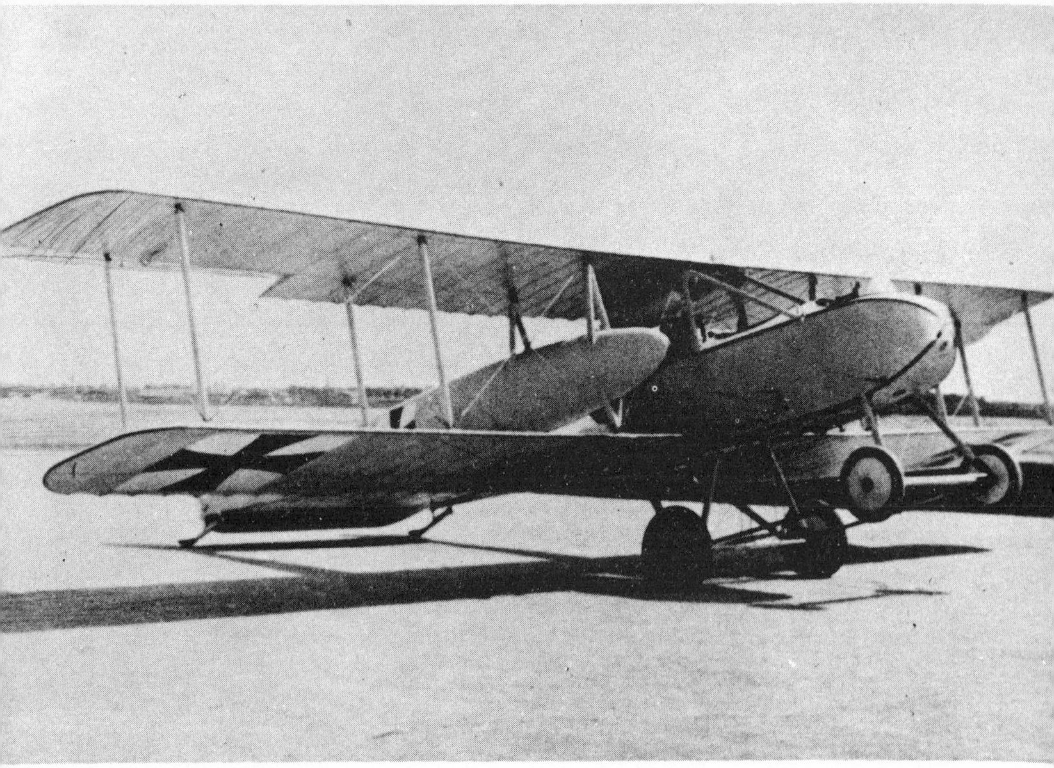

Above: Bleriot XI
Below: AGO C II

2 Lt Insall and A.M. Donald (Vickers F.B. *5074*) patrolling between Bois d'Adinfer and Bapaume at about 2.30 p.m. sighted an Aviatik flying south and about 1,000 feet higher. Shots were fired at it with the rifle at long range and it went away south-east. The Vickers climbed and steered south and engaged it near Achiet, when the German increased his speed and made off north-east. The intention of the German was evidently to lead the Vickers over a rocket battery but this intention was detected and by cutting him off east of the battery a drum was fired into him at close range and apparently with success for his engine stopped and he dived down. The Vickers caught up the German when diving through the clouds and another drum was fired into it, when it was observed to land heavily in a ploughed field west of Heninel, one wing down. The Vickers continued to dive 500 feet and the pilot and passenger were seen to land and get out their machine-gun. They were fired at however, and leaving the machine, fled in the direction of Heninel. One was noticed to be running faster than the other and he went back to help his companion so one of them may have been injured. The Vickers circled again and at about 500 feet dropped an incendiary bomb on the Aviatik which when last seen was enveloped in smoke. The Vickers was so heavily fired on that it had to cross the trenches at about 2,000 feet when the petrol tank was pierced and the engine stopped. A landing was effected 500 yards over the lines behind a small wood west of Agny. The enemy subsequently shelled the machine ranging the artillery with an aeroplane but though about 150 shells were fired the machine was not struck. The Vickers was moved a short distance under cover of darkness and a new tank fitted during the night with the help of screened lamps. Though the machine was within range the whole of the night it was not fired on by shell-fire and the pilot succeeded in bringing it home at dawn.

The IIIrd Wing again undertook bombing operations against the huts at Achiet-le-Grand. 13 Sqn was ordered to start at 6.15 a.m. followed by 8 at 11.30 a.m. and 4 at 2.30 p.m. Owing to thick mist 13 did not start until 11.45 a.m. Each party was accompanied by an escort machine and machines from 11 Sqn patrolled the whole front with a view to preventing retaliation and affording protection to the bombing machines on the homeward journey. Twenty-two 100-pound and seventeen 20-pound bombs were dropped. Of these six of the large bombs and seven of the small bombs hit either the huts or houses close to them and four of the 100-pound bombs hit the railway sidings.

November 8th

The Headquarters of the XIVth Reserve Corps at Bapaume were attacked by machines of the IIIrd Wing. Owing to fog the departure of the machines was delayed. Nine 100-pound and twelve 20-pound bombs were dropped. Only one of these was actually observed by the pilots but the last machine to fly over Bapaume (one of the escorting machines) reports the side of a house was damaged, and a crater within 15 yards of the house. The house was easily recognised from a sketch taken from the IIIrd Army Summary.

In the evening an attempt was made to bomb a concert reported to be held nightly at Douchy. The pilot was unable to find the objective and dropped one 100-pound and three 20-pound bombs on anti-aircraft guns at Puzeaux and two 20-pound bombs on Achiet-le-Petit all of which were unobserved.

Six machines of 7 Sqn each carrying two 100-pound bombs attacked the aerodrome at Gits at 2 p.m. No sheds received an actual hit. Two bombs fell about 100 yards away, the remainder falling on or near the aerodrome. Two machines returned without dropping their bombs, one having failed to find the objective and the other being unable to drop bombs owing to clouds.

HOSTILE BIPLANE SEEN BY 14 ANTI-AIRCRAFT SECTION, EAST OF ARMENTIERES, ON NOVEMBER 4TH

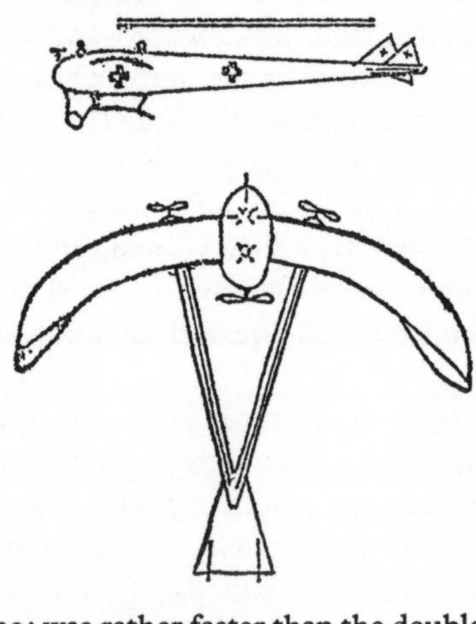

Very large, fast machine; was rather faster than the double-engined machine and a big Albatros which accompanied it.
Wings struck on the arc of a circle; not sloped back.
Top of the fuselage above the upper wings.
Double vertical rudder.
Fish tail.
Either a double closed-in fuselage as shown, or a single closed-in fuselage with pusher propellor on each side.

This machine did not approach nearer than 7,000 yards and sheered of, dropping lights when fired at.

10–16 November, 1915

Despite the continued activities of the Fokker monoplanes some of the R.F.C. aircraft were still obliged to operate with the observer's rifle as the only defensive armament.

'Condor' aircraft were occasionally reported by R.F.C. crews during the first eighteen months of the war. The Kondor Flugzeug-Werke, of Essen, was one of the lesser-known German aircraft companies and none of its designs were selected for large-scale production. The Kondor WI two-seater may have been in operational use during 1915. It is possible, however, that the name 'condor' may have been loosely applied to some other type.

The unidentified aircraft reported by Capt Grenfell, 1 Sqn, could have been an A.E.G. BII, which had a superficial resemblance to the Martinsyde.

An ambitiously-planned raid by IIIrd Wing squadrons on Bellenglise aerodrome was much hampered by bad weather. A smaller raid was made on the aerodrome at Gits.

COMMUNIQUÉ NO. 20

November 10th

2 Lt Symington, 7 Sqn, in a B.E.2c on approaching Gits aerodrome for the third time in order to take aim observed a Fokker bearing down upon him from the front and looking behind saw an Albatros approaching him. The Fokker dived under him at close quarters and almost immediately disappeared leaving the Albatros manoeuvring round and firing with a machine-gun. Lt Symington opened fire and a running fight was kept up till near the lines at ranges of from 100 to 200 yards. Eventually the hostile machine turned back to his own lines apparently undamaged.

Four machines of 7 Sqn each carrying two 100-pound bombs again attacked the aerodrome at Gits, between 9.30 and 9.45 a.m. Three machines succeeded in dropping their bombs on and near the aerodrome but no sheds were seen to be hit.

Lt Herring, 8 Sqn, from a height of 3,000 feet attacked a trench and gun emplacement in the Bois de Biez, (*Sheet 37 D, Square L. 1.*). Seven out of nine of his 20-pound bombs fell in the trench.

November 11th

Lt Russell and 2 Lt Rice, 2 Sqn, in a B.E.2c returning from reconnaissance near Lens sighted an Albatros over Mazingarde about 1,000 feet higher than the B.E.2c. Climbing to about 500 feet below the Albatros, the pilot and observer of the B.E.2c both opened fire. The Albatros now manoeuvred with the apparent intention of getting behind the B.E.2c, but failed. After two more drums had been expended, the Albatros turned and glided towards his own lines.

2 Lt Allcock and 1 AM Bowes, 2 Sqn, in a B.E.2c escort to reconnaissance machine, were attacked by a Fokker which dived underneath them opening fire at 300 feet range. Lt Allcock turned and from the back mounting fired half a drum at the Fokker which cleared off. He was then attacked by an Albatros which followed the Fokker after one drum had been discharged at him.

Capt Babington and Lt Chadwick, 2 Sqn, in a B.E.2c during photography near Vendin–le–Vieil, saw three Albatros machines well above them. None of these machines closed to engage and all cleared off after a few rounds had been fired at them.

2 Lt Murray and 2 Lt Gilbert, 2 Sqn, in a B.E.2c returning from Valenciennes reconnaissance, sighted and attacked an L.V.G. over our lines near Loos. The Lewis gun jammed as the third drum was being fired and the second Lewis gun was then put in action on the front mounting. The L.V.G. eventually crossed the lines gliding in the direction of Lens, apparently undamaged.

2 Lt Sanday and Sgt Hodgson, 2 Sqn, in a B.E.2c on artillery registration, when at 4,500 feet saw an L.V.G. cross over to our lines some 4,000 feet above them. Climbing to 7,200 feet Lt Sanday attacked from immediately below the hostile machine. Unfortunately he was only armed with a rifle. After a few rounds the L.V.G. put his nose down and dived in the direction of Lens.

Lt Saunders and 2 Lt Cleaver, 3 Sqn, in a Morane Parasol, when taking photos near La Bassee sighted an Albatros going towards Armentieres. They pursued it cutting it off and fired one drum, the enemy turning and making off towards Douai. A few minutes later they saw a Condor flying 200 feet below them and dived at it firing 15 rounds. The Condor nose dived and flew very low in the direction of Lille. Another Albatros coming from the direction of Lille dropped smoke balls upon which anti-aircraft guns immediately become active. This machine then disappeared in the direction of Lille and another Albatros was sighted over our lines near Bethune, the attention of the pilot being drawn to him by the fire of our anti-aircraft guns. The hostile machine turned down wind to his own lines at very high speed, the Morane firing 15 rounds at it as it passed. Having practically expended all his ammunition Lt Saunders returned to his own aerodrome.

2 Lt Morton, 16 Sqn, in a Bristol Scout went up at 9.45 a.m. in pursuit of an L.V.G. sighted crossing our lines. He eventually engaged this machine over the Bois de Biez but owing to engine trouble was unable to climb up to him. The hostile machine turned away and went off in the direction of Lille.

Capt Grenfell, 1 Sqn, in a Morane, when taking photographs near Armentieres at 7,500 feet saw a hostile machine of the following description some 700 feet above him.

Very deep, narrow fuselage, like the Martynsyde Scout and R.E.; fish tail similar to the Albatros; B.E. type undercarriage: no extensions to wings; estimated speed 88 to 90 m.p.h. Crosses on the wings appeared thus—and are reported as dark blue.

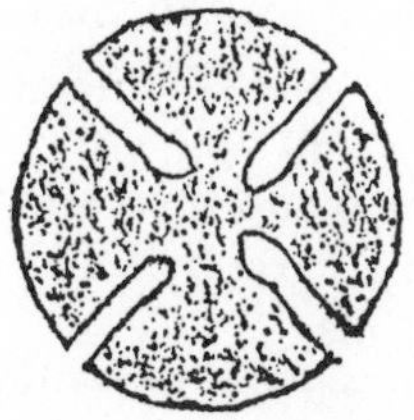

Armament, one machine-gun as far as could be ascertained. This machine passed over the Morane and Capt Grenfell thought it to be the new Martinsyde Scout. After passing, the observer in the hostile machine opened fire. Our anti-aircraft guns then engaged it, but their shells burst 1,000 feet below the Morane. Over Perenchies the German was joined by two more hostile machines and all three turned and bore down on the Morane which was unable to outclimb them. Coming west of Armentieres Capt Grenfell climbed to 11,200 feet and again crossed the line. He found two of the hostile machines still above him and both dived to attack him. Putting the nose of the Morane down, he attacked the third machine, an Albatros, which turned and went down over Lille followed shortly afterwards by the remaining two.

An attempt was made by machines of the IIIrd Wing to bomb the aerodrome at Bellenglise, about 26 miles east of Albert. The intention was for 4, 8 and 13 Sqn to send all available aeroplanes to attack the aerodrome simultaneously, each squadron providing its own escort. Half the machines carried a passenger and half-load of bombs, the remaining machines without passengers and a full load of bombs. 11 Sqn patrolled the areas lying between Peronne and St Quentin and the objective with four aeroplanes to prevent interference by any hostile machines. At reconnaissance height there was a very high north-east wind and over the German lines the weather was thick and cloudy and navigation very difficult. The result was that few aeroplanes found their objective, practically no damage was done, and all machines had great difficulty in finding their way back to their aerodrome.

November 14th

Lt Ashby and Lt Preston, 7 Sqn, in a B.E.2c while flying over Roulers sighted a twin-fuselage pusher machine coming towards them from Menin at about 11,000 feet. Lt Preston opened fire at a range of 500 yards, the German replying and hitting Lt Ashby in the thigh. The hostile machine was about 250 feet above the B.E.2c, the observer standing up and firing. Lt Preston fired six bursts at the hostile machine, the propeller of which was seen to stop, the German gliding down and disappearing. Lt Ashby landed his machine at Abeele aerodrome successfully.

2 Lt Merton and 2 AM Milne, 16 Sqn, in a B.E.2c while taking photographs over the lines opposite Le Maisnil, saw an Albatros approaching them and pass about half a mile away, on their right, firing as they passed. He then turned and fired a few rounds at long range, Lt Merton continuing his photography. The hostile machine shortly afterwards flew off towards Lille.

Three machines of 6 Sqn carried out a bombing attack on a hostile captive balloon in *Square Q. 15, Sheet 28.* The balloon was sighted in the air while the machines were getting height but was pulled down before the balloon was reached. The bombs were dropped in various places but no hits were secured on the balloon.

November 16th

Capt Gordon Bell, 10 Sqn, in a Bristol Scout, patrolling near Lens saw a small tractor two-seater biplane of the Scout type. Climbing to 13,000 feet, Capt Gordon Bell attacked, but after firing one drum he had difficulties with loading his machine-gun, and the hostile machine went off apparently undamaged.

Later in the day, when escorting a photographic machine near Lille, Capt Gordon Bell engaged a large Albatros. After firing a drum the Albatros broke off the fight, diving steeply. Anti-aircraft guns became active as soon as he dived.

Lt Milne and Lt Buckley, 16 Sqn, in a B.E.2c engaged a double fuselage machine over Loos. Climbing to 2,000 feet, Lt Milne noticed that the hostile machine was descending and dived towards him. At 6,000 feet the enemy fired a Very light and anti-aircraft guns immediately opened fire. The hostile machine turned towards Lille and descended to his aerodrome, followed by the B.E.2c to 4,500 feet, firing altogether a drum and a half. Upon returning, Lt Milne met an Albatros and a Fokker. The latter disappeared in the direction of Douai, the former was engaged over Don but showed little fight and made off in the direction of Lille. Lt Milne is of opinion that the fire of the anti-aircraft batteries was directed by the German machines.

Capt Mansfield and Lt Moffat, 7 Sqn, in a B.E.2c when flying in the neighbourhood of Roulers were passed by an Albatros at about 9,000 feet and about 500 yards away. Without fighting the hostile machine descended to 2,000 feet and Capt Mansfield continued his reconnaissance. A little later the Albatros turned and followed the B.E.2c, the latter turning and firing a burst at him. Whilst turning, a smaller hostile two-seater tractor biplane was seen about 500 feet above them and 500 yards away. The observer fired three bursts at him and he banked steeply and disappeared. Capt Mansfield now made for the Albatros and after an exchange of shots the hostile machine went down in a steep spiral, followed by the B.E.2c. At 2,000 feet the hostile machine flattened out and made towards Gits.

Capt Mills, 7 Sqn, in a Bristol Scout in the vicinity of the Foret d'Houthulst saw an Albatros flying north about 2,000 feet below him. He overtook it and diving on it, fired one round with the Lewis gun, when this weapon jammed. The hostile machine replied with a burst of about 15 rounds. Capt Mills was unable to right his machine-gun and broke off the fight.

Lt Morrison and 2 Lt Grant, 13 Sqn, in a B.E.2c when over Harbcourt returning from reconnaissance, sighted a Fokker monoplane, single seater, flying straight towards them and passing over the right wing about 20 yards away, without firing. Lt Grant tried to open fire but the Lewis gun jammed. The monoplane now approached from behind and opened fire at 200 yards, when the second gun jammed. The hostile machine then went off. Both the jams of the Lewis gun were caused by excessive oil.

18–28 November, 1915

Various inconclusive air combats were reported, and the Fokker monoplanes still seem disinclined to press home their attacks.

Reports from agents suggested that the bombing raid on Gits aerodrome 8 November was more effective than the pilots' accounts indicated.

COMMUNIQUÉ NO. 21

November 18th

Capt Porter and Lt Davey (2 Sqn, B.E.2c *1732*) whilst returning from escort duty to a long reconnaissance, were attacked by a single-seater Fokker monoplane, which fired through the propeller. The Fokker overhauled the B.E.2c and when it was within 100 yards, the observer fired half a drum. The Fokker dived beneath the B.E.2c, went away and did not return.

Perenchies Station was attacked on the 18th November by machines of 5 Sqn. The buildings are reported to have been set on fire.

November 20th

2 Lt Cave and 2 Lt Thomas (B.E.2c *1713*, 6 Sqn) whilst on artillery observation near Bixschoote saw an Aviatik about a mile north. The hostile machine first turned towards the B.E.2c but after the latter had fired two drums, it sheered off and went away.

Later in the day the same two officers, while doing artillery work over Hollebeke, saw an Aviatik over Polygon Wood at a lower altitude. The B.E.2c made for the hostile machine which dived steeply through the clouds. The B.E.2c then sighted an Albatros over Zandvoorde, chased it, and got within 100 yards of the Albatros and opened fire. The hostile machine put its nose down and dived through the clouds. The B.E.2c having expended all its ammunition gave up the chase.

2 Lt Bolton and 2 Lt Price (6 Sqn, B.E.2c, *2764*) also saw the second Aviatik encountered by Lts Cave and Thomas and engaged it at the same time. The Aviatik was firing over its tail, the shots going wide.

2 Lt Symington and 2 Lt Boyton (B.E.2c, 7 Sqn) were attacked by a Fokker monoplane over Zarren. The hostile machine came up from behind on the same level and overhauled the B.E.2c. When it had come within 200 yards half a drum was fired at it when it broke off the fight and descended.

November 25th

2 Lt Whitelock and 2 Lt Balmain (B.E.2c, *2001*, 4 Sqn), while on artillery co-operation between Bray and Albert encountered a small hostile machine, type not recognised, 100 feet below them. This machine made off without fighting after a couple of bursts from the Lewis gun. Later an Albatros appeared about 1,000 feet above the B.E.2c. After firing two drums from the Lewis gun, the hostile machine was driven off. A third hostile machine, an Albatros, was now encountered and driven off; and having expended all his ammunition Lt Whitelock returned to his aerodrome.

On November 25th the huts at Achiet Le Grand were attacked by 20 machines of the IIIrd Wing. The place is reported to be practically wrecked. Some pilots who took part in previous attacks are of opinion that some of the huts have been removed to another site.

November 26th

2 Lt Cooper and 2 Lt Insall (Vickers, 11 Sqn) while on Army patrol and photography over Bray observed an Albatros flying 200 feet above them. The Vickers was turned and about 15 shots fired from the Lewis gun without effect. The German opened fire apparently from a trap door in the floor of the machine, and accelerating, made for the lines. Another drum was fired without effect. Engine failure forced the Vickers to give up the chase and when last seen the German was heading for Peronne.

2 Lt O'Malley and Flt Sgt Harrison (B.E.2c, 13 Sqn) when returning from escort to reconnaissance observed an Aviatik about 7,000 feet below them. They managed to get above and behind the German machine without being seen and at 25 yards fired half a drum. Steam was noticed coming from the engine and the machine dived very steeply, followed by the B.E.2c which again opened fire at a range of 100 yards. More steam was seen coming from the engine and the hostile machine was last seen nose diving into a cloud at 2,000 feet just over the lines at Fricourt.

Lt Milne and Capt Storey (B.E.2c, 16 Sqn) when returning from long reconnaissance saw an Albatros over Arras. The hostile machine immediately turned and made off in the direction of Douai followed by the B.E.2c firing a drum. At Douai the hostile machine dived down, the B.E.2c following to 6,000 feet firing another half a drum. The B.E.2c being short of petrol broke off the engagement.

November 27th

Capt Sanders (Morane, 1 Sqn) during artillery co-operation encountered an Albatros flying towards Warneton at about 7,000 feet. By diving across his line Capt Sanders managed to close to 200 yards. The German opened fire a few seconds before the Morane and then dived steeply towards Quesnoy, followed by the Morane firing some 20 rounds. The hostile machine eventually drew out of range and went down towards Lille apparently undamaged.

Later, a second hostile machine of the Albatros type was encountered over Comines. The German approaching from the direction of Halluin at about 12,000 feet. Climbing steeply Capt Saunders got within range and opened fire at 300 to 500 yards, the enemy turning and making off in the direction of Tourcoing. About 10 minutes later, a machine believed to be the same returned but made off as soon as fire was opened on him, planing down towards Menin.

2 Lt Godwin and Lt Jacks (Morane, 1 Sqn) during a reconnaissance sighted an Albatros coming from Lille which passed within 250 yards and below them. The enemy machine-gun could be distinctly heard. At the same time a second Albatros appeared from the west and circled round also firing. After firing one and a half drums both hostile machines made off. Later another Albatros was sighted and attacked. The Morane dived from 11,000 feet, the pilot opening fire with a fixed gun. The observer opened fire with a second gun as the Albatros passed and the hostile machine, after being engaged for about two minutes, dived down towards Menin.

Twenty-one machines of the Ist Wing attacked Don railway station and the vicinity on the 27th instant. Considerable damage to the lines and some rolling stock is reported. A bomb struck a barge which sank.

Miscellaneous

Agents report that bombs dropped on the aerodrome at Gits on November 8th, wounded 30 to 40 men, and destroyed five motor cars. These bombs were dropped by machines of 7 Sqn. On November 10th, bombs dropped by 7 Sqn at Gits are reported by agents to have fallen among 48 military vehicles, and to have done much damage.

The pilot of the German machine which landed in our lines on the 19th instant, stated on examination that he had heard that holes had been made in one of the sheds at the Gits aerodrome by bombs recently dropped by Allied aeroplanes; the bombs seemed unusually large.

It is reported by agents that on the 11th instant, a British and German aeroplane fought over Rolleghem and that both machines fell there. One of the English aviators was killed, and the other wounded. The German aviator was wounded.

This probably refers to Lt Kelway Bamber and Lt Howey of 6 Sqn. At 11.30 a.m. the aerodrome at Abeele was bombed by German machines. Only two actually reached the aerodrome and they dropped four bombs, the total casualties being three cows and one Belgian workman wounded. The bombs appear to have been 20-pounders, making a crater about 6 foot across. No military damage of any sort was done.

28 November – 2 December, 1915

Some of the combats reported in this communiqué suggest that despite its shortcomings, a well-handled B.E.2c could prove a formidable opponent. The various brackets to which the observer was obliged to switch his gun during a combat still placed it at considerable disadvantage.

COMMUNIQUÉ NO. 22

November 28th

2 Lt Lillywhite and Lt Sherwin (Morane, 3 Sqn) returning from photography encountered an Aviatik over Bethune. Fire was opened at about 400 feet as the hostile machine passed immediately over the Morane, but the Lewis gun jammed after the sixth round. The Aviatik crossed the lines apparently undamaged.

Lt Henderson (Morane Scout, 3 Sqn) left the aerodrome at 9.30 a.m. to attack a hostile machine reported over Noeux Les Mines. He found an Albatros at 8,000 feet which made off. The Morane soon reached the same altitude and overhauled the Albatros, which turned and attacked. Lt Henderson dived at him, passing over him at 50 feet and firing continuously. The enemy machine was seen to be descending rapidly and was pursued by the Morane firing as opportunity occurred. The Albatros went down to about 1,500 feet over Vendin Le Vieil, where he dropped a smoke ball and was lost to view. Proceeding towards Lille with the intention of intercepting hostile aeroplanes re-crossing the lines, Lt Henderson found at 8,000 feet, a B.E.2c being attacked by an Albatros and a second German machine, type not recognised. These two machines were attacked in turn, the latter making off after half a drum had been expended against it. The Albatros showed more fight but was eventually also driven off. During this time a hostile machine stood off about half a mile east, and an Aviatik was directly above but took no part in the action. The latter was pursued to La Bassee and was last seen at 13,000 feet making for Lille.

Capt Gould and 2 Lt Vaucour (B.E.2c, 10 Sqn) chased an Albatros from near La Bassee to Aire where having expended all their ammunition they turned for their aerodrome.

Capt Gordon Bell (Bristol Scout, 10 Sqn) attacked a double-engine biplane over the Bois de Biez at 12,000 feet. His Lewis gun jammed after 18 rounds and the fight was broken off.

Capt Mitchell and Capt Bruce (B.E.2c, 10 Sqn) when returning from reconnaissance attacked an Aviatik which approached from La Bassee at approximately the same height. As the enemy passed, the observer fired half a drum at him from the back mounting. The Aviatik turned and made off towards Pont a Vendin.

Lt Milne and Capt Strong (B.E.2c, 16 Sqn) gave chase to an Albatros which they found flying over the lines towards Armentieres. At Armentieres the enemy turned towards Lille and was joined by two Fokkers coming from our lines. For some time Lt Milne managed to head off the Albatros from Lille. The B.E.2c was now at approximately the same height as the enemy and engaged him from the front mounting at very close range. The Albatros nose dived and eventually came to earth near Sequedin, the machine apparently turning completely over. By this time the two Fokkers had been joined by an Aviatik and another Albatros, and a Morane Scout was in hot pursuit of one of the enemy machines. All four machines now attacked the B.E.2c simultaneously, which for a considerable time was under fire from all of them. A steady fire was, however, maintained from the B.E.2c and the enemy machines eventually sheered off. Lt Milne now joined the Morane Scout in the pursuit of one of the hostile aeroplanes, abandoning the chase when near Pont a Vendin.

2 Lt Morton (Bristol Scout, 16 Sqn) while patrolling towards Armentieres sighted a German machine which was also being pursued by a Morane but manoeuvred to head him off and fired half a drum. Turning he got immediately underneath the German and fired another half drum at him. The hostile machine started to go down and while reloading Lt Morton lost sight of him.

2 Lt Tillie and 2 Lt Hardie (F.E., 16 Sqn) attacked an Aviatik approaching from the direction of Lille at 8,000 feet. Climbing to meet it the F.E. discharged one drum at the Aviatik which disappeared in the direction of Lille.

Lt Eastwood and Lt Gould (F.E., 16 Sqn) attacked an Albatros over our lines at Bethune. It immediately went away over its own lines.

Lt Strouer and 2 Lt McKenna (Vickers, 18 Sqn) encountered two hostile machines, a D.F.W. and an L.V.G. They dived at the L.V.G. from 9,600 feet. The hostile machine turned east, nose diving very steeply. At the same time the D.F.W. fired at the Vickers from above, but when attacked turned and disappeared eastwards.

Capt Cunningham and 1 AM Smith (Vickers, 18 Sqn) attacked an L.V.G. which appeared to be unarmed, in the vicinity of La Bassee. Diving from 8,000 feet, the observer of the Vickers opened fire on the hostile machine, which apparently had not up to this time noted the presence of the British machine. He nose dived steeply and the chase was abandoned at 4,000 feet.

Lt Powell and Lt Lubbock (Vickers, 5 Sqn) while patrolling north of Ypres noticed an Aviatik being fired at by our A.A. guns. The German was crossing our lines at about 10,000 feet. Lt Powell manoeuvred to cut him off but the German continued to fly westwards. The Vickers followed the Aviatik from Armentieres to Bailleul, Godewaersvelde, L'Abeele, Watou, Hondschoote, Merckem, keeping on the inside of the circle with the intention of cutting him off. When he turned towards his own lines at Hondschoote, the Vickers gained about 300 feet and opened fire, but after a few rounds both the Lewis guns jammed and the chase was abandoned east of the Forest of Houthulst.

Capt Halahan and Capt McLeod (B.E.2c, 4 Sqn) while taking photographs of Clery and the observer doing a special reconnaissance, encountered a Fokker about 200 yards away. The enemy approach was at first unnoticed, but the Lewis gun was soon brought to bear on him and the B.E.2c headed straight for him. The enemy, after a few rounds, turned sharply to his left and headed for Peronne followed by the B.E.2c. The hostile machine eventually disappeared apparently without sustaining damage.

Lt Douglas (B.E.2c, 8 Sqn) when dropping bombs at La Chapelette saw a Fokker 200 feet below him. Lt Douglas's Lewis gun jammed after the first round owing probably to the freezing of the oil and he was forced to return to his own lines pursued by the Fokker.

2 Lt O'Malley and Flt Sgt Harrison (B.E.2c, 13 Sqn) on escort duty to a reconnaissance machine, the latter owing to engine trouble had to return and 2 Lt O'Malley decided to continue the reconnaissance. When nearing Bapaume they saw a Fokker about 2,000 feet above them. The German machine dived at them firing all the time. In order to get the rear gun in action the *Vickers** dived and Flt Sgt Harrison opened fire at about 200 yards. The Lewis gun jammed three times. Flt Sgt Harrison twice managed to correct the jams during which time he was subjected to heavy fire from the Fokker. Owing to the height of the Fokker above the *Vickers** the front gun mounting could not be brought into action and the fight was abandoned.

November 30th

Lt Cave and Lt Stubbs (F.E., 6 Sqn) between Zonnebeke and Moorslede attacked an Aviatik which appeared 300 feet below them. They dived at it and at a range of 30 to 50 feet emptied one drum into it. The Aviatik dived for about 3,000 feet and was last seen descending towards Roulers. The F.E. was then attacked by a Fokker. Lt Cave reserved his fire until

* This is a mistake: the aircraft is described above as a B.E.2c.

the Fokker nose dived close in front of them and then fired half a drum at him. The hostile machine turned and attacked from the rear, firing apparently through its propellor. Turning to the left the F.E. expended another drum at 150 yards range after which the Fokker made off towards Roulers. The F.E. was hit in several places including all the cylinders of the engine necessitating a forced landing near Poperinghe.

Capt Gordon Bell (Bristol Scout, 10 Sqn) engaged a L.V.G. near Lens at 11,500 feet. After expending two drums at ranges of from 20 to 100 yards, the German machine turned in the direction of Douai. Noticing that it was flying in rather an erratic manner and rather nose down Capt Gordon Bell followed and saw it fall from about 4,000 feet in a series of side-slips into a field near Henin Lietard.

Capt Birch and Lt Long (Morane, 3 Sqn) attacked an Albatros which, throughout the fight, kept some 500 feet above them. After expending three drums of ammunition, the German machine had drawn out of range.

Capt Gould and Lt Vaucour (B.E.2c, 10 Sqn) encountered a large hostile tractor biplane near the Bois de Biez. The enemy showed little fight and after a drum had been fired at him went away towards Don.

The quai and stores at Miraumont were successfully bombed by 20 machines of the IIIrd Wing on November 30th.

The attack was carried out in a very high wind. Very considerable damage was done to stores, buildings and the railway line, and men were observed to leave the quai for the trenches in the vicinity so it is probable there were some casualties. An escort of two Vickers fighters accompanied the bombing machines. All the machines returned safely.

2–9 December, 1915

Lt Max Immelmann, one of the leading Fokker monoplane pilots, is mentioned for the first time in this communiqué. He had scored his first combat victory in a Fokker on 1 August.

An effective bombing raid against Don railway station was mounted by the 1st Wing.

COMMUNIQUÉ NO. 23

December 2nd

Capt Carthew and Lt Milne (B.E.2c, 2 Sqn) when engaged on artillery work, observed a hostile machine coming towards our lines. When approached, the hostile machine turned and opened fire over his tail at long range. The B.E.2c gave chase as far as Pont-a-Vendin and drove off the hostile machine.

While patrolling north-east of Don, an Albatros was observed being attacked by a Morane. As the hostile machine turned they engaged it at close quarters, the enemy replying vigorously. Two drums were fired at it, when the observer's gun jammed. The hostile machine then dived and was lost sight of, apparently undamaged.

2 Lt Allcock (B.E.2c, 2 Sqn) while bomb-dropping at Don, was attacked by an Albatros which passed underneath him and opened fire at a range of 200 feet over its tail. 2 Lt Allcock manoeuvred into a position which enabled him to use the pilot's rear-gun bracket when he fired one drum at the enemy machine at 300-foot range. The German dived and went away due east and 2 Lt Allcock continued to drop his bombs.

Capt Porter (Bristol Scout, 2 Sqn) when over Don, acting as escort to the bombing machines, pursued a hostile machine believed to be an L.V.G. He fired a drum at him while diving towards him. Capt Porter having changed his drum, returned to the attack and met the hostile machine coming towards him. The Bristol Scout dived and another half a drum was fired at the enemy, who dived steeply and disappeared from view. Capt Porter is of opinion that the hostile machine was hit, but cannot say if it was forced to land or not.

2 Lt Gethin and Lt Shepherd (B.E.2c, 10 Sqn) whilst on artillery work over La Bassee saw an Albatros at about 10,000 feet approaching from the east. They eventually engaged him near Bethune at about 200

yards range, the German replying. The hostile machine then turned east and disappeared in the direction of Douai.

Lt Henderson (Morane Scout, 3 Sqn) when escorting the bombing machines to Don engaged a hostile tractor biplane of the Morane type which approached from the direction of Douai at 8,500 feet. The Morane Scout was flying just ahead of the B.E.2cs of 2 Sqn. As the German approached, Lt Henderson turned to go in the same direction and dived at him, opening fire at 150 yards. The B.E.2cs then came into the field of fire. The German machine dived, Lt Henderson diving after him and overhauling him fired a whole drum at short range. While changing the drum, the German turned sharply right-handed and at the same time Lt Henderson was hit by a bullet just above the right eye. His goggles were broken, and being temporarily blinded by blood, he was forced to discontinue the engagement and returned home. He landed his machine safely.

On the 2nd instant, twelve aeroplanes of the Ist Wing, accompanied by seven escorting machines attacked the station at Don.

All the machines flew together and many of the bombs found their mark. A very large explosion occurred; fires were observed to break out and the railway was hit in the vicinity of the station. All the machines returned safely. Lt Henderson (Morane Scout, 3 Sqn) was slightly wounded in the head. (*See also under 'Bombing', page 102.*)

December 5th

Lt E. H. Cave and Lt Nixon (F.E., 6 Sqn) sighted an Aviatik a quarter of a mile in front and 200 feet above them in the vicinity of Polygon Wood. The German opened fire over the tail of his machine at a range of about 150 yards. After one drum had been expended against it, the hostile machine dived steeply and made off towards Gits.

December 7th

Capt Grenfell (Morane, 1 Sqn) during a reconnaissance in the vicinity of Tournai, encountered three hostile machines. The first was a new type of Albatros. He dived towards it and fired about half a drum. The hostile machine went down, firing continuously at the Morane even after it was well out of range. Capt Grenfell then noticed an Aviatik firing at him from above and close behind. He easily outclimbed this machine and was also faster and soon managed to get above and behind the German, which dived down towards Lille almost immediately.

While over Haubourdin, Capt Grenfell fired at a small Albatros, which, without firing, turned and dived for Lille.

2 Lt Gethin and Lt Shepherd (B.E.2c, 10 Sqn) during a tactical reconnaissance near Pont-a-Vendin, observed a hostile biplane just ahead of them at which Lt Shepherd fired half a drum. The German then got

behind when another half drum was fired at him, and he sheered off. A few minutes later the German attacked again but made off to the south after a few rounds had been fired at him. Over Haubourdin the B.E.2c was attacked by a Fokker monoplane, the pilot firing through his propellor. A running fight was kept up for some minutes, the Fokker eventually sheering off.

December 8th

(*See under 'Bombing' (second paragraph) on page 102.*)

Miscellaneous

The German aviator Immelmann is reported to be on leave in Berlin. It is rumoured he is going to the Eastern Front. (Agent's reports.)

12–15 December, 1915

Fokker monoplanes became more prevalent during this week, and altogether eleven were reported in various combats.

Two R.F.C. crews were engaged in close combat with one of the unorthodox Gotha GI twin-engined biplanes (see Communiqué No. 19). This new sketch illustrates the aircraft's main features with reasonable accuracy.

COMMUNIQUÉ NO. 24

December 12th

Lt Douglas and 1 AM Walker (B.E.2c, 8 Sqn) in the vicinity of Bapaume, encountered an Albatros and a Fokker. They had no difficulty in climbing up to the former and engaged him at 200 yards. The Albatros at once dived and disappeared. The Fokker dived before he could be engaged.

December 13th

Capt Gould with 2 Lt Vaucour (B.E.2c, 10 Sqn) when on artillery work near La Bassee, saw an Albatros 1,000 feet above. They climbed and attacked the hostile machine which went away towards Douai. Pursuit was abandoned owing to the machine-gun jamming. Five other hostile machines were seen, all at a great height, the highest at about 15,000 feet.

Capt Mitchell (Bristol Scout, 10 Sqn) when on patrol, saw an Albatros 3,000 feet above. The Scout climbed and attacked the hostile machine which fled, and pursuit was abandoned owing to the machine-gun jamming.

2 Lt De Crespigny and 2 Lt Insall (Vickers Fighter, 11 Sqn) while patrolling over Bienvillers, sighted a L.V.G. They chased the hostile machine which crossed the lines and made off in the direction of Bapaume.

Lt Norman and Cpl Donald (Vickers Fighter, 11 Sqn) engaged a double-fuselage biplane about 2 miles south-east of Ham. The two machines headed almost straight for each other, the German being about 100 feet higher. He opened fire first, the Vickers reserving fire till within 120 yards. Lt Norman then made a sharp right turn in order to face the hostile machine which had passed overhead. The German was now seen making a very steep descent in which the machine appeared to be out of control, rolling from side to side. After dropping about 2,000 feet it appeared to flatten out into a more normal glide but Lt Norman's attention was attracted by the approach of a Fokker and he was unable to see whether the double-fuselage machine landed or not.

The IIIrd Wing again attacked the huts at Achiet-le-Grand on the 13th, doing important damage to the huts and railway in the vicinity. All the machines returned safely.

December 14th

Capt Mitchell and Capt Bruce (B.E.2c, 10 Sqn) encountered two hostile machines, one being an Albatros and the other a new type. This latter was a large biplane with three passengers, one with a gun to fire ahead, the pilot in the centre and a third with a gun to fire astern. The machine had one fuselage, two engines and two rudders; the planes had a wide sweep with extensions, and were straight with square tips. The pilot and gunners sat very high, well above the top plane. (See sketch on *following page, not to scale.*)

Capt Mitchell and Capt Bruce were escorting the Ist Army reconnaissance machine (Lt Sison and Lt Goodson). The latter, which was in advance, was attacked by an enemy biplane which was apparently driven to ground after being hit. At almost the same time a second biplane (Albatros) was engaged by Capt Mitchell and Capt Bruce in the escorting machine. This was driven off eastwards towards Fondecourt. Very shortly after this, approximately over Seclin, the German machine, as described above, appeared from the direction of Lille, and attacked the reconnaissance machine, which returned its fire. The German then left the reconnaissance machine and flew southwards and to the east of the escorting machine. Capt Mitchell at once gave chase and dived down almost on to the hostile machine, Capt Bruce keeping up a hot fire from the forward mounting. At one time the machines were so close together that the enemy's faces could be clearly seen. The forward gun on the enemy machine was apparently jammed but the gun on the stern mounting kept up a continuous fire. The double-engined machine then began to dive very fast, and almost at the same time another biplane (possibly the one which had already been engaged) appeared some distance behind and threw out a white light. The reconnaissance machine had by now drawn some distance away and the escort, therefore, turned and followed it under heavy anti-aircraft gun-fire.

Lt Sison and 2 Lt Goodson (B.E.2c, 10 Sqn) during a tactical reconnaissance, encountered an Albatros in the vicinity of Don. Lt Goodson opened fire at about 100 yards range, the tracer bullets being distinctly discernable. The hostile machine appeared to be hit and nose dived very steeply, passing the B.E.2c at about 80 feet. Lt Sison dived after him, his observer firing another half drum. During the nose dive the observer of the Albatros kept up fire over his tail, but after about 10 of

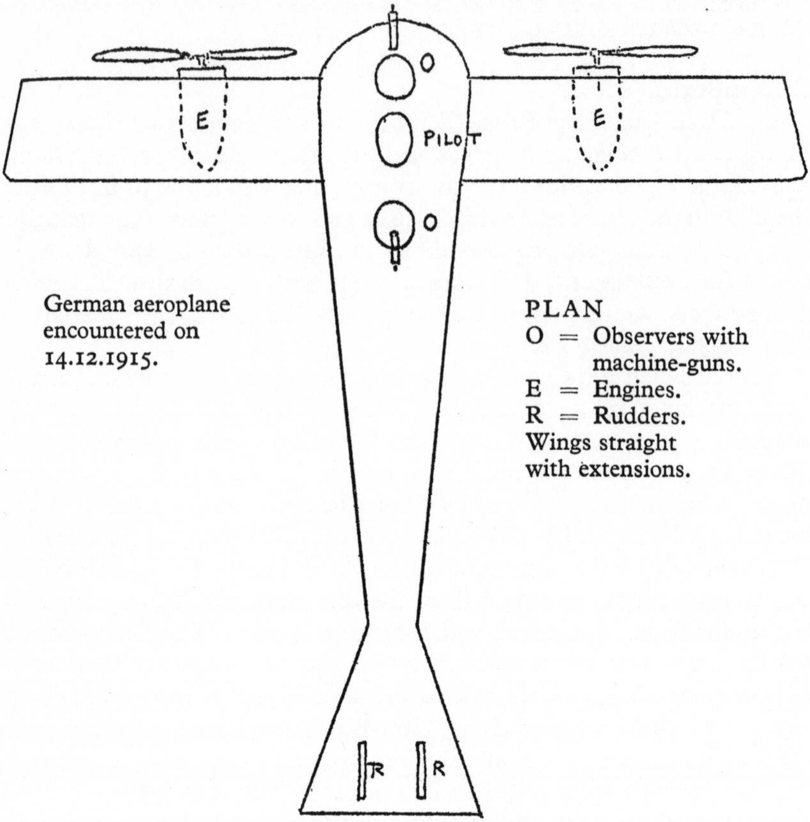

German aeroplane
encountered on
14.12.1915.

PLAN
O = Observers with
machine-guns.
E = Engines.
R = Rudders.
Wings straight
with extensions.

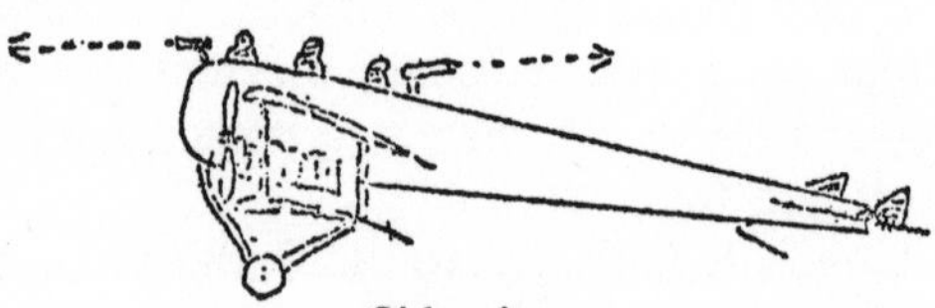

Side view.

our shots he suddenly let go his gun, turned round and sat down in his seat. When last seen, the German was at about 2,000 feet over Pont-a-Vendin, still diving very steeply.

Shortly afterwards the B.E.2c was attacked by the double-engine biplane referred to above. This machine turned towards Tournai when fired on at a range of about 100 yards and it was then attacked by Capt Mitchell and Capt Bruce.

Capt Eastwood and Lt Veitch (F.E., 16 Sqn) during reconnaissance in the vicinity of Douai, were attacked by three Albatroses and 2 Fokker aeroplanes from the west. Shots were exchanged as they passed and one Fokker appeared to be hit. It side-slipped but recovered. These machines were also engaged by a B.E.2c (Capt Beddam-Whethem and 2 Lt Catherall) which was escorting the F.E.

When crossing the lines near Lens shots were exchanged with another Fokker without effect.

Lt James and Lt Perri (Vickers F.B., 5 Sqn) encountered an Aviatik when patrolling east of the Yser canal. They pursued this machine, opening fire at about 600 yards range. After several exchanges of shots the German drew out of range and dived down towards Roulers. When near Langemarck, a Bristol Scout (Capt Read, 5 Sqn) joined in the chase.

Shortly afterwards a Fokker was met about 1,000 feet above them. The hostile machine was eventually engaged at a range of about 60 yards, the Fokker passing directly over the Vickers and offering a good target. On turning, the hostile machine was below and Lt James dived at him. The Lewis gun now jammed and the Fokker flew off towards Roulers. Later in the day, while taking photographs on the VIth Corps front, Lt James and Lt Perri attacked another Fokker. Shots were exchanged at 50 yards range. Three or four tracer bullets were seen to hit the German machine which dived downwards to the east.

Capt Read (Bristol Scout, 5 Sqn) saw an Aviatik and a Vickers (Capt James and Lt Perri) circling round one another near Roulers. On coming up with them, the Aviatik broke off the fight and dived down followed by the Scout.

Later in the day Capt Read attacked an Aviatik, opening fire at 50 yards range, the German apparently not seeing him. Almost immediately fire was opened on the Bristol Scout and the engine and petrol tank were hit. At the same time Capt Read's Lewis gun jammed. A second Aviatik who put himself in a position to cut off the Bristol Scout on returning, dived steeply as soon as Capt Read approached.

2 Lt Fernihough and Lt Moffatt (B.E.2c, 7 Sqn) while passing over Lichtervelde, were fired on by a Fokker which then made off. The hostile machine then turned and followed at about a mile but retreated when fire was opened on him at a range of 400 yards. This was repeated several

times. Eventually he was joined by a second Fokker, the latter diving steeply and disappearing when fired at.

2 Lt Neale and 2 Lt Quested (Vickers F.B., 11 Sqn) while patrolling to the north of Peronne, were attacked by an Albatros. Fire was opened on him at a range of 250 yards but the Albatros gradually drew out of range and the chase was abandoned.

Lt Douglas (B.E.2c, 8 Sqn) after dropping his bombs at Hervilly noticed a B.E.2c being attacked by a Fokker. He turned to assist. The Fokker, which was about 50 feet above him, left the other B.E.2c and dived towards Lt Douglas. A running fight was kept up for some 10 minutes, the Fokker eventually diving down.

On the 14th, fourteen aeroplanes from 4, 8 and 13 Sqns attacked Hervilly aerodrome. No sheds were actually hit but bombs fell sufficiently close to justify expectations of damage to the contents of sheds and several large bombs fell on the aerodrome.

All the machines returned safely.

On the same day, Flt Sub-Lt Graham and Flt Sub-Lt Ince (R.N.A.S.) in a Nieuport, attacked a big German sea-plane off La Panne. The hostile machine was shot down and fell into the sea on fire. The British machine was also forced to descend on to the water, the pilot and passenger being picked up by H.M.S. *Balmoral.* It was not possible to save the pilot or passenger of the German machine.

December 15th

Capt Kinnear (Bristol Scout, 6 Sqn) when patrolling near Poelcappelle, dived from 6,000 feet to encounter a Fokker at 5,000. After two drums had been fired at him, the German made off towards the north but re-appeared after a few minutes. Capt Kinnear now attacked an Aviatik, firing his remaining drum at him. Having no more ammunition, he was then forced to break off the engagement.

Bombing

A deserter confirms the information that, as a result of the air raid on Don on the 2nd December, 10 men were killed, and the railway station was badly damaged. On the day following no rations were received in the trenches.

The aerodrome at Hervilly and a store depot at Miraumont were attacked on the 8th December by 16 machines of the IIIrd Wing. A second attack on Miraumont was carried out on the afternoon of the same day. Considerable damage was done to both objectives. Two pilots claim to have silenced hostile anti-aircraft batteries one of which was a rocket battery. These attacks were carried out in a westerly wind, estimated at 60 m.p.h. All the machines returned safely.

19–21 December, 1915

During the intense air activity of 19 December, two R.F.C. crews reported meeting three Fokker monoplanes operating together.

Omitted from this communiqué were the experiences of the two aircraft which escorted the 3 Sqn Morane Parasol reconnoitring Valenciennes. Air gunner in one of them was Sgt J. B. McCudden, later to become a leading fighter 'ace'. The airfield at Douai, where Capt Mealing reported sixteen aircraft leaving the ground, was a main base for the Fokkers.

Progress in the arming of B.E.2cs is indicated by the reference to a 12 Sqn aircraft fitted with Lewis guns for both pilot and observer.

COMMUNIQUÉ NO. 25

December 19th

German aeroplanes were very active today north of the River Lys, their efforts being evidently directed towards heading off British reconnoitring machines especially from Courtrai and Thielt. In this they were unsuccessful. During the day there were 48 encounters in the air.

Owing to space it is not possible to publish all the reports received. The following are extracts:

Capt Steinbach Mealing and Lt Cleaver (Morane, 3 Sqn) on reconnaissance between Lille and Douai were attacked by a Fokker which they report as firing past the propellor on the left of the machine. The hostile machine dived at the Morane at about 30 yards range and fired about 40 rounds. After a few rounds from the Lewis gun, the enemy put his nose down and went off to Lille. Near Valenciennes another Fokker was fired on but without effect. Capt Steinbach Mealing reports that at Douai 16 machines left the ground none of which, however, attacked.

Lt Lillywhite and Lt Long (Morane, 3 Sqn) fired one drum at a range of about 250 feet into an Aviatik which dived steeply, flattened out near the ground and then turned over and crashed just east of Salome.

Capt Mitchell (Bristol Scout, 10 Sqn) saw an Albatros under A.A. gun-fire proceeding towards Aire at 12,000 feet. He climbed and engaged the German over Bethune, firing a drum at about 100 yards and driving him off. Capt Mitchell then saw two German machines, an Albatros and and L.V.G., both at about 12,000 feet. He intercepted the latter over

Bruay. After a running fight the enemy was driven over to his own side of the line near Arras.

Capt Bell Irving (Morane Scout, 1 Sqn) left the ground at 9.15 a.m. in pursuit of a hostile machine. He could not find it, but later he saw a hostile aeroplane over Perenchies below him and dived on to it. This machine made off for Lille without fighting. Capt Bell Irving then climbed to 11,000 feet and engaged a hostile aeroplane over Quesnoy at close range. The German nose dived and turned gradually to the right, followed by the Morane Scout, Capt Bell Irving emptying a drum at the enemy. The German then dived still more steeply. Large puffs of smoke were emitted from his machine, the volume of which appeared too great for the exhaust, and it had not the appearance of burnt engine oil. The enemy pilot gradually recovered, but at 7,000 feet was still diving steeply when he was lost to view in a heavy mist. It is thought that the enemy made no retaliation as no machine-gun was heard. Capt Bell Irving again climbed to 12,000 feet and saw two hostile aeroplanes going in the direction from Lille to La Bassee. He overhauled these machines and the larger, believed to be an Albatros, was attacked from above. The German dived, the Scout following and keeping up a heavy fire. At the same time, three hostile machines opened fire from above on Capt Bell Irving and he retired from the fight. Heading for Ypres he sighted yet another hostile machine over Polygon Wood. He eventually overhauled the enemy and when within 100 yards, while diving to get into a firing position, Capt Bell Irving was hit in the hand by the splinter of a British anti-aircraft shell. He was unable to shoot so abandoned the chase and returned to his aerodrome.

2 Lt Cooper and 2 Lt Glenny (B.E.2c, 6 Sqn) were attacked over Elverdinghe by a Fokker and two or three other hostile machines, either Aviatiks or L.V.Gs. After a running fight the petrol tank of the B.E.2c was pierced and the fight was broken off.

2 Lt Cave and 2 Lt Duguid (B.E.2c, 6 Sqn) engaged a Fokker over St Julien. A drum was fired on the enemy at about 50 yards range. The hostile machine appeared to be hit. It dived steeply and was last seen still diving at about 1,500 feet over Langemarck. Three minutes later they were attacked by an Aviatik. The Lewis gun jammed after half a drum. Failing to put this right six shots were fired with an automatic pistol, and the encounter was then broken off. The hostile machine fired continuously but did not cross the lines.

Capt Moore and Lt Moncrieff (B.E.2c, 6 Sqn) while observing for hostile flashes near Ypres observed a large German biplane of the pusher type approaching from the direction of Elverdinghe. They manoeuvred to cut him off. The German opened fire at 200 yards and hit the B.E.2c. Capt Moore opened fire at about 100 yards and continued firing as the enemy passed over him at a height of 50 feet. On turning round, large clouds of smoke and steam were seen coming from the hostile machine which was diving steeply and continued to do so until at a very low altitude when it was lost sight of. It was then south-west of Houthulst Forest, approximately *Square U.9*, *Sheet 20*.

N.B. Lt Cave whilst over Langemarck about 12.15 p.m. reports having seen a machine answering the above description on the ground in that locality.

2 Lt Finchan and 2 Lt Price (F.E., 6 Sqn) attacked a Fokker over Bixschoote. The Lewis gun jammed with the first three bullets but then fired normally. The Fokker banked steeply and dived. In the meantime two more Fokkers were pouring a rapid fire at short range into the F.E. from behind, and the petrol tank was pierced. Lt Finchan banked the F.E. steeply to the left and engaged one of the hostile machines which dived steeply. Its flight however could not be followed as two other machines opened fire from above. A drum was fired at the larger of the two machines but without apparent damage. The Lewis gun jammed again and the engagement was discontinued; the hostile machines following the F.E. no further than the lines. During the encounter two Frenchmen in a Maurice Farman endeavoured to assist the F.E. but unfortunately were brought down near Abeele, one of them being wounded.

2 Lt Horsbrugh and Lt Haynes (B.E.2c, 7 Sqn) during a reconnaissance near Zarren were approached by three Fokker monoplanes which took up positions above, below and on the side of the B.E.2c. While these engaged the attention of the B.E.2c, a pusher biplane approached from the west and opened fire from behind at about 80 yards. Lt Haynes replied with a drum from the Lewis gun. The petrol tank of the B.E.2c was pierced necessitating the return to the aerodrome.

2 Lt Horn and Lt Moffatt (B.E.2c, 7 Sqn) when crossing the lines at Dixmude saw an Albatros flying east. They dived and emptied a drum at 100 yards range, the enemy diving down and disappearing. Immediately afterwards another Albatros came up on their left and a third hostile machine attacked from below. Both these shortly made off, but when near Cortemarck the B.E.2c was again attacked by three machines, an Albatros immediately above them, a Fokker behind them, and an Aviatik below them. A running fight ensued, all the Germans eventually being driven off.

Capt Pattinson and 2 Lt Robinson (Vickers, 11 Sqn) while engaged on patrol and photography near Bucquoy sighted three machines over Hebuterne going west. One of these machines, a double-fuselage enemy machine, was seen to dive down and come east. The Vickers turned to head the enemy off. Just before closing up a second machine of a similar type was observed travelling more or less in the same direction but much higher. The first of these machines turned in the direction of the Vickers which opened fire at 300 yards, the tracer bullets being clearly seen. The hostile machine turned and drew out of range, and the Vickers circled to look for the other hostile aeroplane. After more manoeuvring and more expenditure of ammunition both the Germans with their noses down, drew off.

Lt Fairbairn and Capt Perrin (B.E.2c, 12 Sqn) while returning from a reconnaissance to Bruges observed a hostile machine about 2 miles north of Ypres. Lt Fairbairn at once attacked, both pilot and observer using Lewis guns. About a drum was fired from each gun, the Albatros replying strongly. After about 10 minutes manoeuvring and fighting the hostile observer appeared to be hit and stopped firing. Lt Fairbairn was wounded in the arm and descended near Cassel.

28–31 December, 1915

The outstanding combat reported in this communiqué was that between an 8 Sqn B.E.2c, captained by Lt W. S. Douglas (later Marshal of the R.A.F. Lord Douglas of Kirtleside) and three Fokker monoplanes. Lt Douglas followed the only course open to a pilot in such circumstances—descent almost to ground level.

COMMUNIQUÉ NO. 26

December 28th

2 Lt Cave (Bristol Scout, 6 Sqn) while on patrol attacked an Aviatik over Langemarck emptying a drum into it at about 80 yards. The German dived several thousand feet, and was lost sight of. Later, the Bristol Scout was attacked by an Albatros, and after exchanging shots at 120 yards, the hostile machine went off. A third hostile machine was sighted west of St Julien which dived before it could be engaged.

2 Lt Woodhouse (Bristol Scout, 4 Sqn) when over Hebuterne, saw a large German biplane 1,500 feet above him. Climbing to within 100 feet, Lt Woodhouse opened fire with the top Lewis gun directly under the tail of the German machine. The German did not reply but headed straight into a bank of clouds. A few minutes later Lt Woodhouse saw a machine crossing the trenches apparently flying at less than 1,000 feet, and he believes it landed. Later he was attacked by an Albatros, south of Arras. The German turned towards Bapaume losing height and followed by the Bristol Scout.

Capt Crowe and Lt Drenon (B.E.2c, 8 Sqn) engaged and drove off an Albatros which was apparently escorting two other hostile machines which bombed the aerodrome at Marieux.

December 29th

2 Lt Murray and 2 Lt Rice (B.E.2c, 2 Sqn) when on artillery patrol, attacked and drove off a hostile machine. Tracer bullets were seen to hit his fuselage. Later, two Albatros machines were encountered near Lens at which the B.E.2c fired three drums of ammunition, both the hostile machines making off.

Capt Cunningham (Bristol Scout, 18 Sqn) when on patrol, encountered an Aviatik about 9,500 feet over Provin. Diving for about 1,000 feet, the Scout fired a drum at 80 yards range, the German machine diving steeply and disappearing. Shortly afterwards an Albatros was encountered over Pont-a-Vendin. The Scout attacked and the Albatros dived down. While fitting another drum, a further hostile machine attacked the Scout from above. Capt Cunningham, not having reloaded, broke off the engagement. Finally, north of the Bois de Biez a small tractor biplane was pursued but the chase was abandoned as there was no prospect of overhauling the hostile machine.

Capt Horsfall and 2 Lt Bottrell (B.E.2c, 4 Sqn) when escorting bombing machines near Hervilly was attacked by an Albatros. Capt Horsfall reports that the German machine approached in 'an avenue of archies which I think he was obviously firing himself from a Very pistol'. The German opened fire at about 500 to 600 yards' range. The B.E.2c turned to the right and opened fire from the forward gun mounting. A Vickers appearing on the scene, the German dived down and when at about 2,000 feet from the ground, flattened out, apparently none the worse.

Lt Douglas and Lt Child (B.E.2c, 8 Sqn) on escort to Army reconnaissance (Lt Glen and Sgt Jones, B.E.2c, 8 Sqn). About 3 miles west of Cambrai, Lt Glen and Sgt Jones flying at about 6,400 feet, were attacked by two Fokkers. Almost immediately the B.E.2c descended in a very steep spiral to 2,000 feet and then flattened out. The B.E.2c was seen to land and the machine was smashed. The impression which Lt Douglas received was that Lt Glen was wounded with the first burst, and on landing intentionally smashed his machine. Lt Douglas and Lt Child were now attacked by a Fokker from behind. They opened fire and a tracer bullet was seen to hit the Fokker which nose dived and was still diving when three other Fokkers attacked. One Lewis gun jammed at this moment and the second gave a series of stoppages. After fighting for 15 or 20 minutes with the three Fokkers, Lt Douglas went down in a steep spiral to within 20 feet of the ground followed by the three hostile machines to 1,000 feet. The B.E.2c then flew westwards about 15 feet from the ground. One Fokker dived and attacked but retired back to 1,000 feet when met with rapid fire from the B.E.2c. Eventually two of the hostile machines gave up the chase and Lt Douglas climbed to engage the single remaining Fokker. The other two, however, returned and the B.E.2c resumed its original height. Finally all the hostile machines went away and the B.E.2c crossed the lines at 800 feet.

Two successful bombing raids were carried out on the 29th instant. The IInd Wing attacked Comines station with 16 aeroplanes, damaging the station, some sheds in the vicinity and the railway line.

Hostile anti-aircraft batteries were engaged by the Heavy Artillery assisted by wireless machines. As a result, the fire of the enemy's anti-aircraft guns is reported as indifferent.

The IIIrd Wing attacked the aerodrome at Hervilly with 10 machines, and did considerable damage.

In each case all the machines returned safely.

Lt Norman and Cpl Morton (Vickers, 11 Sqn) when escorting the bombing machines to Hervilly, noticed a Fokker approaching them from behind. When the hostile machine had drawn to within 350 yards Lt Norman made a sharp turn which brought the two machines facing each other, the Vickers being about 150 feet higher. The Vickers opened fire at once and dived towards the hostile machine. The Fokker descended with great rapidity but apparently under control. Lt Norman did not pursue owing to the presence of another hostile machine.

Miscellaneous

On the 28th December four hostile aeroplanes attempted to bomb the aerodrome at Marieux. Only two reached their objective and their bombs were ineffective.

5–18 January, 1916

The German air force was now entering a period of marked superiority thanks largely to the wider employment of the Fokker monoplanes.

Although not apparent from this communiqué, British losses were mounting, and on 14 January R.F.C. Headquarters instructed that every reconnaissance aircraft must be escorted by at least three fighting machines.

This communiqué describes a number of determined combats, with indications that at least one Fokker may have been shot down.

The Martinsyde Scout reported in use by 6 Sqn on 17 January was presumably the new G100 single-seater, armed with two Lewis guns and capable of 95 m.p.h. One gun was mounted to fire forward over the top wing and the other on the side of the fuselage to fire backwards. It was still R.F.C. policy to attach the single-seater scouts in small numbers to the bombing and reconnaissance squadrons.

COMMUNIQUÉ NO. 27

January 5th

Lt R. H. Le Brasseur (B.E.2c, 16 Sqn) while on a bombing expedition to Douai was attacked by a Fokker which approached from behind. The B.E.2c endeavoured to elude the hostile machine, but it was too fast, so Lt Le Brasseur turned to attack it. One drum was fired at the German and whilst Lt Le Brasseur was fitting a second drum the Fokker approached to within less than 50 yards. The B.E.2c then fired a few more shots, and the hostile machine went down spinning vertically. Lt Le Brasseur was then attacked by a second Fokker, whereupon he dived and turning, emptied the remainder of the drum at the enemy which also went down spinning vertically. The B.E.2c was much damaged by machine gun fire and made a forced landing at Bruay. Many of the tracer bullets were easily seen to hit the enemy.

Capt C. M. Crowe (Bristol Scout, 8 Sqn) was ordered up to attack two enemy aeroplanes which had been observed near Adinfer. The first, an Aviatik, was sighted at about 6,000 feet and the Scout climbed to attack, but the hostile machine turned and went rapidly away eastwards, Capt Crowe pursuing for some five miles, firing, when the German was lost to view. When returning, the Scout sighted another hostile machine to the south-east and climbing to 9,000 feet went straight for the enemy machine which turned to meet him. One drum was fired at the German at a range of 120 yards when the engine of the Scout stopped, and Capt Crowe glided back and landed safely in our lines, the Aviatik turning eastwards and disappearing.

Successful bombing operations have been carried out as under: Douai aerodrome was attacked by fourteen machines of the 1st Wing on the 5th January and considerable damage was done. On the same day the IIIrd Wing sent eleven machines against the stores dump at Le Sars. Observation was difficult and the extent of the damage is not known.

January 9th

No 2 Kite Balloon Section successfully registered 15 targets. Two telephones were carried for the first time in the basket, and constant communication was maintained with the IInd Army Heavy Artillery.

January 12th

2 Lt Nethersole and 2 Lt Hemming (B.E.2c, 5 Sqn) escort to Army reconnaissance engaged an Albatros over Roulers. After some maneouvring the hostile machine was driven off. He fired a Very light as he withdrew, apparently to summon an Aviatik which was seen approaching. 2 Lt Nethersole now proceeded after the machine which he was escorting followed by the two hostile machines, both of which after further exchange of shots drew off.

January 13th

Lt Wynne-Eyton and Lt Davey, 2 Sqn, carried out some successful artillery work with the 13th Siege Battery in exceedingly unfavourable weather. This battery was ranged on the front line of trenches, three O.K.s and two 'Y's being registered. They then continued firing in their own time with corrections sent down by Lt Davey. The registration started at 5,000 feet and finished in a squall and snow at 1,500 for the last hour. Observation was very difficult. The general effect on the trenches is reported as good. The enemy replied by wild but plentiful anti-aircraft gun fire.

January 14th

2 Lt De Crespigny and 2 Lt Hughes Chamberlain (Vickers F.B., 11 Sqn) sighted a Fokker near Bertincourt at about 8,300 feet. The German immediately began to dive, the Vickers following and firing nearly one drum of tracer bullets. The Fokker was seen to descend with great speed to earth and was last seen in a field. As the day was hazy it was impossible to ascertain if the hostile machine was completely wrecked. An Albatros and another Fokker were sighted at about 2,000 feet, but owing to engine trouble the Vickers was unable to attack and recrossed the lines.

2 Lt Herring and Capt Erskine (B.E.2c, 8 Sqn). While on short

reconnaissance just to the east of Achiet le Grand, Lt Herring noticed that the A.A. guns suddenly ceased firing. On looking round, a Fokker monoplane was seen approaching from the rear. Lt Herring turned towards it and Capt Erskine engaged it from the left front gun mounting at a range of about 150 yards. The pilot then turned again and the observer engaged it from the rear mounting. The Fokker dived on the B.E.2c and Lt Herring was hit twice in the back, Capt Erskine keeping up a steady fire of bursts of 15 rounds. The fight was carried on for some minutes during which Capt Erskine was hit in the leg, and the aneroid, speed indicator, and revolution counter smashed. By this time two or more fresh Fokkers had joined in the fight, one keeping behind and diving on to the B.E.2c, the others keeping on the flanks. A smell of petrol was then noticed and a few minutes afterwards the engine stopped, the tank having been hit. The ammunition (six drums) was by this time finished. The pilot glided down, pursued by the Fokkers firing all the time, and landed just west of our front line of trenches opposite Becourt Chateau, the pilot and observer jumping out into a trench. The Fokkers abandoned the machine as it was over the trenches. A heavy fire was brought to bear on the machine immediately it landed.

January 17th

Lt James and Lt Green (Vickers, 5 Sqn) while taking photographs over Polygon Wood encountered a small Albatros, the pilot sitting in front firing through the propellor. The German opened fire through his propellor at 200 yards. He then turned and his observer opened fire from behind. The Vickers pursued for some distance, but the gun jammed and the chase was abandoned.

Capt Moore and Lt Price (F.E., 6 Sqn) sighted an Aviatik being fired at by anti-aircraft guns over our lines. On seeing the F.E., the Aviatik made for his own lines. The F.E. caught him up and opened fire at 800 feet. An engagement ensued lasting about 10 minutes, during which time four drums of ammunition were fired at him. Having driven the German to his own side of the lines, the chase was abandoned and artillery observation resumed.

2 Lt Bolton (Martinsyde Scout, 6 Sqn) sighted a Fokker biplane over Polygon Wood flying at 10,000 feet. Lt Bolton dived from 12,000 feet and overhauled the Fokker over Gheluvelt, opening fire at a range of 50 feet. After some manoeuvring at close range a jet of flame was seen to come from the enemy's machine and the Fokker dived steeply. Lt Bolton now abandoned the chase as his engine was missing badly. When last seen the hostile machine was seen still diving steeply over Gheluvelt.

2 Lt Wilson and 2 AM Lathean (B.E.2c, 15 Sqn) on escort reconnaissance, saw the reconnaissance machine attacked by a Fokker monoplane.

3—MORANE-SAULNIER SCOUT OR 'BULLET'—110 H.P. LE RHÔNE ENGINE

The French Morane Scout was the first Allied aeroplane to have a machine-gun mounted to fire through the airscrew—accomplished by fitting hardened steel plates to the airscrew blades to deflect those bullets which would otherwise have damaged the screw. Because the 'Bullet' resembled the Fokker monoplane of the period, its spinner, cowling and other metal parts were painted red to help recognition.

Lt Wilson and an escorting B.E.2c dived at and drove off the Fokker which was last seen going down in a spiral.

Returning from reconnaissance a Fokker dived at the B.E.2c firing through the propellor. Fire was opened and the Fokker went away.

2 Lt Bell and Lt Eardley Wilmot (B.E.2c, 9 Sqn) escort to bombing machines, was waiting for two lagging machines when they were attacked from above and behind by a single-seater Fokker firing through his propellor, the pilot in a standing position. The German opened with a burst of three shots at 40 yards. Lt Bell turned the machine and his observer opened fire from the centre mounting with half a drum. The German turned and attacked again. Again the observer fired another half a drum, and the pilot of the hostile machine appeared to be hit. His gun was seen to swing outwards and he dived and was lost to sight.

Capt Lawrence (Bristol Scout, 12 Sqn) at about 10.30–10.55 a.m. a hostile machine was sighted from the aerodrome at St Omer. The Scout left the ground at once and keeping the German in view caught him near Bailleul at 10,000 feet. The Scout attacked from the front, and after firing 20 rounds passed to the rear when the German fired one burst, striking the Scout. The Scout turned in behind and finished the drum, after which difficulty was experienced in reloading. When another drum had been fixed the German had crossed the line and apparently dived quickly as he was out of sight.

Capt Grenfell, escort to a special reconnaissance in a Morane Scout reports as follows: When about 2,000 feet above the Morane which I was escorting, two Fokkers suddenly appeared behind it. I immediately dived and sent one of the Fokkers down after several rounds, and it continued to nose dive for at least 6,000 feet. My attention was then attracted by the second Fokker who was now above and behind me. I climbed and turned above this one getting to within about 100 feet, and after about 30 rounds this machine nose dived very steeply. I followed him down to about 4,500 feet and saw him land in a ploughed field down wind. Climbing again to about 10,500 feet an Albatros was noticed above and behind one of our Moranes. I got above it and drove it north-east of Houthulst Forest until close enough to fire. After half a drum of the tracer bullets which appeared to hit him, he was seen still going down over Houthulst Forest until lost sight of. Returning to my own lines a Fokker was found amongst about six or seven B.E.2cs. This machine was engaged at about 70 feet range. Several tracer bullets could be easily seen to hit the cowl and fuselage of this Fokker who immediately nose dived and was last seen still nose diving at a very steep angle 3,000 feet below.

On the 17th instant the IIIrd Wing again attacked Le Sars with sixteen machines and caused considerable damage to the sheds and stores.

20 January – 6 February, 1916

Items in this communiqué illustrate the hazards of night flying during anti-Zeppelin operations, and also the air traffic control problems which could arise before the existence of radio-telephone communications with aircraft.

COMMUNIQUÉ NO. 28

January 20th
Lt Danby and Lt Price (B.E.2c, 6 Sqn) while carrying out artillery registration over Ypres noticed an Aviatik crossing the line at 6,000 feet. They gave chase and engaged the German at 800 feet range. After firing 30 rounds, the German machine suddenly dropped, turned and made for his own lines, followed by the B.E.2c which emptied the remainder of the drum at him. When last seen, the hostile machine was dropping rapidly over Polygon Wood. The pilot and observer are convinced that the hostile machine was hit.

January 23rd
A hostile aeroplane dropped an incendiary bomb on Beuvry doing no damage. We retaliated by despatching machines from 3 Sqn, carrying 18 incendiary bombs, and machines from 2 and 10 Sqns carrying 112-pound bombs. Owing to the fog these latter had to return without dropping their bombs. 3 Sqn dropped their incendiary bombs on Salome, and attacked and drove down a hostile observation balloon in the same neighbourhood. All the machines returned safely.

January 25th
2 Lt Allcock and 2 Lt Rice (B.E.2c, 2 Sqn) noticed an Albatros crossing the lines north of La Bassee. They gave chase, and eventually the engine of the hostile aeroplane was hit, as it stopped, and the enemy planed down behind his own lines.

Capt Wynne-Eyton (Bristol Scout, 2 Sqn) engaged and drove off two Albatros machines near Bethune. A third Albatros was driven off from over La Bassee, and a fourth was encountered soon afterwards and engaged at a range of 20 yards. Tracer bullets were clearly seen to hit the fuselage and the engine, and the Albatros broke off the combat in haste and turned and glided over his own lines.

The escort to the IInd Army Reconnaissance encountered four Aviatiks, two Albatroses, and four Fokkers. All these hostile machines were driven off, one of the Fokkers being apparently hit in the engine.

Miscellaneous

Information has been received that bombs dropped on Valenciennes station in September last set fire to an ammunition train. The fire lasted for two days. All the coaches were destroyed by the flames or by the explosives they contained. The line was damaged and the fate of a neighbouring depot and the gas works was for a time in doubt. The bombs were dropped by Capt Christie, 12 Sqn.

On the night of the 29/30th one Zeppelin attacked Paris. On its return journey to its own lines this Zeppelin was reported in the neighbourhood of Albert. Two machines of 4 Sqn, pilots—Capts Tennant and Horsfall, were detailed to stand by with bombs, parachute flares, and flying lights for the pursuit of the Zeppelin. At about 2.40 a.m. the Zeppelin was seen flying in an easterly direction over the aerodrome, and Capts Horsfall and Tennant ascended. Capt Tennant climbed for about 10 minutes to a height of about 3,500 feet and then seeing nothing of the Zeppelin and that a thick fog was collecting he returned to the aerodrome. He dropped his flare at about 1,000 over the aerodrome, but the combined light of the ground and parachute flares only illuminated the fog and made it impossible to tell where the ground was. As a result Capt Tennant misjudged his height and ran into the aerodrome wall completely wrecking his machine and engine. He himself was unhurt. Capt Horsfall went up to 10,000 feet but did not see the Zeppelin again. He patrolled over the trench line between Martinsaart and Bray, keeping his bearing by the trench line lights. As the fog appeared to be getting thick he decided to return. He dropped his flare from about 1,500 feet, but was unable to hit off the flares at the first two attempts. Straight over the flares at 500 feet, the flares were distinguishable, but on entering the fog to land the flares were obliterated. Capt Horsfall got down safely at his third attempt at 3.55 a.m. running not more than 100 yards beyond the flares.

On January 27th a pilot practising on a Bristol Scout and another flying a Vickers F.B. decided to land at the same time. Neither pilot saw the other machine and about 150 feet up, while both were gliding down, the Bristol passed over the Vickers tail at right angles to it. The propellor of the Bristol caught the left-hand aileron of the Vickers, almost completely destroying both propeller and aileron, and braking the rear tube of the Vickers tail plane. The rudder of the Vickers was untouched. Both machines landed safely. No other damage than that mentioned was sustained by either machine.

5–9 February, 1916

Two new British fighting scouts received their first positive mention in this communiqué, both attached to existing squadrons.

The De Havilland D.H.2, which scored a combat victory on 5 February, had first flown in July 1915. It was a single-seat pusher design, fitted with a Lewis gun firing forward, and capable of just over 90 m.p.h. The first full squadron of D.H.2s—No. 24—arrived in France on 7 February, but was not reported in action until March. It is surprising to find a D.H.2 working with a Vickers Gunbus squadron at this stage.

The F.B.8, of generally similar design and performance, was a product of the Royal Aircraft Factory. Production was slow, and it was not to enter full squadron service until August.

Two pilots reported a Fokker monoplane with a vertical, stationary engine. This was clearly a Pfalz EV, fitted with the 100 horsepower Mercedes engine. The Pfalz E-series monoplane single-seaters were very similar in appearance to the Fokkers, and it is probable that a good many of the 'Fokkers' reported over the months were in fact the rotary-engined Pfalz EI and EII aircraft.

The IInd Army reconnaissance of 7 February illustrated the methods adopted to counter the Fokker following the instructions regarding escorts and appears to have been completed with notable success.

20 Sqn, reported on escort work, had arrived in France on 23 January. It was the first squadron to be fully equipped with the F.E.2b, which had hitherto been alloted in ones and twos to the bombing and reconnaissance units.

COMMUNIQUÉ NO. 29

February 5th

Capt Cunningham (De Havilland Scout 18 Sqn) when on a patrol near La Bassee met and engaged an Albatros. A drum was fired at the German as he approached the Scout which was about 100 feet beneath him. The tracer bullets were clearly seen to hit the hostile machine, and the engine was apparently damaged, as puffs of black smoke were seen, and the propeller stopped. Nearly all one blade of the propeller was missing. The hostile machine made a forced landing near Carvin. Capt Cunningham was too high to see the result of the landing. Two other Aviatiks engaged by Capt Cunningham were driven off.

Lt Strugnell (Morane Scout, 1 Sqn) attacked and drove off an L.V.G. south-east of Armentieres. Later during patrol an Aviatik was sighted at 9,000 feet going towards its own lines. The Morane Scout overhauled it and opened fire at 400 feet range, eventually closing to much closer range. Tracer bullets were seen to hit the wings and fuselage and apparently the pilot, who appeared to fall forward. The hostile machine then nose dived very steeply into the clouds, not under control.

Capt Powell (F.E.8, 5 Sqn) on three separate occasions during the day left the aerodrome to attack hostile aircraft reported in the vicinity. He drove down a large Aviatik to the Roulers aerodrome under control, though Capt Powell believes the machine to have been hit. A second hostile machine, an Albatros, was driven off from Ypres salient, and a third, an Aviatik, was attacked in the vicinity of Bailleul. After some manoeuvring and a free exchange of shots, the Aviatik dived steeply into the clouds at about 5,000 feet over the trenches near Ploegsteert Wood.

The IIIrd Army reconnaissance was considerably molested throughout its course by hostile aeroplanes.

2 Lt Deighton Simpson and 2 Lt Solby (B.E.2c, 9 Sqn) were attacked by an Albatros which dived past them. The B.E.2c opened fire with both guns, and the tracers were seen to hit the hostile machine. The Albatros stalled, side-slipped and descended out of control, emitting smoke.

Lt Egerton and 2 Lt Scaife (9 Sqn) fired a drum at an Albatros about 200 feet above them and he made off. They were then attacked by another Albatros from above. Fire was opened and the Albatros side-slipped and went to the ground in flames. Another Albatros and a Fokker appeared but made no attempt to attack.

The third escorting machine, 2 Lt Faber and 2 Lt Wynn (B.E.2c, 9 Sqn) attacked an Albatros, hitting the engine and pilot. The hostile machine went down in a spinning nose dive. At 500 feet from the ground it was still diving and out of control. Another Albatros approaching from the right was driven down—several tracer bullets being seen to hit the hostile machine.

Between 11.30 a.m. and 12 noon an Albatros flew over St Omer and dropped three bombs. The patrolling machine of 12 Sqn engaged the enemy over Clairmarais Forest, and he was also attacked by other machines from squadrons in the front line. He managed to escape. As a result of the bombs, two soldiers and a Frenchman were slightly wounded.

No. 3 Kite Balloon Section successfully ranged a 6th Battery on to a hostile kite balloon, obtaining a direct hit on the winch with the fourth round. The German balloon was observed to make a sudden and rapid ascent. It is possible that the airship reported by one of the observers of the IIIrd Wing was this same German kite balloon making a free flight.

February 7th

2 Lt Reid and Lt Billings (20 Sqn) escort to the IInd Army reconnaissance, in a F.E, report that one Fokker attacked a B.E.2c on their left, making a steep spiral round it. The hostile machine then glided out in front of Lt Reid about 300 feet below. As he passed, 35 rounds were fired at him. The Fokker side-slipped and fell rapidly to the rear, smoke coming from the engine. Lt Billings reports the engine of the Fokker was a stationary one with a black cowl.

2 Lt Hudson and 2 Lt Pack (B.E.2c, 15 Sqn) escort to IInd Army reconnaissance, were attacked by one Fokker, firing through his propeller, about 50 yards in the rear. The Fokker was eventually driven off.

While re-crossing the lines over Ypres two Aviatiks were seen flying towards Poperinghe. The B.E.2c dived and attacked the lower machine at about 100 yards range. The German was seen to drop three bombs and he then dived and was driven off across the lines at 600 feet. 2 Lt Hudson gives the following description of the Fokker monoplane: Large vertical engine. Gun fixed over the engine, firing through the propeller. Planes of the Morane-Saulnier type but larger. A gap between the planes and fuselage on both sides. The pilot was very high out of the fuselage, being visible down to the waist.

Capt Powell (F.E., 5 Sqn). A report having been received by wireless from B.E.2c, No. *4085*, of a hostile machine over Ypres, Capt Powell went up and sighted an Aviatik over Poperinghe at 10,000 feet. Climbing to within 800 feet, Capt Powell, opened fire below the Aviatik which turned and manoeuvred to fire on the F.E.8 whilst the latter was changing drums. After a second drum the Aviatik nose dived towards its own lines followed by the F.E.8 to about 6,000 feet. During its dive home the Aviatik was in the most convenient position to fire on the F.E.8 but did not do so. This tends to show that either the gun had jammed or the observer was hit. When last seen the Aviatik was still diving towards its own lines at about 3,000 feet but appeared to be under control.

Capt Jenkins and 2 Lt Mackay (B.E.2c, 15 Sqn) Army reconnaissance machine, on re-crossing the lines after completing the reconnaissance observed two Aviatiks over Boesinghe. They attacked one, which, after dropping three bombs, made for the lines, diving to 3,000 feet, followed by the B.E.2c. Tracer bullets were distinctly seen to hit the fuselage just behind the pilot. He continued to fly downwards very fast and the pursuit was broken off. This Aviatik was also attacked by Sgt Noakes and 1 AM Crossley in a B.E.2c.

The IInd Army reconnaissance crossed the line at 8.20 a.m. in a formation as below:

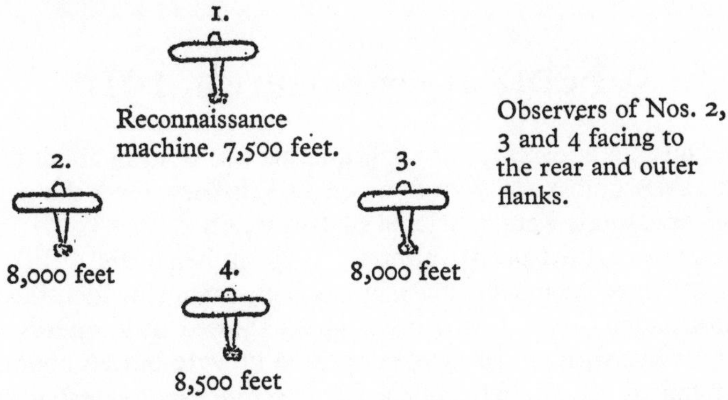

This formation was maintained throughout the reconnaissance at a height of 7,500 to 8,500 feet. The first hostile machine was seen at Roulers and the numbers gradually increased to eight. All these took up station behind the reconnaissance, flying in no definite formation at 9,000 to 10,000 feet.

West of Throughout, two Fokkers appeared. One came in from the right and fired a few rounds at the reconnaissance machine, the other took the left and rear of the escort machines. Six more hostile biplanes came in from the north-west at Cortemarck and followed with the remainder. Over Staden there were fourteen hostile machines following and they continued on till just east of Bixschoote. The reconnaissance machines re-crossed the line at 9.10 a.m. With the exception of the two Fokkers, none of the hostile machines made any attempt to attack. Two hostile aeroplanes were, however, encountered west of the line, one of them having dropped bombs east of Poperinghe. Both were driven off.

Bombing

In September last an Allied aviator (2 Lt Symington, 7 Sqn) dropped a bomb on a troop train travelling from Lille to Valenciennes, as it was passing the level crossing over the Lille–St Amand road. Two men and several horses were killed; traffic on the line was suspended from 1.0 p.m. till 8.0 p.m. This is in addition to the ammunition train previously reported destroyed.

9 February – 4 March, 1916

For reasons not apparent, this communique was reticent about the very considerable combat activity of 20 and 24 February. Over the period as a whole operations were restricted by bad weather.

The twin-engined pusher aircraft, 'very similar to the F.E.', which appears to have been shot down by 20 Sqn, cannot be identified from the information given. German designers showed little interest in the pusher layout, with tail surfaces supported by wire-braced booms. The Otto company of Munich built a few machines in this category, and experimental prototypes were made by several other German firms.

Tracer ammunition, mentioned on 29 February, had been recently introduced by the R.F.C. as an aid to machine-gun sighting.

Five Fokkers, the greatest number so far seen operating together, were reported by 3 Sqn.

COMMUNIQUÉ NO. 30

February 9th

The hutments at Terhand were attacked by eight machines of the 2nd Brigade. Observation was difficult, but considerable damage is believed to have been caused. Twenty huts and a steam lorry were seen to be hit.

February 10th

2 Lt Faber and 2 Lt Way (B.E.2c, 9 Sqn) escort to IIIrd Army reconnaissance were attacked from the rear by a single-seater Fokker who opened fire at 75 yards, gradually closing to 20 yards. Fire was opened on him at 35 yards, and tracer bullets were seen to hit the machine. The German dived and at the same time a second Fokker attacked. 2 Lt Faber was wounded and lost control of the machine which went down in a steep spiral, followed by the Fokker still firing. Two thousand feet from the ground Lt Faber recovered, righted the machine, climbed to 3,000 feet, crossed the lines, and landed his machine safely on the aerodrome.

Lt Egerton and 2 Lt Cox (B.E.2c, 9 Sqn), another of the escort, fired on the second of the Fokkers reported above and clearly saw tracer bullets enter the cowl of the Fokker, which dived steeply and landed safely in a field south of Roisel.

2 Lt Robeson and 2 Lt Scaife, in the reconnaissance machine also fired at this Fokker and saw him dive to the ground.

February 13th

2 Lt Kirton and Lt Billings (F.E.2b, 20 Sqn) drove off an Albatros which attacked them. Later they drove off a biplane which had attacked them. Again, later, during the reconnaissance to which they were acting as escort, they were attacked by a double-engine biplane. Fire was opened on the hostile machine from the back mounting, and a red light was fired from the F.E. as the machine had fallen somewhat to the rear. Eventually he was engaged at 30 yards and is believed to have been hit as he put his nose down steeply and is reported by another observer who came to the assistance as having fallen to the ground west of Mouscron. Lt Billings reports that this hostile machine was a pusher, very similar to the F.E. but with two engines. The O.C., 2nd Brigade reports that the red light fired on this occasion again proved very useful. All the machines of the reconnaissance turned to join in the attack as 2 Lt Kirton's machine was losing distance.

February 20th

During the day there were thirty-four combats in the air. Two hostile machines were driven down by aeroplanes of the 2nd Brigade.

On the night of the 19th/20th February, the aerodrome at Cambrai was attacked by Capt J. E. Tennant and Capt E. D. Horsfall of 4 Sqn. Capt Tennant, carrying seven 20-pound Hales bombs and four incendiary bombs, passed over the line of sheds at a height of 30 feet. He reports that all his seven bombs went through the roof and exploded, the explosions causing his machine to 'bump' appreciably. After dropping the Hales bombs he turned to the left and opened out the throttle to make another attempt with the incendiary bombs. His engine, at first, would not pick up, and Capt Tennant found himself within 10 feet of the aerodrome. Eventually the engine picked up again in time and enabled Capt Tennant to make another attack. One incendiary bomb fell about a foot outside the eastern end of the shed, the other he believes fell into a shed. Capt Horsfall took two 112-pound bombs and glided down to between 1,500 and 2,000 feet. Unfortunately his bombs at first failed to release. Eventually one of the bombs fell but not near the aerodrome. Both machines returned safely.

February 24th

Seven combats. Reports from front line trenches indicate that a hostile aeroplane was forced to descend behind the enemy's lines north of the Ypres–Roulers railway at 12.50 p.m. after being engaged by two of our machines.

February 26th

Twenty-six machines of the 1st Brigade dropped twenty-one 112-pound bombs on Don, many of which hit the target. All the machines returned safely.

February 29th

2 Lt E. W. Leggatt and 2 Lt T. S. Howe (B.E.2c, 10 Sqn) while on patrol sighted an Albatros north of the Bethune–La Bassee Canal, flying towards the lines at about 6,500 feet. They dived to 7,000 feet and fired one drum, the hostile machine turning and disappearing over the lines. While regaining height a second Albatros was sighted flying towards Lillers at 8,000 feet. 2 Lt Leggatt again chased and steadily overhauled the German, opening fire at 150 yards. The hostile machine dived, followed by the B.E.2c still firing. The German's propellor was now seen to slow down, and his machine dived more steeply. The B.E.2c continued diving after him until within 1,000 feet of the ground and keeping up a fire all the time. The hostile machine was seen to land and turn upside down about 2 miles south of Merville. The pilot of the hostile machine was wounded in the leg and he and his observer were taken prisoner. Tracer bullets are reported by Lt Leggatt to have been of considerable assistance.

Capt Powell (F.E.8, 5 Sqn) when flying in the vicinity of Ypres at 10,000 feet saw our anti-aircraft guns firing at a machine over Bailleul. He flew towards it, and passing underneath it at about 50 feet range opened fire. The hostile machine dived towards its own lines followed by the F.E.8. Capt Powell fired three more drums at him at a range of 200 to 400 feet. When at about 7,000 feet Capt Saunders and 2 Lt Joske, in a Morane Parasol, 1 Sqn, joined in the chase. The Morane approached to within 50 to 100 yards, diving steeply, 100 m.p.h. being registered on the speedometer, at an altitude of about 5,000 feet and at about 50 yards range. Tracer bullets were seen to hit the fuselage, and the observer in the hostile machine disappeared from view and ceased firing. After another burst of fire, smoke and flames were seen to come from the engine and the hostile machine was last seen still burning and diving by the woods near Passchendaele.

March 2nd

2 Lt Fincham and 2 Lt Price (B.E.2c, *2127*, 8 Sqn) were persistently attacked by a Fokker biplane when doing artillery patrol in the Ypres salient. The result was indecisive. The pilot reports that he distinctly saw the hostile machine using tracer bullets.

Sgt Bayetto (Morane Scout, 3 Sqn) on escort duty to the Valenciennes reconnaissance reports having been attacked by 5 Fokkers in the neighbourhood of Valenciennes. The reconnaissance machine dived to get clear, but was closely followed by the hostile machines. Sgt Bayetto opened fire on the nearest hostile machine and drove it down, apparently into the woods near Valenciennes. After this engagement he saw no more signs of the reconnaissance machine and returned over Lille where he was again attacked by 3 Fokkers. These he eventually evaded and after circling round Lille for 15 minutes, returned to his landing ground.

Hostile Bombing

A hostile aeroplane dropped bombs on Hazebrouck at midnight, February 18th, wounding nine men of the R.F.C.

Hostile machines attacked the aerodromes of 1 and 7 Sqns at Bailleul on February 24th. No damage was done. In retaliation, five machines of 7 Sqn, each carrying two 112-pound bombs successfully attacked an aerodrome in the vicinity of Lille. Two bombs burst in a large factory by the side of the railway line. This was probably the Kuhlmann Chemical Factory.

Reports of raids

A report has been received that, owing to the destruction by allied aeroplanes of the aviation establishment at Gits, everything has been removed to Beveren.

The aerodrome at Gits was attacked by the IInd Wing and 2nd Brigade on November 8th, 25th, and 28th.

Observation balloons

A hostile observation balloon was reported to have broken loose opposite the IVth Corps at 2 p.m. During the afternoon two hostile observation balloons fell; one near the Naval aerodrome at Dunkirk and the other in the sea near La Panne.

Artillery co-operation

'General artillery action' was in progress on the front of the Vth Corps throughout the day in connection with the attack on the 'Bluff'. Fifty-one hostile batteries were reported and engaged during the day. The G.O.C., Vth Corps reports 'Aeroplane observers have been indefatigable'.

Miscellaneous

2 Lt H. R. Heleshaw and 2 Lt H. F. Mase flew B.E.2cs from Farnborough to St Omer in weather conditions as adverse as they could be for flying. (March 4th.)

On February 21st M. Henderson, 18 Sqn, was wounded by anti-aircraft gun fire, his leg being nearly severed. He managed to land his machine (Vickers) safely and without harm to his observer. Henderson is progressing well.

5 – 22 March, 1916

Bombing operations by 21 Sqn, which had been in France since 23 January, were reported for the first time. The R.E.7, flown by this squadron, was found to be more suited to bombing than its planned reconnaissance role and was being developed to carry the new 336-pound bomb, designed by the Royal Aircraft Factory for use against industrial targets.

The well-intentioned attempt to assist a B.E.2c which had shed a wheel on take-off provides some light relief from combat reports.

COMMUNIQUÉ NO. 31

March 5th

A German machine was seen to fall in flames near Lievin but its destruction cannot tbe raced to a combat.

March 6th

On the night of the 5th/6th March information was received of Zeppelins raiding England. The endeavours to head off the raiders returning to Belgium in the early morning were frustrated, owing to a heavy fall of snow. Seven machines of the 1st Brigade, five of the 2nd Brigade and two machines from G.H.Q. went up, but were forced to return, having seen nothing.

In spite of the adverse weather conditions, some of the pilots reached altitudes of 13,000 feet.

March 8th

Capt Wynne Eyton when patrolling for hostile aircraft between Lens and La Bassee saw two Albatroses going west over Bethune. He overhauled and engaged the rear machine. After firing ½ a drum at it at 150 yards range, the hostile machine turned and made for home, leaving his companion. Capt Wynne Eyton followed him to the lines firing 1½ more drums. The Albatros lost about 4,000 feet in height before he reached his lines, and was last seen over Douvrin. Capt Wynne Eyton then turned and found the other Albatros over the Foret Nieppe, but he had only one drum left, and this was fired without effect. The hostile machine-gun appeared to have jammed, as the Bristol Scout went very close and no fire was opened.

17 Anti-aircraft Section reported that a German machine after being engaged with a B.E.2c, fell behind the German lines. The time coincided with an engagement between a B.E.2c of 7 Sqn and a hostile machine.

Thirty-one machines of the 1st Brigade and 21 Sqn attacked Carvin at about 11 a.m. Over 2 tons weight of bombs were dropped and considerable damage is known to have been done. One bomb is reported by a prisoner of war to have dropped on a parade of soldiers in the street, and to have killed two officers and thirty-five men. On the same date, six hostile aeroplanes attacked the iron works at Isebergues. From a height of 10,000 feet they dropped nine bombs of about 10 kilos. One man was wounded and very little damage was caused.

March 9th

The IInd Army reconnaissance was attacked in the vicinity of Tournai. During the engagement, 2 Lt R. Heywood and 2 Lt D. E. Gayford, 20 Sqn, were forced to land, apparently owing to their engine having been hit. Prior to this, one of the attacking machines was brought down, the German pilot and observer both being killed. 2 Lts Heywood and Gayford were both slightly wounded.

This information was obtained from the pilot of a German machine which descended in our lines on the 12th instant. They also report that Capt Darley is in hospital at Lille. He has lost his thumb, and it is doubtful whether he will regain the use of his arm.

March 12th

Capt Allcock (Bristol Scout, 13 Sqn) attacked two Albatroses recrossing the lines south of Armentieres. After firing one drum he was in turn attacked by a single-seater scout. Having changed his drum, Capt Allcock again attacked one of the Albatroses and apparently hit the engine which stopped, and the machine dived almost perpendicularly. Capt Allcock followed to within 4,000 feet of the ground firing most of the time. The hostile machine landed somewhere between Fort Englos and Lille. Owing to the accuracy and intensity of anti-aircraft gun fire at this height, he was forced to withdraw.

Capt Powell in a F.E.8 attacked a single-seater Fokker monoplane, and claims to have hit it. Clouds of smoke were seen coming from the engine.

A L.V.G. was brought down in our lines near Laventie by anti-aircraft gun fire. The pilot and observer were made prisoners.

Lt F. W. Lerwill (9 Sqn) on leaving the ground in a B.E.2c. lost one of his wheels. Capt Egerton went up after him in a Bristol Scout to attempt to warn him. The machines collided in the air. For a short time they glided down together, but afterwards assumed a steeper dive and crashed, wrecking the machines and injuring both pilots. Both pilots are progressing satisfactorily.

March 13th
An Aviatik with 160 horsepower Mercedes engine made a forced landing in our lines. The pilot, who had started from an aerodrome near Soissons, had lost his way. The machine, which was completely wrecked, contained two machine guns of different pattern.

March 14th
The IInd Army reconnaissance was three times attacked by hostile machines. On each occasion, the attack was driven off by successful combined action, and the reconnaissance was continued and completed.

The 3rd Brigade reconnaissance was heavily engaged throughout its course to Douai and back, being attacked in turn by a twin-tail machine, two Albatroses, one of which was hit, and two Fokkers. All these machines were eventually driven off. During one of the encounters, Lt Van Nostrand's observer 1 AM Parkes was killed. Lt Van Nostrand's machine was badly damaged by the bursting of a shell just below him, which made two holes in the sump and smashed No. 8 cylinder. The engine still carried on, but the machine gradually lost distance and height. While in this condition he was attacked by a Fokker. 1 AM Parkes fired a drum and a half when the gun jammed. He then turned round to change the forward gun to the back mounting, and discovered that this gun had been pierced by a bullet. At this moment he was killed. Lt Van Nostrand dived and made for the lines which he crossed at 1,000 feet with his engine on the point of failing.

March 16th
2 Lt J. Latta (5 Sqn) dropped two 112-pound bombs from a height of 1,800 feet on to the château at Langemarck at 11.15 p.m. He believes that he hit the mark.

A very successful special shoot was carried out by Lt Symington and Cpl Hunt (7 Sqn) with the 1st Canadian Battery, and the 53rd, 35th and 21st Siege Batteries. They successfully engaged anti-aircraft guns firing from emplacements and motor lorries. Anti-aircraft guns firing from the emplacements ceased fire, and a direct hit was obtained on a detached anti-aircraft gun. Other shots which fell within 5 to 10 yards of emplacements were followed by a big spurt of flame and a cloud of smoke. At one stage when numerous anti-aircraft lorries were concentrated near the A.A. Battery ZZ was given with pin point, and was replied to with success by the 1st Canadian Heavy Battery.

March 18th
The IInd Army reconnaissance was heavily attacked. As far as Courtrai the reconnaissance was unmolested, but on turning back from there, hostile aircraft, which had previously been observed, attacked to the

number of 12. A running fight took place all the way back, the reconnaissance machines turning to assume the offensive several times. All attacks were driven off and the reconnaissance successfully completed. One pilot (2 Lt Kirton) was slightly wounded, and two machines badly damaged, but all returned safely to our side of the lines. One Fokker was hit in the engine, but went down under control.

Lt F. H. Thayre and Lt C. R. Davidson (B.E.2c. 18 Sqn) whilst on reconnaissance at about 4.30 p.m., were attacked by three hostile machines. One came round on the left flank from above and behind, and opened fire with about 50 rounds, but failed to do any damage. The second machine attacked from 60 yards in the rear. A drum was fired into the engine of the hostile machine, which immediately dived and disappeared out of sight. Forward observing officers of the 4th Brigade R.G.A. and the 8th Division, General Staff report that the hostile machine crashed vertically to earth after diving steeply to within 200 feet of the ground.

March 19th

Flt Sgt Carlisle and Lt J. McKelvie (Morane Parasol, 1 Sqn) while escorting an artillery Morane over Oostaverne, observed an Albatros diving to attack the artillery machine. Flt Sgt Carlisle turned and attacked at a range of about 300 yards, closing to 150 yards. The hostile machine turned and side-slipped heavily, and was last seen still diving steeply at about 500 feet from the ground. From the fact that the enemy made no attempt to flatten out at all or return the fire, it seems probable that he was badly hit.

Note. The pilot and observer of the artillery machine report that the Albatros went down obviously uncontrolled.

2 Lt R. Collis and Flt Lt Emery (F.E.), while flying over the channel at 8,000 feet, saw a hostile machine being shelled over Dover. They gave chase, but could not get within range. Presently they saw another machine making for Deal. They flew up channel and met this hostile aeroplane on its return. Lt Collis was then at 8,000 feet and the hostile machine at 4,000 feet. Planing down with engine throttled back until within 150 yards, the observer opened fire immediately behind. The hostile machine did not return the fire and made no attempt to manoeuvre out of range. After a drum had been expended the enemy was observed to plunge down towards the sea with a steep right-hand bank and with irregular puffs of smoke coming from the engine. Lt Collis now experienced some difficulty with his engine and during the time that he was changing over the petrol to the service tank, he lost sight of the hostile machine, which was last seen at 1,500 feet diving steeply.

Result of Raids

It is reported that extensive damage has been done by Allied raids in north-east France, especially at Cambrai where several points of military importance were hit.

A refugee from Hamelincourt, Mme Demailly, living at La Vicogne, states that the electric power station and canteen at Monchy were destroyed by bombs from an aeroplane. Date unknown, probably December. (Lt Rowell, 8 Sqn, two 20-pound bombs, December 14th, and Lt Herring, 8 Sqn, one 20-pound bomb—December 9th.)

4—F.E.2b—120 H.P. BEARDMORE ENGINE

The F.E.2b two-seat pusher biplane with its unobstructed forward field of fire shared with the D.H.2 in the eclipse of the Fokker monoplane. The first F.E.2b squadron to go to France was No. 20 which arrived on January 23, 1916. Further squadrons followed,—No. 25 on February 20, No. 23 on March 16 and No. 22 on April 1. Later fitted with the 160 h.p. Beardmore engine, the F.E.2b survived to the end of the war as a night bomber.

20 March – 7 April, 1916

From this date the communiqués are more informative, giving details of the weather and more news of R.F.C. casualties.

This was another period of considerable activity, though few of the combats are covered in detail. On 24 March a D.H.2 of 24 Sqn was reported in action for the first time.

The Army comments on R.F.C. operations underline the moral effect on ground troops of friendly aircraft activity over the trenches.

Ranken darts, referred to on 31 March, were early anti-Zeppelin missiles with explosive heads.

The description of the enemy aircraft furnished by anti-aircraft gunners establishes it as the L.F.G. Roland CII two-seater reconnaissance and escort machine, which was also used for bombing, and had a top speed of 103 m.p.h.

COMMUNIQUÉ NO. 32

March 20th

Ten indecisive fights in the air took place; Lt Latta in a De Havilland Scout engaged four hostile aeroplanes in the Ypres Salient and drove them off. Two emplacements of a hostile battery were destroyed by our 8-inch howitzers working with the IInd Wing, R.F.C.

Capt W. Lewis, R.A. Assistant for Anti-aircraft Duties to M.G.R.A. IIIrd Army reports:

> On the 20th March a B.E.2c was doing a reconnaissance north-east of Arras from about 3.30 p.m. till 6 p.m. During the whole of this time the machine was well over the German lines and under heavy A.A. fire. The Germans must have fired some thousands of rounds at him during this time, and towards the end ceased fire altogether, probably owing to their ammunition not being able to compete with such a demand. Anti-aircraft sections on this side of the lines were very enthusiastic over the performance.

This refers to 2 Lt Hallam Peck, pilot, and 2 Lt Whitehead, observer, 12 Sqn.

The Officer Commanding the 8th Battalion Kings Own Yorkshire Light Infantry has drawn attention to the following flight carried out by 2 Lt Minot and 2 Lt Welsh, 16 Sqn, in a B.E.2c the same day. Between 11 and 11.30 a.m. the aeroplane crossed the trenches occupied by the

K.O.Y.L.I. at an altitude of between 1,000 and 2,000 feet, and, under a heavy fire from anti-aircraft guns, machine-guns and rifles, continued flying backwards and forwards at this low altitude. The Commanding Officer reports that

> The effect of our troops in the trenches and posts was to create the greatest enthusiasm, and the aeroplane was cheered by our men on returning the second time. At no time did the aeroplane appear to be more than 2,000 feet above the ground.

March 21st–March 24th

From March 21st to 24th the weather was very bad and little flying was possible.

March 25th

The weather improved but there was still a strong westerly wind and considerable cloud. Four indecisive combats. 2 Lt Lerwill, 24 Sqn, while on patrol chased a German machine over its own lines. From some cause which is not known he had to make a forced landing behind the enemy's lines near St Quentin and was taken prisoner.

March 26th

A very high south-westerly wind with low clouds, snow and rain. Little successful flying took place.

March 27th

1 and 6 Sqns co-operated throughout the day in the IInd Army operations at St Eloi. Excellent photographs were taken by 5 Sqn at 9 a.m. of the mine craters made the same morning. These were delivered at G.H.Q. the same evening.

March 28th

2 Lt Williams and Lt McClintock, 2 Sqn, took some photographs urgently required by the Ist Corps. They had to fly at 3,000 feet owing to the gale. One of the elevator controls was shot away and the machine was riddled with bullets.

1 and 6 Sqns again did very useful work in connection with the operations at St Eloi in spite of the bad weather, commencing at 4.50 a.m. and continuing till dark. 6 made eight successful artillery observation flights.

March 29th

2 Lt Pinder and 2 Lt Halford of 23 Sqn were brought down by a hostile machine of the Fokker type near Queant while acting as escort to the IIIrd Army reconnaissance. The hostile machine attacked from the rear, first from above and then from directly behind. 2 Lt Pinder is believed to have been slightly wounded and 2 Lt Halford unhurt.

There were eight other combats, after one of which the hostile machine made a forced landing behind his own lines apparently under control.

March 30th

A machine of 8 Sqn (pilot, 2 Lt T. C. Wilson, observer, 1 AM Walker) was brought down in a fight over Monchy au Bois, and it is feared that Lt Wilson is severely wounded and Walker killed. The hostile machine, a Fokker, attacked from behind engaging the right rear escort and centre rear escort (Lt Wilson) in succession. The left rear escort turned back to meet the Fokker, but his gun jammed.

Two machines on photographic duty, one of 11 Sqn (pilot, 2 Lt Castle, observer, 2 AM Coleman) and one of 15 Sqn (pilot, 2 Lt J. G. Welsford, observer, 2 Lt W. Joyce) were also brought down. The first was seen to fall in flames between Fampoux and Monchy le Preux, and 2 Lt Welsford is believed to have been killed in the second, which fell in the same neighbourhood.

There were five other combats, the results of which were indecisive, as far as is known.

March 31st

The squadron from G.H.Q. carried out a reconnaissance over the Menin–Courtrai area. A Fokker attacked the reconnaissance over Hollebeke coming from below and behind. The Fokker put two shots into the propeller and broke the tail boom strut. The pilot turned and fired half a drum into the hostile machine which dived vertically and went out of sight still diving. The Fokker is thought to have been hit.

Another machine of this reconnaissance (pilot, Lt Norris of 25 Sqn) was attacked by a Fokker over Gheluwe. The observer, Capt Segrave was wounded in the leg. The Fokker came from above, diving steeply past the left wing of our machine. A machine of 11 Sqn attacked a hostile machine over Villers au Bois diving down on it and firing four drums. The hostile machine was forced down until close over the German trenches and was last seen almost on the ground, apparently hit.

There were ten other fights with indecisive results.

April 1st

Two machines were sent towards Dunkirk at daybreak in the hopes of intercepting Zeppelins returning from England but saw nothing.

Much artillery work was carried out, fifty-two targets being engaged. 5 Sqn was particularly successful with a battery of heavy howitzers, three targets being very thoroughly dealt with.

Hostile aircraft were very active, twenty-five seen by machines of the 1st Brigade.

Capt Gethin (pilot) and Capt Scott (observer) of 10 Sqn attacked three hostile machines, north of the La Bassee canal firing three drums at one of them at a height of about 10,000 feet. The hostile machine was seen subsequently by our A.A. guns diving steeply at a height of only 4,000 feet.

2 Lt Phelan (pilot) and Cpl Morton (observer) on a machine of 11 Sqn had a protracted fight with an L.V.G., firing five drums at it in all. When at a height of 5,000 feet, the L.V.G. suddenly dived vertically and disappeared from sight.

Fourteen other inconclusive combats took place.

April 2nd

Capt de Crespigny on a machine of 11 Sqn (observer, 2 Lt J. Hughes Chamberlain) while on patrol attacked five L.V.G. biplanes over Lens. He fired two drums at the first at about 110 yards range and three drums at the second at about 40 yards. The latter dived steeply towards the German lines. The other three machines made off. Capt de Crespigny's machine was now completely out of control, the engine having stopped, the propeller being smashed and the control wire shot away. Capt de Crespigny, however, with great skill brought his machine to the ground behind our own lines without any casualty to himself or his observer.

Capt W. Milne, of 25 Sqn (observer, Lt Gilbert) attacked an Albatros over the German lines going in to very close quarters. He hit the German machine but his own petrol tank was hit and his engine stopped.

Major Hubbard on another machine of 11 Sqn from a height of 9,000 feet attacked a hostile machine at a height of 5,000 feet, over the German trenches and drove it down to 2,000 feet firing all the time. The German was still diving steeply when last seen.

There were seventeen other combats in three of which the German machines are believed to have been hit.

Two German kite balloons were attacked by our aeroplanes and forced to descend.

April 3rd

A German Albatros attacked first by Lt Findlay (observer, Lt Scott) and subsequently by Capt Rawcliffe (observer, Sgt Woodfield) was brought down behind our lines south of Souchez, pilot and observer both being killed. The enemy shelled the machine on the ground setting it on fire. There were ten other fights in the air.

2 Kite Balloon ascended to a height of 3,000 feet. Capt Parker, 7 Kite Balloon Section made a successful parachute descent from 1,500 feet.

General

During the Zeppelin raid on the night 31st March/1st April, thirteen of our aeroplanes went up. Three saw Zeppelins and one machine engaged one at 9,000 feet, dropping Ranken darts on it at 9.45 p.m. and again at 10 p.m. His machine was hit many times.

Machines were in the air in two reliefs from 9.12 p.m. to 1.30 a.m. There was only one casualty to personnel; one officer unfortunately being killed as he was leaving the ground. Three machines were damaged.

Total time in the air—18 hours, 40 minutes.

A new type of hostile aircraft is reported by 18 Anti-aircraft Battery. The wings somewhat resemble a Bristol Scout but are more rounded at the ends. The tail plane is similar to that of a Bristol Scout. The fuselage is of the usual German pattern but has a seat for the observer midway along its length. The machine is apparently very fast.

3 – 14 April, 1916

A successful piece of artillery observation work by 7 Sqn was indicated in the references to the 'Clock Code', evolved in 1915 to signal the fall of shells. The target was regarded as the centre of the clock face, with 12 o'clock pointing north and 6 o'clock, south. Imaginary circles round the target at specified distances were lettered; Y = 10 yards, Z = 25 yards, A = 50 yards, B = 100 yards.

The Fokker EIII monoplane which forced-landed on 8 April was the first to fall intact into British hands. It was later tested at the Central Flying School, Upavon, and found to have a top speed of 83 m.p.h. It was dived at 115 m.p.h. and was described as easy to land. These tests finally established that as regards performance the Fokker was a very average machine.

COMMUNIQUÉ NO. 33

April 3rd

Capt Quinnell, of 7 Sqn, carried out a special shoot with the 64th Siege Battery (12-inch Howitzers) on emplacements at Fort Senarmont. Three O.K.s were registered, and the battery was then switched on to another emplacement. Altogether five direct hits were registered, and all the other rounds were within the 'A' and most within the 'Z' circle. The anti-aircraft guns ceased firing for the whole of the period, except one gun on the outside edge of the Fort, which showed slight and feeble activity towards the end of the flight.

April 4th

Very little work was possible on account of low clouds and rain.

April 5th

Observation was again difficult.

Observers reported that on two occasions the following hostile ground signal was observed: an 'X' was laid out on the ground; it was replaced by a 'V', the point of which followed the direction in which the British machine was flying.

The following letter was received by the General Officer Commanding the Royal Flying Corps:

> The Field Marshal Commanding in Chief, Home Forces, desires me to express to you, and through you to the officers and men serving under your

command, his appreciation of the excellent organisation and skilful and daring action of the Royal Flying Corps allotted to the aerial defence of London.

Machines have been up in all weathers and often under very adverse conditions—there is no doubt that the two machines, which, under Lts Brandon and Powell most skilfully attacked one of the enemy's airships on the night of the 1/2nd April, were most successful and that Lt Brandon succeeded in dropping bombs on the ship.

Moreover, the action of aeroplanes at night against airships has been proved to be effective.

April 6th

General artillery action was in force all day on a portion of the IInd Army front owing to the German attack at St Eloi. Aerial observation was hindered by low clouds and mist.

April 7th

Clouds at 1,000 feet. Some successful artillery work was completed by 4 Sqn, four points on the German trenches being registered after 6 p.m., flying at a low altitude.

6 Sqn observed general effect of fire on the hostile trenches at St Eloi, with clouds at times as low as 800 feet.

April 8th

Some successful artillery work was completed, 28 targets being successfully ranged on.

Hostile aircraft

Hostile aircraft were on the whole inactive. The IInd Army reconnaissance was twice attacked, once over Roulers and once again north of Courtrai, on each occasion by four hostile machines. Both attacks were driven off. One F.E. was hit in the main petrol tank, but completed the reconnaissance on the service tank.

A Fokker monoplane with a 9-cylinder 100 horsepower Gnome engine came down in our lines at Renescure. The pilot is an unwounded prisoner. Full particulars of the machine and of information gained from the prisoner have been circulated.

April 9th

4 Sqn working with a battery of 8-inch Howitzers obtained a direct hit on a gun emplacement, completely destroying it.

Few hostile aeroplanes were seen.

2 Lt Leggatt and 1 AM Hooker (B.E.2c, 10 Sqn) chased and drove off an Albatros in the vicinity of La Bassee. When last seen, the hostile machine was diving vertically below the clouds at 5,000 feet.

Capt I. A. J. Duff, observer, 5 Sqn, was slightly wounded by anti-aircraft gun fire.

April 10th

There were eight combats in the air.

Capt H. A. Cooper and 2 Lt Vickery (Vickers fighter, 11 Sqn) whilst engaged in taking photographs near Bailleul, saw an L.V.G. at 8,000 feet flying east. The Vickers dived with the engine off and engaged the hostile machine at a range of 40 yards at 6,000 feet. The observer of the hostile machine was seen to fall back in his seat, and the L.V.G. immediately dived steeply and was lost sight of still diving through the clouds.

Lt-Col D. S. Lewis, D.S.O. and Capt A. W. G. Gale, D.S.O., were killed in a Morane Parasol. The machine received a direct hit by anti-aircraft gun fire at 8,000 feet and fell near the trench lines at Wytschaete.

April 11th

A trench reconnaissance carried out at daybreak on the Ist Army front reported unusual railway movements, activity in the trenches, movements of lorries and carts, and located various gun emplacements. The reconnaissance was carried out at a low altitude. The inactivity of anti-aircraft guns was noticeable.

Practice night reconnaissances were also carried out by the 1st and 4th Brigades, R.F.C.

April 12th

Weather conditions were too unfavourable for flying.

13–30 April, 1916

Further progress in R.F.C. re-equipment with more effective fighting aircraft was disclosed by the report of French Nieuport scouts, operating with 1 and 16 Sqns.

The Nieuport 16, with a 110 horsepower Le Rhône rotary engine, had a top speed of 103 m.p.h. and was highly manoeuvrable. It was armed with a Lewis gun mounted above the top wing.

This week saw some notable operations by the F.E.2bs and provided further evidence of the fighting qualities of the new D.H.2 scouts. One D.H.2 pilot had a miraculous escape when an anti-aircraft shell passed right through the nose of his aircraft.

27 Sqn, now reported in action, was the first (and only) unit fully equipped with the Martinsyde G100. 27 had arrived in France on 1 March. Although designed as a fighting scout, the Martinsyde was a large and unwieldy machine for air fighting—it was nicknamed the 'Elephant'—and was later transferred to bombing duties.

This communiqué made the first specific mention of the German Roland CII.

COMMUNIQUÉ NO. 34

April 13th, 14th and 15th
Unfavourable weather hampered aerial work.

April 16th
2 Lt Read and 2 Lt Lord Doune, 25 Sqn, on Bristol Scouts, engaged a Fokker. Working together, they had all the best of the fight but the combat had to be broken off owing to both their guns jamming.

There were eight other inconclusive fights in the air.

2 Lt W. S. Earle (pilot) and 2 Lt C. W. P. Selby (observer) were brought down in the German lines east of Maricourt as the result of a fight in the air. The machine was apparently on fire. Lt Earle was killed and his observer severely wounded.

Hostile aircraft
Four bombs dropped at Isbergues by night by hostile aeroplanes. Two failed to explode and no damage was done.

April 17th, 18th and 19th

Low clouds, rain and strong wind prevented any successful flying. In spite of this 2 Lts Heleshaw and Goldfoyle flew machines over from England.

April 20th

Weather was again unfavourable. Some successful photography was completed by Capt Williams and Lt Pirie of 2 Sqn, flying at a height of under 3,000 feet.

April 21st

2 Lt McNaughton was wounded in the leg during the IInd Army reconnaissance. He landed his machine safely at Abeele.

Capt James also on the IInd Army reconnaissance, was attacked and forced to land near Kruistraat. He and his observer were unhurt. His machine was shelled and destroyed by the enemy.

A De Havilland Scout of 24 Sqn, piloted by 2 Lt Tidmarsh received a direct hit with anti-aircraft shell. The shell passed through both sides of the nacelle in front of the pilot's legs without touching him or otherwise damaging the machine.

April 22nd

Rain all day. No flying.

April 23rd

Seven combats were recorded.

2 Lt Collison and 2 AM Atwell in a F.E.2b of 25 Sqn, on Ist Army patrol over Fromelles, attacked a hostile machine at about 6,000 feet. AM Atwell fired a drum at a range of about 200 feet, but was hit in the body and lost consciousness while fixing the second drum. 2 Lt Collison opened fire but his machine was hit by anti-aircraft, and he had to make a forced landing near Estaires. AM Atwell was dead when the machine landed.

A Nieuport of 11 Sqn engaged an enemy aeroplane, firing one drum at it. The enemy returned the fire and then dived steeply, being lost to view still diving.

16 Sqn attacked a hostile kite balloon with bombs and incendiary bullets. One machine used bombs and was escorted by two machines using incendiary bullets. The kite balloon was lowered but was not hit.

A hostile aeroplane descended to about 2,000 feet and marked the position of the winch of one of our balloons (2 Sqn) by dropping a shower of silver discs. At the same time machine-gun fire was opened on the balloon. No damage was done.

2 Lt W. C. M. Phelan and 2 Lt W. A. Scott-Brown started on photographic duty at 8.45 a.m. Their machine was brought down as the result

of a fight in the air, and the pilot and observer were taken prisoner.

Miscellaneous

Lt H. S. Ward and 2 Lt H. F. Champion escaped from Germany on the 18 April, and reported to Headquarters, R.F.C. on the 23 April.

Lt H. S. Ward with Lt Buckley of 16 Sqn, were brought down in a combat in the air on the 30 November 1915.

2 Lt H. F. Champion, an observer of 20 Sqn, was taken prisoner on the 29 February 1916. His machine, piloted by 2 Lt L. A. Newbold, had been forced to land near Menin.

April 24th

The IInd Army reconnaissance (five F.E.2bs of 20 Sqn) carried out a running fight during the whole of its course. Just before reaching Roulers, at a height of 9,500 feet, the left front machine was attacked from behind by a biplane. A drum was fired from the back mounting and the hostile machine disappeared. After turning at Roulers, Capt James on the right rear machine was attacked by a Fokker, which was driven off. Immediately afterwards he was again attacked by a biplane from behind. Turning about he fired at close range. The hostile machine went down in a spinning nose dive and was seen to crash on the ground. Shortly afterwards two biplanes attacked the whole formation from the left front, diving through the middle and being fired on by all machines. The rearmost of the two went down steeply, apparently not under control. Confirmation of this is given by the Guards Division who report seeing a hostile machine fall near Passchendaele. From this point onwards there was continuous fighting but the formation worked so well that the reconnaissance machine was enabled to take its photographs successfully. During the whole time there were large numbers of other hostile machines firing on the reconnaissance from long range. Our machines fired over 500 rounds during the reconnaissance. The pilots and observers are as follows:

Pilots	*Observers*
2 Lt Morton	Lt Billinge
Capt Graves	2 Lt Chancellor
2 Lt Scott	Cpl Gawthrop
Capt James	2 Lt Exley
2 Lt Dabbs	Cpl Ward

There were fourteen other combats with indecisive results.

5 Sqn carried out a successful shoot with the 39th Siege Battery, a hostile ammunition store being destroyed. 12 Sqn ranged two batteries on German anti-aircraft battery which was knocked out, flames and smoke being seen.

A hostile machine was shot down by our anti-aircraft west of Ploegsteert Wood. The machine was completely wrecked, pilot and passenger being killed. The machine was a type which hitherto has not been met with on this side, a Roland biplane, a two-seater with the passenger behind. It carried one Lewis gun in a circular gun mounting, and five drums of ammunition.

5 Sqn's aerodrome was bombed in the early morning. Fifteen bombs exploded. The sheds were not hit but slight damage was done to one and the machine in it.

April 25th

There were sixteen combats in the air.

Lt J. S. Andrews and 2 Lt Cowan in De Havilland Scouts of 24 Sqn, when on escort duty to the IVth Army reconnaissance, had engagements with Fokkers. They appear to have had no difficulty in manoeuvring successfully against the Fokkers, and managed to beat off all attacks.

Fifty-nine targets were successfully ranged on. 27 Sqn ranged a 12-inch howitzer on Comines railway station with success. In addition thirteen targets were registered by kite balloon sections.

2 Lts Tyson and Breese of 12 Sqn took 50 photographs in one flight, 49 of which were successful.

99 plates were exposed by the 2nd Brigade.

Hostile bombing at about 4 a.m. in the morning; bombs were dropped near the aerodrome at Abeele. No damage was done.

April 26th

An F.E.2b of 18 Sqn, pilot, Lt J. C. Callaghan, observer, 2 Lt Mitchell, when returning from photographic duty, saw three Fokkers and another hostile machine approaching from Arras. The pilot turned towards the two who were attempting to approach from the rear. The observer fired half a drum at each of the two leading Fokkers, hitting the second. The third Fokker attacked from the rear and put the engine of the F.E. out of action, and the other two Fokkers returned to the attack. The enemy's fire destroyed the fore and aft control, and the observer was hit in the head and killed. Lt Callaghan let his machine take its own gliding angle, and effected a fair landing near the Château de la Haie.

2 Lt Patrick went up from St Omer in pursuit of a German machine, losing it over Ypres. When returning at 7,000 feet over Clairmarais, he saw that the anti-aircraft guns at St Omer were shooting, and made out a hostile machine 5,000 feet above him. Circling round, he got behind and below the hostile machine, opening fire at 200 yards. After firing one drum, he circled to change drums, and attacked again from behind and below, getting to within 30 yards. He repeated this manoeuvre a third time, and after 20 shots the hostile machine went down in a spiral nose dive with the engine full on. The machine, which was a L.V.G. with

160 horsepower engine, fell near Fletre, pilot and observer both being killed by bullets previous to the fall. 2 Lt Patrick was flying a Nieuport with 110 horsepower Le Rhône engine, a Lewis gun fitted on the top plane, having a bowden wire trigger pull to the control lever.

The IIIrd Army reconnaissance was attacked three times. An F.E. was first attacked by three hostile machines, the centre one coming to within 20 yards. The F.E. fired 40 rounds at the hostile machine's engine at this range, and the machine dived steeply. The F.E. was hit in several places. Another F.E. was hit and both petrol tanks put out of action.

A B.E. was also attacked, firing 40 rounds. The hostile machine was seen to dive steeply, but was then lost to sight.

2 Lt S. Dalrymple on a Martinsyde of 27 Sqn, engaged and drove off two hostile machines, and Capt Cairns on a Martinsyde of the same squadron engaged a hostile machine near Souchez. He fired half a drum at about 70 yards and then swerved to avoid collision. He attacked again from behind and below firing the remainder of the drum. The observer of the hostile machine was apparently hit as during the second attack he appeared to be kneeling in the turret doing nothing, and no shots were fired. This hostile machine was subsequently engaged by 2 Lt Tollemache in a Martinsyde who fired a drum at it at about 50 yards range, driving it down towards Douvrin.

A Zeppelin was sighted at daybreak between Menin and Lille. Four Morane biplanes of 1 Sqn ascended but lost sight of the airship in the mist.

2 Lt Mitchell, observer of 18 Sqn was killed in a combat in the air. 2 Lt J. Milner, observer of 10 Sqn was killed by anti-aircraft fire while employed on artillery observation.

April 27th

There were twenty combats in the air.

Lt Maxwell on a F.E. of 25 Sqn sighted six Aviatiks patrolling the enemy's lines over Fromelles. He kept in touch with them and they had turned over Lens when they were attacked by Capt Milne who was patrolling over Hulluch. The Aviatiks were flying in formation, five abreast with one behind, and one on each flank somewhat higher than the remainder. They were joined by two others from the south-east. Capt Bellew and 2 Lt Baines in two more F.E.s joined Capt Milne and Lt Maxwell, and the four F.E.s attacked the Aviatiks, two of which went south at once. The F.E.s went into close quarters and drove a wedge into the Aviatiks, splitting up their formation. A running fight ensued lasting 10 minutes. Capt Bellew and Lt Maxwell drove three to the north-east and headed them off from the others. Capt Bellew drove one to the ground near Illies under control. Lt Maxwell drove one to the ground near

Herlies where it was seen to land in a ploughed field, apparently under control. Of the remainder, two landed at Don and the others disappeared south flying very low. Lt Maxwell's machine was hit but the other F.E.s were not touched.

2 Lt Foggin on a Nieuport of 1 Sqn left the ground on seeing a hostile machine near Bailleul. He quickly overhauled it and fired at close range. Tracer bullets were clearly seen to strike the fuselage. Difficulty was experienced in getting the Nieuport slow enough to keep pace with the German machine without fouling it, and whilst 2 Lt Foggin was doing a half turn to take off speed, one shot hit his machine, the splinters wounding him in the left eye and he had to break off the fight. The German machine had six bombs, estimated at 40-pounds each, strung underneath, three on each side of the undercarriage wheels. The Albatros was observed by anti-aircraft artillery still going down, and was thought to have been hit.

April 28th

Artillery co-operation was very successful, 59 targets being engaged. Direct hits were obtained on three hostile batteries, and several others were fired on with effect.

Few hostile aircraft were seen and only four combats in the air were recorded, all indecisive.

Kite balloons were up all day and engaged six targets.

Miscellaneous

Information has been received from Germany that 2 Lt M. A. J. Orde, a pilot of 8 Sqn (who was missing on March 13th with 1 AM E. Shaw), was wounded in the back and had two of the control wires shot away but managed to land his machine safely. 1 AM Shaw is unwounded.

29 April – 4 May, 1916

It is not possible to put any precise date to the ending of the so-called 'Fokker scourge', but it had certainly passed by the spring of 1916.

The aircraft itself possessed no outstanding qualities and its success was due to its manoeuvrability and forward-firing armament. The maximum number operating on the Western Front has not been established with any certainty, but was probably about a hundred.

By this time the R.F.C. had in France three complete squadrons of single-seat fighting scouts (24 and 29 with D.H.2s and 27 with Martinsydes) and four squadrons of two-seat F.E.2bs, while the general-purpose squadrons still retained a few scouts for escort purposes. The French air force had been using the Nieuport since January, and, as already noted, this excellent little fighter was now being introduced to the R.F.C.

Although the R.F.C. was still losing aircraft to the Fokkers, the latter were also being destroyed in increasing numbers—two losses being reported in this communiqué.

Lt H. O. D. Segrave, 29 Sqn, who drove down an Aviatik on 1 May, was famous in later years as Sir Henry Segrave, holder of land and water speed records.

COMMUNIQUÉ NO. 35

April 29th

Artillery co-operation—much successful work was accomplished. Forty-nine targets were successfully engaged.

2 Lt Lord Doune on an F.E. of 25 Sqn, observer 2 Lt R. V. Walker, when on patrol between Hulluch and La Bassee at a height of 10,000 feet sighted a Fokker 1,000 feet below him. He dived at it, and the observer opened fire at 80 yards. The Fokker attempted to get behind the F.E., and the machines circled round each other several times, the F.E. having the best of the manoeuvring. The third time the two machines approached each other while both pilot and observer were firing at the Fokker at very short range above them, one wing was seen to crumple up, and the Fokker fell in a spinning nose dive, being carried by the wind behind our lines. Five drums in all were fired at it before it fell.

The pilot of the hostile machine belonged to the 18th Flieger Abteilung. He was the son of Prince Ernst von Sachsen-Meiningen.

2 Lt Sampson on an F.E. of 20 Sqn, observer 1 AM Catton, when on escort duty above Messines was attacked by a Fokker from in front. The observer fired half a drum at the Fokker, which then attacked from behind. 1 AM Catton was shot dead and 2 Lt Sampson had his leg grazed by a bullet. The engine and propeller were riddled with bullets, and the engine stopped. 2 Lt Sampson made for Abeele aerodrome, but failed to reach it and landed in a ploughed field near Poperinghe, damaging the undercarriage.

Sgt Carlisle on a Morane biplane, 1 Sqn, engaged a hostile machine at 20 yards. The latter went down diving steeply to his own lines, being followed by the Morane to 2,000 feet. The German did not fire.

A B.E. of 13 Sqn engaged a hostile machine, firing one drum at it. The observer was seen to fall back, and his gun was dropped. The B.E. gave chase, but the hostile machine dived and appeared to make a good landing.

Another B.E. of the same squadron engaged two hostile machines. One drum was fired at one of these which was seen to be hit. The other was pursued, and when the pursuit was given up the first machine had disappeared.

Anti-aircraft artillery on the IIIrd Army front brought down a hostile machine near Maroeuil, the pilot and observer both being killed.

April 30th

Flt Sgt Carlisle on a Nieuport Scout of 1 Sqn, when patrolling between Warneton and Hollebeke at 5 a.m. observed an Aviatik at about 13,000 feet. He attacked it, firing a drum from about 50 yards. The Aviatik appeared to be hit and dived very steeply. Flt Sgt Carlisle followed but lost sight of it at about 4,000 feet. Later another Aviatik was seen being shelled behind the British lines at 12,000 feet. Flt Sgt Carlisle attacked near Ploegsteert and fired a drum at it from below and drove it towards Hollebeke. He followed and fired two more drums, and then had to abandon the chase, having expended all his ammunition.

Capt Pattinson in a Nieuport of 11 Sqn, while patrolling over Arras attacked a hostile machine flying near Ecuire, which was followed by a B.E.2c. The German opened fire at 150 yards, Capt Pattinson closed to 75 yards and fired a drum. He then turned sharply to reload and lost sight of the enemy. The 25th A.A. Battery saw the fight and reported that the German machine came down apparently out of control about *B. 6 Sheet 5lb*. This is confirmed by the 39th A.A. Battery.

2 Lt Tidmarsh on a De Havilland Scout of 24 Sqn, while escorting F.E.s over Peronne, saw a Fokker coming from Bapaume. He attacked it

Above: L.F.G. Roland C II
Below: Bristol Scout

Above: Martinsyde S.1
Below: Albatros C III

from 4,000 feet above, diving straight down at it. The Fokker immediately dived and appeared to get out of control when about 1,000 feet from the ground, crashing on the roofs of the houses at Bapaume. The wings separated, one being thrown a distance of 20 yards. 2 Lt Tidmarsh was never nearer than 500 yards and did not open fire.

Gas came over 7 Sqn's aerodrome in the early morning, and some officers and men were slightly affected.

2 Lt R. K. Shives on an F.E. of 5 Sqn was wounded in the side and in the leg by anti-aircraft fire when on patrol duty. His machine was hit in many places.

May 1st

Artillery Co-operation—66 targets were successfully engaged with aeroplane co-operation, and three by kite balloon sections. An observer of the 4th Brigade directed artillery fire on gun positions, obtaining four direct hits and causing an explosion and a fire.

Capt Grinnell Milne, F.E.2b of 25 Sqn, saw five German machines flying below him at 5,000 feet. One of these detached itself from the rest and flew towards the lines near Hulluch. He dived at it and got to within about 500 feet before it saw him and turned east. The hostile machine then started to dive, but Capt Grinnell Milne got within a few yards of the pilot's back and opened fire. The observer of the F.E., Cpl Waller, fired 34 rounds, and the German swerved sharply, nearly collided, and then went down vertically. The F.E. then had to turn to engage another machine which was attacking him from behind.

Lt Segrave, 29 Sqn, in a De Havilland Scout, engaged and drove down a hostile machine, apparently an Aviatik, which landed in a field near Gheluvelt. Only seven rounds were fired from the German machine. Lt Segrave thinks the observer must have been shot and the pilot wounded.

2nd Brigade report hostile aircraft were unusually active on the IInd Army front, especially in the Salient.

May 2nd

Successful co-operation by all four Brigades. Our artillery, ranged by 12 Sqn, destroyed an anti-aircraft battery, and on the IVth Army front two direct hits were obtained on anti-aircraft guns with the assistance of our machines.

Few hostile aircraft were seen, except on the Ist Army front in the early morning. No hostile aeroplane was seen on the IInd Army front throughout the day.

May 3rd

Low clouds throughout the day hindered aerial activity. Hostile aircraft were inactive, no combats were reported. Some successful artillery co-operation was completed by 8 Sqn, with clouds at a height of 2,500.

4–21 May, 1916

Lieutenant Albert Ball, mentioned for the first time in this communiqué, was to become the first of the famous British fighter 'aces'.

Ball had been flying B.E.2cs in 13 Sqn since February and was posted to 11 on 7 May. His combat in a Bristol Scout on 16 May was not officially confirmed as a victory, though the Albatros appears to have dived past the vertical and is thus unlikely to have recovered.

Two observers—of a 16 Sqn B.E.2c and a 20 Sqn F.E.2b—showed great skill and heroism in landing their aircraft after the pilots had been killed.

COMMUNIQUÉ NO. 36

May 4th

Seventy-seven targets were engaged by aeroplanes, and one by kite balloons.

Lt C. H. Dixon, pilot, and 2 Lt E. R. Davis, observer, in an F.E. of 25 Sqn, attacked two hostile aeroplanes, a Roland and an Aviatik, over Fromelles. The hostile machines came from the north-east at 8,500 and 8,000 feet respectively. Lt Davis steered straight towards them. The Roland opened fire at 150 yards, and 2 Lt Davis at 70 yards. The Roland turned, the observer standing up to fire. Lt Dixon followed, and the Aviatik came up behind him and opened fire. Both pilot and observer of our machine were now firing, being between the two hostile machines. They got within a few yards of the Roland, which ceased fire and dived steeply but apparently under control towards Wavrin. The observer was apparently hit as he disappeared from view and firing ceased. Lt Dixon then turned towards the Aviatik which, however went down in the direction of Wavrin. Lt Dixon's machine was badly damaged, but both pilot and observer were unhurt.

2 Lt S. E. Cowan on a De Havilland of 24 Sqn, sighted a hostile machine flying south at about 1,500 feet between Hem and Clery. He dived down and overtook the German who also dived close to the ground, firing about 12 rounds at a range of 50 yards. The German machine tried to land but hit a wire fence and broke up. 2 Lt Cowan climbed to 200 feet when he again dived firing the rest of his drum at the pilot and observer who were running across the field. One of them fell and the other took

refuge in a shed. Meanwhile 2 Lt Cowan's thumb switch had jammed and he was forced to land, but the bump on landing loosened the spring, and he got off again, crossing the lines at about 500 feet under heavy fire.

2 Lt E. G. Ryckman and Lt J. R. Dennistoun, 7 Sqn, were brought down in the enemy's lines as the result of a combat with a hostile machine.

May 5th

Seventy-one targets were engaged. During a flight of three hours Lt Wigglesworth and Lt Cockrell, 7 Sqn, ranged a battery successfully on to six targets.

A direct hit was obtained on a hostile battery emplacement by one of our batteries, ranged by 12 Sqn.

In the IVth Army area three direct hits were recorded on Clery station, a shed being set on fire.

May 6th, 7th, 8th, 9th, 10th

The weather was unfavourable, and in consequence there was very little aerial activity on either side.

May 11th

Thirty-four targets successfully engaged. 9 Kite Balloon Section registered the 121st Heavy Battery on a farm, which was set on fire and ammunition destroyed.

Capt A. R. Tillie of 16 Sqn, was killed by A.A. fire. His observer, 2 Lt J. G. Howell, climbed back into the pilot's seat and found the rudder jammed. He however managed to land the machine in our lines and escaped unhurt. The machine was shelled on the ground by the enemy.

May 12th

Unfavourable weather.

6 Kite Balloon Section succeeded in ranging a battery on Illies station, causing a large explosion.

4 Kite Balloon Section with two observers attained a height of 4,700 feet.

May 13th, 14th, 15th

Weather unfavourable. On the 14th Capt Burney, 4 Sqn, registered seven targets in one flight from a height of 2,000 feet.

May 16th

Lt R. G. Gold and 2 Lt C. R. Simpson, 10 Sqn, located a hostile battery firing on the 38th Heavy Battery for whom they had gone out to observe. They called upon the 66th Siege Battery to retaliate and obtained a direct hit upon the position from which the hostile guns were firing.

Twenty-seven combats in the air took place.

Lt H. B. Davey and Cpl L. Van Schaick, on an F.E. of 25 Sqn, attacked an Albatros when approaching Lille as escort to the IInd Army Reconnaissance. Half a drum was fired, and the hostile machine spiralled rapidly down, firing occasionally. Later, the same machine was observed climbing again over Lille and following the F.E. at about 500 yards. Lt Davey wheeled sharply and opened fire at close range. The Albatros sheered away to the right, followed by the F.E. still firing at close range. The hostile machine then went down rapidly, and was seen to strike the ground at a cross roads south of Lille. Smoke rose from the spot and only one wing was visible. The F.E. was then attacked by a Fokker monoplane which was driven off.

2 Lt G. R. M. Reid and Lt I. A. Mann on an F.E. of 25 Sqn, saw two hostile machines crossing the lines south of Souchez at 8 a.m. Soon after crossing one of the hostile machines made off. The other was attacked at a height of 8,000 feet, and at a range of about 100 yards fire was opened from two Lewis guns. The enemy dived steeply followed by the F.E. A cloud of white smoke was seen to come from the engine of the hostile machine, which eventually landed in a field north of Vitry. The hostile machine, an Aviatik, was apparently under control when landed, but appeared to run into a ditch and turned sharply to the right. Shortly afterwards another Aviatik was seen and driven off.

2 Lt A. Ball, on a Bristol Scout of 11 Sqn, when flying at 12,000 feet, saw an Albatros at 5,000 feet over Givenchy. The hostile machine turned towards Beaumont, followed by Lt Ball, who opened fire when about 2,000 feet above, and continued until within a few yards. The hostile machine turned and got into a nose-dive, and when about 2,000 feet from the ground was seen to turn upside down.

Lt E. Trafford Jones, 20 Sqn, was killed during a fight in the air. His observer, Capt E. W. Forbes, although himself wounded in the shoulder and lung, managed to land the machine in our lines.

Capt D. Grinnell-Milne and No. 1840 Cpl D. McMaster, 25 Sqn, were forced to land in the enemy's lines near Fournes. The machine was seen to make a good landing. It is probable that the machine was hit by anti-aircraft gun fire.

As the result of a fight in the air Lt Wright and Capt Lucas were wounded. The latter died of wounds the same evening.

2 Lt Mowatt, 11 Sqn, left his aerodrome at 4.55 p.m. in a Bristol Scout. He has not returned.

May 17th

There were thirteen combats in the air, all of which were indecisive.

Capt W. Milne was wounded in the hand, and grazed on the nose by a bullet, during an encounter in the air.

May 18th

Flt Sgt Carlisle on a Nieuport Scout of 1 Sqn, sighted two Aviatiks proceeding north on their own side of the line while he was patrolling between Ypres and Ploegsteert wood. He chased them and caught them up over Zonnebeke. The Aviatiks turned and attacked. Flt Sgt Carlisle fired two drums at about 100 yards without any apparent effect, and a third at 50 yards. One of the hostile machines appeared to be hit, diving vertically and falling about *V2.a. Sheet 20*. The machine was not actually seen to hit the ground, but it never flattened out and there appears to be little doubt but that it was destroyed. The second machine which had been firing all the time, turned and dived towards the German lines.

2 Lt Williams on a B.E.2c of 5 Sqn, observer Cpl Harvey, whilst on patrol at 11,500 feet over Hooge was attacked by a German machine believed to be a Fokker. The B.E. fired half a drum into the Fokker's engine at close range and the remaining half into the Fokker as it turned. The hostile machine appeared to be falling out of control. The B.E. dived down to 5,000 feet but saw no signs of it.

A Nieuport Scout of the 3rd Brigade encountered four hostile machines flying in formation which it attacked, firing at the two higher ones. The Nieuport was then joined by an F.E. which attacked the two lower machines. The formation of the German machines was broken up and they returned home, one being observed diving at a steep angle for some distance until lost sight of.

May 19th

Much successful artillery co-operation was accomplished, 55 targets being engaged by aeroplane and six by kite balloons. Three direct hits were obtained on a hostile A.A. battery on the IIIrd Army front.

Lt Pearse on an F.E. of 20 Sqn, observer 1 AM Hodder, on patrol north-east of Ypres, sighted three hostile machines. He engaged one of them which turned and met him face to face, being slightly below him. Fire was opened and the enemy machine side-slipped and then dived vertically. The F.E. saw no more of the hostile machine.

Sgt J. Noakes on a De Havilland of 29 Sqn, sighted a hostile machine over Bixschoote flying north. He flew towards Langemarck and cut off the hostile machine from its own lines. It was then below him and did not observe him. He dived and fired a drum, but while changing his drum lost sight of the machine. The XIVth Corps report that one hostile machine fell in the enemy's lines about *Sheet 28.C.15*. This was probably the first of the above machines.

Lt Reid on an F.E. of 25 Sqn, observer, Lt Mann, encountered a Fokker. Fire was opened at 50 yards and the enemy machine side-slipped, turned on its back and crashed to earth. Its fall was observed by a B.E. of 2 Sqn.

Capt Cairns and Lt Tollemache on two Martinsydes of 27 Sqn, encountered an Albatros over Festubert and chased him to Fournes. Both the pilots engaged him. When last seen the hostile machine appeared to be out of control.

20–27 May, 1916

The growing R.F.C. superiority was indicated by combats in which up to three British aircraft were available to deal with a single enemy machine.

Intelligent thinking by a 27 Sqn duty pilot caused an enemy aircraft to land intact on Treziennes aerodrome.

COMMUNIQUÉ NO. 37

May 20th

Much successful artillery co-operation was accomplished. Eighty targets were engaged by aeroplane observation, and 8 by kite balloons.

An Aviatik was engaged by three of our machines over Adinfer Wood, viz., two F.E.'s of 23 Sqn, (Capt Adams and 1 AM Chapman; 2 Lt Cloete and Cpl Havens); and a B.E.2c of 12 Sqn, pilot, Lt Farrow, observer, 2 Lt Carden. The B.E. attacked first, firing a quarter of a drum. AM Chapman then dived from 9,000 feet and attacked the Aviatik at 5,000 feet, firing 2½ drums. Capt Adams then closed to within 20 yards and fired two drums at the Aviatik, which went down in a nose dive and crashed into the trees just east of the north end of Adinfer Wood.

An Albatros was attacked by three of our machines over Poziere; a Martinsyde of 22 Sqn, pilot, Capt Summers, and two De Havillands of 24 Sqn, pilots, Lt Wilson and 2 Lt Tidmarsh. Lt Wilson attacked first, opening fire at 50 yards, and turned aside owing to his gun jamming. Capt Summers on the Martinsyde then attacked, firing half a drum at 30 yards range, apparently without effect. Second Lt Tidmarsh then dived on to the hostile machine from above and fired a drum at 40 yards from behind it. The hostile machine burst into flames and fell between Poziere and Contalmaison. Shortly afterwards Lt Wilson sighted another hostile machine, an L.V.G. being fired on at about 12,000 feet, north of Albert. He overhauled it and got within 200 yards. The hostile machine flattened out suddenly at 9,000 feet, and then went down in a spinning nosedive, falling in our lines south of Maricourt, and burst into flames.

2 Lt M. D. Basden, 27 Sqn, in a Martinsyde Scout, was brought down in the German lines as the result of a combat in the air.

May 21st

Sixty-four targets were successfully ranged on by aeroplane observers and 12 by kite balloon observers. Sixty-sixth Siege Battery, co-operating with aeroplanes of 10 Sqn, obtained direct hits on an occupied gun-pit.

Eighteen encounters took place, all of which were inconclusive.

2 Lt A. H. W. Tollemache on a Martinsyde of 27 Sqn, flying at 12,500 feet, saw an Albatros over Fromelles at about 9,000 feet. He dived at it reserving his fire till within close range. Both machines were diving at high speed with engines on. 2 Lt Tollemache having expended one drum, changed and continued the attack. The enemy endeavoured to manoeuvre out of fire, turning in all directions, but 2 Lt Tollemache manoeuvred his Martinsyde and managed to keep the enemy under fire at intervals. At about 4,000 feet over the south-west corner of Lille the machines were so close that they nearly collided. To avoid this the hostile machine turned on one wing and went down in a side-slip and vertical dive. He flattened out near the ground close to the Citadel.

On the night of the 20th/21st Lt Latta dropped two 112-pound bombs from a height of 1,000 feet on the new station at Langemarck. One of these bombs is believed to have hit the mark.

Capt C. E. H. James and 2 Lt H. L. C. Aked, 20 Sqn, on escort duty to the IInd Army reconnaissance, were forced to land in the enemy's lines near Zandvoorde.

Lt Francis, 20 Sqn, was seriously wounded during an attack on two hostile machines. He managed to land safely in our lines.

Miscellaneous

At about 2.45 a.m. on the 21st, the pilot on duty at 27 Sqn's aerodrome at Treziennes was informed that a machine had been heard flying over the aerodrome. The weather was very misty, and he prepared Very lights in order to signal to the aeroplane. About 3 a.m. the machine was again heard, and was seen over Isebergues. Lt J. C. Turner, the orderly pilot, fired one Very light. This was answered from the machine by one white star-light. Lt Turner again fired a red light and the machine again replied with a white star-light. The aeroplane then endeavoured to land but misjudged the landing and went round the aerodrome again. By this time Lt Turner had been able to see that the machine had German markings, but the pilot was evidently under the impression that he was landing at a friendly aerodrome. Lt Turner restrained the guard from firing, and ordered his machine to be got ready. The hostile machine now landed successfully and taxied up to the sheds where pilot and passenger at once surrendered.

May 22nd

Sixty-three targets were successfully ranged on by aeroplane observers and 24 by kite balloon observers. In connection with the hostile attack in the Souchez area, 18 Sqn located the flashes of between 80 and 90 hostile guns. A machine of 12 Sqn registered two of our batteries and one French battery, obtaining 20 O.K.s during one flight. The French battery was then turned on to another hostile battery, and 11 more O.K.s were reported.

Hostile aircraft were particularly active on the front of the Ist Army, as many as eleven being seen simultaneously in the Souchez area. Fourteen inconclusive combats took place. An L.V.G. was brought down in our lines near Cassel by a French aeroplane.

May 23rd

Low clouds and mist made observation difficult. Practically no hostile aircraft were seen, and there were no combats.

Hostile guns were active throughout the day on the Ist Army front. Some successful aeroplane co-operation was carried out at low altitudes.

Several attempts to photograph the area in which fighting was taking place were made by 18 and 25 Sqns.

May 24th

7 and 16 Sqns carried out successful night reconnaissances over Lille and Courtrai. 18 Sqn carried out two reconnaissances on the front of the IVth Corps during the day in connection with the operations at Souchez. The weather was unfavourable throughout the day.

May 25th

Rain and low clouds prevented successful flying.

26 May – 4 June, 1916

Ball was now flying a Nieuport scout, the aircraft which was his favourite mount until he returned for a second tour of combat operations in 1917. Reports of two combats in this communiqué illustrate the difficulties in assessing firm victory scores for the fighter aces. Some of Ball's opponents were forced to land, but it is not established whether they were seriously damaged or their crews wounded. Another was last seen 'diving vertically', its ultimate fate not being known.

A parachute descent from a kite balloon was reported on 1 June. The R.N.A.S. used kite balloons for observation early in the war, and naval balloon sections started working with the R.F.C. in May 1915. Balloon operations were taken over the by R.F.C. in the autumn of that year. The parachutes for the crew were attached to the side of the basket.

COMMUNIQUÉ NO. 38

May 26th

Low clouds interfered with artillery co-operation work during the greater part of the day. Towards evening some useful work was accomplished, 48 targets being engaged by aeroplane observers, and 14 by kite balloon observers.

Hostile aircraft were inactive. As the result of a combat with a machine of the 4th Brigade one German machine was driven down in the hostile lines.

May 27th

Fifty-four targets were successfully engaged by aeroplane observers, and 14 by kite balloons. The weather conditions were unfavourable for this work.

Very few hostile aeroplanes were seen. There were five indecisive combats.

Capt C. J. Mackay, 2 Sqn, was slightly wounded in the leg during a reconnaissance.

May 28th

A fine day favoured aerial work, and many successful reconnaissance and artillery flights were accomplished. Forty-five targets were engaged. Few hostile aircraft were seen. Six of these were engaged in indecisive combats.

In the late afternoon Capt James of 2 Sqn flew over the hostile lines in a Bristol Scout at times as low as 500 feet. He was able to report an important movement of horse vehicles and men.

May 29th

Between 5.30 and 10.30 a.m. six to eight hostile machines were active on the Ist Army front south of the La Bassee Canal. They appeared to be doing artillery and photographic work. Four were engaged without decisive results.

Capt Boulton on a Bristol Scout of 6 Sqn, while on patrol over Ypres sighted a hostile machine over Noordschote being fired on by A.A. guns. After a running fight over Poperinghe, Abeele and Menin, during which four drums were fired, the hostile machine, which had been diving all the time, almost looped and side-slipped badly, but afterwards flattened out. Capt Boulton recrossed the lines at 3,000 feet, being heavily shelled by the hostile A.A. guns.

2 Lt Ball on a Nieuport of 11 Sqn, attacked a hostile machine at 6,000 feet patrolling over Moyenneville. He dived from 10,000 feet firing half a drum at 30 yards range. The hostile machine was last seen diving vertically. Shortly afterwards he sighted an L.V.G. and two Fokkers. He turned towards them, climbing and awaiting an opportunity. Meanwhile two other Fokkers appeared well above the other three machines. The L.V.G. then left the escort, coming towards Oppy. 2 Lt Ball dived, firing half a drum at 50 yards. Getting clear he changed the drum and again engaged the machine, forcing it to land. The escort was last seen making for Douai.

Capt E. W. Parrett, 29 Sqn, while patrolling over Ypres salient on a De Havilland was shot down during a combat in the air with two hostile machines. Capt Parrett had a bullet wound in the head. His machine fell close behind our own lines near St Eloi. One of the German machines was seen to come down a few minutes later out of control.

May 30th

Rain and low clouds until 2 p.m. interfered with observation. Kite balloons were unable to work, but in the late evening 30 targets were dealt with by aeroplane observation.

Few hostile aircraft were seen, and there were no combats.

May 31st

A fine day but thick haze made observation difficult, and little artillery work was accomplished.

The IIIrd Army reconnaissance, consisting of five F.E.2b's and two Martinsydes, was attacked by three Fokkers when over the locality of Cambrai. The enemy were first seen diving at our machines from the rear, with the sun in their backs. Our machines, which were heavily fired at, retaliated as occasion offered, by either firing over the top of the planes to the rear or else by partially turning and bringing the front gun into play. 2 Lt Powell, observer, in one of our F.E.s was shot through the head and instantly killed whilst firing his gun. The machine was safely brought back and landed at its areodrome. Soon after the fight began one of the Fokkers was seen to turn half a loop, side-slip badly and nose-dive. It was last seen nose diving having apparently been hit by the fire from an F.E. Another of our F.E.s, pilot 2 Lt Cairnduff, observer Cpl Maxwell, was last seen soon after the commencement of the fight. Owing to the fact that all the machines were busily engaged in the running fight which was of a persistent nature, the fate of this machine was not observed. About the same time however, 2 Lt Watson, pilot of one of our F.E.s reports that an F.E. apparently out of control, dived over him, almost touching his top plane. No more was seen of this machine. The two remaining Fokkers pursued our reconnaissance, one breaking off the fight or else being compelled to descend before reaching the lines, while the third one followed until within the zone of the advanced German A.A. guns. Several of our machines were badly hit during this encounter. The reconnaissance formation appears to have been kept very well until after our lines were reached.

Except for the above, very few hostile aircraft were seen, and their was only one other indecisive combat.

June 1st

The clear day enabled much successful artillery co-operation to be done. Ninety target balloons were engaged with aeroplanes obervation, and ten with kite balloons.

Lt Gould, of 10 Sqn, in a B.E.2c, with Lt Pearson, observer, while on artillery duty, attacked a hostile machine near Laventie. Fire was opened from the B.E.2c at about 300 yards, but at this moment Lt Gould was attacked by a Fokker from above and behind. The Fokker dived to within 40 yards, when Lt Gould swerved slightly to avoid the enemy's fire. The observer then gave the Fokker a drum at point blank range. The Fokker banked over to the left, and something which looked like a box, fell out. The machine then nose dived and was last seen spiralling down close to earth. 18 A.A. Battery report that the Fokker was seen to nose dive to earth at the north-east corner of Bois de Biez.

2 Lt Latta, in a Nieuport of 1 Sqn, left Bailleul at 2 p.m. in pursuit of a hostile machine seen flying over Armentieres. Catching it up in the neighbourhood of Merville he chased it thence over the lines about one mile south-west of Armentieres, firing four drums apparently without effect.

2 Lt Ball, on a Nieuport of 11 Sqn, attacked two enemy machines consecutively over Douai. The second one was seen to land about a mile west of his aerodrome apparently undamaged.

9 Kite Balloon was carried away by a sudden gust, the cable running off the winch, at 7.25 p.m. The occupants, 2 Lt Gavin R.F.C., and 2 Lt Lancaster, 'C' Battery, 183rd Brigade R.F.A., both made parachute descents, landing safely. 2 Lt Gavin helped Lt Lancaster before descending himself, and consequently landed close to the trenches. Hostile machine-guns opened fire on him but he escaped unhurt. The balloon drifted over the German lines.

June 2nd

5 and 6 Sqns had machines in the air almost continuously throughout the day in connection with the hostile offensive which developed on the front of the IInd Army.

Only one indecisive combat took place.

Kite balloons on the Ist Army front accomplished much successful work with the artillery on the evening of the 1st and during the 2nd. About 5 p.m. on the 2nd 8 Kite Balloon was hit, about 500 holes being made in it. It descended rapidly but without any casualty. Flt Lt Sadd continued to direct fire until the balloon was too low for him to observe his targets.

June 3rd

Twenty bombing machines escorted by six escort machines, all of the 2nd Brigade, attacked Dadizeele and Rossignal at 5 a.m.; and Menin railway station, Divisional Headquarters in Menin, and Halluin railway station at 8.50 a.m., about 4 tons of explosives being dropped. Clouds prevented close observation but the results are believed to have been satisfactory. Lt Goodson L.R.B. was shot down by A.A. fire. He is reported by two other pilots who took part in the raid as having gone down under control. All the other machines returned safely.

Forty-one targets were engaged by aeroplane co-operation and 8 by kite balloons.

5 Kite Balloon reached an altitude of 4,900 feet with one observer.

Few hostile aircraft were seen. There were two indecisive combats.

4–21 June, 1916

The eclipse of the Fokkers was clearly seen in the activity during the period of this communiqué. On 8 June five of them tailed a reconnaissance formation but made no attack. During various combats three Fokkers were destroyed and others driven off.

The Fokker which crashed fatally on 18 June after a combat with the 25 Sqn F.E.2b, crewed by Lt G. R. McCubbin and Cpl. J. H. Waller, was flown by Max Immelmann. The R.F.C. naturally credited the victory to McCubbin and Waller, but the Germans maintained that the crash followed a structural failure of the Fokker. In all Immelmann had scored fifteen combat victories.

The third D.H.2 squadron—32—was reported in action.

Little has been written about the essential and hazardous, though monotonous work of the kite balloon crews. The series of accidents which befell Lt C. W. Hayne shows that the work also had its excitements. The D.H.2 was used to great effect in the aggressive combat by Capt A. M. Wilkinson, 24 Sqn, who destroyed one and forced down two more enemy aircraft. Wilkinson's final victory score was nineteen of the enemy destroyed.

COMMUNIQUÉ NO. 39

June 4th
Unfavourable weather. Few hostile machines were seen. There were no combats in the air. Artillery observation was difficult and hampered successful work. Thirty-two targets were engaged with aeroplane observation, and with kite balloons. A machine of 10 Sqn directed fire with successful results on to two gun pits from which anti-aircraft guns had been firing.

June 5th and 6th
The weather was unfavourable, and no successful flying was possible.

June 7th
Weather continued unfavourable, with few bright intervals, in which advantage was taken to complete some artillery co-operation, and all targets were successfully engaged. A F.E.2b of 25 Sqn, pilot, Lt Lord Doune, observer 2 Lt R. V. Walker, was hit by anti-aircraft gun fire and forced to descend at Essars. 2 Lt Walker was wounded in the face.

June 8th

Much successful work was done with the artillery, 35 targets being registered by aeroplanes, and 4 by kite balloons.

2 Lt Snow, of 10 Sqn, observer Lt Fairbairn, directed the 118th Heavy Battery on to a train at Salome by means of the G.F. (Greeting target) signal. Six direct hits resulted, and the train was set on fire and a shed was seen to be still burning 1½ hours later.

Lt Pentland, 16 Sqn, observer, Capt Walker, ranged the 104th Howitzer Battery on to a railway station. Large explosions were seen in a shed which was totally demolished.

2 Lt Rice and Lt Russell in an R.E.7 of 21 Sqn, were attacked on their return from escorting a reconnaissance of Bapaume. The hostile machine, after following them for some distance of about 11,000 feet, dived steeply at the R.E.7, firing three bursts of about 20 rounds at a time. During the third burst of fire Lt Russell was wounded in the leg, and the petrol pipe was cut. The German then turned sharply away at the same level as the R.E.7, and Lt Russell fired one drum at him at about 50 yards range. The hostile machine dived and disappeared through the clouds at about 1,000 feet from the ground. An officer commanding an A.A. Battery in the IIrd Army reports that the hostile machine was seen to come down apparently out of control near Monchy le Preux.

There were nine other indecisive combats.

Hostile aircraft were more active than of late. About ten were seen on the Ist Army front before 8 a.m. One was engaged and driven east.

Five Fokkers followed the IIIrd Army reconnaissance but did not approach nearer than 300 yards and made no attempt to attack.

Capt Clarke, 29 Sqn, in a De Havilland Scout and Lt Russell, of 21 Sqn, were wounded during combats in the air.

June 9th

Low clouds and some showers interfered with work throughout the day.

Twenty-eight targets were dealt with by aeroplane observation and three by kite balloon.s

Hostile aircraft were inactive, and only one indecisive combat was recorded.

June 10th

Six combats in the air took place.

2 Lt Pentland and Capt W. H. Walker, in a B.E.2c of 16 Sqn, when on artillery duty, saw a Fokker flying over the enemy's trenches. They followed him for about 1½ miles in the direction of Lille, where he turned to attack. Half a drum was fired at the German at a range of about 50 yards. When level with the tail of the B.E.2c the hostile machine turned sharply and dived, and the B.E.2c was able to fire half a drum at him as

he turned. He dived more steeply and was observed by 2 Lt Pentland to crash in a field near Haubourdin.

June 11th

Low clouds and frequent heavy thunder showers hampered work throughout the day.

1 Kite Balloon, passenger, 2 Lt C. W. Hayne and Lt Warlow (attached). At 8.15 a.m. as a storm was approaching from the south-west, the balloon was ordered to be hauled down. At 8.53 a.m. owing to the basket being jerked by the actual hauling down, or by the approaching storm, the stays holding the parachute attached to 2 Lt Hayne broke and the parachute falling out opened to the wind pulling the basket up till it touched the tail. 2 Lt Hayne attempted to cut himself loose from the parachute, but before he could do so, it pulled him out of the basket and he started to descend. While descending he got entangled with the tail line and was held up in the air for about 5 minutes. The tail line ultimately broke and he descended by the parachute and landed on the top of a tree at 9 a.m. In the meantime the stays of the remaining parachute were broken and this too opened to the wind. The strain on the cable was too much for the winch, which stopped. Measured by the winch indicator it was 40 cwts and as the winch could not start owing to the strain, the balloon was hauled down by hand 800 feet. Lt Warlow ultimately freed the second parachute, the balloon descending at 9.5 a.m. The balloon stood the strain well and only slight damage was done. Lt Hayne was admitted to hospital suffering from shock and abrasions of the arm.

June 12th, 13th, 14th, and 15th

Very little work was accomplished on account of unfavourable weather.

June 16th

Artillery Co-operation: mist and clouds made observation difficult. Twenty-five targets were dealt with.

Few hostile aircraft were seen and there was only one indecisive combat.

June 17th

Weather fine; 943 hours of flying.

Seventy-two targets were successfully engaged by aeroplane observation and one by kite balloon.

Hostile aircraft were unusually active. Several hostile reconnaissances in force crossed the lines. On each occasion they were engaged and their formation broken up by our machines.

Lt Chadwick and 2 Lt Wedgwood, F.E.2b, 11 Sqn, left their aerodrome at about 12.45 p.m. to intercept a hostile reconnaissance. Eight hostile machines were observed at 7,500 feet approaching from the direction of Doullens. The F.E. flew towards them, and when almost directly

Above: Fokker E III
Below: Morane-Saulnier BB

Above: A.E.G. G III
Below: B.E. 2e

underneath, 2 Lt Wedgwood fired a drum. The British machine then turned north-east and when at about 400 feet below the German formation, 2 Lt Wedgwood opened fire into one of the tail machines. A few minutes later, this machine was seen to glide down across the trench low, and then land just north of Bois de Biez. Lt Chadwick now endeavoured to cut off the main body of hostile machines before they crossed the trenches. In this he was unsuccessful, but succeeded in catching the last hostile machine just over the trenches at 6,000 feet. When within 100 yards the German dived steeply, followed by the F.E. firing a burst at about 50 yards range. The observer of the L.V.G. appeared to be out of action as no reply was made to the fire from the F.E. Lt Chadwick continued the pursuit until within 2,500 feet of the ground, when the German was seen to land in a field about a mile north-east of Achiet le Petit. The F.E. recrossed the trenches at 2,500 feet.

A B.E.2c of the IInd Wing had a fight with a Fokker at close range. The enemy was last seen in a vertical nose dive.

Altogether there were 30 combats in the air.

On the night of the 16th/17th the balloon of 5 K.B.S. broke away. It descended without injury to its occupants near Beaquesne.

When at 9,000 feet over Pozieres, Lt G. H. Gray in a De Havilland of 24 Sqn sighted a hostile machine flying south-east at 11,000 feet. He manoeuvred to the east of the hostile machine which dived underneath the De Havilland and made for Bapaume. Lt Gray followed him down to 1,000 feet over Pys. The German zigzagged all the way but did not open fire, and flattened out over Pys. Lt Gray fired about ten rounds at point blank range from behind his tail. The hostile machine side-slipped and dived but flattened out again when about 50 or 100 feet from the ground, and continued as far as Reincourt, where he collided with a hedge on landing. As the pilot made no effort to get out, Lt Gray turned and emptied the remainder of a drum into him at about 50 feet. The pilot was not seen to leave the hostile machine, which was apparently undamaged. Lt Gray recrossed the line under heavy fire from machine-guns and rifles.

Capt Wilkinson, in a De Havilland Scout of 24 Sqn, while flying in the vicinity of Arras, observed 6 hostile machines flying west in close formation followed by 3 others. As he approached them from underneath, the formation broke up, two other De Havillands attacking from above at the same time. Capt Wilkinson engaged the nearest machine which promptly turned east and dived. Another of the enemy was, in the meantime, firing at Capt Wilkinson from above, but he continued the pursuit of the first machine which he engaged, and after a considerable amount of manoeuvring, got behind his tail and fired half a drum at about 30 yards range. The German dived almost vertically with his engine on.

Capt Wilkinson, changing drums, continued his pursuit and eventually saw the hostile machine crash in a small field near Achiet le Grand. On his way home Capt Wilkinson engaged and drove down an Albatros, which landed under control in a large field near Grevillers.

He encountered yet a third machine which he pursued and overhauled about Martinpuich. Capt Wilkinson had only one drum left and reserved his fire till within 150 yards, eventually closing to 40. A burst of steam or smoke suddenly came from the hostile machine, which went down in a steep glide with the engine stopped, but landed safely on an aerodrome just east of Bapaume.

June 18th

A great deal of successful artillery co-operation was carried out. Sixty-nine targets were dealt with with aeroplane and kite balloon observation.

An observer of 10 Sqn ranged a battery on some lorries moving between Salome and La Bassee. None appeared to be hit but the convoy was scattered.

There was a marked increase in the activity of hostile aircraft. Three reconnaissances in force penetrated into our lines. On each occasion they were attacked and their formation broken up.

Two F.E.s of 25 Sqn, pilots, Capt Grattan Bellew and 2 Lt Armstrong, observers, Lt Lewes and Sgt Chapman, working together encountered two Fokkers east of Lens at 4.15 p.m. at about 9,000 feet. The F.E.s chased the Fokkers down, diving steeply in small circles and firing all the time. Capt Bellew left his opponent diving vertically at about 2,500 feet, being short of petrol. The other Fokker was shot down by Sgt Chapman and crashed to earth from 4,000 feet.

Two hostile reconnaissances, one of 8 machines and one of 10, were attacked. The first by a B.E. of 13 Sqn, the second by two Scouts of 11 Sqn and two F.E.s of 23 Sqn. One of the enemy's observers appeared to be hit, and one of the machines of the second reconnaissance was forced away from the remainder and driven over his own lines.

Two hostile machines were driven down by machines of the 4th Brigade. One was seen to crash.

Lts Lynch and Long, 3 Sqn, engaged and dispersed a column of infantry in Martinpuich with machine-gun fire.

A machine of the 1st Wing which returned to its aerodrome with engine trouble reports having seen 14 hostile aeroplanes south-west of Arras at about 3.20. p.m Two appeared to be shot down by A.A. guns.

At 5.45 p.m., east of Lens, an F.E. of 25 Sqn, pilot, Lt Read, observer Lt Mann, encountered a Fokker. The hostile machine dived twice at the F.E. which fired about half a drum on each occasion at close range. The Fokker dived steeply into the clouds and was lost sight of.

At 8 p.m. while on patrol near Souchez, 2 Lt Nixon on a De Havilland of 32 Sqn, saw five Aviatiks cross the lines, and attacked the rear one at about 50 yards. After firing a second drum he was hit in the arm, but joined in a fight between another Aviatik and another De Havilland, with an indecisive result.

An F.E. of 25 Sqn, pilot, 2 Lt McCubbin, observer Cpl Waller, when patrolling over Annay at about 9 p.m. attacked three Fokkers seen behind the lines. One of the latter went off. The remaining two made for Lens towards another F.E. of 25 Sqn, pilot, 2 Lt Savage, observer, AM Robinson, which they attacked. Lt McCubbin followed and joined in the fight, diving on to one of the attacking Fokkers which turned away and dived perpendicularly towards the ground. It was seen to crash by the 22nd A.A. battery. (*See also entries for 28 June, page 168.*) When Lt McCubbin turned again the other F.E. and Fokker had disappeared. The second F.E., 2 Lt Savage, is missing and is reported to have landed in the enemy's lines without crashing.

Two F.E.s of 23 Sqn, assisted by some De Havillands of 24 Sqn, engaged a hostile reconnaissance of about 6 machines. One of the enemy's machines was seen to commence a vertical dive and is reported by Capt Wilkinson, on a De Havilland of 24 Sqn, to have crashed in a small field near Achiet le Grand after he had fired half a drum at him. Capt Wilkinson subsequently engaged another machine over Bucquoy and forced it down under control near Grevillers. On return to the lines he saw the third machine about Thiepval, pursued and overhauled it over Martinpuich, where he engaged it. The German machine appeared to be hit but reached its aerodrome near Bapaume.

Capt Crook on a Nieuport of 11 Sqn and 2 Lt Morgan on a De Havilland of 24 Sqn, engaged a hostile reconnaissance of six machines in the neighbourhood of Arras, driving one down near Terre Mesnil east of Doullens, where it landed on its left wing, the pilot and observer being captured. One of them was slightly wounded.

An F.E. of 25 Sqn, pilot, Lt Rogers, observer, Sgt Taylor, is missing. It was last seen west of Souchez and is reported to have landed in the enemy's lines about 3 miles north-north-east of Arras. One of the occupants was seen to get out and go into the enemy's trenches.

Another machine of 25 Sqn, pilot, Lt Savage, observer, AM Robinson, is also missing, and is reported to have been shot down near Wingles in a fight with two Fokkers.

Lt Nixon on a De Havilland of 32 Sqn, was wounded in a fight with 5 hostile machines west of Lens.

June 19th

Low clouds and mist all day. Very little flying.

20–30 June, 1916

A typical example of the excellent work being performed by the F.E.2bs was the running battle by 25 Sqn on 26 June. Capt A. W. Tedder, whose aircraft was damaged, later begame Marshal of the R.A.F. Lord Tedder, Chief of the Air Staff after World War II.

In March it had been decided to withdraw the odd single-seater scouts operating with the bombing and reconnaissance untis and concentrate them into scout squadrons. Although still equipped with some Morane two-seaters, 1 was now in process of becoming a scout squadron, flying Nieuports. Likewise 60 Sqn was building up with Morane Bullets withdrawn from general-purpose units.

The Obituary Notice for Max Immelmann, quoted from the *Frankfurter Zeitung* of 24 June, which appears at the end of this Communiqué is reproduced as it appears in the original text; the translation seems a little inaccurate.

COMMUNIQUÉ NO. 40

June 20th

There was little hostile aerial activity, and no combats in the air took place.

2 Lt Paterson and 2 Lt Cooke in a B.E.2c of 8 Sqn, left their aerodrome at 9.55 a.m. and did not return. The German wireless of the 21st reports a machine having been brought down by A.A. fire at Puisieux, one of the passengers being killed.

June 21st

2 Lt Marnham and 2 Lt Parsons, of 10 Sqn, ranged 38th Heavy Battery on to five lorries approaching Bassee, the fourth shot bursting in the middle of the lorries. A heavy explosion followed, and when the smoke had cleared away the lorries had disappeared.

The 117th Heavy Battery, ranged by Capt Leggatt and 2 Lt Cordon, completely demolished a tower believed to be an observation post.

June 22nd

One hundred and eighty-five targets were dealt with by aeroplane observation and 13 by kite balloons.

Two hostile anti-aircraft batteries were successfully engaged; the ammunition of one being set on fire, continued to burst for 20 minutes.

There was considerable increase in the activity of hostile aircraft on all fronts. At about 2 p.m. 12 aeroplanes crossed the line over Souchez and went to St Pol, which they bombed.

There were 22 combats in the air, mostly indecisive.

Capt C. T. MacLean and Lt Barraclough, in a F.E. of 25 Sqn, attacked a Roland biplane east of Lens at 8 a.m. while on patrol duty at 10,000 feet. The F.E. dived at the Roland, and following it down to 5,000 fired two drums at close range. At 5,000 feet the German dived perpendicularly, the F.E. overshooting it. Subsequently Capt MacLean saw the Roland on the ground.

2 Lt Moore, 1 Sqn, in a Nieuport Scout, had four engagements between 9 and 11 a.m. while on patrol between Messines and Hollebeke. On each occasion the hostile machine was driven off.

2 Lt Armstrong and Sgt Topliffe in a F.E. of 25 Sqn, were brought down in a fight with a Fokker opposite the Loos Salient.

2 Lt L. C. Angstrom of 25 Sqn, was wounded in the foot by A.A. fire.

Capt Sweet in a De Havilland of 29 Sqn was killed in the vicinity of Ypres as the result of a combat in the air.

June 23rd

A hundred and sixty-one targets were dealt with by aeroplanes and kite balloons.

5 Kite Balloon broke loose at 4.10 p.m. but landed in our lines near Dainville. The observers, Lts Jardine and Pape were not seriously hurt. The balloons of 1 and 14 Sections were struck by lightning and destroyed while that of 12 Section had to be ripped. The winch of 12 was also severely damaged.

Three 8-horse wagons were attacked by a machine of the 4th Brigade and were stampeded, from a height of 900 feet.

Lt H. B. Davey, of 25 Sqn, slightly wounded during a fight.

June 24th

The weather was unfavourable, and there was little aircraft activity.

June 25th

Much successful artillery co-operation was carried out. One hundred and thirty-nine targets were dealt with by aeroplanes (101 by the 4th Brigade) and 15 by kite balloons. During the day, aeroplanes of the 4th Brigade co-operating with the artillery obtained 24 direct hits, silenced 5 batteries, and reported 102 active batteries. As the result of the shooting, ing, five fires were started and eight explosions took place.

There were 16 combats in the air, all of a more or less indecisive character. Bombs were dropped by the enemy on a disused railhead at Larbret.

At 4 p.m. a determined simultaneous attack on the enemy's kite balloons was carried out on the front of all four Armies. Twenty-three balloons were reported up. Fifteen were attacked and 6 were brought down. The following Officers made successful attacks:

Lts Moore and Latta of 1 Sqn, 2 Lt Ball of 11 Sqn, and Lt May of 2 A.D.—all in Nieuport Scouts.

The names of the successful pilots of the 1st and 2nd Brigades have not been received.

Sgt Johnson of 23 Sqn, in a F.E.2, was wounded in a fight in the air.

June 26th

All Brigades completed a great deal of successful work.

1st Brigade: Capt Ward with Lt E. W. Bower, 2 Sqn, ranged the 140th Heavies on an A.A. Battery, and completely silenced it.

2nd Brigade: 2 Lt Atkinson and 2 Lt R. Bell Irving, 1 Sqn, ranged a 12-inch Howitzer on A.A. guns, causing a heavy explosion.

3rd Brigade: 8 Sqn carried out 8 trench flights, sending down numerous corrections. They engaged 13 other targets and silenced 10 hostile batteries. 12 Sqn engaged 7 and silenced 5 hostile batteries. In addition they completed much successful trench bombardment observation. 13 Sqn engaged three targets and silenced two hostile batteries, working with the artillery of the XVIIth Corps.

4th Brigade: The 4th Brigade successfully ranged on 83 targets, and obtained a direct hit on the railway, and 23 direct hits on gun emplacements. Several fires were started in two batteries and in villages in the hostile lines. Explosions were observed in Mametz Wood, Martinpuich and four battery positions.

In all 125 targets were dealt with by aeroplane observers and 36 by kite balloons.

Hostile aircraft were again encountered in large numbers on the enemy's side of the line. About 12 Fokkers and 6 to 8 biplanes were at work east of the line during the morning on the 1st Brigade front.

Five F.E.'s of 25 Sqn, pilots: 2 Lt R. Sherwell, Capt Grattan-Bellew, Capt A. W. Tedder, Lt Riley, 2 Lt McCubbin, observers: 2 AM Chadwick, Lt W. Harper, AM Law, Lt E. H. Bird, Cpl Waller. The expedition was returning from Henin Lietard, after dropping their bombs without opposition. The rear pair, Lt Riley and 2 Lt Sherwell, got rather behind, and on nearing the lines, Capt Bellew, Capt Tedder and 2 Lt McCubbin saw Fokkers following up these last machines. Capt Tedder engaged one of these Fokkers and drove it off, but had his main tank pierced by a bullet and returned home. 2 Lt McCubbin engaged two-Fokkers that were coming up. His observer, Cpl Waller, shot down one of them and saw it going down out of control. 2 Lt McCubbin was however hit in the arm and had to return. He landed all right near Beauvray. Capt Bellew then bore the whole brunt of the fighting. He engaged a Fokker which was following up Lt Sherwell's machine and drove it off. He then attacked another that was coming up, and his observer fired two drums into it at 10 yards range. The Fokker heeled over and went down vertically, crashing behind the enemy's lines. Capt Bellew was then at 2,600 feet. He could see three Fokkers going east at 1,000 feet over La Bassee. He waited about, but nothing came within reach, so he came home. 2 Lt Sherwell landed near Cambrin, his machine very badly hit—the rudder controls were broken, most of the tail boom struts and booms hit, and both tanks shot through. His observer, 2 AM Chadwick, was hit three times and died in a few minutes. 2 Lt Riley landed near Mazingarbe, but his machine ran into hidden barbed wire defences, and turned over, being totally wrecked. Lt Riley was thrown on to his head, and has bad concussion. Lt Bird, who was hit in the back, has his wrist broken and his shoulder dislocated.

From the accounts of spectators in the Loos Salient, two Fokkers certainly crashed behind the enemy's lines.

2 Lt L. L. Richardson and 2 AM L. S. Court, F.E.2b., of 25 Sqn, while flying over Douvrin at 7 a.m., saw a number of hostile machines flying low over Billy. The F.E. dropped to 8,000 feet and waited. At 7.25 a Fokker came up through the clouds about 400 yards in front. The F.E. side-slipped and dived to the enemy, who opened fire about 80 yards above him. The hostile machine dived and turned and the F.E. followed, firing half a drum at 60 yards range. The German then dived, side-slipped and landed safely near Annoeullin. 2 Lt Richardson then climbed to 9,000 feet at 7.50 ,where he attacked an Albatros and a Fokker, both of which dived without firing a shot.

Lt N. P. Manfield, on a De Havilland of 24 Sqn, sighted a Fokker at 6,000 feet over Courcelette at 6.30 p.m. on the 25th June. The Fokker turned towards the De Havilland Scout, which dived and fired a few rounds. The German did a big left-hand turn, followed by Lt Manfield, firing a few rounds. The Fokker then dived steeply, but flattened out, and Lt Manfield got nearer and fired the remainder of his drum. The enemy then got into a spiral nose dive, and appeared to be falling to pieces at about 2,000 feet from the ground.

The 2nd Brigade carried out a further attack on hostile kite balloons. Nieuport Scouts piloted by Lts Latta and Moore and Capt Balcombe Brown, all of 1 Sqn, brought-down three in flames.

A hostile machine is reported by two pilots to have been brought down by A.A. fire north-east of Ypres at about 8.30 p.m. on the 25th instant.

Casualties: Sqn 25, *2 AM H. L. Chadwick, observer, killed in a combat* *in the air; 2 Lt G. R. McCubbin, pilot, severely wounded in the arm in a combat; Lt R. G. Riley, pilot, severely wounded in a combat; Lt E. H. Bird, observer, dangerously wounded in a combat;* **23,** *Lt Russell and Lt Dennistoun, left the aerodrome on F.E.2b. 6348 at 8.50 a.m. and have not returned; and 2 Lt Coates,* **9,** *slightly wounded by A.A. fire.*

June 27th

Capt Martin, 8 Sqn, successfully carried out a special reconnaissance to observe the effect of wire-cutting operations in front of Gommecourt Wood, descending to 500 feet to obtain the necessary information. Capt Burney, taking advantage of the low clouds, made a careful examination of the country between the lines and Bapaume.

Very unfavourable weather, but all squadrons took advantage of clear intervals to co-operate with the artillery. Sixty-one targets were successfully dealt with by aeroplane observers, 2 by kite balloons. 8, 12 and 13 Sqns in the 3rd Brigade were especially active, and, in spite of the adverse weather, rendered very valuable assistance. On the IVth Army front 10 direct hits on batteries were obtained, and 157 active hostile batteries were reported.

Casualties: Sqn 2, *2 Lt R. Hilton, observer, seriously wounded in the face by A.A. fire;* **25,** *2 Lt E. H. Bird, observer, died of wounds received the previous day.*

June 28th

Heavy rain and low clouds throughout the day. In the evening it cleared somewhat, and some successful artillery work was accomplished ~ There was no hostile aircraft activity.

Capt Jenkins, 15 Sqn, attacked with machine-gun fire and silenced an anti-aircraft gun.

Extracts from the German newspapers relating to the death of Lt Immelmann make it clear that this pilot met his death at the hands of 2 Lt McCubbin and Cpl Waller of 25 Sqn on the 18th instant.

Extract from *Frankfurter Zeitung* of 24th June, 1916:

Obituary Notice

On 18th June, 1916, there met his death for his country in an aerial combat.

MAX IMMELMANN,

Knight of the Order "pour le Merite" and Commander 2nd Class of Royal Saxon Military Order, Knight and Commander of several high and of several of the highest decorations, holder of the Iron Cross, I and II Class. Royal Saxon 1st Lieutenant and fighting pilot of a Flying Unit. His glory and his name are his country's. In the annals of the German Flying Corps his memory will live as that of a bold flyer, fighter and conqueror.

In the name of the Flying Troops of an Army

STEMPEL,

Royal Bavarian Major and Staff Officer of the Flying Troops of an Army.

29 June – 6 July, 1916

The opening of the Somme battle on 1 July was reflected in the increased air activity. The R.F.C. had now grown to twenty-seven squadrons comprising 421 aircraft.

Extensive photographic reconnaissance had been completed in the preceding weeks and substantial bombing raids were mounted on the opening days of the battle. Although the R.F.C. enjoyed overall air superiority at this stage the B.E.2cs, flying as bombers without air gunners and without adequate fighter escorts, suffered considerable losses. It was later learned that some of their attacks had been very successful. Contact patrols were flown to report on the progress of the British troops and the enemy reactions.

The R.E.7s of 21 Sqn were reported for the first time as delivering 336-pound bombs and the Martinsydes of 27 Sqn were now being used in the bombing role.

The Sopwiths of IXth Wing were the 1½-Strutters of 70 Sqn. The 1½-Strutter (so called because of the peculiar arrangement of the centre-section wing struts) was the first British aircraft fitted with synchronising gear enabling the pilot's Vickers machine-gun to fire between the propeller blades. It was a two-seater, and soon after its introduction the rear cockpit was fitted with the Scarff ring, a great advance on earlier observers' gun mountings.

The B.E.12, mentioned on 1 July, was a makeshift single-seat scout developed from the B.E.2c. It also had a synchronised machine-gun. The first B.E.12 squadron, 19, was not to become operational for another month.

The Le Prieur 'torpedoes' used by a 11 Sqn Nieuport were rockets—and usually designated as such—designed by an officer of the French Naval Air Service. They were mounted on the wing struts and fired electrically. They were primarily intended as an anti-balloon weapon.

The epic battle against an enemy bomber formation on the Ist Army Front by Maj L. W. B. Rees, C.O. of 32 Sqn, in a D.H.2, won him the Victoria Cross. Maj Rees survived the war and retired from the R.A.F. as a group captain.

COMMUNIQUÉ NO. 41

June 29th

The weather was unfavourable, there being low clouds and strong wind all day.

In spite of the weather, a considerable amount of successful artillery co-operation was carried out, though machines were forced to fly low. Seventy-six targets were engaged with aerial observation, and 18 direct hits on gun emplacements were obtained. Fifty-seven active hostile batteries were reported.

There was considerable hostile aircraft activity on the IIIrd and IVth Army fronts.

2 Lt Vaisey on a B.E. of 8 Sqn was attacked by three enemy machines, which suddenly appeared out of a cloud, and wounded in the back. He lost consciousness, but his observer, 2 Lt Pickthorne, climbed out of his seat and roused him, and he landed his machine safely in his own aerodrome. 2 Lt Pickthorne made use of his wireless to summon a doctor during the descent.

A machine of the 4th Brigade attacked a motor car with machine-gun fire, forcing the chauffeur to leave his car. Another machine silenced an anti-aircraft battery with Lewis gun fire.

June 30th

There were again low clouds and high wind, but the weather improved towards the evening ↔ Hostile aircraft activity was again moderate.

Ninety-five targets were dealt with by aerial observation, several direct hits being obtained on batteries, some of which were silenced. Our artillery machines reported a very large number of active hostile batteries.

A pilot of 3 Sqn engaged on artillery registration sighted 5 L.V.G.s and attacked two of them. He brought down one, which was seen to crash on landing. Another L.V.G. was driven down with a damaged engine.

Six machines of 21 Sqn attacked with 336-pound bombs the munition depot and store houses at St Sauveur Station, Lille, in the evening, escorted by 2 Martinsydes and 2 Moranes. Observation was difficult, but two large holes were observed in the roof of two sheds, and one bomb exploded in a house north of the station, blowing it up. Bombs were dropped from a height of 7,000 to 8,000 feet. Hostile anti-aircraft fire was heavy, but we suffered no casualties.

July 1st

A reconnaissance round Cambrai was carried out by four Sopwiths of the IXth Wing at 6 a.m. reporting railway activity normal and no movement on roads. No hostile machines were met with. A second reconnaissance was carried out by a Morane biplane with 4 Martinsydes as escort, all of the IXth Wing, at 9.30 a.m. over Cambrai, Busigny and Etreux, making a similar report. Anti-aircraft guns fired on our machines over Cambrai, and they were attacked by hostile aeroplanes throughout the journey. 2 Lts Dalrymple and Taylor, both of 27 Sqn, each brought down a Roland biplane.

At 7.30 a.m. a general attack was made all along the IVth Army front and on part of the IIIrd Army front. Machines of the 3rd and 4th Brigade Corps Sqns were allotted to counter battery work, a flight to each counter battery area, and to contact patrol and trench bombardment work, a flight being told off for each purpose in each Corps area. Five artillery balloons were up on the front of attack, and 3 balloons carried out tactical reconnaissance, reporting direct to the H.Q. of the Corps concerned.

The attack on St Sauveur Station at Lille was repeated shortly before 6 a.m. by the same number of machines. All 6 bombs dropped from 9,000 feet. Two hit the station and a third hit the railway just east of the station. Reports subsequently received show that one of the sheds was completely demolished.

Five F.E.s of 20 Sqn which were to have met the bombing machines over Armentieres had an encounter with 20 Fokkers before they effected a junction. Only one of the Fokkers succeeded in attacking the bombing machines.

Two Fokkers were brought down in the enemy's lines and at least two more damaged.

27 Sqn, IXth Wing, also carried out a bombing raid on hostile headquarters in Bapaume and on a suspected ammunition dump just south-east of Bapaume. Six Martinsydes did the bombing, carrying two 112-pound bombs each, escorted by two Martinsydes and two Morane Scouts. A fire was started in Bapaume which burned for several hours. One of the bombs carried by Lt J. C. Turner failed to release. Although his engine was running badly, and he was continuously being attacked by two hostile machines, Lt Turner made two more circles over the objective, releasing the bombs at the third attempt. He now found himself at 5,000 feet and recrossed the line at 2,500 feet. The attack was repeated by 6 R.E.s carrying 336-pound bombs later in the day. One bomb fell on the railway, cutting the line completely, and another on a house.

Bombing of the railways north and east of Cambrai, north-east and south-east of Busigny and east of St Quentin was carried out by 12 B.E.s of the 1st Brigade and 8 each of the 2nd and 3rd Brigades respectively. A train was hit in the middle just south of Aubigny au Bac and was set on fire by 2 Lt Gordon Kidd. 2 Lt Ellis, seeing the train on fire, came down low and dropped two more bombs on it, hitting the rear coaches. The fire continued for two hours with continuous explosions. Cambrai Station was hit by two bombs, the lines near it with 5, and the railway bridge in Cambrai by two. Busigny Station was hit once, 8 or 10 other bombs falling near it. A train between Busigny and Wassigny escaped being hit by 5 yards. (*See also page 207, after 'Casualties'*.)

Don was bombed in the early morning by machines of the 1st Brigade. Twelve 112-pound and sixteen 20-pound bombs were dropped. Three fires were caused, one of which burned all day and was still burning at 7 p.m.

Many 20-pound bombs were dropped by machines of all squadrons, on billets, transport, trenches, batteries, etc., in the course of their work. Several batteries were hit.

The machines carrying out the above bombing of trains and railway lines were protected by offensive patrols furnished by 27 and 60 Sqns alternately, which constantly patrolled the area on the far side of the points of attack.

Attempts were made at offensive action on our side of the line opposite the Ist, IInd and IIIrd Armies in the early morning, but subsequently hostile aircraft activity was entirely confined to their own side of the line.

Thirty-five combats took place, 5 hostile machines were brought down on the enemy's side of the line, and at least 5 others driven down, of which two were seen to be damaged. A sixth hostile machine was brought down by A.A. fire.

A party of 8 or 10 hostile biplanes approached the Ist Army front in the early morning near Festubert, and were met by heavy A.A. fire and by 2 of our aeroplanes—Capt Gehlin on a B.E.12 and Maj Rees on a De Havilland. Maj Rees attacked no less than 4 of the hostile machines, and is reported by the A.A. guns to have broken up the German formation single-handed and to have scattered it in all directions. The first machine he attacked was hit between the pilot and observer and returned to its aerodrome. The second was hit and managed to land in its own lines under control. When attacking the third, Maj Rees was hit in the leg, but continued firing until within 10 yards. He then saw the hostile observer was firing wildly into the air, and had evidently been hit. In spite of his wound Maj Rees chased yet another hostile machine and fired his remaining drum at it, but had to break off the fight for want of ammunition.

Lt Cowan, in a De Havilland of 24 Sqn, when on patrol, saw 4 hostile machines. He attacked them, wounding the observer of the first. The second was last seen falling out of control, and disappeared into a low cloud.

Another pilot of 24 Sqn engaged two hostile machines near Grandcourt, one of which he brought down.

The enemy's anti-aircraft fire seemed to have greatly increased, and it is thought that he must have reinforced his A.A. guns.

Very long flights were carried out by machines fitted with extra tanks. Lt Jowett of 4 Sqn, accomplished one flight of 5 hours 10 minutes.

Contact patrols worked continuously on the front of the IIIrd and IVth Armies throughout the day, furnishing most useful information, especially on the front of the IIIrd Army where ground communication broke down from 10.30 a.m. onwards. The information furnished to Corps Headquarters by these machines proved to be very accurate. Capt

C. Hiatt, of 4 Sqn, carried out a special inspection of Thiepval from a height of only 600 feet, furnishing an excellent report.

Casualties: Sqn 32, *Lt J. C. Simpson, killed;* **23,** *Lt A. N. Solly, wounded;* **15,** *Lt A. E. Packe, wounded; Lt N. P. Tucker, wounded;* **32,** *Maj L. W .B. Rees, wounded;* **6,** *Lt G. Cox, missing;* **12,** *2 Lt L. A. Wingfield, missing; 2 Lt C. Van Nostrand, missing;* **13,** *Capt T. Challoner, missing; Lt C. Monckton, missing;* **22,** *Capt G. W. Webb, missing; Lt J. H. Hirstbrook, missing; Lt W. O. Tudor Hart, missing; and Lt Burgess, missing.*

Seven machines missing.

A message was picked up dropped from a German aeroplane that 2 Lt L. C. Angstrom, 25 Sqn, missing on the 22nd June after a fight with a Fokker, was severely wounded. His observer, Sgt Topliffe, was uninjured.

July 2nd

The weather was fine, but there was a good deal of cloud during the morning on the Ist, IInd and IIIrd Army fronts ~ Successful reconnaissances were carried out on all the Army fronts.

Two R.E.s and four Martinsydes of the IXth Wing carried out a reconnaissance over the area Douai–Cambrai–Marcoing–Bapaume in the early morning, reporting a certain amount of railway activity in a southerly direction on the line Douai–Cambrai. Several hostile machines were seen, but kept out of the way.

Between 10.30 and 12.30 this reconnaissance was repeated by two Morane biplanes of 60 Sqn, another two carrying out a reconnaissance over Bapaume–Busigny–St Quentin. One hostile machine was met by the northern reconnaissance and four by the southern, one of which was brought down. There was little activity on roads or railways. Two more reconnaissances were carried out in the evening over the same areas, furnishing a similar report, one by Morane biplanes and Martinsydes, the other by Sopwiths and Martinsydes. The two Martinsydes accompanying the Sopwiths failed to get far, one having engine failure soon after starting, and the other having to land in our own lines after a fight with a Fokker. The Sopwiths completed the reconnaissance alone, the rear one being attacked by six hostile machines. 2 Lts Manly (pilot) and Oakes (observer) fought them off.

The German Headquarters and the railway station at Bapaume were again attacked by six R.E.s of 21 Sqn with 336-pound bombs. A large fire broke out in Bapaume which burned all day and most of the night. 112 20-pound bombs were dropped on points behind the enemy's lines by the machines of all four Brigades.

Much successful work was again done by all the Corps Squadrons and by the kite balloons which ranged on 32 targets. The enemy's anti-aircraft fire again increased at points behind the enemy's lines, which were also found to be strongly defended with rifle and machine-gun fire. His anti-aircraft guns were firing incendiary shell.

Liaison with the Infantry was again well maintained by the contact patrol machines, which flew at very low altitudes.

There was some indication of an increase in the number of hostile machines on the IVth Army front. There were 11 combats on the fronts of the IIIrd and IVth Armies, 4 hostile machines being brought down behind the lines by machines of the IIIrd Brigade.

Casualties: Sqn 32, *Capt H. G. Gilmour, wounded;* **9,** *2 Lt A. L. MacDonald, missing; 2 Lt H. A. Williamson, missing;* **11,** *2 Lt J. W. Toone, missing; and 2 Lt R. P. Harvey, missing.*

Two machines missing.

July 3rd

A fine day with some high clouds ~ There were altogether 30 combats in the air.

The 1st and 2nd Brigades both carried out a reconnaissance in the neighbourhood of Lille. The general impression was that there was increased railway activity at Lille, but not to any great extent.

Reconnaissances were sent out at dawn by the IXth Wing to examine the railways in the area Douai, Valenciennes, St Quentin, Albert. A large number of trains were reported, and there appeared to be a general concentration at Cambrai. A similar reconnaissance in the evening was unsuccessful, owing to low clouds.

A successful bombing attack on Comines Station was made by machines of the 2nd Brigade on the night of the 2nd/3rd, 32 bombs being dropped.

At day-break another attack was made on trains in movement on the Douai–Cambrai line and the lines east of Busigny and St Quentin. The pilots went down under 1,000 feet in spite of heavy fire from machine-guns mounted at the station. Many hits were scored on the stations and on rolling stock in them, and three trains were missed by a few yards only.

Cambrai Station was again attacked in the evening by three R.E.s carrying three 336-pound bombs. A fire was started close to the station.

Many bombs were again dropped on the enemy's billets, batteries and dumps.

Counter-battery work on the front of the IIIrd and IVth Armies continued successfully throughout the day, kite balloons being especially successful, observing 149 targets on the whole British front.

The activity of the enemy in the air increased to a very great degree, but it was confined to localities well behind his own lines. Our machines working near the lines were subjected to a continuous anti-aircraft fire.

A reconnoitring patrol of the 1st Brigade was followed by two Fokkers and a biplane. The escort, two F.E.s of 25 Sqn, having accompanied the reconnaissance back to our own lines, turned to engage the enemy, who had by this time been joined by two more Fokkers. One Fokker was shot down and seen to crash to earth, and a biplane was forced to descend. Lt T. A. Oliver and Sgt Mumford, in a Morane biplane of 1 Sqn, encountered five hostile aeroplanes, driving off four with little trouble. The fifth showed more fight, but was last seen diving vertically with the engine full on, and is believed to have been destroyed.

Machines of the IIIrd Brigade drove down two hostile machines in the German lines, both of which were seen to be wrecked on hitting the ground.

An attack was made on the enemy's kite balloons on the fronts of the IIIrd and IVth Armies, one being brought down in flames by Capt Crook of 11 Sqn in a Nieuport Scout fitted with Le Prieur torpedoes.

The enemy has evidently evolved some new system of defending his kite balloons in view of the success of our attacks upon him. Capt Balcombe Brown, one of the attacking pilots, reports that the enemy got a kind of smoke cloud round the balloon he attacked by means of bursting shell, and subsequently played on the smoke with streams of fire balls about 5 yards apart. The smoke cloud appeared to have the effect of removing the dope from the wings and covering them with moisture. No attempt was made to haul the balloon down, and presumably it was up with ballast as a trap.

Casualties: Sqn 21, *2 Lt R. Sherwell, killed; 2 Lt J. C. Stewart, killed;* **13,** *2 Lt P. R. Meredith, wounded;* **29,** *2 Lt W. Stobart, wounded; 2 Lt L. V. Anderson, wounded;* **4,** *2 Lt R. C. Stoddart, missing; 2 Lt J. F. Quinlan, missing;* **5,** *Lt W. P. Ellis, missing;* **13,** *2 Lt W. F. E. Castle, missing;* **16,** *2 Lt S. H. Ellis, missing;* **24,** *Lt D. H. Gray, missing; and* **60,** *Maj F. Waldron, missing.*

Six machines missing.

The following complimentary orders were received:

(1) The Commander-in-Chief directs that all ranks of the R.F.C. should be informed of his high appreciation of the services rendered by them during the last few days. The work done by the R.F.C. has been of material assistance to the Army, and has contributed in no small degree to the success of the operations.

(2) G.O.C. IVth Army to 4th Brigade R.F.C.: The Army Commander wishes to congratulate all ranks of the 4th Brigade R.F.C., on the excellent work they have carried out during the last few days.

(3) (From a Corps Commander, IIIrd Army:) In our attack yesterday (July 1st) No. 8 Squadron did extraordinarily good work. They never once failed us either as regards getting information or taking photos, and we found that what news they were able to send about the position of our troops was most reliable.

4–12 July, 1916

Extensive bombing was continued during spells of suitable weather and over four days more than 13,000 pounds were dropped on various targets.

Lt Col H. C. T. Dowding, C.O. of IXth Wing, was to achieve distinction as Air Officer Commanding-in-Chief, R.A.F. Fighter Command, during the Battle of Britain in 1940. In 1916 IXth Wing comprised 21, 27, 60 and 70 Sqns.

During the period of this communiqué there was no significant challenge to R.F.C. superiority, though the scale of operations inevitably resulted in a continuing fairly high casualty rate. Since the Somme battle started the communiqués had reported the loss of twenty-four aircraft, with thirty-nine aircrew personnel killed or missing.

The combat by Maj Sidney Smith, C.O. of 27 Sqn, on 6 July illustrated the employment of the single-seater Martinsyde's rear gun.

COMMUNIQUÉ NO. 42

July 4th

Low clouds, rain and thunder. A very unfavourable day for flying.

July 5th

Low clouds all day until the evening.

Two observers of the 4th Brigade reported columns of infantry on the Flers–Bazentin-le-Grand road, and attacked them from 2,000 feet with Lewis gun fire.

July 6th

Weather unfavourable ~ Eight indecisive combats took place.

Owing to the unfavourable weather only a limited amount of work was accomplished. Forty-one targets were registered by aeroplane observers, and 5 by kite balloons. An aeroplane of 9 Sqn reported one battalion of infantry and a motor transport proceeding from Bois de Leuze to Guillemont. A heavy battery was ranged on this target and seven direct hits were obtained on the column. A number of men were seen to fall and the rest scattered in disorder. A direct hit was also obtained on one of the lorries. The infantry was watched for some time, but were not seen to re-form. (*See also page 222, 'Examination of Prisoners'.*)

A brigade of infantry marching into Ginchy was attacked and dispersed

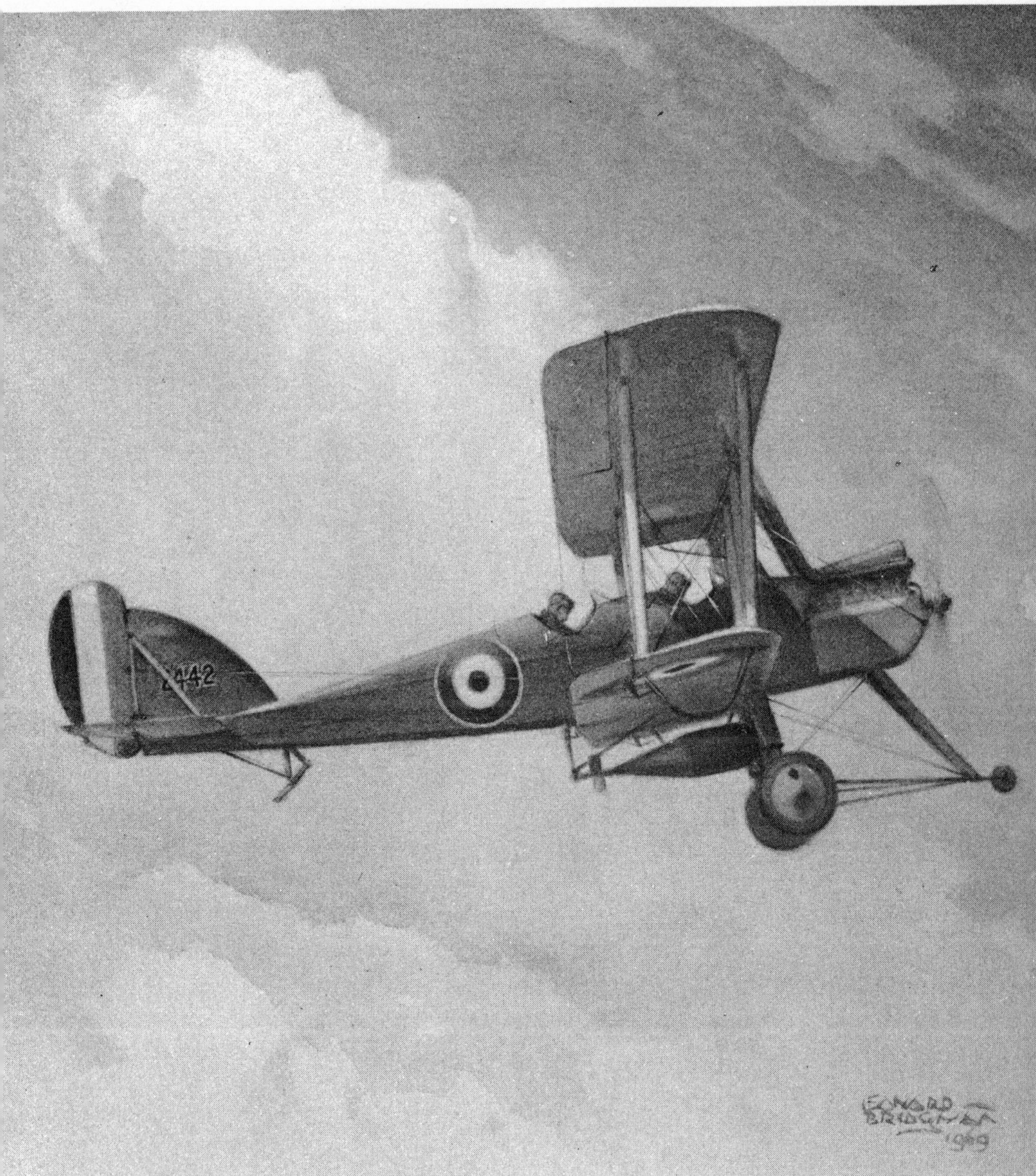

5—R.E.7—150 H.P. RAF.4A ENGINE
The R.E.7 designed by the Royal Aircraft Factory as a bomber, was the first and only RFC aeroplane to carry the Royal Aircraft Factory-designed 336-lb. bomb, a heavy-cased fragmentation bomb containing only 70-lb. of explosive. Its defensive capabilities however, were no better than those of the B.E.2c so that its operational life with No. 21 Squadron, the only fully-equipped R.E.7 unit to go to France, lasted only seven months, from January 23 to the end of August 1916.

by 2 Lts MacDonald and Hill of 9 Sqn with machine-gun fire from 1,200 feet.

Bombs were dropped by the 1st Brigade with success on Wingles, Achville and Lievin.

Six F.E.s of 23 Sqn successfully attacked the aerodrome at Douai. Twenty-seven 20-pound bombs were dropped, 4 of which exploded in the hangars. One hangar was completely destroyed, and it is probable that others were severely damaged. Eight other bombs fell very near the hangars doing additional damage. Eleven bombs exploded in the aerodrome, and two others were seen to explode very near an A.A. battery.

Lts Miller and Long, of 3 Sqn, descended to 300 feet and bombed a troop train from which troops were detraining at Velu station. One bomb exploded in the centre of the train and set it on fire.

Maj Smith in a Martinsyde of 27 Sqn, when over Cambrai on an offensive patrol observed 6 or 8 hostile machines flying west in pairs. He followed them, intending to delay attack till the enemy were nearer the lines, but Lt Pearson, who was above him fired a red light and dived to the attack. Maj Smith conformed, and each one engaged one of the leading machines. In diving at the enemy, Maj Smith slightly overshot the mark, so engaged the hostile machine with the rear gun, firing one drum. He then observed a second machine above him, at which he fired three-quarters of a drum from his top gun. The hostile machine made a very sharp right-hand turn and went down vertically. Maj Smith was unable to observe this machine further as he was attacked by a third hostile machine from behind. Having reloaded his rear gun he fired half a drum, but then found that his machine was temporarily out of control owing to the aileron wires being cut on the left-hand side. He regained control, but owing to the difficulties of control could not work his gun and made for the lines followed by three hostile machines. He landed his machine, which was considerably knocked about, safely on the aerodrome.

Casualty: Sqn 3, *Lt S. A. Tillard, slightly wounded.*

July 7th

Capt Cruikshank on a Sopwith of 70 Sqn, observer 2 Lt Cruickshank, with two other Sopwiths of the same Squadron, reconnoitred the railways radiating from Cambrai, starting at 5 a.m. Capt Cruikshank became separated from the other two machines when over Cambrai, and was attacked by three Fokkers. His observer was wounded, and his aileron controls cut at the commencement of the fight. He carried on a running fight for about 20 minutes, during which one of the Fokkers disappeared. At the end of 20 minutes, after a steep nose dive, he found himself over the trenches, and subsequently recognising that he was over

St Omer, landed there. 2 Lt Cruickshank subsequently died in hospital at St Omer.

The contact patrols of the 4th Brigade continued to do useful work. It was again necessary to fly at low altitudes. Lts Lewis and Cleaver, of 3 Sqn, flying at 800 feet located the enemy's front line in the neighbourhood of the Quadrangle.

Lt Stallibrass, of 3 Sqn also, flying at 900 feet, located the positions of hostile troops in the vicinity of Mametz and Bazentin Woods.

Casualties: Sqn 70, *2 Lt A. J. T. Cruickshank, died of wounds;* **4,** *2 Lt J. H. Ross, wounded in a combat; and Capt G. A. Burney and Lt J. W. Halcrow, killed.*

July 8th

The weather was again unfavourable.

Three reconnaissances flying at low altitudes were successfully accomplished. Nineteen targets were engaged with aeroplane observation and 8 by kite balloons.

Hostile aeroplanes continued their activities, but well to the east of the line. All the reconnaissances were attacked, but without decisive results.

A contact patrol of 9 Sqn reported in detail the positions of the French and our own troops in the neighbourhood of Malz Horn trench and Trones Wood.

Capt Evans and Lt Long, 3 Sqn, attacked and dispersed a column of infantry with machine-gun fire.

Casualties: Sqn 10, *Lt R. G. Gould, wounded during a combat;* **70,** *Capt D. M. Veitch and Lt J. L. Whitty, killed—direct hit from anti-aircraft fire; and* **4,** *Lt E. C. Jowett and Cpl R. Johnston, missing.*

July 9th

Reconnaissances throughout the day along the entire front of the Army kept under observation the railway lines used by the enemy in bringing up reinforcements to the battle area. During the course of these reconnaissances there were many encounters. Nine hostile machines followed a reconnaissance of the IXth Wing throughout its course but did not attack.

A reconnaissance of the 1st Brigade was attacked by Fokkers without decisive result.

Six F.E.s of 23 Sqn, were attacked by 12 hostile machines near Bapaume. A long encounter followed in which two German machines were last seen nose diving very steeply, one emitting smoke. Our machines had expended all their ammunition before returning home.

At 5.45 p.m. 4 Sopwiths of 70 Sqn carried out a reconnaissance round Cambrai. The clouds were very thick, and three of the machines turned back soon after crossing the lines. 2 Lt Manby and 2 Lt Saint, in the fourth Sopwith completed the reconnaissance and rendered a very useful report.

Capt C. J. Mackay and Capt W. J. Pain in a B.E. of 2 Sqn, located an A.A. Battery firing on our machines and obtained a direct hit on it from the 117th Heavy Battery. The A.A. battery ceased firing.

A machine of 3 Sqn, pilot, Capt J. K. Summers, observer, Lt L. S. Williams, directed the fire of our 12-inch howitzers on an enemy battery. Three emplacements were wrecked by direct hits, and the ammunition behind all 4 emplacements was blown up.

Other successful artillery work was accomplished and several hostile batteries were silenced. A large fire was caused in Martinpuich village and station, and another in Bazentin le Petit.

Six R.E.s of 21 Sqn, each with one 336-pound bomb, bombed Cambrai station at 4.30 a.m. Three bombs exploded in the station. The R.E.s were attacked by several hostile machines, and 2 Lt Hewson on one of them failed to return. He is believed to have been brought down by a German aeroplane near Cambrai. At the same time 6 Martinsydes of 27 Sqn with two 112-pound bombs each attacked Bapaume station. Three bombs exploded on or near the railway and one in the south-west corner of the town. 2 Lt Nicholl in one of the Martinsydes is missing. Six Morane scouts accompanied the R.E.s as escort, and the Martinsydes provided an additional escort after dropping their bombs.

At 8 a.m. another 6 Martinsydes bombed Velu, dropping one 112-pound bomb each. Two bombs exploded near the hangars. After dropping their bombs the Martinsydes acted as an offensive patrol.

At 4.30 p.m. another bomb raid was carried out by 5 R.E.s, escorted by 6 Martinsydes and 7 Moranes. Bombs were dropped on the dump at Le Sars and on H.Q. in Le Transloy. No hostile aircraft were seen.

Five F.E.s of 25 Sqn and a De Havilland of 32 Sqn dropped 19 20-pound bombs and one incendiary bomb on Henin Lietard on the evening of the 8th. Three Fokkers were seen, but avoided a combat. 20 B.E.s of the 3rd Brigade carried out a successful raid against a dump at Croisilles at 12 noon, dropping thirty 112-pound bombs, several of which were seen to explode in the middle of the dump. The railway is thought to have been seriously damaged. All machines returned safely in spite of heavy A.A. fire.

An equally successful raid was carried out against a dump at Boyelles in the evening.

Hostile aircraft showed increased activity all along the front. There were 24 combats in all. Hostile machines showed rather more enterprise on the Ist Army front, 5 or 6 crossing 5 or 10 miles over the line. On the rest of the front activity was confined to their own side of the line, but some 20 to 25 were seen on the Ist Army front and two big patrols on the IVth Army front.

Two hostile machines are believed to have been brought down by F.E.s of 23 Sqn during an Army reconnaissance, and two on the IVth Army front in the course of the day, one of which crashed in a field near Bilmcourt.

An F.E. of 11 Sqn was seen by a De Havilland of 24 Sqn, pilot, Lt Knight, to be brought down by a Fokker at 6.40 a.m. in the neighbourhood of Bucquoy.

Another F.E. is reported by an A.A. battery to have been brought down by A.A. fire near Moyenneville.

Special photographs were taken of the German second and third lines at the request of G.H.Q., some 200 plates being exposed.

Casualties: Sqn 11, *Lt N. T. L. Speen and Lt W. A. Wedgwood, missing; Lt D. H. MacIntyre and Lt H. Floyd, missing;* **21,** *2 Lt C. V. Hewson, missing; and* **27,** *2 Lt R. W. Nicholl, missing.*

July 10th

A thick cloud bank east of the line made observation difficult.

Much successful artillery work was done, 78 targets being dealt with by aeroplane observation and 37 by kite balloons.

An ammunition store was hit on the IInd Army front, and 25 direct hits on gun emplacements were obtained on the IVth Army front.

Fires were started in Martinpuich, Longueval and Peronne. The latter burned all day.

Six F.E.s of 25 Sqn, with a De Havilland of 32 Sqn, dropped 24 bombs on Annay on the evening of the 9th. Two hostile aeroplanes were encountered, but driven off. Many bombs were seen to hit the target. On the 10th 58 20-pound bombs were dropped on billets opposite the Ist Army front. Observation was difficult, but a car is believed to have been hit, and some fires were caused. Some of the bombs were seen to land close to battery positions and trenches. In addition one 112-pound bomb was dropped by night.

Four B.E.s of 7 Sqn, dropped 10 bombs on billets and bridges opposite the IInd Army. The effect could not be observed.

F.E.s of 23 Sqn, dropped ten 20-pound bombs on Achiet and Bucquoy.

A German kite balloon was attacked with phosphorus bombs on the IVth Army front. XIIIth Corps report that it fell in flames, but the pilot was unable to see the result of his shot owing to smoke, and the escort was engaged with hostile aircraft.

There were 10 combats in the air. One hostile machine was brought down by a Bristol Scout of 24 Sqn. It was seen to crash in a cornfield south of Grevillers Wood.

2 Lt W. J. Thomson and Capt W. W. Jeffard of 9 Sqn, were brought down by a direct hit from an A.A. gun.

July 11th

A night reconnaissance was carried out by 2 Lt Reid and Lt Billings of 20 Sqn, over the Lille–Tournai–Mouscron area. Train activity was normal. There was little train activity in the enemy's lines, which were kept under observation throughout the day.

Artillery Co-operation

The clouds made artillery co-operation difficult, but 51 targets were dealt with by aeroplane observation, and 15 by kite balloons.

On the IIIrd Army front one hostile battery was silenced and a large explosion caused at another. The emplacements of two batteries were destroyed.

On the IVth Army front two other batteries were silenced. Fires were caused in Peronne, Martinpuich and Longueval.

Bombing

A bomb raid on bivouacs in Bois d'Havrincourt was attempted by the following machines of the IXth Wing:

One B.E., 6 R.E.s and 10 Martinsydes, escorted by Moranes and Martinsydes. The machines were divided into two parties, but the rendezvous was rendered difficult by cloud. Martinsydes reached the objective and dropped 54 20-pound bombs, several fires being started in the wood. Only the B.E. and two R.E.s of the other party crossed the lines, and these were attacked by hostile machines and failed to reach the objective.

Fifty-seven 20-pound bombs were dropped on billets, batteries and railways by machines of the 1st Brigade by day, and 24 20-pound bombs and 10 incendiary bombs on Harnes and Haisnes by night. Successful results were obtained at Fournes, Château de la Vallee, the railway at Lens, Headquarters at Fosse 6, Harnes, and on some lorries moving between Herlies and Aubers.

Machines of the 2nd Brigade bombed by night various billets, obtaining successful results at Moorslede and Oostnieuwkerke. Six 20-pound bombs were dropped on Boyelles by machines of the 3rd Brigade.

Lt Col Dowding and Capt Longridge of the IXth Wing when leading a bomb attack on the Bois d'Havrincourt were attacked by 6 hostile machines. Capt Longridge's gun was hit at the commencement of the engagement and put out of action, and both pilot and observer were slightly wounded. The hostile machines were driven off by Capt Tower and Lt Meintjes in Morane Scouts of 60 Sqn.

Casualties: Sqn 24, *Lt C. Kerr, missing; Lt Col H. C. T. Dowding, wounded; and Capt Longridge, wounded.*

This communique was dated 17 July, presumably in error for 12 or 13 July.

12–19 July, 1916

The bombing offensive was continued against a limited scale of enemy opposition. The communiqué included German prisoners' testimony to the value of earlier attacks.

The technique employed by the Martinsyde pilots of 27 Sqn, in navigating to their target area above cloud, proved most effective and was further developed by this unit during the ensuing months.

COMMUNIQUÉ NO. 43

Between 10 a.m. and 2 p.m. on June 20th about 56 rounds of High Explosive and time H.E. were fired at the balloon and winch of 1 Kite Balloon Section. In the first quarter of an hour 7 rounds of high-explosive shell burst within 20 yards of the winch, one round bursting within a yard of the winch and lifting the back wheels off the ground and damaging the cable. Cpl Jenkins, the driver of the winch, behaved with the utmost coolness throughout, wound in the cable until the frayed portion was on the drum, and then moved the winch slowly up the road away from its original position. The shelling of the balloon and winch continued till 2 p.m. and during the whole of this time Cpl Jenkins moved the winch with the balloon at about 600 feet above it backwards and forwards on the road. But for his presence of mind, both the winch and the balloon would undoubtedly have been seriously damaged, and probably further casualties would have occurred; as it was, the only damage was 4 small holes in the balloon itself.

During the operations on the IIIrd and IVth Army fronts, kite balloon sections have carried out a great deal of useful work (extracts from reports show that between 26 June and 4 July, 239 hostile batteries and 85 other targets were located, 41 and 66 respectively being successfully engaged).

The tactical balloons during the present operations have been useful in reporting movements of trains. Notably, 13 K.B.S. on the 3rd followed and rendered valuable reports on a large train movement from the east to Bapaume.

The following messages were received by 3 Kite Balloon Section on the night of the 2nd/3rd July by lamps, which show possibilities of communication between infantry in the front line and kite balloon sections:

> In contact with German bombing party, about *X.19.b.9.9*. Am unable to push him farther back without a supply of rifle grenades A.A.A. If possible please send a supply without delay. Needed pickets wire and sandbags for consolidation AAA also Very pistols and ammunition AAA O.C.9th.

This message was received at 9.50 p.m. and was despatched by wire at 10.24 p.m. to XVth Corps, 17th Div., and 78th Field Co. R.E., also delivered to 78th Field Co., R.E., by hand at 10.20 p.m.

> Only 2 officers left AAA. Reinforcements of officers wanted, from F.E. at *X.20.a.5.5*.

This message was received at 3.12 a.m. and despatched to XVth Corps, 17th Division, 51st and 58th Infantry Brigades at 3.30 a.m.

Numerous statement made by prisoners captured during the current operations have testified to the value of the many bombing expeditions which have lately been carried out by day and night by the R.F.C. The following is an extract from the Ist Army Intelligence Summary of the 11th July:

> Statements of prisoners show that these raids cause much damage and inflict numerous casualties on the enemy; considerable anger is being expressed by the enemy at the disturbance of their rest and the destruction of their quarters.

Up to and including the 16th instant, 39 tons of bombs have been dropped.

July 12th

Hostile aeroplanes displayed no activity, and no combats took place.

A great deal of counter battery was done by the 4th Brigade. Thirteen hostile batteries were silenced.

In the 3rd Brigade two hostile batteries were engaged and one silenced by 8 Sqn.

Altogether 51 targets were engaged with aeroplane observation and 18 by kite balloon observers.

The machines of the 1st Brigade again carried out a series of successful night bombing attacks against various points of military importance in the enemy's lines. At least 8 searchlights endeavoured to locate our machines, and though they sometimes found them, they were unable to keep them in their rays. The machines were subjected to inaccurate anti-aircraft fire.

On the night of 11th/12th July 18 Sqn (F.E.2bs) made 8 flights, dropping 52 bombs on La Bassee, Douvrin, Pont a Vendin, Lens, Avion, Vimy, Sallaumines, and Henin Lietard. Observers were carried.

Six searchlights were successfully engaged with bombs or machine-gun fire. In one case Lt G. N. Teale, pilot, and 2 Lt A. G. A. Davis, observer, extinguished a searchlight near Harnes, from a height of 300 feet in spite of being caught in the beam and being met with heavy rifle fire. The observer fired at the searchlight with his machine-gun until it was extinguished.

July 13th

Low clouds all day, strong west wind and some rain.

Lt Howard in a F.E. of 22 Sqn, pilot, 2 Lt Courtneidge, carried out a reconnaissance of the German third line between Morval and Le Sars between 11.40 a.m. and 1.40 p.m. and furnished an excellent report. They had to fly at 2,000 feet in order to see anything.

Four Martinsydes of 27 Sqn, pilots, Capt. Boyd, Lt Turner, and 2 Lts Pearson and Taylor, crossed the line in the clouds, and coming down over their objective bombed trains on the lines Douai–Cambrai and Denain–Cambrai. 2 Lt Taylor saw two trains, one going north and another just west Aubigny-au-Bac. He dropped a bomb from a height of 800 feet at the first train which failed to explode. Waiting until the second train pulled up near the junction he dropped his second bomb from a height of 500 feet which fell 10 yards from the railway line near the front end of the train. The tender and two leading trucks were derailed, one truck being overturned and the tender and remaining truck thrown sideways across the rails. A squadron of cavalry on the road Epinoy–Marquion scattered in all directions. Lt Taylor also saw a convoy of transport about 3½ miles long on the Fressines–Cambrai road, the head opposite Blecourt. The exploding bomb caused considerable commotion in the convoy.

Lt Pearson dropped two bombs at a train near Iwuy on the Cambrai–Denain line from a height of 600 feet. The first fell 20 yards from the target level with the centre of the train. The second fell 15 feet from the engine and the train stopped. The pilot could not see the damage. Lt Turner from a height of 800 feet attacked the same train as Lt Taylor first attacked. Both bombs exploded level with the centre of the train 20 yards from it. No damage appeared to be done.

Capt Boyd from a height of 500 feet attacked the same train as Lt Pearson. His first bomb fell about 8 yards from the line level with the rear of the train, and his second on the telegraph wire alongside the line level with the centre. No damage however appeared to be done. The pilot then attacked the engine with machine-gun fire, but no result was apparent. All four machines returned safely.

Machines of the 1st Brigade dropped seven 20-pound bombs on Annay, Hulluch, and Bois de la Folie. A loud report was heard in Annay, and a column of smoke seen.

July 14th

Clouds and mist, no flying till late evening.

In retaliation for the shelling of Poperinghe, 20 machines of the 2nd Brigade carried out a bombing raid on Westroosebecke in the late evening. Each machine carried two 112-pound bombs. Considerable damage was done. A direct hit was obtained on the railway station and the majority of the bombs fell in the town. All machines returned safely. Four Martinsydes of the IXth Wing were sent out at about 6.30 p.m. to bomb trains moving in the railway triangle Epehy–Velu–Marcoing. Owing to the bad light the bombs were dropped without definite results.

At 7.30 a.m. troops having been reported to be moving up to the battle on the Albert–Bapaume road, four Martinsydes were dispatched. These were unsuccessful in locating their target and the bombs were dropped in other localities.

2 Lt Brearley, of 29 Sqn in a De Havilland, while escorting the bombing party of the 2nd Brigade to Westroosebecke saw a hostile machine at about 5,000 feet. He dived at him firing about 6 rounds at a range of about 80 yards. The hostile machine immediately fell sideways and nose dived on to the ground. This is confirmed by a pilot of 20 Sqn.

Casualty: Sqn 9, *Capt. Kelly, seriously wounded by shell fire.*

July 15th

Very misty in the morning—bright clear day after 10 a.m. but observation difficult.

Observation was difficult but 23 targets were engaged with aeroplane observation and 15 with kite balloons.

Two ammunition dumps were set on fire by batteries ranged by machines of the XVth Wing.

During the day the following expeditions were undertaken:

Epehy Station—5 Martinsydes of 27 Sqn with ten 112-pound bombs. The expedition was attacked by 3 machines which were driven off.

Bapaume Station—16 machines of the 3rd Brigade dropped twenty-eight 112-pound bombs and dense smoke was seen rising from the buildings round the station. The escort encountered 4 Fokkers, 2 L.V.G.s and one twin-engine machine. The latter was brought down in flames by Lts Tyler and Turnbull and Lt Hicks and 1 AM Libby.

The 3rd Brigade also carried out highly successful bombing raids at St Leger, the railway siding at Moyenville, and on the railway between Vitry and Douai; also on Achiet-le-Grand, Bapaume and Hendecourt, causing a large fire at the latter place.

In the evening Martinsydes of 27 Sqn dropped bombs on Sailissel, Bois St Pierre Vaast and Bois des Vaux. They also attacked, apparently with success, a Corps Headquarters situated in Beugny.

Five R.E.s of 21 Sqn attacked Le Transloy, dropping two 112-pound bombs each. Houses were set on fire and all bombs appeared to burst in the town.

The 1st Brigade, during bombing expeditions, stampeded some horsed transport.

None of the afternoon or evening bombing raids were interfered with by hostile aircraft.

Lt Asher on a Martinsyde of 27 Sqn, when escorting R.E.s, was attacked by 3 hostile machines. His machine-gun jammed but he drove off a Roland biplane with his revolver, and getting his gun into action again continued the combat with the other machines until they disappeared.

Eight hostile aeroplanes were engaged, 2 Fokkers and a single-seat biplane being brought down; one Fokker by a F.E.2b of 25 Sqn, pilot, 2 Lt Mathewson, observer, AM Booth, assisted by 2 Lt Lewis on a De Havilland of 32 Sqn. The machine was seen to fall by an A.A. battery. The second was brought down by 2 Lt Coleman on a De Havilland of 32 Sqn. The biplane by 2 Lt Godlee of the same squadron.

On the IInd Army front the hostile aircraft activity was below normal and there were two indecisive combats.

On the fronts of the IIIrd and IVth Armies, hostile patrols were encountered well east of the line but this was the only evidence of activity.

There were 12 combats, and in addition to the double-engine machine reported above as being brought down, two others were brought down by the 4th Brigade.

Two machines of 22 Sqn (Capts Swart and Wyncoll and Lts Bowen and Mansell) attacked some infantry on the Flers–Longueval road with machine-gun fire, descending to 2,000 feet. They made 3 attacks causing the enemy to disperse with several casualties on each occasion. Subsequently they attacked some wagons and a gun limber, killing one horse and causing the drivers to bolt.

Casualties: Sqn 9, *Lt H. A. V. Hill, slightly wounded; and* **22,** *2 Lt J. L. Reed, wounded by A.A. fire.*

July 16th

Twenty-five targets were dealt with by aeroplane observation. A large explosion, which is believed to have been an ammunition store, was caused near Wingles. Vimy Station was successfully ranged on. No hostile machines were met with.

During the night 15–16 machines of the 4th Brigade and the XVth Wing attacked several points in the enemy's lines with phosphorus and 20-pound bombs.

A very successful raid was carried out by the 3rd Brigade against the junction of the railways at St Leger where the light railway meets the main line. Thirteen machines exclusive of the escort, took part, and twenty-six 112-pound bombs were dropped. From the resultant smoke and flames it is evident that considerable damage was executed.

A patrol of 22 Sqn fired on a transport wagon causing the driver to run away. A second transport wagon seen in Grandcourt was fired on from 3,000 feet and was hit. The horses galloped in the direction of the trenches and overturned the wagon.

Small parties of infantry were also fired on and dispersed.

Casualties: Sqn 18, *2 Lt H. W. Butterworth and Capt J. H. F. McEwen in a F.E.2b, missing;* **4,** *2 Lt T. L. Brennan, wounded by rifle fire;* **3,** *Lt H. Long, and Capt A. J. Evans, missing; and* **25,** *Pte W. H. Cruisdale, slightly wounded by A.A. fire.*

17–24 July, 1916

Some intensive air combats were reported in this communiqué. The highly manoeuvrable D.H.2 was now in its heyday and operating with great success.

The casualty rate continued fairly high. Nine R.F.C. aircraft were lost and twelve aircrew killed or missing, and ten enemy aircraft were reported destroyed and seven forced down. 21 Sqn suffered heavily, with three of the cumbersome R.E.7s lost on 21 July.

Lt Oswald Boelcke, mentioned by an indiscreet prisoner, had scored his first victory in a Fokker monoplane in 15 August and was currently the leading German 'ace'. He had recently submitted to higher authority far-reaching proposals for German air reorganisation, and his presence on the British Front was no rumour.

COMMUNIQUÉ NO. 44

July 17th/18th

Clouds, mist and rain. Unfavourable weather for any successful flying.

July 19th

Much successful artillery co-operation was carried out, 64 targets being engaged with aeroplane observation and 13 by kite balloons.

Capt Ward, pilot, and Lt Brigham, observer, of the 1st Brigade carried out very successful registration on minenwerfer emplacements.

Contact patrol machines did some good work with battalions in the neighbourhood of Longueval, obtaining their situation from them and a report that all was well.

Activity was normal on the Ist Army front, slight on the fronts of the IInd and IIIrd Armies, and much increased on the fronts of the IVth and Reserve Armies.

On the Ist Army front about 18 hostile machines were working; two crossed the lines and dropped 2 bombs on Chocques and La Gorgue respectively.

A patrol of F.E.s and De Havillands over Provin and Lille encountered 6 Fokkers, one of which was shot down by an F.E. of 25 Sqn, pilot, Lt Mann, observer, 2 Lt Webb. It was seen to fall to pieces and crash in the Provin aerodrome.

2 Lt Godlee of 32 Sqn engaged another Fokker which appeared to go down in a spinning nose dive, 2 Lt Godlee being mortally wounded was unable to make a report.

A hostile aerodrome was located near Provin (*C. 22.c. Sheet 36*). One large shed and Fokkers were seen.

There were no combats on the IInd Army front.

On the IIIrd Army front there were five combats. One hostile machine was forced down.

On the IVth Army front there was a good deal of fighting. Two hostile machines are believed to have been brought down, but owing to the number of machines engaged at the same time it was difficult to observe results. Between 30 and 40 machines were seen, and there were 12 combats.

Bombing operations were continued during the night of the 18th/19th and on the 19th against various points of importance in the enemy's lines.

The 1st Brigade attacked the aerodrome at Ronchin by night. Four bombs were observed to fall on the aeroplane sheds.

At midnight 2 Lt Thayre of 7 Sqn dropped two 112-pound bombs on St Sauveur Station, Lille. Both bombs burst in the station and appeared to cause disorganisation of the traffic.

During the day the 3rd Brigade carried out successful raids against a dump at Biache St Vaast, against the siding at Boyelles and against the aerodrome at Douai. At the latter place twenty-eight 112-pound bombs were dropped. A petrol store was apparently set on fire, and at least one hangar was destroyed and others damaged.

Machines of the IXth Wing attacked Cambrai station, Rocquigny, Gueudecourt, Le Transloy and Beaulencourt. Much damage appeared to have been done in the last two named places.

Casualties: Sqn 32, *2 Lt J. Godlee, wounded in a combat, died of wounds;* **13,** *Lt H. Clements-Finnerty, missing;* **23,** *2 Lt C. V. J. Borton, wounded in a combat;* **3,** *Lt E. R. Manning, wounded in a combat;* **25,** *Lt M. G. B. Copeman, wounded in a combat; Cpl A. Reid, wounded in a combat;* **27,** *Lt A. H. W. Tollemache, missing;* **70,** *Lt H. R. Hele Shaw, missing; and 2 Lt R. C. Oakes, missing.*

Altogether nearly 7 tons of bombs were dropped during the day.

July 20th

Some successful artillery co-operation was carried out by all brigades and XVth Wing, but observation was difficult except in the Ist and IInd Army areas. Forty-five targets were dealt with by aeroplane observation and 8 by kite balloons. An active A.A. gun on a lorry was engaged by our artillery directed by a machine of 15 Sqn. It ceased firing and retired after two or three rounds.

Some successful contact patrol work was carried out by 10 and 16 Sqns during the Ist Army attack on the evening of the 19th.

Very successful contact patrol work was done by 3 and 9 Sqns in the vicinity of Longueval, Delville and High Woods. A good number of flares were seen and reported, also many Brigade and Battalion Headquarters, from some of which messages were received.

Hostile aircraft were inactive until the evening when they became very active, especially on the IVth Army front.

2 Lt Walters on a Nieuport of 1 Sqn, went up to attack a hostile machine over Bailleul chasing it for 10 miles over the line. He got quite close to it, hitting the observer, but although he fired six drums, the German machine managed to escape.

On the Ist Army front about 16 hostile machines were seen in the evening, but only one crossed to our side of the line.

On the IIIrd Army front there was no activity, but on the front of the Reserve Army hostile patrols were more active and came down the line. A machine of 4 Sqn, 2 Lt Randall and 2 Lt Angier, was brought down, the pilot being killed.

Two offensive patrols of the IXth Wing were sent out at 5.30 p.m. and 6 p.m. respectively. The first consisted of 5 Sopwiths, the second of 6 Morane Scouts. The Sopwiths encountered a Roland biplane which was driven down. 2 Lt Manley, pilot of one of the machines was wounded in the face and shoulder. The Morane Scouts saw a few hostile aircraft but had no fighting.

At about 6.15 p.m. four F.E.s of 25 Sqn encountered four Fokker and two biplanes. A fight which lasted for nearly three-quarters of an hour ensued. Eventually one of the Fokkers was driven down and destroyed; a second went away hard hit, and the whole formation was dispersed. Our machines returned undamaged. One pilot was wounded.

Between 8 and 9 p.m. an offensive patrol of four De Havilland Scouts of 24 Sqn encountered 5 L.V.G.s, 3 Rolands and 3 Fokkers over Flers. Capt Chamberlain, who led the patrol, first dived at an L.V.G. which made off east, and he then attacked and drove down a Fokker. The Fokker flattened out low down. Capt Chamberlain was then attacked by a Roland, but he out-manoeuvred it and drove it down. Meanwhile Lt Evans had closed with another Roland which he also drove down out of control. Two Fokkers which attacked Lt Evans nearly collided, and Lt Evans fired his remaining half-drum at an L.V.G. Lt McKay at a lower altitude, after disposing of a Roland which fell in a spinning nose dive, was attacked by a Fokker, and his engine having been hit he was unable to outmanoeuvre him. He therefore descended in a steep spiral. Lt Chapman observing this, dived to the rescue, and engaged the Fokker at 1,000 feet over High Wood. The hostile machine fell to the ground and burst into flames. Eventually all the hostile machines were either driven down or driven off east—except one Fokker which tried to manoeuvre on to Capt Chamberlain's tail. The De Havilland climbed in a spiral to attack, and the last of the hostile formation was driven off. This fight was witnessed by a pilot and an observer of 9 Sqn, who confirms the destruction of 3 hostile machines.

Casualties: Sqn 4, *2 Lt G. V. Randall, killed;* **25,** *2 Lt L. Richardson, wounded;* **70,** *2 Lt J. Manley, wounded;* **23,** *2 Lt D. S. C. Machaskie, missing; and 2 Lt C. I. Sandays-Thomas, missing.*

July 21st

Much successful co-operation with artillery was carried out, especially on the southern half of the line. Ninety-two targets were engaged with aeroplane observation and 25 with kite balloon. Pilots of 15 Sqn obtained several direct hits on emplacements, the ammunition in one continuing to explode for over half an hour. Some very successful work was also done by pilots of 9 Sqn.

A great deal of photography was done by all the squadrons, some 300 plates being exposed. Succeessful photographs were taken of Pozieres and of the German switch line east of it; also of the German third line.

The following points were attacked with bombs:

Epehy Station, by six R.E.s of 21 Sqn escorted by Martinsydes, fourteen 112-pound bombs were dropped. Two burst in the station and others on the line north of it and in the town.

Le Transloy, by a similar number of machines of the IXth Wing. Fifteen 112-pound bombs were dropped, causing fires to break out in the village.

Railway bridge over the canal at Aubigny au Bac—twenty-eight 112-pound bombs. The bridge was not hit, but the permanent way was considerably cut up.

Lt Philpott, 12 Sqn, descended to 200 feet to attack a train. One of his bombs failed to explode; the second missed the train by 10 yards.

An F.E. of 22 Sqn, pilot 2 Lt Bowen, observer, 2 Lt Mansell, on photographic duty, was attacked by a Roland, which came level and then dived and attacked under the tail of the F.E. The F.E. side-slipped until level with the Roland, and fired three drums at it at 40 yards. The

6—D.H.2—100 H.P. GNÔME MONOSOUPAPE ENGINE
With its pusher engine and nose-mounted Lewis gun the D.H.2 was the first single-seat fighter to outfight the Fokker monoplane. It equipped No. 24 Squadron which went to France as the first homogeneous single-seat fighter squadron on February 8, 1916. Two other D.H.2 squadrons followed,—No. 29 on March 25 and No. 32 on May 28.

Roland crashed near Leuze Wood. This fight was witnessed by a De Havilland of 22 Sqn.

An offensive patrol of five De Havillands, pilots: Capt Andrews, Lts Honnet, Pither, Glew and Sgt Piercey, with two F.E.s was attacked near Roisel by five Rolands and five Fokkers. Capt Andrews drove off the Fokker, and Lt Pither drove off another which tried to attack Capt Andrews, and afterwards drove off a Roland. Capt Andrews, seeing the F.E.s heavily engaged, dived to assist, attacking a Fokker which went down near Allaines, where Lt Pither attacked it with Buckingham bullets. The undercarriage was broken, and a group of men ran away when Lt Pither attacked. Lt Honnet attacked another Fokker, but had engine trouble and had to come home, as also had both F.E.s which were badly shot about. Major Hawker on another De Havilland then joined the patrol, which attacked four L.V.G.s, Maj Hawker, Capt Andrews and Sgt Piercey attacking several machines in turn. The hostile formation was broken up.

An offensive patrol in the same area consisting of 6 Martinsydes of 27 Sqn, pilots: Capt Boyd, Lt Usher and 2 Lts Willcox, Forbes, Joy and Letts, was attacked by a hostile biplane which was forced to dive vertically, but flattened out at 1,000 feet. Capt Boyd followed it all the way down. A Fokker met a similar fate at the hands of Lt Usher, Capt Boyd and 2 Lt Forbes, and a second one was attacked by Capt Boyd. Both his guns, however, jammed, but he continued to lead the patrol, which subsequently drove off another Fokker.

Lt Green, pilot, and 2 Lt Brown, observer, in a Morane Parasol of 3 Sqn, while on artillery patrol at 4,000 feet saw 8 hostile aircraft over Bapaume at 9,000 feet. They climbed to this height and were joined by an offensive patrol of 2 F.E.s of 22 Sqn and 3 De Havillands 24 Sqn. The enemy were joined by 5 L.V.G.s and 2 Fokkers. Our machines all attacked, the enemy being somewhat scattered. The Morane and 2 De Havillands dived on to one party, a Fokker falling from 7,000 feet and crashing near Warlencourt, and 2 others being forced to land in a field near Le Transloy. Another machine attacked by 2 Lt Evans in a De Havilland was seen to fall out of control into Combles. A third machine attacked by an F.E., pilot 2 Lt Hackwill, observer 2 Lt Parsons, crashed into a field near Beaulencourt. The fighting lasted over half an hour, and the remaining hostile machines eventually drew off in twos and threes; east and south-east.

This brings the total of hostile machines brought down on the 21st up to six, and at least 3 driven down damaged.

Lt J. L. Chalmers and Lt H. B. Cox of 9 Sqn, saw 50 men walking behind a hedge between Leuze Wood and Guillemont. They dived at them and scattered them with machine-gun fire.

Casualties: Sqn 21, *2 Lt R. W. Wilson Brown, missing;* **20,** *Cpl W. Moore, wounded;* **21,** *Capt J. O. Cooper, missing; Lt A. V. Oliver Jones, missing;* **60,** *Lt H. A. Browning Patterson, missing; and* **27,** *2 Lt F. G. Hogarth, wounded.*

July 22nd

Some useful contact patrol work was done by 3, 9 and 34 Sqns. Lt Lewis and Capt Watson of 3 Sqn identified the position of two Brigade and two Battalion Headquarters of the XVth Corps between 8 a.m. and 9 a.m.

A machine of 9 Sqn carried out a successful reconnaissance of the enemy's position about Falfemont Farm and Ginchy, also the enemy's third line at Comples, Morval, Guedecourt and Flers.

2 Lts Pearson and Blount of 34 Sqn, identified two Brigade and two Battalion Headquarters of the IIIrd Corps, and reconnoitred a new trench line made by the enemy.

Extract from the examination of a wounded officer prisoner of the 44th Foot Artillery Battalion:

> The prisoner openly expressed his admiration of our new infantry and what Lord Kitchener had done in forming the Armies, but especially he admired our aeroplanes. Their work must be splendid he said. It is rumoured that Boelcke had come to this front from Verdun.

22 July – 3 August, 1916

This communiqué reported some more first-class bombing by the Martinsyde Elephants of 27 Sqn.

The Rumplers mentioned on 29 July were probably of the CI two-seater class which had been in service for more than a year, although this was the first specific reference to the type. Accurate identification of the various enemy reconnaissance aircraft was difficult.

Klaxon horns 31 July were originally installed in contact patrol aircraft with the intention of signalling messages in Morse code to our ground troops. It was soon found that such messages could rarely be received above the general noise of battle, and the klaxons were used to signal 'AAA'—a request to the infantry to indicate their most advanced positions.

COMMUNIQUÉ NO. 45

June 22nd

The weather almost entirely prevented work before the evening. 4 Sqn, however, succeeded during the morning in carrying out 6 urgently needed registrations on trenches round Pozieres.

Some useful contact patrol work was done on the morning of the 22nd by 3, 9 and 34 Sqns. Lt Lewis and Capt Watson of 3 Sqn identified the position of 2 Brigade and 2nd Battalion Headquarters of the XVth Corps between 8 a.m. and 9 a.m.

A machine of 9 Sqn carried out a successful reconnaissance of the enemy's position about Falfemont Farm and Ginchy, also the enemy's third line at Combles, Morval, Gueudecourt and Flers.

2 Lts Pearson and Blount, of 34 Sqn, identified 2nd Brigade and 2nd Battalion Headquarters of the IIIrd Corps, and reconnoitred a new trench line made by the enemy.

June 23rd

Fine, but low clouds all day ⌔ Little artillery co-operation was possible ⌔ 38 targets were registered by aeroplanes and kite balloon observers.

Some good contact patrol work was carried out at very low altitudes by the Corps Squadrons of the 4th Brigade and XVth Wing much detailed information being furnished to the Corps concerned.

Casualty: Sqn 15, *2 Lt R. W. Settle, killed.*

July 24th

Clouds were again low throughout the day, making artillery work difficult. Seven hostile batteries reported active by a machine of 15 Sqn were all silenced by 60-pounders in 10 minutes.

Twice during the day machines of 4 Sqn went down to 700 feet and opened machine-gun fire on horsed transport on the roads leading east from Courcelette scattering the transport in both cases. Pilots: Capt Sutton and Capt Whittaker; observers: AM Pateman and Lt Brewis.

July 25th

In spite of the weather 34 targets were dealt with on the IVth and Reserve Army fronts by aeroplane observation and 8 by kite balloon observation, mostly on the IInd Army front. Machines had to fly at about 1,500 feet. German batteries were very active opposite the IInd Corps, and 4 Sqn did a great deal of counter-battery work with considerable success. At one time four machines were working simultaneously. Direct hits with 12-inch, 9.2-inch, 8-inch, and 6-inch Howitzers were obtained on five or more batteries, and ammunition was exploded in three places. On the IVth Army front direct hits were obtained on three targets, one with the French guns.

Casualties: Sqn 9, *2 Lt J. A. Brown, missing; 2 Lt F. Bowyer, missing; and 7, attached to* **4** *Sqn, 2 Lt E. D. Steytler and 2 Lt J. G. Robertson, missing.*

July 26th

Fine with low clouds until the late afternoon.

Flashes of many batteries were reported in the evening on the fronts of the Reserve and IVth Army, but very little ranging could be done owing to the haze. Only 8 targets were dealt with by aeroplane observation and one by kite balloon.

Capt Maltby and Cpl Wilson of 4 Sqn, carried out a successful shoot with the 67th Siege Battery obtaining 9 direct hits on a trench.

Capt Mackay of 15 Sqn, ranged the 62nd Siege Battery on a strong point, obtaining 9 direct hits. The clouds were very low, and he had to return eventually when they came down to 700 feet.

Hostile aircraft were quite inactive until the late evening. A reconnaissance to Cambrai saw some 15 and had a considerable amount of fighting.

Casualty: Sqn 60, *Lt Whitehead, wounded.*

July 27th

Weather continued unfavourable for observation until the evening.

Three offensive patrols were sent out in the evening by the IXth

Wing, two consisting of 4 De Havillands and one of 6 Morane Scouts. The latter had a fight with 7 L.V.G.s at least two of which were brought down, one in flames.

Three Martinsydes of 27 Sqn, escorted by four others, dropped three 112-pound bombs on Sailly-Saillisel in the evening, some of which appeared to burst in the village. Lt Forbes on one of the bombing machines engaged and drove off two hostile aircraft. Capt Boyd on one of the escort machines engaged several hostile machines, driving them off.

Hostile aircraft became active on his own side of the line in the evening.

Lt Cowan of 24 Sqn, dived at 5 hostile machines which were attacking a B.E. between Le Sars and Martinpuich. All the hostile machines were driven off.

July 28th

Although the weather cleared in the afternoon there was still a considerable amount of ground haze, which made observation difficult. Thirty-six targets were dealt with by aeroplane observation (20 of them by the XVth Wing), and 2 by kite balloons. 15 Sqn obtained 9 direct hits on batteries.

At 12.30 p.m. four Martinsyde Scouts, carrying between them two 112-pound bombs, and three 20-pound bombs started to attack the railway station at Mons where large quantities of ammunition have recently been reported. They were accompanied as far as St Amand by four Sopwiths. East of the line clouds were below 5,000 feet, which considerably favoured the expedition. The bombing machines arrived over Mons between 2 and 2.30 p.m. and all four machines descended to heights of from 2,000 to 4,000 feet to drop their bombs. The station was crowded with rolling stock, and the sheds, which had been reported by agents as containing ammunition, were attacked. The sheds were hit and several hits were observed among the rolling stock. The pilots remained for a considerable time flying round the target, and fires were seen to be started at 4 different points. It is probable that considerable damage was done. The expedition was practically unmolested by anti-aircraft guns or hostile aeroplanes, and all machines returned safely. The last pilot to leave Mons was fired at by A.A. guns a few times after he had got well away from the station.

Two of the machines returned home via the north of Douai, and two to the line to the south, and all four machines landed on the aerodrome Fienvillers within four minutes of one another. Pilots: Lts Darwin, Joy, Usher, and Willcox of 27 Sqn.

The railway bridge at Aubigny-au-Bac was attacked by 15 machines of the 3rd Brigade, thirty 112-pound bombs being dropped causing extensive damage to the permanent way in the vicinity of the bridge. The formation was subjected to very heavy A.A. fire and was attacked by four Fokkers. The latter were easily driven off, and the machines returned safely.

Further details of the 3rd Brigade bombing raid at Aubigny-au-Bac on the 28th state that the escort was first attacked by two Fokkers, one of which was driven down badly damaged. Several other hostile machines then came up and the fight became general, another Fokker being driven down emitting smoke. The formation was followed as far as the lines by 8 Fokkers and one Roland, all of which kept at a safe distance.

Four Martinsydes, each carrying two 112-pound bombs, attacked Le Transloy at 5.15 p.m. A fire was started in the centre of the village. One hostile machine was engaged and driven off. A formation of hostile machines seen over Bapaume made off at once.

The enemy's aircraft on the fronts of the Ist, IInd and IIIrd Armies has considerably decreased. During the day there were 14 combats.

The Morane Scouts of 60 Sqn engaged and brought down a L.V.G.

Offensive patrols from 32 and 60 Sqns were active over the enemy's lines throughout the day and had a considerable amount of fighting.

112-pound and 20-pound bombs were dropped at the railway junction north-east of Avion and on Wavrin by machines of 1st Brigade in the late evening of the 28th. Eight bombs fell on the railway and 13 in the village. The effects of the bombing could not be observed.

Casualties: Sqn 15, *Lt G. K. G. Kerr, wounded;* **23,** *Lt L. N. Gould, wounded;* **8,** *Lt H. H. Watkins, wounded;* **23,** *2 AM F. Collinson, wounded; and* **32,** *2 Lt E. L. Lewis, wounded.*

July 29th

Much successful artillery work was done, 83 targets being engaged with aeroplane reconnaissance and 27 with kite balloons.

15 Sqn ranged 12-inch Howitzers on a battery of two 5.9 Howitzers which was destroyed.

4 Sqn ranged 9.2-inch Howitzers on to another battery, destroying one emplacement and causing explosions which lasted for an hour.

9 Sqn ranged a Siege Battery on to a dump, causing a great deal of damage.

Many other batteries were successfully ranged on all fronts, ammunition being exploded in several instances.

On the 29th the 1st Brigade bombed the village of Fournes and Provin Aerodrome, and also various other points opposite the Ist Army front. Thirteen bombs were seen to burst in Fournes and the aerodrome was hit in several places.

At 1.30 p.m. on the 29th, Douai aerodrome was bombed by 16

machines, each carrying two 112-pound bombs. One bomb was seen to fall on a machine on the ground at the aerodrome. Two sheds were hit and extensive damage done. The remaining bombs fell on the aerodrome. No hostile machines interfered but A.A. fire was heavy.

In the early afternoon four Martinsydes with 112-pound bombs escorted by 4 Sopwiths attacked Hervilly aerodrome, several bombs dropping on the aerodrome. Capt Boyd was attacked by a hostile machine which he at first mistook for a Sopwith. His side gun jammed but he got above the enemy and fired a drum from his top gun. The enemy side-slipped and dived. Capt Boyd lost sight of him as he was watching another machine but Lt Joy saw the machine fall out of control until within 2,000 feet of the ground.

At 6 p.m. 11 Martinsydes, escorted by four De Havillands, dropped 112-pound bombs on Beaulencourt and Thilloy, most of the bombs falling on or near these villages. On the return journey Lts Darwin, Usher and Smith saw 5 Rolands flying up the Peronne–Bapaume Road. They attacked and broke up their formation scattering them in all directions.

Some 15 hostile aircraft were working on the Ist Army front, four being engaged.

2 Lt MacDonald, pilot, and 2 Lt Arkle, observer, on an F.E. of 18 Sqn, had a fight at close quarters with a hostile machine over Provin about 4.30 p.m. The observer appeared to be shot and the German machine broke off the fight. The F.E. was hit in several places.

On the IInd Army front 7 hostile aircraft were seen.

Capt Read, pilot, and 2 Lt Scott, observer, on an F.E. of 20 Sqn, attacked two Rumplers over Zandvoorde, firing one drum at one of them, while banking, at a range of 20 yards. The right wing of the enemy machine was shot away, and it fell to the ground near Zandvoorde. There was little activity on the IIrd Army front, and no decisive combats. On the Reserve and IVth Army fronts there was much activity which increased towards the evening. There were many combats.

Four De Havillands of 24 Sqn, on offensive patrol with some F.E.s between 1 p.m. and 2 p.m. had a great deal of fighting round about Bapaume. Later, four hostile machines were encountered over Morval. One, a Roland, was attacked by Lt Cowan at very short range, and went down in a nose dive with its engine full on. The remainder were driven off eastwards. Subsequently, the machine in a badly crashed condition was reported to be on the ground just west of Bois des Vaux.

At 7.10 a Morane Parasol of 3 Sqn, pilot, 2 Lt Lynch, observer, 2 Lt Rickards, assisted by two De Havillands, engaged four machines east of Ginchy. The hostile formation was broken up, and the Morane drove down an Aviatik in a damaged condition, which is believed to have crashed. Subsequently, the Morane engaged and drove off a small single-seater scout.

On the evening of the 29th Wavrin was bombed by machines of the 1st Brigade, several bursting in the houses, and one in the station. Twenty-two 112-pound bombs were dropped by machines of the 2nd Brigade on Courtrai Station. Many of them fell on the buildings and sidings. One building in the station was set on fire and it is presumed to have been an oil store, from the way it blazed.

Lts E. G. A. Brown and W. S. Mansell on an F.E. of 22 Sqn, attacked 50 infantry marching on the Albert–Bapaume road with machine-gun fire, scattering them in all directions.

July 30th

Much successful artillery work was done, 84 targets being dealt with by aeroplane observation and 28 by kite balloons.

A heavy battery of the Ist Army was successfully ranged on transport moving along a road.

On the Reserve Army front 6 or 8 gun-pits were destroyed and two ammunition dumps exploded.

On the IVth Army front 14 batteries were successfully engaged, two emplacements being destroyed and two explosions caused. Troops reported by aeroplanes marching along roads were engaged and scattered on two occasions.

Epehy junction was attacked about 2 p.m. by 8 Martinsydes, 4 carrying two 112-pound bombs each. These were successfully dropped in the station and on the stores. The formation was heavily attacked by hostile aircraft throughout the raid. Two machines are missing. About the same time thirty 112-pound bombs were dropped by machines of the 3rd Brigade on the railway junction at St Leger. One pilot dropped a bomb on a moving train causing it to blow up. Another explosion was observed in a dump, the railway lines being severely damaged. All machines returned safely. At 3 p.m. the railway at Henin Lietard was bombed by the 1st Brigade with one 112-pound bomb and twenty-four 20-pound bombs were dropped on Ascq, near Lille, by the 1st Brigade. Sheds near the railway were hit and a very large explosion resulted which threw up a dense cloud of smoke. The explosion was heard and felt by machines flying 9,000 feet above it. Fires were burning when our aeroplanes left. One hostile machine was seen and attacked with an indecisive result.

Seven Martinsydes, escorted by 4 Sopwiths, all of the IXth Wing, started to bomb Marcoing Station at 6 p.m. The mist was very thick and the machines failed to reach their objective. One had a forced landing south of Amiens, the remainder returned safely.

About the same time machines of the 3rd Brigade bombed the villages of Rocquigny, Villiers-au-Flos and Martinpuich. Sheds and houses were set on fire in Rocquigny and at Martinpuich a very large explosion was caused, the smoke rising to 8,000 feet and a fire started which burned for some hours.

There was practically no activity of the enemy on the fronts of the Ist, IInd and IIIrd Armies. On the Reserve and IVth Army fronts they were very active, a great many machines being seen and fighting being continuous from midday onwards, principally south-west, south and south-east of Bapaume. Some 25 machines in all appear to have crossed short distances over our lines, but the work of our Corps machines was not interfered with.

The enemy dropped one bomb in the Caterpillar Valley, wounding a few men. No decisive results of the fighting were seen, as the fights followed one another so quickly. The fighting was all in our favour, however, and the enemy formations in every case were dispersed and driven off. Two of his machines are believed to have been destroyed, but there is no confirmation. Several were driven down.

The following account has been received from Lt R. H. C. Usher, 27 Sqn, wounded on the 30th July:

> After dropping bombs on Marcoing, I turned round and almost ran into an L.V.G. I fired a drum at him and he passed underneath me. I saw a Sopwith engage him, and while changing drums, I was attacked in front by a Roland. I fired a drum at this machine, and hearing a machine-gun behind me, looked round and saw three Rolands on my tail. I was hit in the leg almost immediately, but managed to give the hostile machines a drum from my side gun, on which they went away. My engine started spluttering, and I saw a hole in my petrol tank. My engine then stopped and I then started gliding down, thinking I should have to land. The petrol was flowing over my left leg, but I managed to put my left knee over the hole in the petrol tank. It occurred to me that by pumping I might be able to get a little pressure. When I was only 200 feet up my engine started. I was then about 15 miles from my lines. I kept pumping hard and just managed to keep enough engine to keep going, though I thought I should have to land three or four times. Once I had actually flattened out to land when the engine picked up just in time, and I managed to cover the 15 miles to the lines at an average height of only 50 feet. I had lost myself, and was so low that I could see very little of the country. So seeing a French biplane flying low, I followed it and eventually landed at Moreuil aerodrome, crashing the machine on landing. I was feeling very weak as I had lost a lot of blood, and was exhausted by having to pump for so long. During the time I was flying so low, I was subjected to a lot of rifle and machine gun fire.

Casualties: Sqn 4, *2 Lt A. Hughes, wounded by A.A. fire;* **60,** *Lt L. E. Whitehead, wounded; Lt W. E. G. Bryant, wounded; Capt L. G. Charles,* *missing; Lt G. Williams, missing; 27, Lt E. R. Farmer, missing; Lt L. N. Graham, missing; and Lt R. H. C. Usher, wounded.*

July 31st

Eighty targets were registered by aeroplane observation but only 5 by kite balloons owing to the haze.

Successful results were obtained on the Reserve and IVth Army fronts, many emplacements being hit direct and ammunition exploded on 9 different occasions. The emplacements of one battery on the IVth Army front appeared to be practically destroyed.

Some good contact patrol work was done by Squadrons of the XVth Wing and 4th Brigade.

Co-operation with the infantry is improving daily. The Klaxon horn appears to provide a successful method of asking the infantry to light their flares and the latter are being more freely used. Detailed reports of the enemy work were furnished by all the squadrons although machines had to fly as low as 900 feet on account of the haze.

Bombs were dropped on Martinpuich at 10.30 a.m. by machines of the 3rd Brigade. The results could not be seen owing to the mist but the village was still burning from the attack of the previous night. Machines of the 2nd Brigade dropped thirty-eight 112-pound bombs on the canal, wharf, barges and dump at Wervicq. One barge was set on fire, bombs fell on motor vehicles, one on the landing stage and one in hutments on the bank. All our machines returned safely. In addition sixteen 112-pound bombs and sixty-four 20-pound were dropped by machines of the 1st Brigade on trenches, houses, batteries, etc., on the Ist Army front. Martinsydes of 27 Sqn attempted to carry out a second raid on Gouzeaucourt Station at 6 p.m. but failed to find their objective, owing to the thick haze.

Other bombing raids were carried out by the 1st and 2nd Brigades against Wavrin, Beauchamps and the Sugar factory at Marquillies.

27 Sqn attacked the stations at Marcoing and Cambrai. Bombs were seen to burst in each station.

There was little hostile aircraft activity again on the fronts of the Ist, IInd and IIIrd Armies. Two crossed the lines on the Ist Army front. Only four were seen in all, and there was one indecisive combat. On the IInd Army front there were 3 combats, all indecisive. On the IIIrd Army fronts two of our machines on artillery work had fights, first with 4 Fokkers and then with a single machine on patrol. In the first combat a B.E. fired a drum at one of the enemy machines which was last seen diving out of control. The remaining combats were indecisive.

Activity was greatest on the Reserve and IVth Army fronts during the middle of the day and there were 8 combats, mostly consisting of several separate fights. One Fokker was engaged by Lt Saundby near Roisel. Lt Saundby first attacked a Roland, but finding a Fokker behind him, turned and manoeuvred under his tail. He fired one drum at very close range and the Fokker nose dived and went down in a spin, the machine being seen still spinning near the ground by another pilot.

Another machine was driven down near Manancourt emitting smoke. Several other machines are thought to have been damaged.

Casualties: Sqn 18, *Capt J. Callingham, slightly wounded;* **24,** *2 Lt R. H. M. Saunders, slightly wounded;* **22,** *2 Lt C. G. Riley, severely wounded; and Pte L. C. Welford, wounded.*

1–9 August, 1916

The long-distance raid on Zeppelin sheds at Brussels on 2 August, with various diversionary attacks to split the enemy defences, represented one of the most carefully planned and intricate bombing operations attempted to date. The successful rendezvous by the 20 Sqn F.E.2ds, escorting for part of the return journey, was a tribute to good flight planning and accurate navigation by all concerned.

24 Sqn's vigorous battle on 3 August was clearly a victory—although no enemy aircraft were confirmed as destroyed—and was one of the most protracted 'dog fights' reported to date.

A German prisoner testifies to the havoc caused by the B.E.2cs' bombing attack on St Quentin on 1 July.

COMMUNIQUÉ NO. 46

August 1st

Very successful artillery co-operation was carried out, especially on the IVth and Reserve Army fronts. Eight-seven targets were dealt with by aeroplane observation and five by kite balloons. The haze made observation from the latter very difficult. Much damage was done to the enemy's emplacements by our artillery, ranged by machines of the XVth Wing and 4th Brigade, co-operation by the XVth Wing being particularly successful. Several explosions were caused among the ammunition, one a very large one.

The following bombing raids were carried out on the night of July 31st/August 1st: 1st Brigade attacked a cinematograph shed at Provin, many bombs were seen to fall near the target.

The 3rd Brigade on the 31st dropped thirty-two 112-pound bombs on the dump at Corons; the railway, a bridge over the road, and some of the station buildings being hit. The same Brigade, at 1.30 p.m. on the 1st dropped thirty 112-pound bombs on the aerodrome at Queant. One shed was set on fire and another damaged. The railway station which adjoins the aerodrome was also hit.

Machines of the 1st Brigade attacked the aerodrome at Ancoisne and hit 2 sheds.

Sixteen machines of the 2nd Brigade with an escort of 11 machines attacked the station sidings and dumps at Ledeghem, causing much damage and starting 3 fires.

Hostile aircraft were much less active on all fronts. On the Ist Army front only 10 were seen, and there was only one combat. Two crossed about a mile on our side of the line, but quickly returned. On the IInd Army front there was no activity except during the raid on Ledeghem Station when enemy machines came up in force. Altogether there were 7 combats, in one of which a Fokker was brought down by an F.E. of 20 Sqn—pilot, 2 Lt Dabbs, observer, 1 AM Stewart. The Fokker crashed into a ploughed field south of Poelcappelle.

On the IIIrd Army front a few single machines were seen patrolling behind their own lines. Five were encountered, one of which was seen to dive very steeply after a fight with an F.E. of 11 Sqn—pilot, Sgt Thompson, observer, Sgt Clarkson. It was not, however, definitely seen to be out of control.

On the IVth and Reserve Army fronts there was slightly more activity during the morning, but it became notably less in the evening. Altogether there were 8 indecisive combats. In two cases a few machines crossed our lines for a short distance, but our artillery and other machines working on the lines suffered no interference.

During 8 offensive patrols carried out by squadrons of the IXth Wing, no combats occurred and only 5 hostile machines were seen.

2 Lt Vinson and Capt Murray attacked some transport on the Beaumont–Hamel road with machine-gun fire and dispersed it.

An F.E. of 22 Sqn attempted a similar attack on some limbers near Courcellette, but the gun jammed after firing half a drum.

Casualties: Sqn 15, *Lt S. Stretton, wounded by A.A. fire;* **25,** *2 Lt J. B. Hinchcliffe, wounded by A.A. fire; and* **22,** *Capt W. A. Summers and Flt Sgt N. C. Clarkson, missing believed killed by A.A. fire.*

August 2nd

Eighty-six targets were engaged with aeroplane observation and 8 with kite balloon with very successful results.

Twelve batteries were successfully dealt with by the Reserve Army artillery observed by machines of the XVth Wing, and 7 by the IVth Army and 4th Brigade.

Direct hits were seen on 9 gun emplacements, and explosions were caused in nine cases, one being very extensive.

Some very successful contact patrol work was done by Capt Maltby of 15 Sqn.

Six machine-gun emplacements were located, and a detailed report of new trenches and wire was rendered.

At 11.30 a.m. six B.E.s and three Morane biplanes of the 2nd Brigade started to attack the Zeppelin sheds at Brussels. One B.E. failed to get its height. The machines came under heavy A.A. fire at Ledeghem, and one machine, apparently hit, turned west and is missing. Pilot, Capt Snook of 5 Sqn. Two machines had been detailed to each of the sheds reported, but only two sheds could be found. No direct hits were observed on the sheds, but four 112-pound dropped on Etterbeek fell within 10 to 50 yards of their objective. The bombs on Evere fell within 100 yards north-east of the shed. A.A. gun fire was opened on our machines during the attack (the machines having gone to 1,000 feet to drop their bombs) but was inaccurate. One hostile machine was seen but did not attack. The B.E.s met, after dropping their bombs, at the appointed rallying place at Strytham cross roads covered by their escort, and started on the return journey. Between Audenarde and Courtrai they met an escorting patrol of five F.E.s within five minutes of the appointed time, and the 12 machines returned over the lines safely. The whole journey took five hours.

The 2nd Brigade carried out a second bombing raid against Courtrai station with 13 machines of the IInd Wing, with a view to assisting the return of the Brussels raid. The escort reports 3 hits on rolling stock, 2 on buildings close to the station, 4 bombs on the railway yard, and one on the main line. Two columns of smoke were seen ascending from the railway sidings. All machines returned safely. The A.A. fire was very heavy during this attack, and a considerable number of hostile aircraft were engaged by the escort.

The R.N.A.S. co-operated in the day's work by attacking the aerodrome at St Denis Westrem, and the ammunition dump at Meirelbeke, both of which were bombed with excellent results.

The 3rd Brigade carried out 3 bomb raids, the first on Bapaume station where eight 20-pound bombs were dropped, 2 of which fell on the railway south of Bihucourt.

In the second raid thirty 112-pound bombs were dropped on Brayelle aerodrome. A large explosion occurred, and one shed was set on fire, many bombs falling on the aerodrome.

There were no decisive combats. The enemy confined his activities to his own side of the line, and our Corps machines were hardly interrupted at all.

During a photographic reconnaissance on the evening of the 2nd, machines of 23 Sqn encountered four Fokkers over Douai. In the resulting fight, one Fokker was brought down by two of the F.E.s' pilots—Capt Watson and Lt Gopsill, observers—2 Lt Blake and Lt Osmaston. The Fokker was seen to turn on its back and fall quite out of control. A second Fokker was forced down under control.

There were 9 other indecisive combats on this front.

Casualties: Sqn 20, *2 Lt D. H. Lascelles, wounded by A.A. fire;* **60,** *Sgt A. Walker and 2 Lt L. L. Clark, missing, believed killed by A.A. fire; Lt J. A. N. Ormsby and 2 Lt H. J. Newton, missing—A.A. fire; and* **5,** *Capt C. W. Snook, missing—A.A. fire.*

The following is an extract from the examination of a German prisoner, and evidently refers to the bombing of St Quentin Railway Station by machines of the 3rd Brigade on July 1st. Neither of the four machines concerned returned:

> At the end of the month of June, the 22nd Reserve Division was at rest in the neighbourhood of St. Quentin. On the 1st July the Division was warned to proceed to the Somme front.
>
> About 3.30 p.m. the 1st Battn. of the 71st Res. Regt and 11th Res. Jaeger Battalion were at St. Quentin Station ready to entrain, arms were piled, and the regimental transport was being loaded on to the train. At this moment English aeroplanes appeared overhead and threw bombs. One bomb fell on a shed which was filled with ammunition and caused a big explosion. There were 200 wagons of ammunition in the station at the time; 60 of them caught fire and exploded; the remainder were saved with difficulty. The train allotted to the transport of the troops and all the equipment which they had placed on the platform were destroyed by fire.
>
> The men were panic stricken and fled in every direction. 100 men of the 71st Reserve and 80 men of the Reserve Jaeger Battalion were either killed or wounded. It was not till several hours later that it was possible to collect the battalion of the 71st Reserve Regiment; it was then sent back to its billets at Etriellers. The next day it was entrained at another station and sent to Ham, where it was re-equipped. From there it was sent to Peronne and placed in the Reserve near the Peronne-Eterpigny Road.

August 3rd

One hundred and fourteen targets were dealt with with aeroplane observation and 13 by kite balloons, the haze interfering considerably with the latter. Sixteen barriers were successfully engaged on the IVth Army front, and 22 on the Reserve Army front, gun pits being destroyed, and ammunition blown up.

An explosion in a battery in Courcelette caused smoke to rise to 2,000 feet.

At 11.30 a.m. 8 Martinsydes escorted by four Sopwiths, all of the IXth Wing, left Fienvillers to attack the Ronet Sidings at Namur and the airship sheds at Cognelee. Three of the Martinsydes dropped out for various reasons before crossing the lines, but the other five reached their objective, escorted as far as Conde sur l'Escaut by the Sopwiths. At the Ronet sidings one bomb fell in the engine shed, one in the power house, one on the main line, destroying a house close by, two on rolling stock in the sidings, and one in a field just to the south of the sidings. The machines came down to 800 feet to drop their bombs, and were able to see men running about wildly in all directions. Of the machines that went to the airship shed, one is missing, pilot, Lt Turner; the other came down and released both his bombs. The shed he had been ordered to attack was seen to be empty through the open door. He therefore attacked another, the corner of which he hit with one bomb. Seeing a company of infantry in the open in front of the shed, he attacked it with machine gun fire, causing some casualties. This pilot saw the missing machine over its objective, the third airship shed. Only one hostile aircraft was seen during the raid. There was no anti-aircraft fire at the railway sidings, but a good deal at the airships sheds.

Machines of the 1st Brigade dropped 106 bombs, mostly 20-pound on the evening of the 2nd and during the 3rd on Mericourt, Don, the aerodrome at Tourmignies, and various objectives in front of the Ist Army. Very few hostile aircraft were seen, and no casualties were sustained. The railway line was hit at Mericourt and at Don, and the station at Rouvroy. The aerodrome at Tourmignies, and the château and houses on the edge of it were also hit. One aeroplane was seen on the aerodrome.

Machines of the 3rd Brigade dropped sixteen 112-pound bombs and 48 incendiary bombs in the Bois de Loupart on the evening of the 2nd, which were seen to burst in the wood. Twenty-eight 112-pound bombs were dropped over Grevillers about midday. Many appeared to hit the target, but the haze rendered observation difficult.

Much successful photography was accomplished, over 200 plates being exposed. On the late evening of the 2nd a photographic reconnaissance by 23 Sqn encountered 4 hostile machines.

An F.E. of 20 Sqn, pilot, Capt Maxwell, observer, AM Stewart, while carrying out a height test, sighted a hostile machine over Ypres and attacked it. The fight lasted 10 minutes the F.E. firing 12½ drums of ammunition. The hostile machine was driven down from 11,000 to 5,000 feet, when it appeared to be out of control, and finally crashed to earth in a field near Gheluwe. Another F.E. of the same Squadron, pilot, 2 Lt Reid, observer, Capt Dixon Spain, attacked two hostile machines, an Aviatik and a Fokker over Hollebeke. The Fokker was first attacked and dived underneath the F.E. The Aviatik was then attacked and driven off. The Fokker was then attacked again and was last seen in a spinning nose dive.

On the IVth Army front four De Havillands of 24 Sqn—pilots, Capt Andrews, Lts Cowan, Glew, and Sgt Piercey, encountered 7 hostile machines near Flers. Capt Andrews fired a double drum into one at 100 yards range, which disappeared in a nose dive, but was unable to follow it owing to the proximity of the other machines. The other pilots also attacked, and the hostile machines scattered east. Lt Cowan drove one down near Sailly, and pursued two others driving them down at Velu aerodrome. Returning, he encountered another machine at which he fired several bursts from above and behind. The machine ceased fire and began to manoeuvre wildly. Lt Cowan saw the observer hanging head downwards over the side of the fuselage. After he had fired a few more rounds it commenced to spiral, gradually descending more steeply and faster. Lt Cowan did not see it reach the ground as he was engaged with another machine which he also drove away east.

Meanwhile Capt Andrews and Lt Glew pursued the remaining machines towards Manancourt. When over Sailly Lt Glew engaged one machine, firing a drum at close range. The machine turned on its side and went down in a nose dive. Two hostile machines had meanwhile attacked Lt Glew from behind. Capt Andrews fired a double drum into one of them at 20 yards, and saw the observer collapse into the cockpit. Being himself attacked, he was unable to watch what became of the machine, which, however broke off the fight.

Sgt Piercey engaged another hostile machine, which was high above the remainder, preventing it from attacking our machines.

The fight lasted altogether 45 minutes.

3rd Brigade attacked Oppy at 9 p.m. on the 3rd instant. Eight 112-pound bombs were dropped and a fire was started in the village.

Casualties: Sqn 27, *Lt J. C. Turner, missing;* **25,** *2 Lt K. Mathewson and Pte E. M. Dostresay, missing; and* **60,** *2 Lt C. A. Ridley, missing.*

August 4th

Ninety-one targets were registered by aeroplane observers and 45 by kite balloon observers.

On the IVth Army front 24 targets were registered and 9 hostile batteries were successfully engaged. All four emplacements of one battery on this front were hit.

On the Reserve Army front 10 points were registered and much damage done to trenches, in particular direct hits being obtained along a length of 50 yards of trench north-west of Pozieres. Ten gun pits were destroyed and 7 others considerably damaged. Three ammunition pits were blown up and hits scored on three other battery positions. Many hostile batteries were engaged and silenced. Forty-one active hostile batteries were reported on the Reserve Army front, of which 33 were in the IInd Corps area.

There was considerable activity on the fronts of the Reserve and IVth Armies, on other fronts practically none.

There were no decisive combats. One L.V.G. was driven down damaged.

August 5th

On the 1st and 2nd Brigades' fronts some successful co-operation was accomplished. Lt F. R. Hardie and Lt F. G. Pearson working with the 136th Heavies engaged a hostile battery of four guns firing on our trenches. Eighteen O.K.s were obtained and an ammunition store was set on fire. The ammunition continued to explode for over an hour. The explosions were confirmed by 10 K.B.S. observers and forward Artillery Observing Officers.

3rd Brigade successfully engaged 21 targets and obtained several direct hits on gun emplacements.

On the front of the 4th Brigade 38 targets including 13 batteries were dealt with successfully. Many of them were silenced. Several pits were destroyed and ammunition was exploded at several batteries and dumps. The XVth Wing carried out 26 shoots on gun positions. Six gun pits were destroyed and 9 damaged. Four others were hit by 60-pounders. Five ammunition pits were blown up and four hits with shrapnel were scored on A.A. guns. Active hostile batteries engaged were quickly silenced.

In the course of the day 63 active batteries were reported. Altogether 115 targets were successfully ranged on.

Opposite the IIIrd and Reserve Army fronts several indecisive combats took place between patrols east of the line. During a bombing raid carried out by the XVth Wing against Grevillers station our machines were attacked by several L.V.G.s and Fokkers and the escort was fighting continually. One of our machines was shot down.

On other fronts there was little or no activity.

3rd Brigade repeated their attack on the village of Oppy with six 112-pound bombs which burst well in the village.

At 6 p.m. the same Brigade dropped twenty 112-pound bombs in Croisilles causing a fire to break out in the town.

The XVth Wing attacked the railway station at Grevillers with fourteen 112-pound bombs.

The balloon of 7 Section was fired on and hit by hostile artillery. The case of the shell and several bullets pierced the envelope and so rapid was the escape of gas that the occupants Capt Parker (Commanding the Section) and Lt Beaton had to make parachute descents. They both landed unharmed. This incident occurred about 11 o'clock when a battery was being ranged. By 6 p.m. a new balloon had been inflated and Capt Parker ascended and completed the registration.

Casualties: Sqn 40, *2 Lt H. C. Davis, killed—accident;* **18,** *2 Lt E. Y. Maclean, wounded; and* **4,** *Lt H. W. Thomas, missing.*

6–13 August, 1916

Air fighting continued at a fairly high intensity, with the R.F.C. still maintaining a clear superiority.

On 6 and 8 August, German bombing formations were completely routed before they could cross into Allied territory.

The engagement of 8 August showed that despite its generally good performance for the period, the Roland CIII was a very ineffectual aircraft in combat.

The use by troops of mirrors and sheets of tin to indicate their position to contact patrol aircraft (8 August) was soon discontinued, as it also gave away their positions to the enemy.

Buckingham bullets (9 August) were phosphorous incendiaries, primarily for use against balloons and airships.

COMMUNIQUÉ NO. 47

August 6th

Some successful registration was done by the 1st and 2nd Brigades, 10 targets being registered by the 1st and 11 by the 2nd.

On the Reserve Army front 20 points were registered, the railway line at Miraumont was much damaged by 15-inch Howitzers, and much successful trench bombardment was completed—23 shoots on gun positions, 9 of which were active during part of the time. Ten gun pits were destroyed, 5 badly damaged, and two others badly damaged by 60-pounders. Three ammunition pits were blown up and hits scored on 7 other battery positions. On the IVth Army front 10 hostile batteries were successfully engaged.

On the fronts of the Ist, IInd and IIIrd Armies there was little activity. Five indecisive combats took place.

The enemy continued his aerial activities on the fronts of the Reserve and IVth Armies, but in the majority of cases well inside his own lines. Corps machines were not interfered with by hostile aircraft. 2 Lt W. V. Sherwood in a De Havilland Scout of 29 Sqn, when on patrol duty at a height of 13,000 feet observed a hostile machine at about 9,000 feet in the neighbourhood of Poperinghe. He dived at it and chased it towards the lines, where he met and attacked a second L.V.G. This machine dived steeply and stopped firing. It was lost sight of in the clouds. The

Adjutant of the 24th Artillery Group and three independent witnesses of 29 Sqn who saw the fight state that they followed the falling machine as far as the bottom layer of clouds.

Lt T. A. Oliver in a Nieuport Scout of 1 Sqn attacked a hostile machine over Kemmel which in appearance was very much like a Martinsyde. The Nieuport closed to within 150 feet of the hostile machine and fired two drums under the tail. The engine of the hostile machine was seen to stop, and it dived steeply. Five drums in all were fired at the German, whose machine was followed down to 3,000 feet with its propeller stopped. It is believed that the observer of this machine was also hit.

At 9.15 a.m. Lt Evans of 24 Sqn attacked a L.V.G. (fast type) which with other machines was patrolling the Bapaume–Peronne road. Diving, he fired a drum at 75 yards range. The observer was apparently hit, or his gun jammed, as he ceased to fire and waved his arm. Lt Evans changed drums and signalled to the hostile machine to come west. This was ignored, so Lt Evans again opened fire. The hostile machine at once nose dived, turned over and over, and finally crashed east of Bois des Vaux.

Later Lt Tidmarsh and Lt Manfield made several attacks on H.A. in the same vicinity, but owing to stoppages in the guns, were unable to effect any result.

At 6 p.m. an offensive patrol of 70 Sqn, led by Capt Sanday, with Lt Busk as observer, saw an Albatros near Gouzeaucourt. Capt Sanday dived at the hostile machine, which went down towards an aerodrome at Hervilliers. At about 6.45 the patrol encountered ten German machines carrying bombs east of Bapaume and flying due west. The Sopwiths got between them and our lines and attacked. A hot fight ensued, the German machines turning northwards and finally eastwards without ever having succeeded in crossing the line. Capt Sanday and Lt Mase having fired all their ammunition, returned for more. 2 Lt Blain and 2 Lt Griffiths continued the pursuit of the German machines until one of them fired a red light, and all were seen to land. In the course of the engagement one machine was seen to land outside an aerodrome and it is believed that a second did likewise. The hostile bomb raid was completely frustrated.

An offensive patrol of 27 Sqn in the vicinity of Epehy saw six L.V.G.s, all very low. A Fokker attacked their formation from above, and was engaged by all four Martinsydes and driven down out of control. He disappeared into a cloud, so his ultimate fate was not seen. One of our machines suffered slight damage.

The Bois de St Pierre Vaast was attacked by 27 Sqn with success. The majority of the bombs fell in the north-west corner of the wood, where billets had been reported by prisoners. The 3rd Brigade carried out a further bombing raid against Oppy, dropping six 112-pound bombs. They also attacked Grevillers, where over 2 tons of bombs were dropped and very considerable damage done.

Machines of the 3rd Brigade dropped thirty-eight 112-pound bombs on Grevillers with much success on the evening of the 6th, and during the night machines of 13 Sqn dropped 24 incendiary bombs on Oppy.

Casualties: Sqn 29, *Capt E. R. Baisey, wounded; and* **22,** *2 Lt W. F. Mansell, wounded.*

August 7th

Bethune was shelled about midday by a gun from the neighbourhood of Santes. The flashes of the gun were roughly located by Capt Rodwell and 2 Lt Bickerton of 10 Sqn, and later accurately located by 2 Lt O'Hara Wood and 2 Lt Parsons of 10 Sqn. The position was subsequently bombed with twenty-two 112-pound bombs and twenty 20-pound bombs. An explosion was caused in the vicinity of a gun position. Lt McArthur and Lt Carden of 12 Sqn silenced a hostile anti-aircraft battery.

On the IVth Army front 14 hostile batteries were successfully engaged. One pit was seen to be destroyed and explosions caused in two ammunition pits.

On the Reserve Army front there were 16 shoots on gun positions; nine direct hits on pits, and five others were damaged. Three ammunition pits were blown up. Forty-seven active batteries were reported. A party of 100 men on the road were dispersed and a wagon destroyed. In all 94 targets were engaged with aerial observation and 72 with kite balloons, the bulk of the latter being on the IIIrd and IVth Army fronts.

Hostile aircraft were not very active and no decisive combats were recorded.

Lt Yates on a De Havilland of 24 Sqn met 5 hostile aircraft over Clery. He attacked two which were flying very high above the remainder. The observer of one ceased firing and collapsed into his cockpit.

An offensive patrol of 19 and 27 Sqns engaged and drove down in a damaged condition a Fokker and a Roland.

Casualties: Sqn 70, *2 Lt E. W. Blain and 2 Lt Griffiths, missing.*

August 8th

The 2nd Brigade carried out a reconnaissance via Menin, Ingelmunster and Deynze to Ghent between 6.10 and 7.20 a.m. Railway activity was considerable, especially about Ghent, where there were 25 trains with steam up, and rolling stock for 30 trains. Infantry, estimated at about two battalions, were seen marching south-east at Machelen, and others, estimated at 3 battalions, assembling at Deynze.

Much successful artillery co-operation was accomplished; 102 targets were dealt with by aeroplane observation and 58 by kite balloon.

Twenty-six hostile batteries were engaged on the IVth Army front, direct hits being scored on six pits and 16 explosions of ammunition caused.

On the Reserve Army front seven gun pits were hit, four others damaged, and three explosions caused in ammunition pits. In addition one battery position was completely destroyed, all four gun pits being blown up, and several lots of ammunition exploded. A direct hit was obtained on the bridge at Miraumont with 12-inch Howitzers.

5 K.B. ranged five heavy batteries, a round from one of which caused a large explosion.

Two successful contact patrols were carried out by machines of 9 Sqn during the fighting round Guillemont. The first patrol was out from 8.40 to 11.5 a.m. Pilot, Lt Anderson, observer, Lt Begg, obtained contact with Battalion H.Q. and obtained the position of our troops by means of mirrors and sheets of tin on men's backs. A map was dropped to Corps H.Q. giving the position of our troops.

The second patrol, pilot, Lt Collier, observer, Lt Begg, was sent out to clear up the position at 3.25 p.m. Messages were sent to Battalion H.Q. by lamp and answers received by panel. Three Battalion H.Q. were located.

The 1st Brigade attacked Pont-a-Vendin at 1.30 p.m. A barge in the Canal was hit, and two bombs fell on the railway line close to the bridge.

During the course of patrols, machines of this Brigade attacked various objectives, among them an A.A. battery which was hit. The 2nd Brigade dropped sixteen 112-pound bombs on the sidings and railway station at Roulers. Many of the bombs were seen to explode among the rolling stock in the sidings.

Machines of the 3rd Brigade carried out two bomb raids on the station and sidings at Boyelles, one about 1 p.m. on the 7th, the other about 1 p.m. on the 8th. Twenty-six 112-pound bombs were dropped on the first mentioned, falling on the dump outside the station and on the railway and station buildings. In the second raid thirty-two 112-pound bombs were dropped, and a train in the siding was set on fire. The railway appeared to be badly damaged, and other fires were started.

27 Sqn dropped forty-three 20-pound bombs on Gouzeaucourt Station about midday. Some 15 were seen to hit the station and sidings, in which there was a train and some rolling stock.

Hostile aircraft were more active. On the Ist Army front about 15 were seen. Six Roland biplanes were encountered over Bethune about 6.40 a.m. by three F.E.s of 25 Sqn. The F.E.s attacked, Lt Collinson on one of them driving the two highest Rolands east. They dropped their bombs over their own lines. An empty drum bounced out of the nacelle and broke the propeller, and Lt Collinson had to return home. Lt Woollven drove off another Roland, which also dropped bombs, into his own lines. Seeing this, he thought it might be a British machine, and turned his attention to another. His observer, Lt Nelson, fired two drums at it, and last saw it diving vertically into the mist.

Lt Chadwick on the third F.E. chased the fifth Roland to Pont-a-Vendin. His observer, Lt Hopper, fired three drums at it. Both pilot and observer saw it heel over and strike the ground in a vertical nose dive. They then chased away the remaining Roland. When our machines returned a thick mist had arisen. Two had to make forced landings.

There was one other indecisive combat.

On the IInd Army front 14 hostile aircraft were seen, and there were five combats.

2 Lt Moore on a Nieuport of 1 Sqn, from 17,000 feet observed an Albatros circling between Armentieres and Lille. He waited until it had made two circuits and then dived and attacked it from behind and below. A long shaft of flame burst from the hostile machine, and the Nieuport had to turn quickly to avoid the flame, the heat of which was felt by the pilot. The machine fell and hit the ground near Frelinghem, one of the occupants having already fallen out. The other four combats were indecisive.

On the IIIrd Army front there was little activity, and only one indecisive combat.

On the IVth Army front from 10 to 20 hostile machines were patrolling well behind their own lines most of the day. They were continually attacked by our patrols, but showed little fight.

Lt A. Evans on a De Havilland of 24 Sqn, attacked four over Bapaume, engaging one from underneath and forcing it down in a nose dive. This machine was seen to crash east of Bapaume by 22 Sqn. Though his machine was badly damaged, Lt Evans regained our lines safely. Other combats were indecisive.

During two offensive patrols carried out by the IXth Wing in the Bapaume area, both consisting of Martinsydes and B.E.12s, there were six combats in all. Two machines at least appeared to be damaged. Lt Hicks of 27 Sqn attacked single-handed three L.V.G.s attempting to cross our lines, and turned them all back.

Casualties: Sqn 27, *Capt R. H. J. Lee, wounded;* **22,** *2 Lt W. B. Parsons, wounded; Lt G. H. A. Hawkins, wounded;* **15,** *Lt T. K. Johnstone, slightly wounded; and* **29,** *2 AM E. Howell, wireless operator, wounded.*

August 9th

There was much successful artillery work, 135 targets being dealt with by aeroplane observation and 42 by kite balloons.

On the IIIrd Army front three direct hits on emplacements were observed.

On the IVth Army front one observer engaged three hostile batteries and obtained 16 direct hits in one flight. Altogether direct hits were obtained on four emplacements, and ammunition was exploded in four cases. Twelve other battery positions were hit.

On the Reserve Army front 10 gun pits were destroyed, 17 others damaged, and three ammunition pits blown up. Six other battery positions were hit.

Six machines of 13 Sqn attacked Oppy on the night of the 8th/9th at 9.15 p.m. Three of these machines dropped 12 phosphorus bombs. A short time later the remaining three machines dropped six 112-pound bombs on the same spot. All the bombs were seen to drop in the village.

The 2nd Brigade with 10 B.E.2cs escorted by four Morane biplanes dropped seventy-seven 20-pound bombs on the huts and billets at Tenbrielen, causing three fires.

The 3rd Brigade dropped twenty-eight 112-pound bombs on Beugny where fires broke out. Some of the bombs dropped on the railway west of the village, and some wagons on the road were hit.

Two pilots of 8 Sqn attacked two hostile kite balloons with machine-guns and Buckingham bullets. The observer of one balloon was seen to jump out with a parachute. No balloon was destroyed, but both were quickly hauled down.

Activity of the enemy was normal. Some indecisive combats were recorded on all fronts, and several of the enemy's machines were driven down damaged.

Offensive patrols of the IXth Wing had a considerable amount of fighting.

2 Lt Holden and Cpl Winterbottom on an F.E. of 22 Sqn fired five drums at active hostile batteries from 5,000 feet, temporarily silencing them.

Casualties: Sqn 24, *2 Lt S. E. Cowan, slightly wounded;* **70,** *2 Lt R.M. S. Shepherd, missing; 2 Lt J. W. Gunton, missing;* **25,** *Lt C. J. Hart, missing; Lt J. A. Mann, missing; and* **2,** *Capt E. W. Leggatt, missing.*

August 10th

Rain and low clouds throughout the day.

In the late evening of the 9th instant some successful co-operation with artillery was carried out. 2 Lt G. K. Palmer and Lt H. L. Waite of 2 Sqn registered seven O.K.s on a hostile battery position, a large explosion occurring in one of the gun pits.

Twelve targets, including 8 batteries, were successfully engaged with aeroplane co-operation by the 4th Brigade.

On the Reserve Army front six points were registered and trenches damaged by direct hits. Ten gun pits were damaged, four were destroyed and two lots of ammunition blown up. Three motor lorries were damaged, and a small party of men and wagons were successfully ranged on with shrapnel.

At 9 p.m. on the 9th instant three machines of 13 Sqn attacked the Château at St Leger with six 112-pound bombs. Observation was difficult, but some of the bombs were seen to fall near the objective.

Capt Walser dropped 30 phosphorus bombs on an M.T. park near Le Sars. Owing to ground mist, it is uncertain whether the target was hit, but a fire was started and was still burning when the pilot returned to his aerodrome.

Information has been received that the following are prisoners of war in Germany: **Sqn 5,** *2 Lt G. W. Snook;* **9,** *2 Lt W. J. M. Tomson;* **11,** *2 Lt D. H. Macintyre; 2 Lt J. W. Toone; 2 Lt E. B. Harvey;* **24,** *2 Lt C. Kerr;* **27,** *2 Lt R. W. Nichol; and* **9,** *Capt W. W. Jefferd.*

11 – 18 August, 1916

Indifferent weather permitted little air activity in the period of this communiqué.

B.E.12s were reported in combat for the first time with 19 Sqn. One aircraft from a patrol of four was shot down.

Comments from the enemy side paid tribute to the effects of the R.F.C. bombing offensive during the first phase of the Somme battle.

COMMUNIQUÉ NO. 48

August 11th

Little artillery co-operation could be done owing to the weather. Some registration was accomplished, and five gun positions were engaged, direct hits being obtained in three cases, and one explosion caused in an ammunition pit.

Hostile aircraft were inactive. There were four indecisive combats on the Reserve Army front, where two hostile patrols were met by De Havillands of 32 Sqn. In the first encounter Capt Jones engaged a Fokker at very close range, and saw it go down apparently out of control, but lost it in the mist.

August 12th

The haze made observation difficult, but 85 targets were dealt with by aeroplane observation, the majority of them on the fronts of the Reserve and IVth Armies. On the Reserve Army front 11 hostile batteries were engaged successfully, two gun pits destroyed and five others hit. Two ammunition pits were seen to blow up.

On the IVth Army front four batteries were successfully engaged, one pit hit and two explosions caused. One pilot obtained seven direct hits on strong points and trenches. Five direct hits were obtained on Morval Church tower, which was knocked down.

Pont a Vendin was attacked by the 1st Brigade at midday and at 4.30 p.m. Many bombs fell on the railway, the station, and houses near the station.

The 2nd Brigade dropped seventy-two 20-pound bombs on the enemy's billets at Houthem, doing considerable damage.

Machines of the 3rd Brigade attacked Beugny at about 3 p.m. with twenty-six 112-pound bombs, the majority of which exploded in the village.

An offensive patrol of 23 Sqn dropped bombs in Oppy and Bailleul, damaging the railway.

St Leger, Boisleux and Boiry were also attacked by 11 Sqn. A train in the sidings at St Leger was damaged.

Seven Martinsydes of 27 Sqn, carrying four 112-pound and forty 20-pound bombs, attacked the railway and factories at Blanc Misseron, east of Valenciennes, with very successful results. Three buildings were hit, also two trains and the railway line. One machine, which overshot the mark, dropped four bombs on an A.A. gun, silencing it. Some machines went down as low as 300 feet to drop their bombs. On the way back, two Fokkers attempted to attack the formation but were driven off, one appearing to fall out of control.

With the exception of the Reserve and IVth Army fronts, there was little activity and no decisive combats took place. On the IVth and Reserve Army fronts a good many machines were encountered throughout the day, the majority of them flying well east of the line, and very low. Fifteen indecisive combats took place, but the hostile machines for the most part descended as soon as engaged.

The enemy appears to be doing artillery work at very low heights.

Casualties: Sqn 32, *Sgt E. Dobson, missing; and* **10,** *2 Lt J. M. Harris, wounded by A.A. fire.*

August 13th

The weather was against successful artillery co-operation, but 60 targets were dealt with by aeroplanes and 15 by kite balloons.

An anti-aircraft battery and two other hostile batteries were successfully engaged by machines of the 1st Brigade, and three heavy explosions were caused at Salome Halt.

On the IVth Army front 11 batteries were successfully engaged, one observer obtaining seven direct hits on two batteries. Many trench points were registered, five direct hits being obtained.

On the Reserve Army front four batteries were engaged, three pits being destroyed and three damaged, and two ammunition pits blown up. Several lengths of trench were registered.

A machine of the XVth Wing on contact patrol work reported a concentration of hostile troops for a counter-attack on the IInd Corps front. A very successful barrage was brought to bear by the artillery.

A machine of 34 Sqn on contact patrol located Brigade and Battalion H.Q., and the positions of our troops between Pozieres and High Wood.

Douai Aerodrome was bombed three times during the day by machines of the 3rd Brigade. Twenty-six 112-pound bombs and sixty 20-pound bombs were dropped. Observation was difficult on the first two occasions, but several bombs were seen to burst on the aerodrome on the second occasion, several being close to hangars. On the third occasion three hangars were seen to be hit, many bombs fell on the aerodrome, and one on the railway line south of the aerodrome.

The 1st Brigade carried out attacks against Wavrin and Pont a Vendin.

No decisive combats took place. A patrol of four B.E.12s of 19 Sqn attacked four hostile aircraft over Bapaume, dispersing them. The B.E.s were in turn attacked from above by two hostile machines, one of which was seen to side-slip after a short encounter, and was lost sight of.

One of our machines failed to return.

The 1st Brigade again attacked the cinematograph theatre at Provin on the evening of the 13th. Many bombs fell close to the objective.

Casualty: **19 Sqn,** *2 Lt G. Geen, missing.*

August 14th

Low clouds all day, some showers and strong southerly wind.

Sixty-four targets were engaged with aeroplane observation and thirty-six with kite balloons, mostly on the evening of the 13th. Three direct hits on hostile batteries were obtained on the Ist Army front, and five on one battery on the IVth Army front. On the Reserve Army front 13 battery positions were engaged, six gun pits being destroyed and twelve others damaged. Six explosions were caused in ammunition pits.

August 15th

Weather continued unfavourable with a few bright intervals.

Artillery Co-operation

Rain and clouds at 1,000 feet practically debarred artillery work. Several attempts had to be abandoned after firing a few rounds, which could not be seen.

On the IVth Army front only one hostile battery was engaged.

On the front of the Reserve Army six targets were successfully ranged on, and 31 active batteries reported. A body of men was dispersed on the Pys–Courcellette road by a heavy battery, which also engaged four lorries on the same road. One lorry was put out of action by a Howitzer shell.

In spite of very adverse weather conditions some good photographs were taken from a height of about 3,500 feet.

The following extracts from prisoners' letters, other captured documents, from Agents, and from the foreign Press, give some information as to the value of the work which has been done by the R.F.C. during the current operations. A young German officer who was among the prisoners recently taken, said:

He would not admit that Germany was beaten, but talked frequently about their difficulties, and cursed our airmen. He said that our raids over the German lines had not been responsible for many deaths, but they had smashed up the direct lines of communication. They had cut up the railway, played the deuce with the stations, and altogether upset the plan of shifting troops at a moment's notice from one place to another.

Morning Post, August 1st

Extract from letter received concerning the air raid on St Quentin, written by a French lady residing in that town:

You have probably read the English communiqué of the 4th July, stating that successful raids had been made on the important railway centres of Comines, Combles and St Quentin. My mother's letter must therefore refer to this raid, but the expression she uses (tremblement de terre) makes me think that the damage in the town was caused by the explosion of the ammunition depots, of which there were a considerable number in the neighbourhood of the station. This would explain walls falling down and the glass in a large part of the town being broken, for I do not imagine for one moment that the British aviators dropped their bombs in the middle of the town.

Extracts from Army Summaries: Reserve Army. 25th July 1916. Prisoner's statement:

Our successes so far gained are attributed in a large measure to the skill and daring of the British airmen in depriving the enemy of all means of aerial observation. It is stated that the German Flying Corps have lost heavily in prestige as a result of recent operations.

Reserve Army. 26th July 1916:

Prisoners state that our Flying Corps is far superior to the German Flying Squadrons opposed to them on the Second Army front. They put down largely our successes to our superiority in this arm. The officers admit great confusion in the Pozieres Sector, no entrenching work being possible owing to the constant interference of our artillery, and of the watch kept by the Flying Corps.

Ist Army. 27th July 1916:

Aeroplane bombs are said to have a much greater effect on the morale of the troops than shell fire. The N.C.O. has experienced them personally. An officers' party is said to have suffered 16 casualties from this cause, and other casualties are indefinitely spoken of in billets.

Extract from the examination of a prisoner (well educated man):

He expressed his admiration for our Flying Corps, and admitted that the German airmen had for some time been completely outclassed and out-fought. He ascribed this not to the inferiority of German machines, but to the wide extent of front which they had to cover, both on the Western and Eastern fronts, while machines also had to be sent to the Balkans and to assist the Turks.

From a captured order:

Dumps are to be protected from aerial observation by means of wiring and green shrubs.

Extracts from the examination of prisoners:

Officers of the 3rd Guard Division state that the Division detrained about Marcoing and thence marched via Flers to the front. One battalion of the Lehr Regiment suffered losses to the extent of 50% from our artillery and aeroplane fire before they reached the second line trenches.

This battalion was probably the battalion on which our heavies obtained seven direct hits south of Ginchy, 6th July.

Prisoners of the 190th Regiment state that they detrained about June 30th and had a two days' march to Flers. During these two days they were much delayed by our aeroplanes, having been forced continuously to halt and leave the road to avoid detection.

From German officers' diaries and statements it appears that in fine weather troops on the march are considerably delayed by the presence of British aviators. Columns on the march are halted as long as our aeroplanes are in the neighbourhood. On certain occasions German machines are detailed to guard troops on the march.

The following are extracts from the diary of a man of the 5th Division:

10th July: Left (Valenciennes) for St Quentin, arrived 8 p.m. march till 11 p.m. to Vermand, billeted in a barn, aircraft bombs on the village.

11th July: Air fighting in neighbourhood.

19th July: Last night we marched nearly to Geudecourt. Fierce air fight, about 40 hostile aircraft engaged. Some of our companies had casualties through bombs. We changed our position at midday.

21st July: Three enemy aeroplanes brought down in our neighbourhood (Presumably Geudecourt), one of them in flames. Unfortunately two of ours were also brought down.

The *Morning Post*, 15th August, 1916, states:

The Telegraaf learns from the frontier that in the recent air raids on Belgium bombs were dropped on the Station at Mons (Hainault). This was the second time the station had been bombed in a fortnight, and on both occasions it was crowded with military trains. Especially during the first raid, and even before the airmen had appeared, much confusion prevailed at the Station, the officials having received orders and counter-orders, so that they did not know which trains were destined for the Somme and which were to go via Brussels to Germany, presumably for the Eastern front. Wagons were destroyed by the air raid and railway traffic was hampered for a long time, with the result that the arrival of much ammunition for the front was delayed. The German authorities are very uneasy about the raid. They immediately ordered searches and the examination of documents in the town, presuming that there were foreigners who gave information to the enemy. Some civilians living in the vicinity of the station were injured. The repeated air raids on Ghent, Zeebrugge, Evere, and Mons have led to a still more vigorous limitation of traffic.

Extracts from prisoner's letter:

. . . Each of us crouches in a little hole that he has dug out for himself as a protection against possible splinters and stares at nothing but the sky and the back wall of the trench . . . and the airmen circle over us and try to do some damage, but only enemy ones, for a German airman will not dare to come here—far too much afraid—only behind the front a great crowd and here not one makes an appearance.

16–22 August, 1916

A notable feature of this communiqué is the reappearance of Albert Ball, 11 Sqn. Flying a Nieuport Scout he scattered a formation of Rolands, forcing two of them down.

For some weeks past, on instructions from R.F.C. Headquarters, Ball had been resting from active combat flying—the 'rest' taking the form of artillery observation work, piloting B.E.2cs and B.E.2ds in 8 Sqn.

COMMUNIQUÉ NO. 49

August 16th

Very little work was done until the evening on account of low clouds. Thirteen hostile batteries were successfully engaged on the fronts of the IVth and Reserve Armies.

2 Lt Scott and 2 Lt Matthew, of 4 Sqn, ranged two heavy Howitzer batteries on two hostile batteries south-east of Pys, observing in all 70 rounds. During the whole time they were flying at 3,000 feet at a considerable distance on the enemy's side of the line.

There were 14 combats, 10 of which were on the front of the IIIrd Army. 2 Lt Ball, of 11 Sqn, in a Nieuport Scout attacked five hostile machines. He attacked a Roland, causing it to dive, then climbed and dispersed the remainder, two of which he forced to descend.

4 F.E.s of 11 Sqn attacked two Rolands and one L.V.G., one of the former being driven down emitting smoke.

Casualty: Sqn 24, *Capt R. E. A. W. Hughes Chamberlain, wounded.*

August 17th

In spite of the weather, 87 targets were dealt with by aeroplane observation and 52 by kite balloon. Aeroplanes for the most part had to fly low.

Eight hostile batteries were engaged on the Ist Army front, and direct hits obtained on five gun pits.

A hostile battery was silenced on the IInd Army front with balloon observation.

On the IIIrd Army front one battery was engaged and one emplacement hit.

Above: Fokker D III
Below: Vickers FB 5

Above: Aviatik C III
Below: R.E.5

On the IVth Army front 18 batteries were engaged, and one direct hit obtained which caused two separate explosions.

On the Reserve Army front 13 batteries were engaged, 14 pits damaged, and four explosions caused.

A very successful shoot on Switch Trench was carried out by a machine of 34 Sqn (Lts Paget and Buller) with the 39th Siege Battery, many direct hits being obtained.

Twenty-four 112-pound bombs were dropped by machines of the 3rd Brigade in the valley between Irles and Warlencourt, where there are many hostile gun positions.

A hostile machine was brought down in flames just behind our front line trenches near Pozieres after a combat with two F.E.s of 22 Sqn, pilots, 2 Lt Duffus and Capt Swart, observers, Cpl Winterbottom and 2 Lt Cook. The hostile machine approached our two machines from behind. The F.E.s turned and engaged the enemy at about 200 yards, and the hostile machine, turning east, almost immediately burst into flames and fell vertically.

2 Lt Holder and Cpl Winterbottom drove down another machine under control near Barastre.

Casualty: Sqn 9, *2 AM J. Pearce, wireless telegraph operator, wounded.*

August 18th

Weather was unfavourable, and hostile aircraft showed practically no activity. A few indecisive encounters took place. One hostile machine appears to have been shot down by infantry or a passing shell and crashed to earth in a nose dive near High Wood and was burnt.

Artillery Co-operation was considerably hampered by the weather, but 49 targets were successfully engaged by aeroplane observation and 20 by kite balloon.

Sgt Pateman, of 4 Sqn, took some successful photographs from 2,000 feet in very bad weather conditions.

During the night of the 17th/18th the 1st Brigade dropped four 20-pound and 12 incendiary bombs on Pont a Vendin, some of the bombs falling on or near a train. Bombs were also dropped on Courrieres. On the 18th the 1st Brigade attacked Annay, Noyelles and a château near Marquillies. The latter was hit.

Four machines of 27 Sqn each with eight 20-pound bombs attacked Sailly Saillisel between 2 and 4 p.m.

At 2.40 p.m. 4 machines of 27 Sqn left to attack the railway sidings at Annay. Thick clouds were encountered in the vicinity of Arras and the machines lost touch, two of them returning without having dropped their bombs. Lt E. D. Hicks after flying for 20 minutes over the line had engine trouble and was forced to return. He dropped his bombs close to a railway. 2 Lt B. D. Frost dropped bombs from 1,500 feet on a station about 20 miles over the line. He succeeded in wrecking three coaches in the middle of the train, besides doing considerable damage to the station. Having fired a drum of Buckingham bullets into the station he returned to the aerodrome, crossing the line at between 2,000 and 3,000 feet.

On the night of the 17th/18th at about 1 a.m. 13 Sqn carried out a night bombing raid against the Château at St Leger with three machines, six 112-pound bombs being dropped with great success. They were seen to explode round the château.

Capt Mills and Lt Cleaver attacked several parties of infantry with machine-gun fire, and Lt Bowen and Lt Ambler attacked infantry in trenches with machine-gunfire.

August 19th

Weather continued unfavourable until the evening, when some artillery work was accomplished. 3 and 7 Sqns carried out some good contact patrol work, and supplied their Corps with valuable information concerning the situation about Delville Wood, Guillemont and Mouquet Farm.

An offensive patrol of 70 Sqn between 4,30 and 7.30 p.m. engaged two machines which endeavoured to get between the patrol and the lines. Capt Cruikshank drove one down 6,000 feet, but lost it in the clouds.

During a bomb raid on Rocquigny Lt Sherren of 27 Sqn attacked a hostile machine which was presently joined by 5 others. Lt Sherren had his radiator, petrol tank and engine shot through, but returned safely.

Six 112-pound and 4 incendiary bombs were dropped on Fournes on the evening of the 19th by machines of the 1st Brigade. Two machines which became separated from the raid dropped their bombs on Marquillies sugar factory and on Don. All three targets were hit.

A dump near Beaucamps was attacked about the same time with sixteen 20-pound and 7 incendiary bombs, several of which hit the dump.

There was no opposition in either of the above raids.

August 20th

Sixty-four targets were dealt with by aeroplane observation and 8 by kite balloon.

On the IVth Army front 12 hostile batteries were successfully engaged, 4 direct hits being obtained on emplacements.

On the Reserve Army front 14 batteries were engaged, 11 gun pits were damaged, 3 being completely destroyed, and 2 ammunition pits blown up, one causing a very large explosion.

Machines of the 3rd Brigade dropped twenty-three 112-pound bombs on the valley between Warlencourt and Courcelette on the evening of the 19th. Some of the machines which failed to reach this objective dropped their bombs on hostile trenches in the neighbourhood of Gommecourt.

Some useful contact patrol work was done by 3, 9 and 34 Sqns. Detailed reports on the situation opposite Switch Trench, Delville Wood, and south of Guillemont being obtained and sent to the Corps concerned. Flares were lighted by the infantry west of Delville Wood when called for by a machine of 3 Sqn by means of the Klaxon horn.

Nine indecisive combats took place.

1 Kite Balloon broke loose about 6.30 p.m. and drifted over the enemy's lines, where it was brought down by A.A. fire. All the instruments and maps were thrown out, and 2 Lt Moxon descended safely in a parachute. Capt B. H. Radford was killed.

Casualties: 1 Kite Balloon Section: *Capt B. H. Radford, killed; and* **Sqn 2,** *2 Lt R. T. Griffin and Lt H. H. Whitehead, missing.*

The following information has been obtained as to the results of bombing raids:

Douai. An ammunition train (10 trucks) was destroyed here at the end of June. (Agent's report.)

Mons. The railway lines at Mons were badly damaged by the raid on the 4th August. Thirteen soldiers were killed. (Agent's report.)

Courtrai. During the raid on the 2nd August bombs were dropped on the barracks, several soldiers being hit, and much damage was done. The 'Congo' station was also hit. 60,000 kg. of oil were set on fire and destroyed. Four bombs aimed at a bridge missed it by 30 yards. One bomb dropped on the workhouse which was occupied by the military.

Bombs dropped by the 1st Brigade on Sainghin caused 17 casualties to the 247th Reserve Regiment, all killed.

Bombs dropped on the Marquillies sugar factory caused much damage to the pioneer park. Much material and the entire saw mills were destroyed by fire.

Extracts from captured German letters:

> 6.45 p.m. We are now sitting here under terrible artillery fire, and eagerly awaiting orders for our relief .We can count as many as 30 aeroplanes over us at a time. Our losses were again heavy to-day.
>
> The war is starting in real earnest, all the villages all shot down. No captive balloons of ours dare go up—at once airmen come and shoot them down, if they do. Only a little while ago, 5 went thus . . . No rest you may imagine. 8 days' intense fire—indescribable.

21 August – 1 September, 1916

The Fokker biplane reported on 22 August was clearly one of the D-series Scouts designed to replace the now obsolescent monoplanes. The Fokker DI and DIV had water-cooled engines and the DII and DIII were powered by air-cooled rotaries. Contemporary with these new Fokkers were the Halberstadt DII and DIII. Little is recorded as to the dates when these Scouts were introduced, but they had been distributed among the reconnaissance squadrons for escort duties from early summer. The small Scout reported on 29 July (Communiqué No. 45) was probably a Fokker or a Halberstadt.

The first two regular fighting squadrons of the German Air Force had now been formed—Jagdstaffel No. 1 on 23 August and No. 2 on the 30th. Capt Oswald Boelcke, who had strongly urged the formation of such specialist fighter squadrons for some time past, commanded Jasta 2 and Capt Martin Zander, Jasta. 1 These units were initially equipped with the Fokker and Halberstadt biplanes.

On 22 August Albert Ball played a leading part in 11 Sqn's battle with a large formation of L.V.G.s and Rolands, destroying two of the enemy and sending down another out of control. The enemy force was routed, and the description of aircraft landing in all directions suggests a state of near panic.

19 Sqn's B.E.12s, having proved to be ineffective fighters, made a disastrous debut in their new bombing role on 26 August, with five out of eleven machines missing.

COMMUNIQUÉ NO. 50

August 21st

Fifty-seven targets were engaged with aeroplane observation, principally on the Reserve and IVth Army fronts, and five by kite balloons. Three hostile batteries were engaged on the 1st Army front and 12 on the Reserve Army front, where 14 gun pits were destroyed or damaged and one ammunition pit blown up. Fourteen batteries were engaged on the IVth Army front, and 30 direct hits were obtained. One battery was silenced under the area call system. Eighty-five active hostile batteries were reported by the XVth Wing, and 86 by the 4th Brigade.

Some good contact patrol work was carried out by Squadrons of the

4th Brigade west of Delville Wood, west of High Wood and about Guillemont. In the latter case 2 Lts Hollinghurst and Scaife descended to 1,000 feet and examined Guillemont and the Quarry for 15 minutes under heavy rifle fire.

A patrol of 24 Sqn attacked three hostile machines over Sailly Saillisel on their way back from our lines. They engaged two, but were unable to get to close range. Shortly afterwards ten hostile machines carrying bombs were attacked over Grandecourt. When attacked, they released their bombs (some of which fell in the German lines), and made off east.

Many other indecisive combats took place.

August 22nd

Some successful artillery co-operation was carried out, 31 targets being dealt with by aeroplane observation and 15 by kite balloons. The 1st Brigade registered the Heavy Artillery on three hostile batteries, obtaining a direct hit on one gun pit, and the Siege Artillery on three trench targets. Fifteen batteries were successfully engaged by the 4th Brigade, 17 direct hits obtained, and 4 explosions caused. Lt Leman obtained seven direct hits on one battery, destroying an emplacement and causing an explosion.

XVth Wing reported four points registered, six shoots on gun positions, one gun position destroyed, five others damaged, and four ammunition pits blown up.

Capt J. T. P. Whittaker with 2 Lt Stevens of 4 Sqn was attacked in turn by a Fokker biplane and an L.V.G., both of which were driven off. Between Le Sars and Pys they successfully engaged a Fokker which fell apparently out of control. The 67th A.A. Battery confirm this report.

Seven hostile machines which attempted to cross our lines were prevented from doing so by Capt Wilkinson and Lt Wood of 24 Sqn. Lt Sibley of 24 Sqn engaged a hostile machine over Le Sars. The hostile observer was hit, and the machine descended vertically into a cloud and was lost to view. Later a German machine was seen on the ground in this neighbourhood.

On the front of the 3rd Brigade an offensive patrol of 11 Sqn encountered a formation of about 15 German machines, chiefly Rolands and L.V.G.s. These were engaged by our F.E.s, assisted by one Nieuport Scout. The engagement became of a general nature, all of our machines being engaged. 2 Lt Morris, pilot, and Lt Rees, observer, singled out one machine which was seen to side-slip and plunge to earth out of control, and was seen on the ground in a wrecked condition. Three others were driven down by the combined attacks of our machines, and appeared to be completely out of control, although lost to view before hitting the ground. Of these, one, a Roland Scout, was seen to be emitting clouds of smoke, as though on fire. This latter machine had been engaged by Capt Price, pilot, and Lt Libby, observer. Three other machines were seen to land under control, and the whole hostile formation was completely broken up. On the front of the 4th Brigade nine indecisive combats took place. Two hostile machines were seen on the ground.

The following is an account of a fight given by the pilot, 2 Lt Duffus, and the observer, Cpl Winterbottom of 22 Sqn:

> While on defensive patrol we saw an F.E.2b doing photography north of Le Sars. We followed this machine, going east of it, when we saw 5 H.A., type E., coming from Bapaume, evidently with the intent to attack the photographic machine. We dived at the H.A., opening fire at 500 yards. The H.A. immediately split up their formation, diving and making off in all directions. We closed with one machine, firing two drums into it and actually set it on fire, but a after few seconds the flames went out. The hostile machine dived rapidly for the ground. We then engaged another machine, firing one drum at it, but could not get close to it. All five hostile machines made for the ground.

2 Lt Curphey of 32 Sqn, while on offensive patrol, engaged three L.V.G.s north of Bapaume. The centre machine was engaged, two drums being fired. The enemy machine went down apparently out of control, but the pilot was unable to see whether it crashed, as his attention was diverted to the other machines.

2 Lt Jarvis of 4 Sqn, observer 2 Lt Collenette, when on artillery patrol, engaged an L.V.G. near Courcelette, following it towards High Wood and firing two drums .The enemy machine appeared to fall north-west of High Wood, but our machine was obliged to return, as two flying wires were shot through and other damage done. The fall of the enemy machine was afterwards corroborated by two witnesses on the ground.

After a fight today with two hostile machines amongst clouds, 2 Lt King of 32 Sqn, saw a crashed machine on the ground at *N. 14*, below the scene of a fight near Thilloy. This machine was also seen an hour later by Capt Aizlewood. It is not certain that this machine was brought down by 2 Lt King, as clouds prevented him seeing the result of the fight.

The escort to bombing machines of the 3rd Brigade encountered about 20 hostile machines flying in three formations, which were engaged separately. Lt Ball on a Nieuport first engaged the rear machine of a formation of seven Rolands, into which he emptied 1½ drums at a range of about 15 yards. The enemy machine was seen to crash and turn over on its side. Lt Ball then turned his attention to five more Rolands, discharging two drums into one from underneath. The enemy machine turned, diving very steeply out of control with fire and smoke coming out of the fuselage. The German formation was broken up, but Lt Ball got level with another machine and discharged the remainder of his ammunition into it. The enemy machine fell out of control and crashed on to some houses in the village below. During all this the F.E.s were busy fighting hard, and managed to disperse what remained of the hostile formation. Numerous enemy machines were seen to descend and land in all directions. Lt Ball returned to one of our aerodromes for more ammunition and went back to the scene of the battle, where he engaged and dispersed such enemy machines as had remained in the vicinity.

Casualties: Sqn 7, *2 Lt W. R. E. Harrison, slightly wounded;* and **10,** *2 Lt H. C. Markham and Lt C. L. Tetlow, missing.*

On the 22nd instant 27 Sqn attacked Le Transloy, and many bombs were seen to burst in the village. On the same day the 3rd Brigade dropped twenty-nine 112-pound bombs in the valley between Irles and Warlencourt. Many explosions were observed, and at least one dump or battery was hit. The 3rd Brigade also attacked the village of Thilloy with success.

August 23rd

1st Brigade engaged 4 hostile batteries with heavy artillery, obtaining direct hits on three gun pits and 3 A.A. batteries, causing ammunition to explode in one case, and obtaining O.K's on 2 guns.

2 Lt P. Huskinson and Pte Bidmeade of 2 Sqn ranged on to a house in which a party of infantry had taken cover, obtaining three direct hits.

2nd Brigade successfully registered 18 targets, including one hostile battery, and caused an explosion amongst the ammunition.

On the front of the 3rd Brigade 5 trench targets were registered by 8 Sqn.

Thirteen batteries were successfully engaged by the 4th Brigade, and three direct hits obtained. A direct hit was also obtained on a balloon winch. Thirty-four active batteries were located.

Fifteenth Wing obtained 13 direct hits on enemy batteries, and exploded an ammunition pit.

At 5.40 p.m. a patrol of 24 Sqn, pilots: Capt Wilkinson and Lts Wood, Morgan and Knight, encountered nine hostile aeroplanes flying west over Le Sars. Attacked and dispersed.

On the 23rd Aulnoye Station was attacked by machines of the IXth Wing. Bombs were dropped from a height of 400 feet. An engine was blown up, and much damage caused to rolling stock.

Casualties: Sqn 13, *Lt W. H. Bragg, slightly wounded;* **34,** *2 Lt L. T. S. Smith, slightly wounded; 2 AM E. C. Skinner and 2 AM C. C. Playle, wireless telegraph operators, both seriously wounded;* **15,** *2 Lt G. S. Wood, slightly wounded;* **10 Kite Balloon Section,** *2 Lt C. G. Ronaldson-Clark, injured in accident; and* **34,** *2 Lt H. M. Probyn, slightly wounded.*

August 24th

Fifty one targets were registered by aeroplane observation and 4 by kite balloons.

On the Reserve Army fronts 19 shoots on gun positions were obtained, 7 gun pits destroyed and 11 damaged, and ammunition was blown up in five cases. Four other battery positions were hit, and 12 direct hits were obtained with 9.2-inch howitzers on a battery under trees. On the IVth Army front, 7 batteries were successfully engaged.

A patrol of the IXth Wing under Capt Henderson was fighting continuously, and dispersed several hostile formations. One machine is believed to have been brought down, and others were damaged.

On the 24th instant the 3rd Brigade again attacked the valley between Irles and Warlencourt with thirty 112-pound bombs. A hut was demolished, and several bombs were seen to fall within 25 yards of an active battery, which at once ceased firing. This Brigade again attacked Ligny-Thilloy and Thilloy.

The following is an account of the experiences of Lt Vaucour and Lt Bott of 70 Sqn.

> Whilst on an offensive patrol south-west of Cambrai on the 24th instant, Lt Bott discovered that the fuselage was on fire. A burning wad from an A.A. shell had fallen inside the fuselage and was lying on top of a longeron. He immediately tore off the surrounding canvas and beat out the flames with his hands. Just previously the machine had been hit by machine-gun fire in a combat, and the engine was firing on 8 cylinders only, and the pressure pump propeller had one blade broken off. When near Bapaume Lt Vaucour fired a white light, and turned west as the engine was missing badly. East of Le Sars he saw and dived at two enemy machines, engaging and driving them off. He now discovered that the petrol pressure piping had been shot through. He glided over the lines, crossing them at 1,500 feet and landed one mile south of Carnoy.
>
> The following morning Lt Vaucour left for his aerodrome with 1 AM Warminger as passenger. About 3 miles south-west of Albert they were attacked by three H.A., one attacking from the front and two from the rear. During the combat, Lt Vaucour's machine was hit by high explosive, presumably from A.A. guns, and 1 AM Warminger was seriously wounded. The machine became uncontrollable for a time, the petrol tank being pierced and the engine stopped, but it was eventually safely landed.
>
> 1 AM Warminger behaved with great pluck he died the same evening in hospital.

Casualties: Sqn 25, *Lt M. T. Barnes and Lt W. E. Harper, slightly wounded;* **70,** *Capt R. G. Hopwood and 23942 Gr. C. R. Pearce, missing; and* **15,** *2 Lt C. D. Kershaw, wounded.*

August 25th

One hundred and twenty-seven targets were engaged with aeroplane observation and 25 by kite balloons.

On the 4th Brigade front 31 hostile batteries were engaged and 24 direct hits obtained. Sixteen emplacements were damaged, and a gun was knocked out of its emplacement into the road.

On the Reserve Army front 22 shoots on gun positions were carried out. Seven positions were destroyed, 10 were damaged, 4 ammunition pits were blown up, and damage was caused in 8 other battery positions. An active A.A. battery was engaged and both pits destroyed.

On the IIIrd Army front a hostile machine was hit by A.A. fire and turned over several times in the air, but apparently flattened out before reaching the ground.

In all there were 21 combats, 9 of which were fought by the escort to a bombing raid in the locality of Bapaume. Captain Price and 2 Lt Libby of 11 Sqn engaged an Aviatik, which was seen falling out of control, but it was lost to view before it reached the ground. On the IVth Army front, hostile aircraft were active. Offensive patrols had numerous encounters, and Lts Mackay and Bowerman of 22 Sqn brought down a hostile machine. This was confirmed by an A.A. Battery.

An A.A. Battery observer, and also an observer in the trenches, report that an aeroplane, nationality unknown, fell in flames just north of Douvrin about 6.30 p.m. on the 24th. Cause of the fall unknown.

On the 25th instant the 1st Brigade dropped twenty-eight 20-pound bombs on a dump near Beaucamp. Six bombs were seen to burst in the dump. During the operation one of our machines was hit by A.A. fire, but returned safely to our lines. Numerous other small bombing raids were carried out against various objectives on the Ist Army front, and a considerable amount of damage done to railway lines, stations, etc.

The 3rd Brigade repeated their attacks on the valley between Irles and Warlencourt, dropping twenty-nine 112-bombs, and causing several explosions.

The IXth Wing attacked Busigny Station where a heavy bomb hit a factory or gas works, and considerable damage was done to the railway track and rolling stock.

Casualties: Sqn 4, *2 Lt G. R. Bolitho, wounded;* **60,** *2 Lt J. M. Drysdale, wounded;* **70,** *1 AM H. P. Warminger, 3538, wounded A.A. fire, since died;* **22,** *Lt R. D. Walker and 2 Lt C. Smith, missing;* **24,** *2 Lt S. J. Sibley, slightly wounded;* **22,** *No 1922 Sgt B. F. Murray, died of wounds;* **3,** *Capt E. C. Miles, wounded; and* **29,** *2 Lt K. K. Turner, missing.*

August 26th

Weather was unfavourable for flying till late in the afternoon, when artillery work was continued with success.

Late in the evening when the weather had cleared, 11 machines of 19 Sqn proceeded on a bombing raid to attack the Bois de Havrincourt.

After leaving the rendezvous, they encountered thick weather, but some of them managed to drop their bombs on the objective. On the return journey a heavy storm was encountered, and five of the machines failed to return.

Hostile machines became moderately active after 6 p.m. on the 26th. At 7 p.m. on the 26th, one hostile machine, L.V.G. type, was engaged by 2 Lt Walters of 60 Sqn, on a Nieuport, who fired one drum at it at close range. The enemy machine was seen to fall out of control, but was lost sight of in the clouds. 2 Lt Walters was then attacked by a number of other German machines, who were again lost sight of in the clouds.

Casualties: Sqn 4, *Capt J. T. Powell Whittaker, slightly wounded;* **70,** *Lt J. C. Taylor, slightly wounded;* **19,** *Lt S. P. Briggs, missing; 2 Lt R. Talbot, missing; Lt H. M. Corbold, missing; 2 Lt A. W. Reynell, missing; and Lt E. Callaghan, missing.*

August 27th

The weather was unfavourable for flying all day.

In the late evening some artillery work was accomplished. The XVth Wing carried out 7 shoots on gun positions, destroying two pits and damaging 7 others. Two ammunition pits were blown up, one of which caused a heavy explosion.

3rd Brigade carried out a bombing raid against the Bois de Loupart about 10.15 a.m. on the 27th with 112-pound bombs, the majority of which burst well within the wood.

At 3 p.m. 3rd Brigade attacked Grevillers with eleven 112-pound bombs. Great damage was caused in the centre of the village. Several pilots reported that practically the whole centre of the village had collapsed in a state of ruin.

At 5.30 p.m. a second attack on the Bois de Loupart was carried out. Twenty-six 112-pound bombs exploded in the wood.

28 August – 5 September, 1916

First sighting of the new Albatros DI Scout, which, more than any other single aircraft type, was destined to swing the tide of air superiority in Germany's favour, was the most significant item reported in this communiqué.

Some authorities have recorded 17 September as the date on which the initial Albatros Scout sorties were made. In fact this was the date when Boelcke's Jasta 2 first flew them into action. The description of the aircraft encountered by 24 Sqn on 31 August—'streamline propeller boss' and 'very large and rounded tailplane'—leaves no doubt as to their identity, and these machines must therefore have belonged to Jasta 1. The British account also admitted their superiority in speed and climb to the D.H.2.

Not reported, but perhaps more important, was the Albatros installation of two synchronised machine-guns firing between the propeller blades—double the armament of the British fighters. The reference to a rearwards-firing gun is puzzling, for this was not fitted in regular squadron use. It may have been an early experimental installation, or the British pilots may have mistaken the side-mounted radiators of the Albatros for a gun bracket.

The DII model, which followed shortly afterwards, had a slightly different arrangement of the wing-centre section struts. Performance was virtually the same, and the two versions were almost indistinguishable at a distance.

Albert Ball had now moved to 60 Sqn, one of the new regular Scout units. His combat of 28 August illustrates one of his characteristic techniques—to fly directly underneath an enemy and pull his Lewis gun down on its mounting to fire upwards.

The D.H.2s continued to give a good account of themselves, and the combat of 31 August suggests that some enemy units were still unaware that their guns were moveable in the vertical plane.

COMMUNIQUÉ NO. 51

August 28th

Late in the evening Lts Turk and Scott, of 11 Sqn encountered and attacked a formation of 7 hostile machines. One of them was brought down out of control near Ligny-Thilloy. The destruction of this machine was reported by an A.A. Battery.

Lt Keen and Capt Glenday, of 70 Sqn, engaged a hostile machine successfully. It was driven down completely out of control. Capt H. G. Salmond and Lt Stewart, Sopwith of 70 Sqn, engaged a number of hostile machines, one of which was driven down apparently out of control.

2 Lt Ball, Nieuport Scout of 60 Sqn, attacked 4 hostile machines. He manoeuvred underneath the nearest of the hostile machines and emptied one drum into it. The German immediately went down in an uncontrolled dive, closely followed by Lt Ball, who fired another drum into it at about 20 yards range. 2 Lt Ball followed his opponent to within 500 feet of the ground and saw him crash just east of Ayette. Previous to this Lt Ball had engaged three enemy machines two of which were seen to make forced landings.

Capt Wilkinson, of 24 Sqn, observed a hostile machine and a Morane Scout engaged near Le Sars. He fired at the German, who went down vertically in a steep spiral and finally crashed.

A machine of 32 Sqn forced a hostile machine to land in a cornfield.

4 Section's balloon broke loose and drifted east. The observer, Lt Jenson, landed safely in a parachute from 1,500 feet.

On the night of the 28th/29th 20-pound and incendiary bombs were dropped on Avion, Henin Lietard and Sallaumines by the 1st Brigade. It was impossible to observe results.

On the evening of the 28th the 3rd Brigade dropped twenty 112-pound bombs on the Bois de Loupart, where numerous explosions were seen. At about the same time ten 112-pound bombs were dropped in the village of Grevillers.

Casualties: Sqn 15, *Lt H. F. Mase, missing; Lt V. G. Odling, missing; and* **60,** *2 Lt B. M. Wainwright, missing.*

August 29th

In spite of very unfavourable weather a lot of very useful artillery work was carried out.

1st Brigade engaged 5 hostile batteries, obtaining direct hits on two gun pits. Siege artillery engaged two batteries, obtaining direct hits on a gun pit, the first of which caused a heavy explosion.

4th Brigade engaged 17 hostile batteries, obtaining three direct hits on batteries, and three on dug-outs. Fifty-five active batteries were located.

5th Brigade: during registration Pys church was registered and hit. Many successful trench shoots were carried out, and an ammunition dug-out was set on fire.

There was very little hostile aircraft activity. At about noon four hostile aircraft were seen by Lt Glew, of 24 Sqn, attacking a B.E.2c over Serre. Lt Glew attacked and fired half a drum at the lowest machine which turned and went off north-east. He then attacked a second machine, emptying a drum into it. This machine went down vertically and is believed to have crashed.

A Bessoneau hangar of 21 Sqn was blown away by a storm. Five machines in the hangar were completely wrecked.

Casualties: Sqn 15, *Lt R. Burley, missing; 2 Lt R. C. Harry, missing;* **34,** *2 Lt D. S. Cairnes, missing; and* **2,** *Lt K. E. Tulloch, missing;* **3,** *2 AM Hobbs, wireless operator killed by shell fire.*

August 30th
Low clouds and driving rain all day.

August 31st
1st Brigade engaged 5 hostile machines one of which was driven down.

Capt Reid and 2 Lt Scott, F.E.2d of 20 Sqn, had several indecisive engagements with hostile aircraft during artillery patrol. Eventually they were attacked by a Fokker biplane, which on four occasions dived at them firing through the propeller. On the fourth occasion the engine of the hostile machine was apparently hit. Clouds of blackish smoke came from the machine, which dived steeply and was not seen to flatten out although it made several unsuccessful attempts to do so.

2 Lt G. P. S. Reid and Capt G. Dixon-Spain, whilst on patrol encountered and drove off several hostile aeroplanes, one of which appeared to be hit.

The morning bombing raid of the 3rd Brigade encountered a large formation of 10 or more German machines over the locality of Bapaume. The whole of our escort became engaged, and four of the B.E.s were enabled to fire as opportunity offered, but the escort completely prevented the enemy from molesting the bombers. As the result of this prolonged fight one German machine was last seen in a vertical nose dive out of control. This machine had been heavily engaged by Lt Hood, pilot, and Cpl Meakin, observer, of 23 Sqn, and its uncontrollable attitude was confirmed by a number of pilots. At least two of the hostile machines were driven down, and the whole formation scattered. About the same time one of our offensive patrols encountered a German formation of some half a dozen machines. A general engagement followed, as the result of which two German machines were driven down, one apparently out of control.

Machines of the 4th Brigade had a number of successful engagements with hostile aircraft. Lt A. G. Knight on a De Havilland of 24 Sqn, saw 9 hostile aircraft approaching from the south-east at 10,500 feet. He attacked the nearest machine over Ginchy, diving and firing a drum at close range. The H.A. went down vertically with engine full on, later getting into a steep spiral. Owing to the proximity of the other hostile aircraft Lt Knight was unable to observe the machine strike the ground. The remaining H.A. dispersed east on the approach of other De Havillands.

Capt Andrews and Lt Glew, in two De Havillands, of 24 Sqn, encounterered three hostile machines of a new type, extremely fast and climbing quickly. They were biplanes, with stream-line propeller boss, apparently single-seater, but firing both in front and over the tail, from what appeared to be a rear mounting on the left-hand side. The tail plane was very large and rounded, not a fish tail. The H.A. kept above the De Havillands, diving, firing and climbing again. The encounters lasted 30 minutes, during which time the De Havillands were only able to fire a few rounds owing to their inferior position underneath, and their inability to outclimb the hostile machines. At the end of half an hour the hostile machines turned away east. Ten minutes afterwards another hostile machine of the same type returned, and was engaged over Curlu at 7,000 feet. Capt Andrews dived and fired a double drum at 100 yards range. The H.A. dived steeply into a cloud, pursued by Capt Andrews. Lt Glew, who was above Capt Andrews, dived over the cloud and attacked the hostile machine as it emerged from the cloud, still diving steeply. He fired half a drum at close range, about 20 yards, and left it in a nose dive over Clery.

Capt Wilkinson and Lt Capon, on two De Havilland Scouts, of 24 Sqn, observed 11 hostile aircraft attacking three F.E.s and some B.E.12s near Grevillers, but the De Havillands were underneath. Climbing, Capt Wilkinson attacked the nearest, a Roland, which was engaged with an F.E. He fired 50 rounds at some 60 yards range, and the H.A., leaving the F.E. dived east under the De Havilland. Capt Wilkinson followed, but was attacked from behind by another Roland. This he succeeded in out-manoeuvring by climbing upwards, finally getting on the H.A.'s tail, firing 40 rounds at about 80 yards. The H.A. dived almost vertically and was afterwards seen on the ground near Villers.

Lt Capon, diving at a Roland, was shot through the leg below the knee; he finished his drum at close range, and returning, landed successfully at Chipilly. Three more Rolands approached to attack, but Capt Wilkinson climbed, and they made off east as soon as he reached their height. Later, Capt Wilkinson saw an L.V.G. approaching High Wood. He dived, keeping to a flank, and when within 70 yards, turned on to the

H.A.'s tail. At this moment Capt Wilkinson was fired on from behind, but he continued his attack on the L.V.G. under heavy fire from four Rolands, firing 50 rounds at about 20 yards range. The L.V.G. dived almost vertically under the De Havilland, and probably crashed, but Capt Wilkinson had to turn to meet the attack from behind. The four Rolands were just above, and manoeuvred to take advantage of the De Havilland's fixed gun, but Capt Wilkinson raised the mounting and engaged three of them with short bursts. Apparently taken by surprise, the H.A. immediately retired east, one going down steeply, but apparently under control. Capt Wilkinson then retired, owing to shortage of petrol, his emergency tank having been shot through. Also two struts were damaged, 2 main spars pierced, and 6 wires cut through.

The 5th Brigade had a considerable number of combats, all indecisive. During the bombing raid on Bois de Havrincourt by 19 Sqn, Capt Wilkinson observed 6 hostile machines attacking two of ours, and at once returned to their help, and soon brought down one of the hostile machines apparently out of control, with the observer hanging out over the side. One of our pilots having been hit, and another having both guns out of action, the three proceeded towards our lines, Capt Henderson endeavouring to ward off attacks from the remaining five of the enemy.

Casualties: Sqn 27, *2 Lt M. H. Strange, missing; 2 Lt A. J. O'Bryne, missing; Capt A. Skinner, missing;* **24,** *2 Lt R. S. Capon, wounded;* **23,** *2 Lt F. G. Mackintosh, missing; 2 Lt J. D. A. Macfie, missing;* **27,** *Capt, O. L. Whittle, missing; and* **19,** *2 Lt S. W. Carline, wounded.*

31 August – 10 September, 1916

On 6 September Flt Sgt J. B. McCudden (see Communiqué No. 25) now a D.H.2 pilot in 29 Sqn, scored the first of his 57 combat victories.

Lt G. H. Bowman, of the same unit, whose aircraft was damaged in collision with one of the enemy three days earlier, ended the war with a victory score of 32 enemy aircraft destroyed.

Albert Ball continued his aggressive campaign against the enemy two-seaters, scoring two more victories on 31 August.

Lt R. M. S. Saundby, 24 Sqn, who destroyed an enemy aircraft on 6 September, was well-known in World War II as Air Marshal Sir Robert Saundby, deputy Commander-in-Chief, Bomber Command.

Combat reports summarised in this communiqué suggest that despite heavier opposition the R.F.C. was still destroying more enemy aircraft than were being lost by its own squadrons.

COMMUNIQUÉ NO. 52

August 31st

2 Lt Ball, on a Nieuport Scout of 60 Sqn, encountered a formation of 12 Rolands near Cambrai between 6.30 and 8.20 p.m. on the 31st August. He climbed, and, getting to the rear of the formation, dived in amongst them, firing one drum. The formation was broken up, and 2 Lt Ball then got under the nearest machine and fired one drum at 15 yards under the pilots seat, causing the machine to plunge to earth south-east of Bapaume. Shortly afterwards, some more hostile aeroplanes came up in formation. Lt Ball attacked one, which went down and landed in a gap between two Woods south-east of Bapaume. Several other machines were engaged with indecisive results, and, having expended all his ammunition, Lt Ball returned.

About 6.45 p.m. on the 31st August, Lt Latta of 60 Sqn attacked one of a group of 8 L.V.G.s. The machine side-slipped and went down in a spin, falling near Bapaume.

Lt Byrne, on a De Havilland of 24 Sqn, attacked and drove down a damaged hostile machine near Bapaume.

September 1st

Machines of the 1st Brigade engaged 3 hostile batteries. Two gun pits

Above: B.E.12
Below: L.V.G. C V

Above: A.E.G. C IV
Below: Nieuport XII

were hit, and a large explosion of ammunition occurred behind one of them.

Two hostile batteries were successfully engaged by machines of the 2nd Brigade.

1 Sqn engaged two hostile batteries, and two emplacements were hit.

28 Sqn engaged a hostile battery, causing a large explosion and several minor explosions. A kite balloon reported that a fire continued burning for an hour after this explosion occurred.

A.A. batteries were engaged by 13 Sqn.

Forty-one hostile batteries were engaged by machines of the 4th Brigade. Ten emplacements were damaged or destroyed, a fire caused, and three explosions took place in a battery position. Four gun pits were destroyed, 9 damaged and 2 ammunition pits blown up by fire directed by machines of the 5th Brigade. Five other battery positions were hit, 9 houses believed to contain three guns of a battery near Le Sars were ranged on, 2 being entirely destroyed. Two direct hits were obtained on Pys Church with 9.2-inch Howitzers. Seven active hostile batteries were accurately registered with 4.5-inch.

2 Lt N. W. Webb and Lt C. S. Workman, in an F.E.2b of 25 Sqn, attacked two hostile balloons. They crossed the line in clouds, and after flying for about 10 minutes, descended and found themselves about 2 miles from one of the balloons. 2 Lt Webb dived, and his observer fired five drums of tracer ammunition at the balloon, and also dropped 4 bombs on it when it was nearly on the ground. Tracers were observed to hit the balloon. The bombs fell very close. They then attacked the second balloon, which was about a mile distant. This balloon was also hit, and drawn down. They then recrossed the lines at 1,200 feet, their machines having suffered considerable damage from A.A. fire.

2 Lt F. L. Barnard and 2 Lt Doughty, 18 Sqn, fired 2 drums at the pit head at Haines from a height of 800 feet. One man was seen to fall.

Lts Da Costa and Stalker, 22 Sqn, fired two drums into the enemy's support line at Haines.

Lts Duffus and Amber of 22 Sqn, fired on the second line hostile trenches south of Beaumont-Hamel, and also into the trenches at Thiepval.

Casualties: Sqn 18, *Lt G. K. MacDonald, wounded in combat; Lt F. S. Wright, wounded in combat; and* **34,** *2 Lt S. A. Gibbons, slightly wounded by A.A. fire.*

September 2nd

The 3rd Brigade engaged one hostile battery, which was silenced. Two direct hits were observed. The 4th Brigade successfully engaged 8 batteries. Two emplacements were damaged. Eighty-six hostile batteries were located.

Considerable damage was done to trenches by fire directed by machines of the 5th Brigade. Ammunition was exploded and A.A. guns silenced by machines of 4 Sqn. One gun pit was destroyed and two others damaged, and a large explosion was caused.

2 Lt Vaucour and 2 Lt Bott of 70 Sqn, while on patrol near Cambrai, encountered six H.A. While diving at the hostile patrol leader, three hostile machines dived on to the tail of Lt Vaucour's machine. One of the enemy machines was engaged by another pilot while Lt Bott engaged another, and fired 2½ drums into it as it passed across the tail of his machine. This enemy machine then made a vertical dive with a stream of smoke pouring out behind it. Lt Vaucour turned and opened fire on the third machine with his front gun, firing about 20 rounds at it. The pilot turned and got under the tail, and Lt Vaucour also turned and fired another 20 rounds into it, after which he was seen to dive vertically out of control, and turn on his back. The remaining hostile machines dispersed, and were observed to land west of Cambrai.

Sgt Pateman and Lt Duke of 4 Sqn, engaged a hostile aeroplane over Pys, and drove it down apparently out of control.

Lt Glew of 24 Sqn, attacked a hostile machine near Delville Wood. This machine was reported by 11 A.A. Battery to have crashed this side of the lines.

Capt Andrews, of 24 Sqn, drove down an enemy machine over Les Boeufs, which seemed to be out of control. A machine was also driven down by Lt Byrne of 24 Sqn.

Further details of the fighting on the IVth Army front on the evening of the 2nd show that the machine attacked by Capt Andrews of 24 Sqn over Les Boeufs was wrecked just north of that village. Lt Byrne of the same patrol saw two F.E.s attacking three hostile machines near Villers. Another machine approached to join the enemy. Lt Byrne attacked it, firing 20 rounds at 50 yards range. The hostile machine banked steeply, offering a good target, and Lt Byrne fired the remainder of his drum at very close range. The German machine side-slipped, and went down in a steep dive towards Beaulencourt. Owing to the continued fighting, Lt Byrne was unable to see whether it reached the ground.

Fifty-six bombs were dropped by 19 Sqn on hutments and on an ammunition dump in Bois de Havrincourt.

Capt Mackay of 4 Sqn, whilst engaged on Artillery observation, opened fire on a fatigue party of about 50 men entering Pys, and dispersed them, inflicting some casualties.

On the IIIrd Army front an offensive patrol of 11 Sqn encountered five Rolands over Bapaume late in the evening of September 2nd. Lt Quested, pilot, and 2 Lt Wyatt, observer, were attacked by 4 of the enemy, but turning sharply emptied one drum of ammunition into the nearest at 20 yards range, causing it to fall sideways completely out of control. Lt Quested then attacked another Roland which was just above him, firing 1½ drums at close range. The Roland turned a complete cart-wheel on its right wing tip and fell out of control. During the fight, one of our machines, pilot, 2 Lt Burton, observer, 2 Lt Griffiths, was driven down in the enemy's lines. The machine was subsequently seen by a French pilot standing on the ground head to wind, and appeared to have landed safely.

2 Lt Joyce, of 60 Sqn, on a Morane Scout, engaged a double fuselage machine, diving on it from the front. The hostile machine fell, and was seen to crash.

Casualties: Sqn 11, *2 Lt G. N. Anderson, wounded in combat; 2 Lt G. M. Allen, killed; 2 Lt E. Burton, missing; 2 Lt F. W. Griffiths, missing;* **32,** *Capt R. E. Wilson, missing* [Capt Smith and Lt Rennie of 4 Sqn, saw a De Havilland land apparently under control in hostile territory. Capt Wilson appears to have set fire to his machine after it landed]; **19,** *Lt G. G. Downing, slightly wounded; 2 Lt R. H. Johnson, slightly wounded;* **70,** *Capt H. G. Salmond, missing; and Lt D. Stewart, missing.*

September 3rd

One hundred and thirty-two targets were dealt with with aeroplane observation and 22 with kite balloon.

Seven hostile batteries were engaged on the Ist Army front, and three gun positions hit.

2 Lt Barnard and Capt Head, of 18 Sqn, ranged an 18-pounder on some infantry collected round a dump. Four very good salvoes caused much confusion.

On the IInd Army front two hostile batteries were engaged, and one gun hit.

On the IIIrd Army front 16 batteries were engaged.

On the IVth Army front 33 batteries were engaged and 18 emplacements were damaged and 4 explosions caused. Lts Blunt and Pearson, of 34 Sqn, attacked a battery with a machine-gun from 2,200 feet and caused it to cease fire.

On the Reserve Army front 19 batteries were engaged, 17 pits damaged, and four explosions caused.

The following bombing attacks were carried out: 1st Brigade—seventy-three 20-pound bombs on La Pouillerie aerodrome, and seventy-four 20-pound bombs on Phalempin Aerodrome. Good results were seen in both cases, especially in the former, where many of the bombs hit sheds. 2nd Brigade—nineteen 112-pound bombs on Mouscron Railway Station and sidings. The majority of the bombs fell on or near the sidings with good results. 3rd Brigade—twenty-nine 112-pound bombs on

Bois de Loupart and 10 on Grevillers, both with satisfactory results.

The IXth Wing attacked Le Transloy with fifty-six 20-pound bombs. Eight Martinsydes of 27 Sqn, which set out to bomb Sailly Sailissel, encountered rain storms and clouds, and their formation was somewhat broken up. Six of the machines reached their objective.

Some very good contact patrol work was done by all three Corps squadrons of the 4th Brigade. While our troops were digging in east of the road running south from Ginchy, Lts Kidd and Phillips, on a machine of 3 Sqn, saw the enemy massing in the trenches opposite. They got the artillery on to the trench by wireless, and made some very good shooting, direct hits being obtained on 4 different bays of trench which were full of Germans at the time.

Some useful contact patrol work was also done by 7 Sqn. Lts Pollard and Scaife, of 9 Sqn, while on contact patrol, saw our infantry being held up by a German machine-gun, which they attacked from the air, and enabled the advance to be continued.

2 Lt Dabbs and 2 Lt Dewar, on an F.E.2d of 20 Sqn, engaged a Fokker over Rumbeke. Fire was opened at 200 yards, and the German immediately dived steeply. The F.E. finished one drum, by which time the Fokker was spinning and eventually crashed into the bank of a canal east of Roulers.

In the course of a combat a Fokker struck a De Havilland of 29 Sqn flown by Lt Bowman. The aileron king post of the De Havilland was broken off and the aileron control shot away. Lt Bowman recrossed the line at 2,500 feet.

On the IVth Army front there were many combats, and our machines were very successful in keeping the enemy well east of the battle area and preventing any interference with artillery and contact patrol work. One offensive patrol of six F.E.s of 22 Sqn was fighting practically the whole time from 8 a.m. to 10.30 a.m., firing 48½ drums of ammunition.

Lt Knight, on a De Havilland of 24 Sqn, attacked a single-seater machine escorting an L.V.G. north of Le Sars. After a few rounds the hostile machine went down in a spiral followed by the De Havilland. The hostile machine turned underneath Lt Knight, who dived almost vertically, and fired the remainder of the drum at about 5 yards range, almost colliding with the enemy machine, which went down in a nose dive disappearing into a cloud apparently out of control. Many other machines were driven down on this front.

Six F.E.s of 23 Sqn, whilst on photographic duty, were heavily engaged by 20 hostile machines. Two of the F.E.s during the fighting became detached and were attacked by 5 hostile machines. One hostile machine was brought down and was seen to crash in a field. One of the F.E.s was also brought down.

2 Lt Brearley on a De Havilland of 29 Sqn, crossing the lines at 11,500 feet, got directly above a German kite balloon, and, pretending to be in trouble, fell in side stalls to 1,500 feet, whence he dived at the balloon which was close to the ground. He opened fire at 500 yards with Buckingham bullets, and continued firing until he almost touched the balloon. Just as he passed over it, the balloon burst into flames, and was completely destroyed in a few seconds.

Casualties: Sqn 10, *Pte J. B. W. Phillips, A.S.C. (Attached), observer wounded;* **8,** *2 Lt A. P. V. Daly, pilot, wounded;* **24,** *2 Lt H. C. Evans, pilot, missing;* **4,** *2 Lt H. E. McCutcheon, pilot, killed; 2 Lt F. W. Rennie, observer, wounded;* **23,** *2 Lt E. A. H. Sams, pilot, missing; 13958 Cpl W. Summers, observer, missing;* **27,** *2 Lt P. A. Wright, wounded; and* **9,** *15704 2 AM S. C. Jenner, wireless operator, wounded.*

September 4th
Weather was unfavourable, with low clouds and showers all day.

Two targets were registered by the 2nd Brigade and 7 direct hits obtained on a hostile battery.

Two hostile batteries were silenced, explosions occurring in both, by the 4th Brigade.

The 5th Brigade ranged on gun positions. One pit was destroyed and four damaged. Two batteries were silenced. Capt Jenkins of 15 Sqn ranged a 60-pounder battery on to an A.A. gun mounted on a lorry. A house close by was wrecked, and the gun withdrew. Capt Jenkins then went down and fired a drum with his machine-gun at the A.A. gun.

Night Flying: a pilot of the 1st Brigade after dropping bombs lost his way in the darkness and sounded his Klaxon horn. Numerous Very lights and rockets were sent up, which enabled him to pick up his bearings.

The balloons of 1 Kite Balloon Section were shelled twice during the night of the 3rd/4th. Slight damage was done to the balloon.

September 5th
Weather continued unfavourable.

Some successful artillery work was accomplished on the fronts of the 4th and 5th Brigades.

Lts Curphey, Hunt and Bainbridge, of 32 Sqn, while on offensive patrol encountered 13 hostile machines which they attacked. In the course of the fight, Lt Bainbridge was brought down.

September 6th
Artillery working with machines of the 5th Brigade destroyed 2 pits and

damaged 5, 4 of which were badly damaged. The weather was not favourable for artillery work.

2 Lt C. Gordon-Davis and Cpl Birch, in an F.E.2d of 20 Sqn, engaged and drove down a hostile machine over Passchendaele. The observer of a second hostile machine was hit. A third hostile machine, engaged by 2 Lt Reid and 2 Lt Golding, also of 20 Sqn, was driven down apparently on fire.

Flt Sgt McCudden, of 29 Sqn, on a De Havilland Scout, engaged a hostile machine over Houthem. The Ist Anzac Corps report that this machine crashed.

A patrol of 24 Sqn encountered 8 hostile machines over Le Sars. Lt Saundby attacked one, which was seen to crash near Flers. Capt Norris of 21 Sqn attacked an L.V.G. near Peronne. Having fired 150 rounds at it, the hostile machine went down completely out of control.

A reconnaissance of 70 Sqn encountered several hostile aircraft west of Busigny. After a considerable amount of fighting, Capt Sanday hit a hostile machine, which caught fire and crashed near Elincourt.

An offensive patrol of 70 Sqn engaged 4 hostile machines north-east of Bapaume. Two of these were attacked by Lt R. B. Mansell and 2 Lt G. N. Cousans, and one of them was apparently hit. It turned over, side-slipped and went down in a spinning nose dive.

Capt Cruikshank, of 70 Sqn, engaged 4 Rolands, one of which was forced to land and ran in to the parapet of a trench near Flers. Later on, he attacked 3 Rolands, one of which he drove down.

Machines of the 1st Brigade dropped 114 20-pound bombs on the following places: Lievin, Meurchin, Auchy, Annoeullin. The results were not always observed, but in many cases the objectives were hit, and considerable damage done.

The machines of the 2nd Brigade dropped fifty-four 112-pound bombs on a factory at Quesnoy which was hit, and a big explosion occurred. A fire was observed at the point where the road and the canal converge. Twenty-six 112-pound bombs were dropped on hutments at Westroosebeke.

Sixty-two 112-pound bombs were dropped by machines of the 3rd Brigade at Achiet le Grand. The railway station was hit on several occasions, and considerable damage was done to the town.

Machines of the 5th Brigade attacked the group of aerodromes at Bertincourt and Velu. As the machines approached their objective, the Germans wheeled all their aeroplanes out of the sheds. One of the machines was destroyed on the ground by a bomb, and the remaining bombs did considerable damage to the aerodrome. No sheds were actually seen to be hit. Two machines of this Brigade did not return.

The station and rolling stock at Aulnoye Junction were attacked by machines from G.H.Q. Squadrons, twenty-four 20-pound and eight 112-pound bombs being dropped. All the machines came down to 500 to 800 feet, and all the bombs with one exception hit the objective. Pilots report that an immense amount of damage was done to the rolling stock and the Station. Bombs were also dropped on Le Transloy, and a large explosion was seen in the village.

Casualties: Sqn 19, *Capt C. G. A. Williams, slightly wounded;* **25,** *2 Lt J. L. Robertson and 2 Lt C. E. Kemp, missing;* **42,** *2 Lt C. S. L. Thomas, missing;* **70,** *2 Lt T. K. Tullis and 2 Lt J. C. Taylor, missing; and* **15,** *Lt F. Hodgson, wounded.*

September 7th

Machines of the 1st Brigade successfully registered on two trench targets. Siege artillery obtained a direct hit on one pit and caused an explosion of ammunition.

4th Brigade engaged 16 hostile batteries, obtaining 4 direct hits on emplacements, and causing two explosions. Several direct hits were obtained on trenches and strong points.

5th Brigade registered 34 trench points, doing considerable damage. Five gun pits were destroyed and 10 damaged. Two ammunition pits were blown up, 3 other battery positions hit, and 3 batteries silenced.

2 Lt Scott, with Lt Bird, of 4 Sqn, on seeing a hostile machine land, obtained 3 hits before it could leave the ground. The machine was set on fire and completely destroyed.

Machines of the 1st and 2nd Brigades had ten indecisive combats.

On the IIIrd Army front the enemy's activity was considerably above the average. Several of his machines attempted to cross the lines for a short distance. One was brought down by A.A. fire and was last seen diving steeply behind Adinfer Wood.

An offensive patrol of 24 Sqn engaged five hostile machines which were patrolling in the neighbourhood of Bapaume. Lt Wood got to close quarters with one and drove it down.

An offensive patrol of 32 Sqn, composed of 2 Lt Mare-Montambault, Lt Curphey and 2 Lt Bentley, encountered a number of hostile machines near Puisieux with which they were engaged for 15 minutes. One of the enemy's machines was certainly hit. During the course of the fight, 3 more machines reinforced the enemy. These were attacked by Lt Bentley, and eventually all the enemy machines were driven off. Late on the evening of the 6th, Capt Mackay, of 4 Sqn, was attacked by a hostile aeroplane. He opened fire, and the enemy dived down apparently out of control. Two other machines saw the hostile aircraft pass under them, and as long as it was observed it was out of control.

1st Brigade—157 20-pound bombs and one 112-pound bomb were

dropped on the following places: Cross roads Lievin, Tourmignies Aerodrome, hostile battery Le Pietre, junction of the second line trenches, distillery, La Bassee, Meurchin, Auchy, Canteleux, Aubers, Angres and Phalempin Aerodrome.

2nd Brigade—The following aerodromes were attacked twice during the day: Beveren, Rumbeke, Coucou (Menin), Reckem, Wasquehal, Mouveaux. In addition to 20-pound bombs, 68 incendiary bombs were dropped.

3rd Brigade—Machines of the 3rd Brigade dropped bombs on Oppy and the aerodromes at Douai, Valenciennes and Saultain. Machines of 27 Sqn dropped forty-five 20-pound bombs on Beaucamp Aerodrome.

Casualties: Sqn 22, *2 Lt F. W. Holder, wounded; Lt E. Ambler, wounded; and* **15,** *2 Lt C. R. Cook, wounded.*

7–17 September, 1916

This is the first communiqué to be printed, instead of typewritten and duplicated.

Lt Max von Mulzer, presumably the intended victim of the elaborate decoy plot reported on 6 September, was a leading German 'ace' of the time. Although the report is not specific, the aircraft was presumably one of the new Fokker biplanes, as very few of the old E-series monoplanes were still at the Front. If the pilot was von Mulzer, he certainly survived this encounter, for he was killed in an Albatros accident on 26 September, when his victory score was 10 Allied aircraft destroyed.

The F.E.2b squadron involved in the plot cannot be identified from the information given, but the F.E.8 may have been from 40 Sqn, which had arrived in France on 25 August.

Bad weather restricted flying during the period of this communiqué, but in the limited combat activities which were reported the gap between British and enemy losses appeared to be narrowing.

COMMUNIQUÉ NO. 53

September 7th

12 Sqn carried out a successful bombing raid on the aerodromes at Valenciennes and La Briquette. On reaching Hamel, on the outward journey, the ground became totally obscured, and Capt Tyson, the leader, took the course entirely by compass. After seventy minutes a clear patch in the clouds was reached over the aerodrome, and considerable damage was caused.

September 8th*

1st Brigade ranged on a hostile battery, causing a large explosion. Siege artillery obtained five direct hits on two other batteries, in addition to causing several small explosions. Trenches were considerably damaged by artillery ranged by machines of the 5th Brigade. One gun pit was destroyed, five damaged, and an ammunition pit blown up.

A scheme was arranged by the 1st Brigade to try to catch Lt Mulzer. Capt Dixon, flying at 9,000–10,000 feet, patrolled from Provin to Meri-court. Capt Lloyd and 2 Lt Webb, flying at 15,000 feet and 14,000 feet respectively, patrolled just west of the lines, keeping Capt Dixon in sight.

* September 6th in original text.

At about 5.20 p.m. a Fokker which had been getting height for about twenty minutes, was east of Carvin, and Capt Dixon at about 10,500 feet over Provin. Each time Capt Dixon turned towards the Fokker he sheered off. At 5.35 p.m. anti-aircraft shells burst very close to Capt Dixon, who pretended he was hit and started going down in circles, stalling from time to time. The Fokker immediately turned towards Capt Dixon, who gradually got nearer the lines, still going down. At 5.40 p.m., and when at 7,500 feet up, Capt Dixon put on his engine and started fighting the Fokker which was then about 500 feet higher. Capt Dixon engaged the hostile machine until 5.45 p.m., getting off four drums. When over Hulluch the Fokker suddenly saw Capt Lloyd and 2 Lt Webb, followed by an F.E.8 diving on him. All three F.E.2bs fired at the Fokker, who sheered off eastwards, closely followed at about 30 yards by 2 Lt Webb, who got off one drum. Capt Lloyd, who was above and about 50 yards away, fired a drum and a half. The hostile machine nose dived sharply, and was last seen going vertically through the clouds. Anti-aircraft gunners report that at 5.50 p.m. a hostile machine was seen apparently out of control and still in a nose dive just above Pont-á-Vendin.

The following places were bombed by machines of the 1st Brigade: Lievin, Haisnes, Hulluch, Givenchy, Auchy La Bassée, Provin Station and town, and on other places of importance. Wingles and La Bassée were bombed by night.

3rd Brigade dropped thirty 112-pound bombs on a dump near the railway line between Achiet-le-Grand and Miraumont. Five machines of 21 Sqn bombed Velu aerodrome and destroyed one shed. Ten 20-pound bombs were dropped by machines of the 5th Brigade on Grandcourt and the Grandcourt-St Pierre–Divion road. A successful bomb raid was carried out by machines of 27 Sqn on the Beaucamp aerodrome. Considerable damage was done to hangars, sheds and ground.

At 9 a.m. on September 8th, Lt Philpott, 12 Sqn, went out alone in thick fog, and followed the road at about 100 feet to Arras. He flew up and down the German front line trenches for about thirty minutes, firing his Lewis gun at groups of Germans from about 50 to 100 feet. Although fired at a great deal by machine-gun and rifle fire, his machine was not hit.

Casualties: Sqn 24, *2 Lt A. E. Glew, killed;* **22,** *Lt E. A. Bowen, missing; Lt R. M. Stalker, missing;* **20,** *2 Lt D. H. Dabbs, wounded; 8865 2 AM R. Anderson, wireless operator, killed.*

September 9th

1st Brigade ranged on and silenced an A.A. battery, 4 direct hits being obtained. Machines of the 2nd Brigade successfully ranged on one hostile battery, and machines of the 4th Brigade ranged on 10 active hostile batteries, silencing them and causing 4 explosions. Forty direct hits were obtained on trench points. Machines of the 5th Brigade registered 6 trench points, causing considerable damage. Seven gun pits were destroyed, 6 damaged, and 4 ammunition pits blown up.

2 Lt N. W. Webb and Cpl L. C. Court, 25 Sqn, while on a bombing raid engaged a hostile machine over Pont-á-Vendin. Cpl Court fired a whole drum at about 30 yards range, and the hostile machine ceased firing. The engine stopped, and the machine went down out of control, and was eventually seen to be wrecked.

Lt W. H. Dore and 2 Lt R. M. Collingwood, 1 Sqn, engaged a Fokker near Menin which they drove down in a spinning nose dive. They also engaged and drove down an L.V.G.

On the evening of the 8th, 2 Lt T. M. B. Newton and 1 AM O'Lieff engaged and damaged a Fokker over Ypres. The engine of the hostile machine stopped and the aeroplane descended in a series of vertical dives. In the course of further fighting a Fokker was brought down and seen to crash near St Julien by Lt W. H. Hubbard and Lt H. B. Rickards of 5 Sqn.

A formation of about 20 hostile machines was engaged by machines of the 3rd Brigade near Miraumont. In the course of the combat, which assumed a general character, two hostile machines engaged by Lt Harvey and 2 Lt Cathie, 11 Sqn, were driven down damaged. 2 Lt Molloy and Sgt Allen, also of 11 Sqn, drove down another enemy machine, apparently out of control. One hostile machine was seen to make a forced landing near Bapaume.

An offensive patrol of De Havillands of 32 Sqn, composed of Capt L. P. Aizlewood, 2 Lt Henty and 2 Lt Mare-Montembault, engaged five hostile machines over Thiepval. In the course of the fight, Capt Aizlewood dived at one of the hostile machines, reserving his fire until within 20 yards, when he fired a complete drum. He got so close that he ran into the tail of the hostile machine, thereby breaking the under-carriage and propellor of the De Havilland, and damaging the tail-booms. His machine became almost uncontrollable, but he succeeded in regaining our lines and landing near Aveluy without injury to himself. The hostile machine was seen to crash near Miraumont.

3rd Brigade attacked a dump at a railway station between Achiet-le-Grand and Miraumont. A great number of the bombs fell on the dump and railway, and caused considerable damage. Miraumont Station was attacked with success by the 5th Brigade with thirty-two 20-pound bombs. 27 Sqn dropped sixty-four 20-pound bombs on Le Mesnil. Results were mostly unobserved owing to thick haze.

Machines of the 1st Brigade bombed the following places: Carvin, Bauvin, Billy Montigny, a distillery, Bois de Biez, Rue d'Enfer, Rouvroy siding, station and dump, La Bassée Station, and Sallaumines. A number of bombs were seen to hit the mark and do considerable damage. Machines of the 2nd Brigade bombed by night billets in Zonnebeke and a dump, both of which were hit.

In spite of the very unfavourable weather some very good contact patrol work was done by machines of the 4th Brigade. The progress of our attacks and the movements of enemy troops were closely followed by our aeroplanes, flying at low altitudes.

Lt Robarts with Lt Williams of 22 Sqn, observed a number of men working near Beaumont-Hamel. They dived down to 2,500 feet and fired at them.

Lt Blount with Lt Pearson of 34 Sqn, dived down to 800 feet whilst on contact patrol work, and fired a drum into a crater in which the enemy were seen.

Casualties: Sqn 11, *2 Lt W. H. C. Buntine, wounded;* **24,** *Lt N. P. Manfield, missing;* **22,** *Lt H. Strathy Mackay, killed; Lt A. J. Bowerman, killed;* **70,** *2 Lt H. A. Howell, wounded; 2 Lt G. W. Cousans, killed;* **8,** *2 Lt Stainer, wounded.*

September 10th

The weather was unsatisfactory for observation. Fifteen trench points were registered by the 5th Brigade and during the course of fire on gun positions, two pits were destroyed, one was damaged, and an ammunition pit was blown up.

5th Brigade again attacked Miraumont with thirty 20-pound bombs.

Casualty: Sqn 34, *2 Lt C. J. Campbell, slightly wounded.*

September 11th

The weather continued unfavourable for the greater part of the day.

Some successful artillery co-operation was carried out by machines of the 4th and 5th Brigade.

On account of the weather there was little activity. Lt Horswell and Lt A. P. Maclean of 70 Sqn, while on offensive patrol in the Bapaume area engaged several hostile machines, one of which they drove down completely out of control.

Casualties: Sqn 9, *2 Lt D. L. Reed, slightly wounded;* **24,** *Lt L. R. Briggs, missing;* **23,** *2 Lt G. J. Firbank and 2 Lt L. G. Vernon, both missing.*

September 12th

Low clouds all day with occasional showers.

One heavy battery was successfully ranged on by machines of the 2nd Brigade. The 4th Brigade completed some successful trench shoots. Four gun pits were damaged, 4 ammunition pits blown up and 3 active batteries silenced by artillery ranged by machines of the 5th Brigade.

2 Lt Horridge and 2 Lt Scutt, on a B.E.2d of 7 Sqn, engaged a hostile machine near Pozieres. After several bursts of fire from the B.E.2d, the German machine burst into flames and fell to the ground in our lines near Pozières.

On the night of the 12th/13th, 4 machines of 13 Sqn set out to bomb Achiet-le-Grand Station. Owing to adverse weather conditions, only 2 machines reached their objective.

The 5th Brigade carried out a bombing attack against Courcelette and Miraumont Stations.

Casualty: Sqn 60, *Capt F. E. Goodrich, killed.*

September 13th

Low clouds and rain throughout the day, in consequence of which there was little aerial activity on either side.

4th Brigade succeeded in ranging on and silencing 4 hostile batteries, and the 5th Brigade ranged on to 2 hostile batteries, in one of which an ammunition pit was exploded.

September 13th

Unfavourable weather.

Casualty: Sqn 9, *2 Lt C. S. Hollinghurst, wounded.*

September 14th

Heavy artillery was ranged on an A.A. battery by a machine of the 1st Brigade, and direct hits obtained. The Divisional artillery was also ranged on an A.A. battery which was silenced.

Machines of the 3rd Brigade ranged on 2 hostile batteries and 3 direct hits were obtained by our artillery.

Fourteen batteries were engaged through machines of the 4th Brigade and 5 direct hits were obtained. The guns were chiefly employed on trench work and did a great deal of damage to the trenches.

A house containing a machine-gun in Thiepval was ranged on and destroyed with machines of the 5th Brigade. Two gun pits were destroyed, 4 damaged, 1 ammunition pit was blown up causing a very large explosion, and 6 battery positions were hit. In addition to these, enemy trenches were much damaged.

A considerable amount of valuable contact patrol work was done during the day. On two occasions Lt Coller with Lt Scaife used a Klaxon horn, and each time signals were immediately put forth, which showed the pilot the exact locality of our men.

There was a considerable amount of fighting on the fronts of the 3rd, 4th and 5th Brigades. Capt Price and Lt Libby, 11 Sqn, drove down a hostile machine apparently out of control. 2 Lt Morris and Lt Rees, 11 Sqn, also drove down a hostile machine which appeared to be out of control.

Machines of 11 Sqn, acting as escort to bombing machines, successfully prevented the enemy from interfering with the bombing party, and drove off all hostile attacks.

Capt Wilkinson, Lts Knight, Morgan, Bowring and Sgt Cockerell, on De Havilland Scouts of 24 Sqn, when north of Bapaume, saw 4 hostile machines about to attack some F.E.s. They immediately attacked the Germans, who soon discontinued the fight and turned east. Four H.A. were encountered over Fremicourt. Sgt Cockerell at once opened fire and Lt Knight followed up, getting on to the H.A. and fired about 15 rounds at very close range. The German pilot fell forward, and flames were seen to come out of the cockpit, which gradually enveloped the whole machine. After falling 1,500 feet the wings came off, and the remains hit the ground near Manancourt. The other H.A. turned east and disappeared.

Capt R. H. G. Neville of 21 Sqn, was returning from a bomb raid on Le Transloy when he nearly collided with an L.V.G., going north-east. He pursued and fired at him, and noticed that the hostile machine had no observer. He followed him to within 1,000 yards south-west of Velu aerodrome. The hostile machine stalled over a hedge and dropped into a field. Capt Neville is convinced that the German was hit, and no one was seen to get out of the machine.

An offensive patrol of 27 Sqn attacked and dispersed 5 hostile machines, one of which was observed to land amid shell holes about a mile behind the front line trenches near Sailly Saillissel. Later they engaged two L.V.G.s. 2 Lt Forbes fired a full drum at very close range into one machine, which dived vertically and was lost sight of. Shortly afterwards, however, a hostile machine was seen to fall in flames in the Bois des Vaux.

2 Lt A. M. Vaucour and 2 Lt A. J. Bott, on a Sopwith of 70 Sqn,

drove off three hostile aeroplanes which attacked them near Havrincourt. One of these was driven down and seen to land in the open country.

Machines of 70 Sqn, while returning from a reconnaissance over Bapaume, were attacked by 6 hostile aeroplanes. Capt Patrick, with Lt Burke, turned and dived at one of the enemy, and a general engagement ensued, in which Lt Gale's machine was brought down and Lt Burke was killed.

Bombs were dropped by the 1st Brigade on Avion, where billets near the railway were hit. Other rest billets were also attacked by this Brigade. 3rd Brigade attacked a railway dump west of Irles. Observation was difficult, but many bombs appeared to burst on and around the dump. Machines of the 5th Brigade attacked Courcelette, Le Sars, and Miraumont.

Sgt J. Drew and 2 Lt J. A. Gorges, 16 Sqn, observing a batch of men walking along the railway at Lievin, descended to 1,500 feet and fired two drums at them.

Casualties: Sqn 70, *2 Lt S. H. Gale and 285, Sapper Strathey, missing; 2 Lt E. W. Burke, killed in combat;* **24,** *2 Lt J. V. Bowring, missing.*

15 – 24 September, 1916

Clear warnings were now visible that Germany was entering into a second period of air superiority. In addition to the formation of the new Jagdstaffeln with their markedly superior fighting aircraft, more squadrons of all types were being concentrated on the Somme.

On 15 September, B.E.2cs, B.E.12s and Martinsydes, made some very successful bombing attacks, and the escorting fighters, when employed, were able to beat off enemy opposition. On the 17th it was a very different story. The raid on Marcoing station by 12 Sqn B.E.2cs, with an escort of 11 Sqn F.E.2bs, was heavily engaged on the homeward journey and six R.F.C. aircraft were lost. Five of the British machines were shot down by Jasta 2 making its first operational sortie with Albatros DIs. Boelcke himself claimed one victim, and a new pilot, Lt Manfred von Richthofen, scored his first victory against one of the F.E.2bs. Von Richthofen's final victory score of 80 Allied aircraft destroyed was the highest on either side in World War I.

During the period covered by this communiqué more than 20 R.F.C. aircraft were lost. Four more combat victories for Albert Ball were recorded.

An unusual incident on 15 September was the destruction of an L.V.G. two-seater by a 60 Sqn pilot using his Le Prieur anti-balloon rockets.

COMMUNIQUÉ NO. 54

September 15th

1st Brigade—Heavy and Siege Artillery were ranged on 8 hostile batteries, O.K.s being obtained on 6 gun pits. On the IInd Army front 7 hostile batteries were successfully engaged, and one explosion caused among ammunition. On the IIIrd Army front 8 Sqn successfully ranged the 91st and 93rd Siege batteries, obtaining several O.K.s on hostile gun positions. On the IVth Army front 70 hostile batteries were engaged, and 159 active batteries were located, 29 of which were silenced. Thirteen direct hits were observed.

5th Brigade: four infantry targets by use of the 'area call', 3 of these were seen to be scattered, and casualties inflicted. Clouds prevented observation in the fourth case, in which the target consisted of 2 battalions. Batteries were constantly silenced throughout the day by the use

7—NIEUPORT TYPE XVII SCOUT—110 H.P. LE RHÔNE ENGINE

Before the days of synchronised guns, the French Nieuport Scout was one of the most successful single-seat fighters. Its Lewis gun was mounted on the upper wing to fire forward clear of the airscrew disc. For shooting down enemy observation balloons electrically-fired Le Prieur rockets were sometimes mounted on the Vee interplane struts. The first Nieuports were received by the RFC in France in March 1916 and were attached to Nos. 1 and 11 Squadrons.

of the 'area call'. Twelve gun pits were destroyed, 15 damaged and 4 ammunition pits blown up. Out of 51 targets ranged on, 15 Sqn dealt successfully with 30.

During the day over 8 tons of explosives were dropped by our machines with highly satisfactory results. 1st Brigade attacked Provin Aerodrome and Billy Montigny, causing considerable damage in both cases. Zonnebeke Chateau and Quesnoy factories were attacked by the 2nd Brigade, both with satisfactory results.

3rd Brigade carried out three successful raids. At the Chateau at St Leger many bombs fell close to the target, and fires broke out in the village. At Bapaume Station 38 bombs were dropped from heights of from 200 to 800 feet by 12 Sqn with an escort of 11 Sqn. One train, several trucks and the station buildings were repeatedly hit, and the railway line badly damaged. At Velu Station three trains were hit, several coaches derailed, and a large store by the side of the line was set on fire. At Bertincourt Aerodrome, where 16 bombs were dropped, the results were unobserved owing to clouds.

IXth Wing—At 4.50 a.m. two machines of 19 Sqn left to attack Havrincourt Château. Four 112-pound bombs were dropped from a height of 1,400 feet. Capt G. W. D. Allen reports that one of his bombs exploded in the south-west corner of the Château, knocking out one of the walls. 2 Lt Edwards did not observe the burst of his bombs. At the same time two machines of 27 Sqn attacked Bourlon Château. A small fire was started among the outhouses. Between 7 and 10 a.m. Bourlon Château was again attacked by 27 Sqn. Four bombs dropped from a height of 6,000 feet hit the Château.

Shortly after 2 p.m. 8 Martinsydes of 27 Sqn attacked trains in the vicinity of Cambrai. A 112-pound bomb dropped from a height of 500 feet exploded and blew up an ammunition train, one bomb having previously hit the engine. Another 112-pound bomb dropped in the midst of a mass of troops, who got out of the train. A truck of another train was also hit. During this raid some of the pilots attacked transport, which was alongside the train, with machine-gun fire. Damage was also done to trains at Bantouzelle, Epehy and Achiet le Grand. 2 Lt L. F. Forbes, of 27 Sqn attacked with success troops and transport on a road leading to Le Transloy.

Bapaume and Achiet le Grand were attacked by 11 Sqn late on the evening of the 15th.

An offensive patrol of 60 Sqn encountered several hostile machines, chiefly Rolands, near Bapaume about 9.30 a.m. 2 Lt Cole fired one drum into a Roland, which was last seen falling in an uncontrollable spin. Lt

Ball brought down one Roland, which was seen to crash east of Beugny. 2 Lt Walters, 60 Sqn, on a Nieuport, was engaged in an attack against 8 hostile kite balloons. Finding that the balloon allotted to him was not up, he attacked an L.V.G., firing his Le Prieur rockets, one of which entered the enemy's fuselage. The L.V.G. at once burst into flames and fell to earth.

12 Sqn's bombing raid to Bapaume Station was heavily engaged. The bombers came very low to take good aim, and were well protected by the escort. Four German machines were brought down and seen to crash. They were accounted for by the following pilots and observers: Lt Harvey with 2 Lt Cathie, 2 Lt Bowman with Sgt Walker, 2 Lt Molloy with Sgt Morton, Capt Foot with 2 Lt Welsford, and Lt Quested with Cpl Monk. Two others were driven down out of control. Lt Philpot, in one of the bombing machines engaged a hostile aeroplane and apparently hit the observer, who was seen to fall forwards.

11 Sqn's reconnaissance was attacked by about 10 machines near Velu. A very vigorous fight ensued, and two of the Germans were seen to go down out of control.

One hostile kite balloon was brought down by Lt Bell-Irving, 60 Sqn, on the evening of the 14th, and another by Lt Gilchrist, 60 Sqn, on the 15th. From pilots' reports, it seems almost certain that a second balloon was brought down on the morning of the 15th. This was probably done by Capt Summers, who was taking part in the attack and has not returned.

Lts Byrne, Mackay and Nixon, of 24 Sqn, whilst on offensive patrol near Morval, encountered 17 hostile aeroplanes at various heights. They dived into the middle of the hostile formation and attacked. Lt Byrne got to very close quarters with one machine, which burst into flames and was seen to crash. He then attacked a second machine, which was driven down and crashed in a field. Lt Knight, also of 24 Sqn, attacked a hostile machine over Flers, into which he fired half a drum. The German machine went down vertically and was seen to crash.

Lt Gould and Lt Turnbull, of 23 Sqn, while on offensive patrol, attacked 11 hostile machines near Bapaume. One of the hostile machines was destroyed. Sgt Irwin with 2 Lt Cox, 23 Sqn, whilst on an offensive patrol near Bapaume, at 9.45 a.m., met 4 L.V.G.s flying north. They fired a drum into one machine, which left the others and went down in a nose dive. They were unable to see it crash, but 2 Lt Blake saw what he took to be an L.V.G. crashed on the ground at about the spot where this machine would have to come to ground.

2 Lt Mare-Montembault, 32 Sqn, while on offensive patrol, dived at 5 hostile machines and was at the same time attacked from behind by a Roland. He turned and got behind the hostile machine, kept on its tail and drove it down. Lt Bentley, of the same patrol, saw a hostile machine descending in flames.

The machines of 27 Sqn, which attacked Bourlon Château, were heavily engaged for about 30 minutes. In the engagement one hostile machine was destroyed and two others driven down. The others were dispersed.

2 Lt A. M. Vaucour and 2 Lt H. A. Bott, of 70 Sqn, engaged and drove off a hostile machine. During the engagement they lost their formation, and were later attacked by 3 machines, 2 of which attacked from below, the third from above. The latter was fired at by Lt Bott, whereupon the enemy lost height and tried to get under the Sopwith. In endeavouring to do so, he collided with one of the other Germans, who crashed to earth. The two remaining machines, one of which was damaged, then left them. Shortly afterwards, Lt Vaucour was attacked by several Germans, one of which he drove down. Capt C. K. C. Patrick and Capt F. G. Glenday, of 70 Sqn, dived at two hostile machines which were attacking another Sopwith. One of the Germans was driven down and crashed. Captain Patrick attacked the second German, but was forced to break off the fight, as his observer was wounded. Capt Glenday died in hospital as the result of his wounds.

The course of the infantry advance was watched throughout the day by contact patrol machines of the 4th and 5th Brigades and IXth Wing. The task of these machines was greatly facilitated by the large number of flares lighted by the infantry.

The movements of the 'tanks' (armoured cars) could be easily observed, and were reported throughout the day.

2 Lt Irons, of 21 Sqn, observed infantry on the Bapaume–Le Sars Road. He dived down to 200 feet and attacked them with his machine-gun, firing about 100 rounds, and causing great panic and many casualties. He was subjected to very heavy rifle fire.

Maj Carthew and 2 Lt Brewis, 4 Sqn, attacked with their machine-guns two anti-aircraft guns on lorries.

On many occasions German infantry were engaged with machine-gun fire from aeroplanes, and one battery was temporarily silenced.

On the 15th instant the IInd Corps Counter Battery Group, Reserve Army, took in from aeroplanes of the XVth Wing 179 'area calls' for active batteries and 9 'area calls' for infantry targets, one of which was an LL call.

Casualties: Sqn 70, *2 Lt C. J. Beatty, killed; Capt F. G. Glenday, killed;* **3,** *2 Lt H. Tatton, wounded;* **12,** *Capt E. J. Tyson, wounded; 5569 Sgt G. B. Walker, wounded (died of wounds);* **70,** *Capt G. L. Cruikshank, missing; Lt R. A. Preston, missing; 2 Lt F. H. Bowyer, missing; 2 Lt W. B. Saint,* *missing;* **27,** *2 Lt C. J. Kennedy, missing;* **60,** *Capt A. S. M. Summers, missing;* **21,** *2 Lt C. Elphinstone, missing;* **11,** *2 Lt F. E. Hollingsworth, missing; and 2 Lt H. M. W. Wells, missing.*

September 16th

Machines of the 3rd Brigade ranged the 93rd Siege Battery and obtained 12 direct hits, causing an explosion of ammunition in a hostile battery. The 128th and 143rd Siege Batteries were also successfully ranged on to emplacements.

Aeroplanes of the 4th Brigade ranged our batteries on to 45 hostile batteries, causing several heavy explosions and obtaining direct hits on numerous strong points, infantry and transport.

On the 5th Brigade front 17 trench points were registered; 2 gun pits were destroyed and 15 damaged. Sixty-one ammunition pits were blown up and a large number of batteries silenced.

An 'area call' was sent down to open fire on a hostile battery being withdrawn from its position south-west of Le Sars. Within three minutes heavy fire was opened, and one gun was hit.

2 Lt S. E. Cowan, 24 Sqn, drove down one hostile machine enveloped in smoke and flames over Sailly Saillisel. 2 Lt P. C. Campbell and 2 Lt W. A. Mackay, 18 Sqn, damaged and drove down an L.V.G. near Combles. By the combined action of English and French machines, two of the enemy's aeroplanes were driven down, and were seen to make forced landings near Bapaume.

Bombing attacks were carried out as under:

By machines of the 1st Brigade—Douai Railway Station and aerodrome. By the 3rd Brigade—Bapaume Station. Considerable damage was done to the station. An offensive patrol of 11 Sqn attacked a dump at Vis en Artois.

The attack on hostile kite balloons carried out by 13 Sqn was unsuccessful.

Contact patrol work continued successfully, and in many instances pilots descended to low altitudes to attack troops and transport with their machine-guns.

2 Lt L. C. Haywood and 2 Lt P. J. Smythe, 18 Sqn, fouled the cable of 6 Kite Balloon Section. 2 Lt Haywood was injured, and 2 Lt P. J. Smythe died of injuries. The kite balloon was cut adrift, and the observer, Lt C. E. Cooper, was killed.

Casualties: 6 Kite Balloon Section, *Lt C. E. A. Cooper, killed;* **Sqn 15,** *Capt K. A. Brooke Murray, wounded;* **2,** *2 Lt D. Cushing, missing;* **21,**

Lt G. Klingenstein, missing; and 11, *2 Lt A. L. Pinkerton and Lt J. W. Saunders, missing.*

September 17th

Observation was difficult owing to clouds. Machines of the 3rd Brigade successfully ranged several Siege Batteries on to hostile emplacements, obtaining some direct hits and silencing guns. On the IVth Army front, 35 active hostile batteries and many trench, infantry, and transport targets were engaged by our artillery with aeroplane observation by machines of the 4th Brigade. Ranged by machines of the 5th Brigade, our artillery destroyed 9 gun-pits, damaged 17, blew up many ammunition pits and dispersed infantry.

Capt R. S. Maxwell and 2 AM A. Stanley, of 20 Sqn, attacked and destroyed a hostile machine.

A bombing raid carried out by machines of the 3rd Brigade was heavily engaged by about 20 hostile machines on its return from Marcoing Station. No details of the fighting are procurable. Four machines of 11 Sqn and 2 of 12 Sqn, which took part in the raid, did not return. A Roland was engaged and driven down out of control by Sgt Thompson and Sgt Clarkson, of 11 Sqn.

2 Lt J. W. Brophy, 21 Sqn, attacked a hostile machine over the Bois de St Pierre Vaast. A burst of flame was seen to come from the hostile machine as it went down in a steep dive.

2 Lt Lynch and 2 AM Clarke, 3 Sqn, forced an enemy machine to land near Bapaume.

An offensive patrol of 24 Sqn encountered 3 hostile machines over Beaumont Hamel. Shortly after the fight one of the enemy's machines was seen in a wrecked condition on the ground near the scene of the fight.

One hostile machine dropped two bombs near Marieux without causing any damage. Late on the evening of the 17th, Capt E. D. Johnson, of 21 Sqn, attacked and drove off a hostile machine. The enemy observer was hit, and seen to collapse in his machine.

The 1st Brigade attacked Douai Railway Station and Rouvroy during the night of the 16/17th. Machines of this Brigade carried out a further attack on Douai Railway Station on the morning of the 17th.

Poelcappelle rest billets were attacked by the 2nd Brigade by night. In Marcoing Station a very large explosion occurred as the result of bombs dropped by the 3rd Brigade. The rolling stock and the permanent way were seriously damaged. Miraumont was also attacked by this Brigade.

The 4th and 5th Brigades attacked numerous places of importance in the enemy's lines, and the IXth Wing attacked Havrincourt Château, and the Railway Stations at Valenciennes and Cambrai.

Casualties: Sqn 25, *Lt R. Spicer, wounded;* **21,** *2 Lt E. S. Duggan, wounded;* **11,** *Capt D. Gray, missing; Lt L. B. Helder, missing; 2 Lt L. B. F. Morris, missing; Lt T. Rees, missing; 2 Lt H. Thompson, missing; Sgt J. E. Glover, missing; 2 Lt T. P. L. Molloy, missing; Sgt G. J. Morton 2173, missing;* **23,** *3389 Sgt B. Irwin, missing; 2 Lt F. G. Thiery, missing;* **12,** *2 Lt A. F. A. Patterson, missing; Lt R. R. Money, missing;* **70,** *2 Lt O. Nixon, missing; Lt R. Wood, missing; and* **27,** *Lt W. H. S. Chance, missing.*

September 18th

In spite of heavy rain throughout the day, a certain amount of successful artillery work was accomplished by machines of all Brigades ◇ There was little aircraft activity.

A machine was driven down out of control by 2 Lt Caldwell and Capt Welchman, of 8 Sqn.

September 19th

Very little flying until after 3 p.m. on account of adverse weather ◇ Some successful co-operation with artillery was accomplished by the 4th and 5th Brigades.

A reconnaissance of F.E.s of 11 Sqn, escorted by Scouts of 60 Sqn, was attacked by between 20 and 25 hostile machines. Fighting was continuous from Queant homewards, but the escort succeeded in a very large measure in preventing the reconnaissance machine from being molested. 2 Lt Latta, of 60 Sqn, drove down one of the hostile machines out of control. Capt Tower was heavily engaged. His machine was brought down by a Roland. This latter was attacked by Lt Harvey and 2 Lt Cathie, of 11 Sqn, and eventually driven off. 2 Lt Cathie was wounded, and Lt Bowman's machine was hit in the engine, and he only just succeeded in crossing the lines. His observer, Cpl Munk, was wounded in the arm.

The following bombing attacks were carried out: La Bassée on the night of the 18th/19th, and Lens on the 19th by the 1st Brigade, Langemarck Station by the 2nd Brigade, where considerable damage was done to the station and permanent way. Machines of the 5th Brigade dropped bombs on Miraumont in the course of their other duties.

Casualties: Sqn 11, *2 Lt A. J. Cathie, wounded; 3436 Cpl G. Munk, wounded; and* **60,** *Capt H. C. Tower, missing.*

September 20th
Rain during the greater part of the day.

During the fair intervals some successful co-operation with artillery and a little bombing were accomplished. Lt Gawler and 2 Lt Gorges, of 16 Sqn, from a height of 3,000 feet fired on three anti-aircraft guns, two of which immediately stopped firing.

Casualties: Sqn 22, *2 Lt R. W. Carter, missing; and 2 Lt W. J. Gray, missing.*

September 21st
Machines of the 2nd Brigade directed artillery fire successfully on three hostile batteries and caused an explosion of ammunition.

Machines of the 5th Brigade, in co-operation with artillery, registered 11 trench points. Several direct hits from a 12-inch howitzer were recorded on Pys church, which was set on fire. Three gun-pits were destroyed and 2 ammunition pits blown up.

Lt Ball, 60 Sqn, having dispersed, a formation of 6 Rolands by firing his rockets with which he set out to attack a kite balloon, got underneath the nearest machine, and emptied a drum of ammunition into it. The enemy went down and landed, apparently under control. Lt Ball then attacked a second machine from underneath and fired two drums into the pilot's seat. The German was seen to crash. Later in the evening Lt Ball destroyed a second hostile machine.

2 Lt G. T. R. Hill, 29 Sqn, attacked and brought down a hostile kite balloon with Buckingham bullets. At 3,000 feet, when over Comines, he dived at the balloon which was then rapidly descending. He opened fire at 400 yards and finished his drum as he passed about 20 feet over the balloon, which by that time had caught fire.

Lt Phillipi, of 60 Sqn, drove down a hostile machine out of control.

Late on the evening of the 21st Lt Byrne, 24 Sqn, engaged an L.V.G. near Miraumont. After fighting for 25 minutes, the German ceased firing and was seen to make a forced landing. Lt Byrne followed him down to 2,000 feet and fired at the machine on the ground. Also on the evening of the 21st, 2 Lt King, 32 Sqn, assisted by a De Havilland, of 24 Sqn, drove down a hostile machine.

2 Lt Jameson and 2 Lt Landry, 42 Sqn, while acting as escort to machines attacking kite balloons, fired three drums of ammunition from a height of 150 feet at a team of horses hauling down a balloon. One of the horses fell.

22 – 30 September, 1916

Although not alarmingly apparent, the R.F.C. squadrons continued to suffer an increased casualty rate and the assessment of confirmed aircraft losses appeared to show a balance in the enemy's favour. 19 Sqn underwent a bad period, losing five of its B.E.12s.

On 30 September Trenchard wrote to the War Office stressing the necessity for an increased supply of efficient fighters to prevent the development of a serious situation.

A well-planned interdiction operation on 25 September by aircraft of Ist Brigade met with notable success.

Several unusual incidents were recorded during the week—the surrender of some German troops to a contact patrol aircraft, a successful crash-landing by an F.E.2b pilot while unconscious and an attempt by the pilot of a damaged Martinsyde to minimise a crash-landing impact by aiming for a tree. This particular Martinsyde had earlier collided with an aircraft of Jasta 2 during a combat which gave von Richthofen his second victory.

COMMUNIQUÉ NO. 55

September 22nd

Heavy artillery ranged by machines of the 1st Brigade obtained four direct hits and caused a heavy explosion in a gun-pit. Trench targets and trench mortars and an anti-aircraft battery were also successfully ranged on. Machines of the 4th Brigade registered on 50 targets, including 28 batteries. On the 5th Brigade front, the spire of Pys Church was demolished. Ten gun-pits were destroyed, and five ammunition pits exploded.

Capt Walser and Lt Bird, 4 Sqn, registered 10 O.K.s., 15 Ys and 30 Zs for the 13th Siege Battery.

Capt D. O. Mulholland, 40 Sqn, dived at a Fokker which was engaging an F.E.2b. The German was driven down in a spinning nose dive and seen to crash.

Sgt T. Mottershead and 2 Lt C. Street, 25 Sqn, when returning from a bombing raid, were attacked in rear by a Fokker. The F.E. turned and attacked the German, who went down in a spinning nose dive and was destroyed.

Lt Quested and 2 Lt Welsford, 11 Sqn, encountered several formations of four or five Germans in the locality of Bapaume. They brought down an Aviatik, which fell in the Bois de Logeast.

An offensive patrol of 60 Sqn engaged three hostile machines, one of which is believed to have been brought down by Lt Ball.

2 Lt Stewart, 19 Sqn, drove down a hostile machine east of Bapaume. This machine was seen by several pilots to burst into flames, and was doubtless destroyed.

Numerous other encounters took place, in the course of which six hostile machines were driven down in a damaged condition. Their complete destruction cannot be verified.

On the evening of the 22nd Capt R. H. G. Neville, 21 Sqn, was attacked from behind by a hostile machine. In order to better his position he looped, and thus getting behind the enemy, drove him off.

2 Lt H. J. Finer and Cpl Winterbottom, 22 Sqn, attacked a hostile machine on the evening of the 22nd near Sailly Saillisel. The German was driven down, and appeared to be out of control. Later, when near Morval, they attacked two hostile machines, one of which succeeded in getting a position in rear of our machine. The pilot stalled the machine, and the observer stood up to use the rear gun, but he had barely pulled the gun up into position when he was hit in the head and killed. The gun fell down, as the stand had not been clipped into position, and struck the pilot on the head. The pilot remembers nothing distinctly until he recovered consciousness on the way to a French Army Headquarters.

Somain Station was attacked by the 1st Brigade. An ammunition train was blown up, and the rolling stock, permanent way, station and sheds were considerably damaged. The 2nd Brigade hit Zonnebeke Château and Westroosbeke billets. Machines of the IXth Wing attacked Havrincourt Forest, the railway works and sidings at Quievrechain, and the aerodromes at Vely and Bertincourt.

Lt Hall and Lt Randall, 18 Sqn, while on photographic reconniassance, had their machine hit by A.A. fire. The pilot, Lt Hall, was wounded and became unconscious. Lt Randall took control and landed the machine in our lines. Lt Hall died on the way to hospital.

Casualties: Sqn 22, *Cpl A. Winterbottom, killed;* **25,** *Lt K. F. Hunt, missing; 6537 Cpl L. O. Law, missing;* **19,** *2 Lt G. Hedderwick, missing; 2 Lt R. D. Herman, missing; 2 Lt R. H. Edwards, missing;* **18,** *25124 Sgt Jones Cox, missing; and 2 Lt F. A. Hewson, missing.*

September 23rd

Artillery of the Ist Army, in co-operation with machines of the 1st

Brigade, obtained four direct hits on gun pits and two on an anti-aircraft battery, both of which caused explosions. Two hits were obtained by siege artillery on a hostile battery. Trenches were damaged and some lorries west of Vimy were hit. Machines of the 2nd Brigade registered artillery on five hostile batteries. In co-operation with machines of the 3rd Brigade, direct hits were obtained on several hostile emplacements and batteries. Artillery in co-operation with machines of the 4th Brigade destroyed six emplacements and caused five explosions of ammunition. Machines of the 5th Brigade ranged artillery on to Pys Church. Several gun-pits and a number of trenches were severely damaged, and nine ammunition pits blown up.

Lt S. Alder and 1 AM Alexander, 20 Sqn, offensive patrol, engaged and drove down a hostile machine, which crashed south-east of Roulers.

While acting as escort to a bombing raid Lt Bell Irving, of 60 Sqn, observed a Roland attacking an F.E. He dived at the German machine and destroyed it.

Capt Jones, of 32 Sqn, engaged two hostile machines over Warlencourt. He emptied a drum into one of them at a range of five yards, the German machine crashing near Eaucourt l'Abbaye.

In a sharp engagement, which resulted in the loss of three Martinsydes of 27 Sqn, 2 Lt L. F. Forbes collided with a German machine. The latter fell abruptly to earth. One wing of 2 Lt Forbes machine collapsed and the Martinsyde was practically uncontrollable. He, however, succeeded in reaching 24 Sqn's aerodrome. He found that without full engine his machine would not fly. He therefore decided to run into a small tree. In doing so he sustained serious injuries.

Machines of the 1st Brigade dropped 132 bombs, doing considerable damage to Fresnoy, Lens Station and St Sauveur Station, Lille. 2nd Brigade machines attacked Courtrai Station, Poelcappelle and other places of importance. A successful bombing raid was carried out by the 3rd Brigade at Queant, where many explosions and a fire at the station were caused. Douai railway station was also attacked. A fire and an explosion were caused at Roisel Station, which was bombed by the 4th Brigade. Bapaume Station was attacked and considerably damaged by the 5th Brigade. The Zeppelin shed at Maubeuge was attacked by 27 Sqn. The shed was not hit.

Lt Ball, of 60 Sqn, engaged four 2-seater Rolands at about 6 p.m. on the 23rd instant. Approaching from behind Lt Ball scattered his opponents by firing one drum at them. He then got underneath the nearest machine into which he fired 90 rounds. The machine caught fire and was seen to crash.

The 2nd, 3rd and 5th Brigades carried out bombing raids by night.

Casualties: Sqn 27, *2 Lt L. F. Forbes, wounded;* **34,** *2 Lt P. B. Pinsent, died of wounds; Lt J. A. R. Buller, wounded;* **27,** *2 Lt E. J. Roberts, missing; 2 Lt O. C. Godfrey, missing; 17018 Sgt Bellerby, missing;* **21,** *Lt J. M. Kenny, missing;* **18,** *2 Lt J. L. Tibbetts ,missing; and Lt W. G. Warn, missing.*

September 24th

A portion of trench railway was wrecked, and trench targets damaged by Siege artillery working with the 1st Brigade. The 2nd Brigade co-operated with artillery in destroying ammunition and damaging a hostile battery.

Lt S. Alder and Lt R. W. White, of 20 Sqn, attacked and brought down a hostile machine, which crashed south-west of Courtrai. Capt G. R. M. Reid and 2 Lt L. H. Scott, and Lt A. D. Pearce and 2 Lt W. F. Findlay, 20 Sqn, destroyed a German machine south of Rumbeke.

2 Lt J. Gilmour, of 27 Sqn, while on offensive patrol, attacked a Fokker near Bois d'Havrincourt. The German machine was destroyed.

Machines of 22 Sqn while on offensive patrol, encountered a number of hostile machines, one of which was destroyed by Lt Robarts and 2 Lt Williams. This pilot and observer then attacked a second machine which they hit and drove down.

During a general engagement between an offensive patrol of 23 Sqn and several aeroplanes, one of our machines was driven down and the pilot, Lt Osmaston, was killed. Lt Gopsill and 2 Lt Vickery attacked the German and succeeded in driving him down out of control.

There were many other combats during which more of the enemy's machines suffered damage.

The 1st Brigade dropped 52 bombs on Seclin railway station. setting fire to the main station building and hitting the railway bridge. Bombing raids were also carried out by the 2nd, 3rd, 4th and 5th Brigades against ammunition dumps at Vyfwegen and Irles, the aerodrome at Reckem and other places of military importance.

Casualties: Sqn 23, *2 Lt R. S. Osmaston, killed;* **19,** *2 Lt T. West, missing; 2 Lt G. Edwards, missing; and* **27,** *2 Lt E. H. Wingfield, missing.*

September 25th

Machines of the 4th Brigade ranged artillery on to 47 hostile batteries, 34 of which were silenced. Sixteen direct hits were obtained; one battery was completely destroyed, and three large explosions caused in batteries. A column of troops was dispersed and trenches damaged.

Artillery assisted by the 5th Brigade obtained direct hits on Miraumont church with a 15-inch howitzer. They also destroyed 9 gun-pits, damaged 7, and blew up 3 ammunition pits.

2 Lt C. J. Creery, of 21 Sqn, attacked an L.V.G. near Le Transloy. He opened fire at about 50 yards range. At the first burst the observer fell forward, the hostile machine went down and was seen to crash.

Lt Duguid and 2 Lt Van der Byl, 23 Sqn, drove down a hostile machine near Le Transloy.

A German machine was driven down out of control north-east of Peronne by 2 Lt H. A. Taylor, of 27 Sqn.

2 Lt C. H. C. Woolven and 2 AM G. R. Horricks, 25 Sqn, drove down a hostile machine near Freton on the 25th. A hostile machine has been seen in a wrecked condition at this place, and is believed to be the German whom Lt Woolven engaged.

First Brigade bombing raid on Libercourt—the following scheme which was planned to intercept traffic on the Douai–Lille main line, was carried out on September 25th.

The railway station at Libercourt, sidings and rolling stock were to be bombed, and an attempt made to attack trains going south, in the hope that they might be carrying troops or ammunition towards the Somme battlefield.

Patrols, each of 2 F.E.2b aeroplanes of 25 Sqn, and a F.E.8 aeroplane of 40 Sqn, were first sent to attack the aerodromes at Tourmignies, Phalempin and Provin, to prevent German aeroplanes from coming up to interfere. They dropped phosphorous bombs at intervals to keep the aerodromes enveloped in smoke, and from time to time, a 20-pound high explosive bomb to show that they were still there.

Two more F.E.2bs of 25 Sqn, each protected by a F.E.8 of 40 Sqn, were then to descend and attack the trains. The first train to appear was seen leaving Libercourt at about 1.40 p.m., and the F.E.2bs dived down to attack it. While descending, a second train was seen coming up the Henin Lietard branch line towards Ostricourt where it joins the main line, and one of the F.E.2bs diverted on to it.

Capt Chadwick, with Sgt Brown, attacked the first train from a height of about 800 feet near Ostricourt. Six 20-pound bombs were dropped, the engine was hit, became derailed and two or three of the front coaches partly telescoped. German soldiers immediately began to alight, were fired on, and ran towards Ostricourt village and woods. There were so many men that Capt Chadwick said it would have been hard to miss them and a large number were either killed or wounded.

Meanwhile, the second train came to a standstill near the junction as the wrecked train on the main line was blocking its way. The other F.E.2b, pilot Lt Woolvern, with Lt Workman, attacked it with six 20-pound bombs, two of which hit the train and one the engine. Troops also began to descend and were fired on. They ran towards Envin village.

Altogether, between 600 and 700 rounds were fired by the two aeroplanes and many German soldiers were hit.

Neither of the 2 F.E.2bs were fired on. Capt Chadwick said he was tempted to land, in order to obtain identifications, as the ground was suitable, but he refrained from doing so. The 2 F.E.8s descended to 3,000 feet to protect the 2 F.E.2bs in case of interference by hostile aircraft.

As soon as the attack on the trains began, the main raiding party, which was composed of 7 B.E. aeroplanes of 16 Sqn with 6 F.E.2bs of 25 Sqn, and also F.E.8s of 40 Sqn, attacked Libercourt station at about 2 p.m., where fourteen 112-pound and thirty-four 20-pound bombs were dropped. Station buildings, sidings and rolling stock were hit, some carriages were wrecked, and one coach was afterwards observed to be lying crossways over the line.

The patrol over Provin aerodrome destroyed a hangar in the course of its work, and that over Phalempin caused a fire which spread over the northern part of the village in a blaze, which is believed to have been caused by a petrol store being hit. The fire was still burning at 6.45 p.m. that evening.

One hostile aeroplane came on the scene during the proceedings, but was easily driven off.

Casualties: Sqn 16, *2 Lt R. S. Howard, wounded; 16168 2 AM H. S. P. Rolfe, wounded (since died);* **4,** *2 Lt N. E. S. Simon, wounded; and* **11,** *Capt A. W. Field, wounded.*

September 26th

Artillery co-operating with the 1st Brigade obtained 4 direct hits on an A.A. battery. Siege artillery destroyed 4 gun-pits and obtained a number of hits on hostile batteries. Through machines of the 2nd Brigade three hostile batteries were successfully engaged. In co-operation with machines of the 3rd Brigade, artillery caused a large explosion of enemy ammunition, and obtained several direct hits on batteries and emplacements. Machines of the 5th Brigade ranged artillery on to 62 trench points, many hostile batteries, and a large body of infantry.

A contact patrol machine flew over Gird trench at between 300 and 400 feet during the morning. The Germans in the trench held up their hands and waved white handkerchiefs. This information was transmitted to the ground station, and the Germans shortly afterwards surrendered to our troops.

2 Lt Livingstone, with 1 AM Dearing, 20 Sqn, engaged a hostile machine over Ypres. Lt Livingstone and his observer were both wounded and their machine considerably damaged. He just succeeded in crossing the lines and landing. Information has been received that an Albatros fell near where Lt Livingstone's combat took place.

Capt Ball, 60 Sqn, while on offensive patrol on the evening of the 25th, attacked an Albatros into which he emptied 90 rounds from underneath at about 15 yards' range. The German machine was seen to crash.

Lt Coleman, 32 Sqn, assisted by a De Havilland of another squadron, destroyed a hostile machine near Le Transloy.

2 Lt J. Gilmour, 27 Sqn, lost contact with the machines of an offensive patrol, and followed two machines which proved to be hostile, and which attacked him. Lt Gilmour succeeded in driving one down out of control and driving away the second. Lt P. C. Sherren, 27 Sqn, engaged and hit an enemy machine near Velu. The German was last seen side-slipping and nose-diving.

Other hostile machines were engaged and damaged by Sgt Noakes, 29 Sqn, and Lt Beanlands and Lt Good, 70 Sqn.

The 1st Brigade carried out a number of successful bombing raids during the night of the 25th–26th and on the 26th. The station of Lille was attacked on the night of the 25th–26th by the 2nd Brigade. During the day they bombed with considerable success the rest billets and station at Poelcappelle.

Lagnicourt aerodrome was attacked by the 3rd Brigade.

Successful bombing raids were carried out by the 4th and 5th Brigades. 19 Sqn attacked the Divisional Headquarters at Barastre. A number of bombs were observed to explode in the village.

60 Sqn made an attack on hostile kite balloons with Nieuport Scouts at 11 a.m. These Scouts were armed with Le Prieur rockets. Lt Phillippi brought down one balloon in the locality of Bapaume, and Lt Hill brought one down near Boisleux-au-Mont. Lt Phillippi was wounded in the head by a piece of shell during his attack. Both balloons went down in flames.

2 Lt Hudson and 2 Lt Manville, 15 Sqn, on three separate occasions engaged and dispersed small bodies of infantry with machine-gun fire. Many men were seen to fall. Lt Streatfield and Lt Barry, 9 Sqn, fired three drums into German infantry.

Lt Byrne, 24 Sqn, attacked a wagon and six horses from 2,000 feet.

He then attacked an A.A. battery, and finally two horsemen. Capt Walser and Lt Bird, 4 Sqn, came down to a 1,000 feet and attacked hostile batteries with machine-gun fire.

Lt Thompson and Capt Taylor, 15 Sqn, attacked German infantry moving along a communication trench, and Lt Gordon Kidd and Lt Dighton, 7 Sqn, dispersed a working party with machine-gun fire. 2 Lt Vinson with 2 Lt Laird, of 15 Sqn, also attacked infantry with their machine-gun.

Casualties: Sqn 20, *2 Lt A. F. Livingstone, wounded; 9882 1 AM F. Dearing, wounded;* **60,** *2 Lt G. Phillippi, wounded;* **8,** *Capt P. E. Welchman, wounded;* **70,** *2 Lt F. J. N. Echlin, missing; 1 AM Grundy, missing;* **9,** *Lt B. T. Coller, missing; and 2 Lt T. E. G. Scaife, missing.*

September 27th

Unfavourable flying weather. Clouds and rain.

Batteries were ranged on several bodies of infantry and horse transport by machines of the 5th Brigade, causing many casualties. An ammunition pit was blown up, nine gun-pits totally destroyed, and ten damaged.

Machines of 25 Sqn, escorting an Army photographic reconniassance, engaged two hostile machines over Tourmignies. Lt V. W. Harrison, with Sgt L. S. Court, drove one machine away and destroyed the other.

On the IVth Army front a hostile machine was driven down by a Nieuport Scout (probably French), near Rocquigny.

The 1st Brigade carried out bombing raids both by day and night. A sugar factory was set on fire, and other damage was observed. Bombs were dropped on hutments at Houthem on the night of the 26th/27th by the 2nd Brigade.

The 4th Brigade dropped fifty-six 20-pound bombs on points of importance. Miraumont, Warlencourt and Grandcourt were bombed by the 5th Brigade.

A hostile kite balloon drifted over our lines from the direction of Bapaume. Capt Hill, 40 Sqn, pursued it and got directly over the balloon at a height of about 6,000 feet. The balloon was rapidly descending, and the observer was half-way up the rigging between the car and the envelope, waving a white handkerchief. Capt Hill refrained from firing, and keeping very close signalled to the German to go down. When the balloon had descended to about 1,200 feet from the ground a De Havilland Scout came up and fired into the balloon with Buckingham tracer bullets. It caught fire and fell near Mont Kemmel.

2 Lt Franklin with 2 AM Wadey, of 16 Sqn, attacked a motor-car with Lewis gun fire.

Lt Le Gallais and Lt Cleaver, 3 Sqn, attacked a company of Germans with machine-gun fire, and drove them into Thilloy.

2 Lt Buckingham, with Lt Clark, Capt Binning with Lt Carre, 2 Lt Hudson with 2 Lt Bradford, and 2 Lt Binson with 2 Lt Laird, all of 15 Sqn, attacked infantry, horse and motor transport, from heights varying from 1,000 to 2,000 feet with machine-gun fire.

Capt Mackay and Pte Napier, 4 Sqn, on artillery registration from 1 to 4 p.m. reported:

> At 2.20 p.m. observed about 80 infantry walking down sunken road at *R. 14 b 6.4*, towing 11 small carts—zone call sent down. On fire being opened they ran about 200 yards to some dug-outs and huts on side of road, leaving the carts on the road. At 2.45 p.m., on their coming out of the dug-outs and huts, zone call again sent—fire in response very accurate—many casualties were caused—the remainder left their carts and ran back about 400 yards to the woods near the river—2 bombs dropped on Warlencourt.

Casualties: Sqn 27, *2 Lt B. V. S. Smith, wounded;* **70,** *2 Lt M. S. Faraday missing; Lt J. H. Lowson, missing;* **27,** *2 Lt H. A. Taylor, missing; 2 Lt S. Dendrino, missing.*

September 28th

In spite of unfavourable weather, much successful co-operation with artillery was accomplished.

On the Reserve Army front, 16 gun-pits were destroyed, 15 damaged, and 9 ammunition pits blew up. One hostile battery appeared to be completely destroyed.

Lt Dickie and Lt Hanlon, observing a body of infantry, sent down the area call. A direct hit caused many casualties. Capt Walser, 4 Sqn, ranged a 9.2-inch howitzer battery on a hostile battery. Nineteen direct hits completely destroyed several pits and set fire to ammunition.

A 9.2-inch howitzer battery, in co-operation with Lt Clapperton and 2 Lt Stevens, 4 Sqn, destroyed four pits out of eight in one battery position, and exploded several lots of ammunition. An 8-inch howitzer battery, for which 2 Lt Fawkner, 15 Sqn, was spotting, demolished four gun-pits, all of which were left burning. A 12-inch howitzer battery, with which 2 Lt Steele, 15 Sqn, was working, destroyed four pits, using only 18 rounds.

Lt Curphy, 32 Sqn, destroyed a L.V.G. near Miraumont.

8—MARTINSYDE G.100 SCOUT—120 H.P. BEARDMORE ENGINE

The Martinsyde G.100 was originally designed as a long-range fighting scout and although used for escort duties, it was as a bomber that it was principally employed. The G.100 carried one 112-lb. bomb but the later G.102 development with the 160 h.p. Beardmore engine carried twice the bomb load of the earlier version. No. 27 Squadron, which arrived in France on March 1, 1916, was the only unit to be completely equipped with the Martinsyde Scout, or 'Elephant' as it came to be nicknamed.

Late on the evening of the 28th Capt Ball, 60 Sqn, on offensive patrol near Bapaume, engaged three hostile machines. He emptied a double drum into one at 15 yards range. The German went down in a spin and was seen to crash. Capt Ball afterwards attacked several more hostile machines, two of which he forced to descend. Capt Foot, 60 Sqn, flying a Spad, dived at a formation of four hostile machines, one of which he destroyed.

Douvrin was attacked by the 1st Brigade during the night of the 27th/28th instant.

The 2nd Brigade made a successful attack on Ledeghem station. Lt Acland and 2 Lt Davis, 15 Sqn, dropped bombs in the midst of infantry. The infantry dispersed and were then attacked by machine-gun fire from the aeroplane.

Casualties: Sqn 42, *Lt Anderson, wounded;* **16,** *2 Lt R. V. Franklin, wounded;* **5,** *Lt A. T. Easom, missing.*

29 September – 8 October, 1916

During a week when bad weather curtailed flying operations Albert Ball claimed several more combat victories before his posting back to England on 4 October.

Although it is impossible to assess with complete accuracy Ball's victory score at this point, the communiqués suggest that since he started Scout flying in May, he had destroyed 11 enemy aircraft and driven down another 18, damaged and apparently out of control, or deliberately force-landed by their pilots. At this time he was unquestionably the leading fighter pilot of the R.F.C.

Lt S. F. Vincent, 60 Sqn, who was mentioned on 30 September, retired from the R.A.F. after World War II as an Air Vice-Marshal. During the Battle of Britain, 1940, he commanded the fighter station at Northolt.

COMMUNIQUÉ NO. 56

September 29th
Low clouds and rain prevented flying throughout the day.

2 Lt J. B. Brophy, 21 Sqn, engaged and destroyed a hostile machine which fell into the Bois au Dessus. In the course of other engagements he forced another German to land.

Casualties: Sqn 18, *27512 2 AM W. Syme, wounded.*

September 30th
Aeroplanes of all brigades continued to co-operate successfully with artillery. Many direct hits were registered on the enemy's gun pits and trenches. A 9.2-inch howitzer with which 2 Lt Fowkner, 15 Sqn, was working, destroyed three pits of an active hostile battery.

During a bombing raid carried out by the 3rd Brigade against Lagnicourt aerodrome the escorting machines engaged and drove off several of the enemy. 2 Lt Roberts and Lt Collins, 11 Sqn, and Capt Ball, 60 Sqn, attacked and destroyed one, and 2 Lt S. F. Vincent, 60 Sqn, brought down a second which was seen to crash near Villers au Flos. A third German machine was brought down in flames near Thilloy by 2 Lt

Harvey and Lt Black, 11 Sqn, and a fourth driven down out of control by Lt Bell-Irving, 60 Sqn.

Three L.V.G.s were attacked by Capt Aizlewood and Lt Curphey, 32 Sqn. Capt Aizlewood fired a drum at close range at one of them, and it went down in a spinning nose dive. He flattened out after going down about 5,000 feet. On seeing this Lt Curphey dived at him, and the German again got into a spinning nose dive and was seen by an observer of 23 Sqn to crash.

On the evening of September 30th, a patrol of the 3rd Brigade encountered many hostile machines. A formation of seven Rolands near Bapaume were dispersed, two of them being driven down out of control.

The 1st Brigade attacked the aerodromes at Phalempin and La Pouillerie. At the former damage was done to the buildings on the edge of the aerodrome, and one 112-pound bomb fell on a machine which had just landed. The 3rd Brigade attacked Lagnicourt aerodrome, causing damage to the aerodrome and buildings, and many bombs falling near hangars. Bois Loupart, Miraumont and Achiet le Grand were bombed by the 5th Brigade.

Over 500 photographs were taken during the day.

Lt Bryne, 24 Sqn, on three occasions attacked with machine gun fire and dispersed troops and transport.

Casualties: Sqn 11, *Lt E. C. Lansdale, missing; and 3149 Sgt A. Clarkson, missing.*

October 1st

Heavy and Siege Artillery of the Ist Army, in co-operation with machines of the 1st Brigade, dealt successfully with a hostile battery and an anti-aircraft battery. Two direct hits were obtained on trench mortars and an explosion of ammunition caused. Field Artillery were ranged with success on trench targets.

On the IInd Army front 15 hostile batteries were engaged, and ammunition exploded in two instances. The 4th Brigade recorded 139 active batteries, several of which were successfully dealt with. Artillery of the Vth Army in co-operation with the 5th Brigade, accomplished some successful wire cutting and trench shoots. One gun pit was destroyed, ten were damaged and an ammunition pit blown up.

Between 3 and 6 p.m. the IInd Corps Counter Battery Group received 67 zone calls from aeroplanes and 39 active battery reports from kite balloons.

2 Lt I. Curlewis, 29 Sqn, with the use of Buckingham bullets brought down a hostile balloon in flames.

On the 1st instant, Capt Ball, 60 Sqn, drove down two patrolling machines out of control near Gommecourt. He afterwards waited and attacked three hostile machines which came up from Lagnicourt aerodrome, forcing one to land and dispersing the remainder.

2 Lt Roberts and Lt Jones, 3 Sqn, when taking photographs, were attacked by 7 Rolands. The attack was driven off with the assistance of two F.E.s who, joined the fight. One of the Rolands, apparently hit by fire from one of the F.E.s, fell in a nose dive and crashed.

A patrol of 32 Sqn was engaged with hostile machines over Bapaume. Capt Martin attacked one and fired a drum at 100 yards range, the German diving down, followed by Capt von Poellnitz, who fired at a range of about 50 feet. The hostile machine dived steeply and appeared to be on fire.

Capt Binning and Lt Carre, 15 Sqn, drove down a hostile machine apparently out of control.

On the evening of the 1st instant Capt Jones and Lt King, 32 Sqn, had their machine considerably damaged during combats. A hostile machine engaged by Capt Jones was driven down emitting large clouds of smoke.

Orchies station was bombed by the 1st Brigade, many bombs falling on the permanent way and rolling stock. The 3rd Brigade attacked Miraumont station with twenty-five 112-pound bombs. Damage was done to the station, buildings and permanent way and a fire started in the station which burned for several hours. 19 Sqn attacked Bois d'Havrincourt. Many bombs fell in the wood, which is known to be used extensively by the enemy for rest billets.

Casualties: Sqn 18, *2 Lt F. C. Biette, wounded; and* **70,** *Capt H. T. Harris, wounded.*

October 2nd to October 6th

During this period the weather was continually unfavourable for aerial operations, strong westerly and south-westerly wind prevailing, and on the majority of the days heavy rain falling ∽ *In spite of this considerable amount of work was accomplished. One hundred and twenty-eight targets were dealt with by aeroplanes in co-operation with the artillery, more than 100 photographs were taken, and nearly two tons of bombs were dropped on various points of importance in the enemy's lines.*

Lt Duguid and 2 Lt Van der Byl, 23 Sqn, engaged 7 hostile machines over Le Transloy. One of the hostile machines was seen to crash by pilots and observers of the 4th Brigade.

On the 5th instant by means of the zone call, shrapnel fire was brought to bear on the enemy's trenches north of Thiepval within two minutes of the call being sent down by Lt Dickie and Lt O'Hanlon, 4 Sqn. 13th Siege Battery (9.2-inch howitzers) co-operating with Capt Walser, 4 Sqn, in very difficult weather conditions, succeeded in destroying one pit and setting fire to ammunition.

On October 6th Lt Thwaytes and Lt Brewis, 4 Sqn, fired 4 drums from 1,200 feet on an active A.A. gun on a lorry. The gun ceased firing and the lorry was withdrawn.

Casualties: (October 2nd): Sqn 15, *Lt W. D. Miller, missing; and Lt W. C. Carmichael, missing.*

7–14 October, 1916

Weather continued to restrict air operations.

The fast Scouts resembling the French Spad, reported by 70 Sqn on 10 October, may have been Fokkers or Halberstadts, though since these types had been in use for some time it is strange that they were not more positively identified. No other new German aircraft with any similarity to the Spad was introduced around this time.

Two examples of skilled airmanship were reported—the 32 Sqn pilot who managed to crash land a D.H.2 with most of its controls shot away, and the 23 Sqn observer who landed an F.E.2b after his pilot had been mortally wounded.

COMMUNIQUÉ NO. 57

October 7th
A stormy day, unfavourable for flying.

Artillery of the IVth Army, in co-operation with aeroplanes of the 4th Brigade, engaged 45 hostile batteries. Eleven emplacements were destroyed or damaged, and 6 explosions of ammunition occurred. One hundred and twenty-three active batteries were located, 15 of which were engaged, and many direct hits obtained.

Aeroplanes of the 5th Brigade, working with artillery of the Reserve Army, registered 45 trench points. Two gun pits were destroyed, 6 were damaged, and an ammunition pit was blown up. The area call again proved its value—a working party south of Grandcourt was dispersed.

The 1st Brigade attacked several places of importance. The permanent way and a railway shed at Lievin were much damaged. Bombs were dropped on Miraumont, Warlencourt, Bois Loupart and Pys by the 5th Brigade.

Despite the very unfavourable weather, contact patrols from the 4th and 5th Brigades and the IXth Wing did good work.

Over 100 photographs were taken during the day.

Casualties: Sqn 15, *2 Lt A. Rice-Oxley, wounded;* **21,** *2 Lt J. A. Stewart,* *wounded;* **34,** *2 Lt S. A. Gibbons and 2 Lt R. St J. Hartley, wounded;* **21,** *2 Lt W. C. Fenwick, missing.*

October 8th

Artillery of the IVth Army engaged 4 hostile batteries, two of which were silenced.

The 5th Brigade co-operated with artillery in the destruction of trench points. Capt Scott and Lt Fagan, 4 Sqn, in rain and clouds, registered a Siege battery on to trench targets from a height of 200 feet. Capt Walser and Lt Brewis, 4 Sqn, in addition to sending down many zone calls, co-operated with the 13th Siege Battery on a hostile battery near Irles; 8 O.K.s were obtained, and a fire and small explosion were caused. They also flew low, and fired a drum of ammunition into the trenches near Grandcourt.

Hostile aircraft were inactive, and no decisive combats took place.

October 9th

Observation was difficult throughout the day on account of low clouds.

On the Reserve Army front 26 points, including 4 hostile battery positions, were registered. On two occasions effective shrapnel barrages were brought to bear on hostile infantry in trenches by means of the zone call. Two gun pits were destroyed, 5 damaged, and 3 ammunition pits were blown up. Several active hostile batteries were engaged, by means of the zone call, and silenced. Capt Walser and Flt Sgt Halstead, 4 Sqn, after directing the fire of a battery and obtaining a direct hit on a hostile battery target, directed shrapnel fire on a collection of the enemy in the trenches near Pys. On another occasion they flew low and fired 6 drums at the enemy's infantry.

Aeroplanes of the 4th Brigade co-operated successfully with the 12th, 78th, and 141st Siege Batteries. Hostile gun positions and the enemy's trenches were successfully engaged.

Several indecisive combats took place during the day.

2 Lt F. A. Coward and Lt R. Johnstone, 9 Sqn, drove down a hostile machine into which they had fired half a drum of Buckingham bullets. The machine was not seen to crash.

2 Lt Barnard and Sgt Lauder, 18 Sqn, fired into the enemy's trenches from a height of 300 feet.

Lt Brill and Lt Bayley, 8 Sqn, while on artillery patrol, engaged with a Lewis gun, and dispersed, a party of infantry on the Ransart–Bellacourt road.

Casualties: Sqn 3, *2 Lt C. T. Cleaver, wounded;* **16,** *2 Lt V. Kennard, and 4043 1 AM Digby, missing.*

October 10th

The 1st Brigade ranged Siege Artillery on a house believed to be a headquarters: five direct hits were obtained. The 3rd Brigade ranged artillery on six hostile batteries, obtaining several direct hits on emplacements. Aeroplanes of the 4th Brigade co-operated with success with several siege batteries of the IVth Army. Two emplacements were destroyed, 14 were damaged, and an explosion of ammunition was caused. Some good trench shoots were also carried out.

On the front of the Reserve Army, artillery in co-operation with the 5th Brigade carried out successful shoots on trenches, bodies of infantry, and hostile batteries. Nine gun pits were destroyed, 17 were damaged, and six ammunition pits blew up. A number of hostile batteries were silenced and working parties were dispersed. The 94th Siege Battery (9.2-inch Howitzers) with observation by 2 Lt MacNeill and 2 Lt Cotton, 7 Sqn, destroyed all the four pits of one battery. In another hostile battery, two explosions of ammunition occurred and three pits were destroyed. The 33rd Siege Battery (8-inch Howitzers), co-operating with 2 Lt Cave and Lt Duke, 4 Sqn, obtained eight direct hits on three pits of one battery, and exploded ammunition. Capt Walser and Lt Brewis, 4 Sqn, working with the 13th Siege Battery, obtained seven direct hits, entirely destroying two and badly damaging the remaining two pits of a hostile battery.

A hostile machine was brought down by rifle fire from the trenches, and fell near Souchez.

On the fronts of the IIIrd, IVth and Reserve Armies there was considerable activity.

A hostile machine was driven down out of control by Lt Harvey and 2 Lt Libby, 11 Sqn. Capt E. F. Norris, 21 Sqn, also drove down a hostile machine, which was last seen nose diving in the clouds 2,000 feet from the ground.

Lt Pender and Lt Duncan, 5 Sqn, had six encounters between 7 a.m. and 8.45 a.m. whilst on artillery patrol. In an encounter with three L.V.G.s, one German dived emitting clouds of smoke, having been engaged at 20 yards range. The remaining machines declined close combat.

2 Lt Mare-Montembault, 32 Sqn, in the course of an encounter with several hostile machines, had all the controls of his machine, with the exception of the rudder, shot away. His machine turned a somersault, and was wrecked near Pozieres. The pilot was unhurt.

An offensive patrol of 70 Sqn was attacked by seven fast hostile machines which, pilots report, closely resemble the Spad. F.E.s and De Havillands joined in the fight, and our machines succeeded in driving off all the hostile aircraft, one of which is believed to have been destroyed.

Oppy was twice bombed by 25 Sqn, 71 bombs dropping in the village or in the wood west of it. In the second attack six hostile machines were encountered, and one of our machines failed to return.

13 Sqn accomplished highly successful raids against railway trains and stations at Queant, Cambrai, and Bapaume at about 11 p.m. on the night of the 9th/10th instant. A train entering Cambrai was attacked by Lt Thorne and wrecked, a bomb being observed to hit the first carriage behind the engine. His second bomb hit the station buildings, whereupon all the lights were extinguished.

18 Sqn attacked railways, billets and an active battery during the night of the 9th/10th. Capt Callaghan and Cpl Ankers, 18 Sqn, twice attacked searchlights with machine-gun fire. One of the searchlights was extinguished.

In the course of the day one hundred and ten 20-pound bombs were distributed by the 5th Brigade on Bois Loupart, Miraumont, Pys, and Achiet le Petit.

Velu Station and wood were bombed by 27 Sqn.

Over 500 photographs were taken during the day.

During a combat in the air on the 10th, Capt R. N. Adams and 2 Lt Ogg, 23 Sqn, carrying out an offensive patrol and photography, were heavily engaged with six hostile machines near Bapaume. Capt Adams was shot in the groin and became unconscious. 2 Lt Ogg, the observer, seeing that his pilot was unconscious, leaned over and held Capt Adams back with one hand, worked the control lever with the other, and managed to land the machine in our lines near Morval. In landing, the machine was wrecked in a shell hole. Capt Adams never recovered consciousness. 2 Lt Ogg was unhurt.

Casualties: Sqn 23, *Capt R. N. Adams, killed;* **70,** *2 Lt F. M. Corry, wounded;* **16,** *2 Lt R. V. Franklin, wounded;* **24,** *2 Lt N. Middlebrook, missing;* **11,** *649 Flt Sgt E. Haxton, and 3023 Cpl B. G. F. Jeffs, missing;* **70,** *Lt J. B. Lawton and 2 Lt F. M. Lawledge, missing;* **25,** *2 Lt M. Hayne and Lt A. H. M. Copeland, missing.*

October 11th

Weather was unfavourable for observation ⌔ Hostile aircraft displayed little activity. A few indecisive combats were recorded.

On the IVth Army front six hostile batteries were engaged, and 14 active batteries were located.

The 5th Brigade, in co-operation with artillery of the Reserve Army, registered 26 points. Sgt Pateman and 2 Lt Buckeridge, 4 Sqn, carrying out contact patrol, observed a large number of infantry in Regina Trench. Zone call was sent down, and an excellent barrage was turned on, causing casualties to the enemy and driving them east, where they were again caught by our artillery fire. Much of the artillery work was carried out at altitudes of from 700 to 1,000 feet, and many shoots had to be abandoned owing to low clouds.

Marcoing Station was bombed by Capt Allen and Lts Buck and Cronyn, 19 Sqn, on the night of the 10th/11th. The station was hit.

A night bombing raid was carried out by 13 Sqn at about 11.30 p.m. on the night of the 10th/11th. Capt Brunwin-Hales dropped twelve 20-pound bombs on a train in Vitry Station. Capt Sheridan dropped ten 20-pound bombs on the aerodrome at Douai, all the bombs falling around the sheds. He dropped the remainder of his bombs on a column of infantry on the Gavrelle–Fresnes Road, scattering the formation. A third machine did not return. (*See also page 317, November 18th.*)

A successful night bombing raid was also carried out by the 4th Brigade, 18 Sqn, at Cambrai Station.

2 Lt F. P. Kane, 29 Sqn, fired a drum of ammunition from 1,400 feet at a closed touring car. The car immediately stopped, and three people got out of it and ran away.

Casualty: Sqn 13, *Lt G. Wadden, missing.*

October 12th

No hostile aircraft activity.

On the IVth Army front six targets were successfully engaged. 5th Brigade registered 23 points, including three direct hits on dug-outs, with a 9.2-inch howitzer. Thirty-three active batteries were reported, for all of which the zone call was sent down. Accurate artillery fire was brought to bear in most cases, and many were silenced.

Casualties: Sqn 3, *2 Lt L. C. Kidd, killed; 2 Lt F. E. S. Phillips, killed;* **24,** *1491 Sgt S. Cockrell, wounded;* **15,** *L/Cpl G. Pilkington, wounded;* **9,** *2 Lt S. M. Smith, wounded.*

October 13th

Low clouds all day with wind and occasional rain ~ In spite of this, some successful work was accomplished by 4 Sqn with registration of siege batteries on 10 trench points.

14–22 October, 1916

20 October was a day of intense activity, with more than 80 combats reported.

The IIIrd Army reconnaissance by 11 Sqn F.E.2bs was a typical example of the excellent work still being performed by these slow but formidable old pushers, despite the greatly increased enemy opposition.

Roland Scouts were reported in action on 17 and 20 October. The Roland DI had entered limited production towards the end of 1916, but it is more likely that the aircraft referred to were in fact Albatros DIs or DIIs. There was frequently a time lag of some weeks before new aircraft types were correctly identified, and it is significant that the communiqués had not yet mentioned the new Albatros Scouts by name. These bore some superficial resemblance to the Roland CI two-seater, and it would be reasonable for R.F.C. pilots to assume that they were products of the same firm. When the Hannover two-seater entered service in 1918 it was reported as a Roland or an Albatros.

The Fokker monoplane shot down must have been one of the last remaining on the Western front.

COMMUNIQUÉ NO. 58

October 14th

The 160th Siege Battery, in co-operation with Lt Smith and Capt Duff, 6 Sqn, obtained nine direct hits on a hostile battery, causing ammunition to explode for five minutes. The 86th Siege Battery, co-operating with aeroplanes of the 3rd Brigade, obtained 15 direct hits on three trench targets.

On the IVth Army front a number of hostile batteries were successfully engaged, and three were silenced. Four direct hits were obtained on a strong point near Les Boeufs, and a series of small explosions ensued. Artillery, co-operating with machines of the 5th Brigade, did considerable damage to trenches, and carried out some successful wire-cutting operations. A party of the enemy near Grandcourt was dispersed, and several hostile batteries were silenced by the employment of the zone call.

In spite of the unfavourable weather throughout the day, some bombing was carried out by the 4th and 5th Brigades, and some successful contact patrol work was accomplished.

Lt Dickie and Lt O'Hanlon, 4 Sqn, reported accurately on the position of infantry at Schwaben and Stuff Redoubts.

Casualty: Sqn 6, *Capt T. R. Duff, wounded.*

October 15th

Aeroplanes of the 2nd Brigade co-operated with artillery of the IInd Army in 8 successful shoots on hostile batteries. Machines of the 3rd Brigade directed artillery fire on to many hostile batteries and on to two railway bridges. A building near one of the bridges, believed to be an ammunition depot, was hit, and a heavy explosion resulted. Direct hits were also obtained on two anti-aircraft batteries. On the IVth Army front the 75th Siege Battery, working with Lt Barker, 34 Sqn, obtained 3 O.K.s and 19 Ys on one battery and 2 O.K.s and 20 Ys on a second.

Forty-four points were registered by machines of the 5th Brigade. Many dug-outs were damaged, 70 yards of railway were destroyed, 2 gun pits were damaged, and 6 ammunition pits blown up. Capt Walser, 4 Sqn, observing for the 13th Siege Battery, reported 23 O.K.s and 23 Ys. All the four emplacements of a hostile battery were badly knocked about, and an ammunition store behind the battery position blew up.

There were a few indecisive combats.

The 1st Brigade attacked Avion Station and dump. Motor transport, station buildings and the dump were hit. Minor bombing operations were carried out by the 2nd and 5th Brigades.

2 Lt Macdonald, 9 Sqn, attacked and dispersed a company of infantry near Le Transloy from 800 feet.

Casualty: Sqn 24, *2 Lt W. E. Nixon, wounded.*

October 16th

Aeroplanes of the 1st, 2nd, and 3rd Brigades co-operated successfully with artillery against hostile batteries, trench and other targets. On the 4th Brigade front 22 batteries were engaged; 11 direct hits were obtained and 5 emplacements damaged. The 65th Siege Battery (12-inch howitzers) with observation by Lt Larkin and Lt Power, 5 Sqn, damaged and set fire to targets in Puisieux.

Artillery of the Reserve Army, co-operating with aeroplanes of the 5th Brigade, destroyed 11 gun pits, damaged 13, and blew up 6 ammunition pits. The 13th Siege Battery, for which Capt Walser, 4 Sqn, was observing, obtained 7 O.K.s and 15 Ys on a four-gun battery. The position was so damaged that the pits were not easily distinguishable. In the same flight, the same battery destroyed two pits in another target. The 94th Siege Battery, with observation by Lt Haig and Lt Scutt, 7 Sqn, knocked out two emplacements and set fire to a dug-out.

On the Ist Army front one machine was driven down out of control. Two hostile balloons were attacked; one is believed to have been destroyed.

A machine attacked by Capt Andrews, 24 Sqn, was destroyed near Villers.

2 Lt Baines and 1 AM Bayes, 23 Sqn, engaged three machines, one of which crashed near Beaulencourt. Four French machines joined in the fight, which resulted in the destruction of a second German machine. An offensive patrol of 23 Sqn encountered four of the enemy's machines near Biefvillers. They dived at the hostile formation and in the course of the fight one of the machines attacked by 2 Lt Horswell and 2 Lt Fyfe fell out of control. It was seen by a pilot of 4 Sqn to be completely wrecked.

A hostile aeroplane dropped a bomb on 9 Sqn's aerodrome. Two air mechanics were wounded, one machine was wrecked, and a second damaged.

Other hostile machines were driven down out of control by Lt C. C. Godwin and Lt P. C. Ellis, 1 Sqn, and Capt G. R. M. Reid and 2 Lt L. H. Scott, 20 Sqn.

One hundred and thirty-three bombs were dropped by the 1st Brigade. Billy Montigny and Avion were attacked at night. Bois Bernard, reported to be full of troops, was attacked. The majority of the bombs fell in the village, destroying a large wooden hut and causing a fire.

During the night of the 15th/16th, Douai Aerodrome and Bucquoy were attacked by the 3rd Brigade. Night bombing operations were carried out by the 4th Brigade.

5th Brigade dropped bombs on Loupart Wood, Star Wood, Pys and Miraumont. Hermies Station and Aerodrome were attacked by the IXth Wing. An expedition against the Bois d'Havrincourt was abandoned owing to clouds over the objective.

In the course of the day 600 photographs were taken.

Casualties: Sqn 15, *Sgt F. Barton and Lt M. Carre, killed;* **42,** *2 Lt V. Hugill and 2 Lt A. Douglas, killed;* **9,** *7429 1 AM C. Gale, wounded; 13719 2 AM W. Lamb, wounded;* **3,** *6527 Cpl R. B. Bolton, wounded;* **34,** *2 Lt C. K. M. Douglas, wounded;* **4,** *Lt C. R. Clapperton, wounded;* **18,**

2 Lt A. R. Crisp and 3467 1 AM H. A. Hardinge, missing; **1,** *2 Lt C. M. Kelly and 2 Lt T. G. G. Sturrock, missing;* **24,** *Lt P. A. L. Byrne, missing;* **19,** *Capt C. R. Tidswell and 2 Lt J. Thompson, missing.*

October 17th

Heavy artillery of the Ist Army obtained a direct hit on an A.A. battery, and Siege artillery, co-operating with aeroplanes of the 1st Brigade, were successful on two trench mortar targets. Artillery of the IVth Army, co-operating with machines of the 4th Brigade, silenced three hostile batteries and caused a large explosion. On the 5th Brigade front considerable damage was done to trenches, gun pits and ammunition.

Five hostile machines were met by aeroplanes of the 1st Brigade returning from bombing raids to Denain and St Amand. One of these was pursued and dived down. Although no shots were fired at it by our machines, it got into a nose dive and crashed into a lake about 10 miles south of Douai.

The IIIrd Army reconnaissance was heavily attacked over Mory by about 20 German machines. An Aviatik, attacked by Capt Price and 2 Lt Libby, 11 Sqn, was last seen falling in a spinning nose dive and out of control. A Roland Scout was driven down by 2 Lt Turk and 2 Lt Allen, 11 Sqn. Two of our machines did not return.

During a general engagement, Lt Knight, 24 Sqn, drove down a hostile machine, but owing to the severity of the fighting he was unable to watch it to the ground. He then attacked a Roland in which the pilot was seen to collapse and the machine descended steeply. Lt Knight followed and was about to open fire again when the German observer stood up and waved. The machine appeared to descend out of control but was lost to sight.

A reconnaissance of 23 Sqn drove off an attack by 10 hostile machines. The same 10 machines were in their turn attacked by a formation of De Havilland Scouts and driven away in disorder.

Simultaneous attacks were carried out by the 1st Brigade on St Amand and Denain. At St Amand bombs burst in the station yards, station, among the rolling stock and in a factory. Two explosions were caused. At Denain damage was done to the station buildings, sidings and rolling stock, and a moving train was hit near Lourches. A raid by the 2nd Brigade against an ammunition depot at Bisseghem was abandoned owing to weather.

1 Sqn attacked hutments with 20-pound and incendiary bombs, all of which fell about the objective. A siding and dump to the north of Bapaume were attacked by the 3rd Brigade with nineteen 112-pound bombs. A heavy explosion occurred in a building near the dump.

During the day 13 targets were successfully engaged with kite balloon observation. Miraumont station was damaged by a 6-inch Mark VII gun with observation by 5 K.B.S.

Casualties: Sqn 60, *Lt N. McL. Robertson, killed;* **11,** *Lt W. P. Bowman, missing; 2 Lt G. Clayton, missing; 2 Lt C. L. Roberts and 2 Lt J. R. Pulleyn, missing;* **23,** *Lt J. K. Barker and 2 Lt J. C. Wilson, missing;* **1,** *Lt C. C. Godwin and Lt P. E. Ellis, missing.*

October 18th

Unfavourable weather. Low clouds and showers throughout the day ∽ In spite of this some successful artillery co-operation was accomplished and aeroplanes flying at low altitudes were able to do some contact patrol work.

Capt Walser, 4 Sqn, working with the 13th Siege Battery, observed 114 rounds on a 4-gun active battery. Six direct hits were obtained. Two pits were destroyed, a third damaged and two explosions caused.

October 19th

Very little flying owing to unfavourable weather conditions.

Casualties: Sqn 18, *2 Lt R. L. Dingley and Lt W. H. N. Whitehead, missing.*

October 20th

Reconnaissances were carried out by all Brigades.

The IIIrd Army reconnaissance of six machines made a wide circle round Douai, taking photographs. Here they experienced violent anti-aircraft fire. Having completed the photography, the leader, Capt Davey, headed south-west followed by two or three hostile scouts. Nine or ten more hostile scouts approached the reconnaissance formation from the direction of Arras, and all of our machines became heavily engaged. Capt Davey headed for Arras in order to fight within gliding distance of the lines. One of our machines (2 Lt Pommeroy and 2 Lt Black) was brought down before the line was reached. Lt Harvey was badly wounded and his machine wrecked near Arras. The enemy having withdrawn, Capt Davey headed south in an endeavour to complete the reconnaissance. He was accompanied by only two escorting machines. He made for the Bois d'Havrincourt in order to pick up a Nieuport patrol who were on the look-out for them in that neighbourhood. On the way south the reconnaissance was again attacked and another machine (2 Lt Turk) retired with engine and propeller badly shot. The Nieuport formation was not picked up, and the escort now being reduced to one, Capt Davey turned homeward surrounded by hostile machines, and recrossed the line at 10.15 a.m. The formation was well kept throughout the flight.

Aeroplanes of all Brigades continued to co-operate successfully with artillery. For the first time our artillery machines were somewhat seriously interfered with by hostile aircraft. One hundred and forty-one targets were dealt with with aeroplane observation, and 27 by kite balloon observers.

On the 5th Brigade front a working party near Miraumont was twice dispersed by artillery, the party suffering many casualties.

On the Ist Army front 23 combats took place. A Roland Scout was brought down and destroyed by Sgt J. H. R. Green and Cpl W. P. Gilbert, 25 Sqn. A Fokker monoplane which crashed at Bauvin was shot down by Sgt G. J. Mackie and Sgt Horrocks, also 25 Sqn. Three other enemy machines are believed to have been shot down by Capt D. O. Mulholland, 40 Sqn, 2 Lt E. L. Benbow, 40 Sqn, and 2 Lt E. S. P. Hynes and Sapper L. N. Smith, 25 Sqn.* They were not actually seen to crash. Five others were driven down and in three cases seen to land.

The 2nd Brigade record 9 indecisive combats. A machine of 20 Sqn was forced to land near Armentieres.

3rd Brigade. Fourty-one combats took place. An offensive patrol of 11 Sqn had three encounters. One hostile machine fell out of control in the neighbourhood of Gommecourt after being engaged by Capt Price and 2 Lt Libby, and Lt Dowling and Lt Harrow-Bunn. The machine appeared to be on fire.

An offensive patrol of 60 Sqn had 6 combats, as the result of which one German machine was seen to heel over and fall out of control after being attacked by 2 Lt Gilchrist. Capt Grenfell, 60 Sqn, attacked 8 machines, one of which fell out of control in the vicinity of Rocquigny, and three others were driven down.

4th Brigade: a German machine attacked by De Havillands and F.E.s fell in High Wood. Details of this machine have not yet been received.

A hostile machine attacked by Lt Hackwill and 1 AM Edwards was seen to go down out of control near Grevillers.

On the front of the Reserve Army the 5th Brigade had 15 combats, in the course of which two of the enemy's aeroplanes were forced to land. In other encounters the hostile machines were driven off.

At Petit Hantay, where the first Brigade dropped 19 incendiary and sixty-six 20-pound bombs, huts were set on fire and tents and houses hit. The 2nd Brigade attacked the ammunition sheds at Bisseghem. Some of

* See also page 291, 'further evidence'.

the sheds were hit. 27 Sqn successfully raided Aulnoye Station and sidings. Station buildings and permanent way were damaged, and four trucks were derailed.

Seven hundred and fifty-four photographs were taken during the day.

2 Lt C. D. Bennett and 2 Lt E. H. Kann, 2 Sqn, attacked with machine-gun fire, and temporarily silenced, an anti-aircraft gun.

2 Lt Franklin and Lt Peach, 16 Sqn, attacked and scattered motor transport and motor cars with machine-gun fire.

Casualties: Sqn 11, *2 Lt G. K. Welsford, killed;* **19,** *2 Lt A. B. Drewery, killed;* **3,** *2 Lt R. Davis, killed;* **11,** *Lt R. P. Harvey, wounded;* **1 AD,** *2 Lt C. H. Stokes, wounded;* **20,** *2 Lt G. G. Collender, wounded;* **27** *Capt O. D. Filley, wounded;* **3,** *2 Lt W. B. Young, wounded;* **11,** *2 Lt N. de Pomeroy, missing; 2 Lt W. Black, missing; and* **21,** *2 Lt C. J. Cherry, missing.*

21–28 October, 1916

24 Sqn's protracted and indecisive battle with a large mixed enemy formation on 26 October showed that the D.H.2 could still hold its own against the new enemy scouts despite their better overall performance. But in single combat between two pilots of equal ability the German aircraft would normally hold the advantage—thanks to its superior fire-power and the ability to break away at will and outpace its opponent.

It is difficult to identify the 'two-seater Scouts of Bristol and Nieuport types' reported to have taken part in this combat. The enemy operated no aircraft answering to this description and their light two-seaters in the CL category were not introduced until 1917. The Roland CII, which had a tailplane roughly similar to that of the Bristol Scout, was already a very familiar type.

The Spad operating with 19 Sqn was probably an early example undergoing evaluation trials. This excellent French Scout, capable of nearly 120 m.p.h., did not enter full R.F.C. squadron service until 1917.

A B.E.2c, armoured for protection against ground rifle and machine-gun fire, was employed on a low-level reconnaissance on 24 October.

COMMUNIQUÉ NO. 59

October 21st

During the day 153 targets were engaged with aeroplane observation and 31 by kite balloon observers.

2nd Brigade carried out a number of successful registrations, obtaining 33 O.K.s during the day. 8, 12 and 13 Sqns, co-operating with artillery of the IIIrd Army, registered many direct hits and severely damaged hostile emplacements, a building and an anti-aircraft battery. On the IVth Army front 24 batteries were engaged; three emplacements were damaged and two ammunition stores exploded. Several trench targets south of Le Transloy were much damaged. On the front of the Reserve Army 28 shoots with aeroplane observation were carried out on gun positions. Ten pits were destroyed, 14 were damaged and 7 ammunition pits were blown up. Many active hostile batteries were engaged and silenced by means of the zone call. During the attack on the Regina Trench by the IInd Corps, Capt Walser, 4 Sqn, observing for the 13th Siege Battery (9.2-inch howitzers) engaged 5 active batteries, all of which were silenced and some damaged. During the same attack the 80th Siege Battery (12-inch howitzers) with observation by Capt Scott, 4 Sqn, damaged and silenced 4 active batteries. In a later flight, the same battery, again working with Capt Scott, silenced another 2-gun battery.

Nineteen combats took place on the Ist Army front.

A Roland scout was shot down by Capt Mapplebeck, 40 Sqn, and was seen to crash into a wood near Ascq. Lt C. O. Usborne, 40 Sqn, attacked a Fokker, which is believed to have been destroyed. The German machine stalled, side-slipped, nose dived and fell vertically emitting a large volume of black smoke. An L.V.G. was brought down in flames by 2 Lt E. D. Spicer and Sgt S. Birch, 20 Sqn.

Further evidence tends to confirm that the machine attacked by 2 Lt E. S. P. Hynes and Sapper L. N. Smith, 25 Sqn, on the 20th instant was destroyed.

Capt G. R. M. Reid and 2 Lt L. H. Scott, 20 Sqn, destroyed an L.V.G. near Comines. Capt Parker and 2 Lt Hervey, 8 Sqn, had two combats whilst on artillery observation. A hostile scout, which they engaged at very close range, appeared to be hit and was last seen falling out of control.

11 Sqn, escorting bombing machines of the 3rd Brigade, had 6 combats. One of our machines did not return from the raid and was seen diving steeply over Bullecourt, followed by a German. 2 Lt Turk and 2 Lt Allan, 11 Sqn, on offensive patrol, brought down 2 machines. One was seen to fall in the Bois de Logeast. The destruction of this machine is confirmed by an anti-aircraft battery. The second machine fell in flames.

Offensive patrols of 60 Sqn had 9 combats, in the course of which 6 German machines were forced to descend, all apparently under control.

The activities of hostile aircraft were somewhat above normal on the IVth Army front. 2 Lt Aspinall and 2 Lt Taylor, 22 Sqn, shot down a machine which fell near Beugnatre.

Offensive patrols on the front of the 5th Brigade had many combats. 32 Sqn attacked and drove down a hostile machine. 23 Sqn forced 2 German machines to land, 1 near Favreuil, the other in a field near Fremicourt. 19 Sqn, whilst on a bombing raid, escorted by Martinsydes and a Spad, had several encounters and succeeded in driving down 4 of the enemy's machines.

Raids were carried out by the 1st Brigade by night on Fournes and Wavrin. By day they attacked Haubourdin station, where most of the bombs appeared to hit the sidings and rolling stock. The escorting machines were heavily engaged, but sustained no casualties. Bombs were dropped on other places of minor importance. Huts were hit at Petit

Hantay and a large explosion was caused at Marquillies Sugar Factory. The 2nd Brigade attacked hutments, causing a fire. A dump and some transport were also hit. The 3rd Brigade dropped thirty 112-pound bombs on Queant station. Many bombs burst around the station and on the permanent way. Billets, railways and aerodromes were attacked by the 4th Brigade and Bois Loupart, Star Wood, Miraumont and Pys by the 5th Brigade.

A highly successful attack was made by 27 Sqn on an ammunition depot at Ath. Ten 112-pound bombs were dropped by Lt McAlery, Lt Shirlaw, 2 Lt Spanner, 2 Lt Caster and 2 Lt Chappell, some of them from heights of 300 feet. The majority of the bombs appear to have hit the sheds which were set on fire. All the machines returned safely.

9 Section's balloon was attacked with machine-gun fire by a hostile aeroplane and brought down in flames. The pilot, Lt Nops, who remained in the basket, was killed. The observer, Lt Formby, 90th Heavy Battery, made a successful parachute descent.

On the night of the 20th/21st German machines dropped bombs at Querrieu, Corbie and Amiens.

Casualties: Sqn 7, *10023 2 AM J. Banks, wireless operator, killed;* **11,** *2924 Flt Sgt J. Helingoe, wounded;* **7,** *9557 2 AM W. Horsley, wounded;* **45,** *2 Lt M. J. Fenwick and 2 Lt G. H. Bennett, wounded;* **10,** *2 Lt J. A. Simpson, wounded (died of wounds);* **24,** *W. E. Nixon, wounded;* **12,** *2 Lt A. Raymond Barker, missing.*

October 22nd

During the day artillery were successfully registered on 141 targets with aeroplane observation; kite balloon observers registered on 27 targets.

Lt Wright, 6 Sqn, directed fire on to hostile anti-aircraft guns. Six O.K.s were obtained, and a pit destroyed.

On the IVth Army front 27 hostile batteries were engaged. Sixty-six batteries were located. All the emplacements of two batteries were badly damaged. In one instance six direct hits were recorded on the emplacements of an active battery. Other emplacements and trenches were badly knocked about.

The 5th Brigade registered 29 points and co-operated with artillery in wire cutting operations and in 18 shoots on gun positions. Six gun pits were destroyed, 11 were damaged, and 3 ammunition pits were blown up.

7 Sqn took part in several successful counter-battery shoots. The 33rd Siege Battery with observation by 2 Lt Carroll and 2 Lt Fagan, 4 Sqn, destroyed 2 emplacements, and set fire to ammunition which continued

to explode in small quantities for an hour. 2 Lt Sworder and Lt Bird, 4 Sqn, co-operated successfully with the 13th Siege Battery in the destruction of 2 pits and the damage of 2 others.

In 22 combats in which aeroplanes of the 1st Brigade took part, 6 hostile machines were shot down.

2 Lt Hay, 40 Sqn, destroyed one near Pont à Vendin, which fell in flames.

Sgt Matheson and Lt W. G. Meggitt, 25 Sqn, brought down a hostile machine near Seclin. This machine was seen to crash by a pilot of 10 Sqn. A German machine attacked by 2 Lt J. L. Leith and Sgt L. S. Court, 25 Sqn, ceased firing, dived vertically, and landing down wind in a ploughed field was wrecked.

2 Lt E. L. Benbow, 40 Sqn, destroyed a hostile machine near Lens. It burst into flames and crashed to earth. North-west of Lille a German attacked by 2 Lt D. S. Johnson and Lt W. G. Meggitt, 25 Sqn, went down in a vertical nose dive with frequent bursts of flame issuing from its fuselage. It crashed to earth nose first.

Capt R. J. Mounsey and Capt R. E. Saul, 16 Sqn, joined in a fight that was taking place near Arras between 3 F.E.s of the 3rd Brigade and eight or nine Roland biplanes. Capt Mounsey and his observer engaged 5 of the enemy machines, and shot down and destroyed 1.

On the IInd Army front in the course of a combat, 2 Lt Holborn, 29 Sqn, was brought down near Polygon Wood.

On the 3rd Brigade front 26 combats were recorded. In many instances the enemy machines were driven away and their formations broken up. One of our machines did not return.

A machine attacked by Lt Knight, 24 Sqn, was forced to land near Bapaume. Another machine, attacked by Capt Andrews, 24 Sqn, was driven down.

Lt Bonnell, 32 Sqn, engaged and destroyed a hostile machine. The destruction of this machine is confirmed by the 67th A.A. Battery. Lt H. Corby, 32 Sqn, dived on to an L.V.G. and followed it down to 1,000 feet. He emptied a drum into the tail of the hostile machine at a range of 100 feet. The German is believed to have been destroyed. A wrecked machine was seen later on the ground in the vicinity of the fight. During the day, De Havilland Scouts of 32 Sqn and F.E.s of 23 Sqn, did excellent work in dispersing hostile formations. 2 Lt Capper, 19 Sqn, in a Spad, shot down a hostile aeroplane out of control near Louveral.

Before daybreak on the morning of the 22nd, bombs were dropped by the 1st Brigade over several billetting areas. At 9 a.m. Seclin Railway Station was bombed. A train steaming into the station was hit, and bombs also fell on the station buildings and rolling stock. 42 Sqn attacked and hit a dump near Fournes. The 3rd Brigade dropped thirty-five 112-pound bombs on the railway station at St Leger. A large number of the bombs fell in and around the station. One hundred 20-pound bombs were dispersed over various places of importance by the 5th Brigade during the day.

On the 22nd instant 2 Lt F. L. Barnard, with Lt F. S. Rankin, 18 Sqn, engaged seven hostile machines near Bapaume. Two of the enemy were hit, and one of them went down out of control. During the engagement Lt Rankin was killed, and, the machine being badly damaged, 2 Lt Barnard had some difficulty in returning to our side of the lines.

2 Lt H. Griffiths and Lt F. Surgey, 45 Sqn, while on offensive patrol, on the 22nd encountered six hostile aeroplanes. Lt Surgey was wounded in the head at the commencement of the fight, but continued fighting for a considerable time, and drove down one of the enemy's machines out of control.

The following interesting report of a fight in which 2 Lt J. B. Graham and Lt L. F. D. Lutyens, 11 Sqn, were engaged, has been received from Gunner W. A. Franklin, B Battery, 302nd Brigade, R.F.A.:

> On Sunday, October 22nd, I was on air scout duty in the Battery, and in the afternoon I saw 5 F.E.s come over the Battery and go well over the German lines. About 4.30 I saw 4 of them coming back, and just about over the lines they were attacked by 9 Roland Scouts coming from the south, about 4,000 feet up. They were fighting for about 10 minutes or a quarter of an hour. I saw one F.E. chasing a Roland down to within 100 feet of the ground until they disappeared from sight behind some trees. I never saw that Roland get up again. This happened behind the German lines, and the whole time the F.E. was under heavy rifle and machine gun fire from the German trenches. Another Roland detached itself from the other fight and followed the F.E. down, and the F.E. came back over the lines very low (could not have been more than 150 feet) and landed close to the Battery with the propeller broken (two blades shot away). As soon as they landed the Roland turned to chase a B.E., but was stopped by Lewis gun fire from F.E. which was on the ground. When the two Rolands fell out of the formation the others dispersed and the F.E.s came back.

Casualties: Sqn 18, *Lt F. S. Rankin, killed;* **22,** *2 Lt A. Crapper, killed;* **6,** *2 Lt A. Koch, wounded;* **45,** *Lt Surgey, wounded;* **19,** *2 Lt P. G. Robinson, wounded;* **10,** *2 Lt J. M. Harris, wounded;* **21,** *2 Lt W. T. Wilcox, missing;* **11,** *2 Lt A. L. M. Shepherd and 1 AM N. Brain (17094), missing;* **29,** *2 Lt J. N. Holtom, missing;* **3,** *2 Lt F. G. W. Marchant and 2 Lt C. C. Hann, missing;* **19,** *2 Lt R. Watts, missing;* **45,** *24715 P. Snowdon, missing; 2 Lt F. Fullerton, missing; 2 Lt O. J. Wade, missing; 2 Lt W. J. Thuell, missing; Capt L. Porter, missing; and 2 Lt G. B. Samuels, missing.*

2 Lt J. A. Simpson, 10 Sqn, who was wounded by A.A. fire on the 21st, has since died. Although mortally wounded, he succeeded in bringing his machine and his observer safely back to his own aerodrome.

October 23rd
Unfavourable flying day.

Reconaissances were carried out by the 1st, 2nd and 4th Brigades.

Artillery work was greatly interfered with, and at times it was impossible owing to fog. Twenty-five targets were successfully engaged with aeroplane observation and three by kite balloons.

October 24th
Rain throughout the day; practically no flying.

A special reconnaissance of a new crater near The Bluff was carried out by Lt Smith, 6 Sqn, in an armoured B.E.2c at a height of 300 feet.

October 25th
Raining most of the day ⌓ There was little aerial activity ⌓ Some artillery work was accomplished by the 4th and 5th Brigades.

Reconnaissances were carried out, and a few minor bombing operations were carried out by the 1st and 4th Brigades.

Casualties: Sqn 4, *5710 1 AM H. Thake, killed; 2 Lt S. N. Williams; and 2 Lt G. R. Bolitho, missing;* **7,** *2 Lt W. Fraser; and 2 Lt J. Collen, missing;* **21,** *2 Lt A. J. Fisher, missing.*

October 26th
Clouds and rain interfered with artillery work. Some successful shoots with aeroplane observation were carried out on the fronts of the IVth and Reserve Armies. Lt Macdonald, 9 Sqn, recorded 5 O.K.s and 10 Zs for the 105th Siege Battery on trench targets near Gueudecourt. The 5th Brigade dealt with 31 targets. A mill on the River Ancre was well knocked about by a 15-inch howitzer Battery. Three gun pits were damaged and several ammunition pits were blown up.

An attack made by a patrol of 60 Sqn dispersed a German formation. As a result of the engagement 2 of our Nieuports had forced landings in our lines and a third is missing. The German formation, consisting of 6 machines, attacked and brought down a B.E.2c over Serre. Capt Foot, 60 Sqn, dived at the leader, but was too late to assist the B.E.2c. Capt Foot's Nieuport was considerably shot about, his gun-mounting was put out of action, and he only just succeeded in recrossing the lines. He landed with his machine on fire. A patrol of 32 Sqn appears to have joined in this fight, and one of the enemy's machines brought down by Lt Coleman crashed to the ground close to the B.E.2c.

Lts Mackay, Knight, Crawford, Wood and Pashley, 24 Sqn, were heavily engaged with about 20 of the enemy's aeroplanes, mostly Halberstadt Scouts and two-seater Scouts of Bristol and Nieuport types. When the patrol crossed the line at about 7.15 a.m. 3 hostile formations, each of 5 or 6 machines, were flying south of Bapaume at different heights. As the De Havillands approached, the top patrol dived to the attack. They were driven down to the level of the second patrol. The De Havillands attacked and drove the whole to the level of the third patrol. A general engagement at close quarters ensued, and so close was the fighting that it was not possible to observe results, but the enemy's machines gradually diminished in numbers, until when over Bertincourt only 9 or 10 remained in the fight. The De Havillands were now running out of petrol and had to fight their way back to the line against a strong wind. All attacks made on the way home were beaten off. In the course of the fight Lt Knight drove down 2 Halberstadts to 5,000 feet, but, being attacked, was unable to see their ultimate fate. He noticed several other enemy machines having a bad time with De Havillands well on their tails. A machine engaged by Lt Mackay went down vertically, but flattened out very low down and appeared to land. He also drove down a second. A German attacked by Lt Pashley spiralled down with his engine stopped. Lt Crawford was slightly wounded early in the fight but continued the patrol, and emptied a drum into a machine which fell 2,000 feet out of control, but was lost to sight. Though superior in speed and climb, the Halberstadts appeared to lose height on the De Havillands while turning. The De Havillands were thus able to out-manoeuvre them.

While on a test flight, Capt A. M. Vaucour and Lt Elliott, 70 Sqn, saw 10 hostile machines close to the lines. They attacked and chased the enemy back to Bois d'Havrincourt. Two of the enemy's machines appeared to be hit, and their formation was broken up. Eventually Capt Vaucour's gun jammed after firing about 200 rounds, and he turned to the lines followed by two of the hostile machines. Lt Elliott fired two more drums at close range and both of the Germans made off, one of them apparently hit.

The 1st Brigade made a successful attack on Henin Lietard Station. Bombs burst in the middle of the station and on buildings west of the station. A train entering the station was hit, and other bombs fell among lorries.

Casualties: Sqn 15, *2 Lt L. C. Fawkner, killed;* **5,** *2 Lt J. C. Jervis, killed;* **41,** *2 Lt C. O. Bean, wounded;* **9,** *1 AM E. H. C. Foot (wireless operator), wounded;* **24,** *2 Lt K. Crawford, wounded;* **5,** *2 Lt J. S. Smith, wounded;* **60,** *Lt W. M. Carlyle, missing;* **7,** *2 Lt F. Parsons and 2 Lt G. A. Palfreyman, missing;* **18,** *2 Lt P. F. Heppell and 2 Lt H. B. O. Mitchell, missing.*

October 27th

Unfavourable weather ⌔ Nothing to report.

28 October – 5 November, 1916

Capt Oswald Boelcke, one of Germany's greatest airmen, was killed on 28 October when his aircraft collided with that flown by one of his own squadron pilots, Lt Erwin Boehme, during a dog-fight with 24 Sqn D.H.2s. Boelcke was credited with 40 combat victories at the time of his death. He was flying an Albatros DII—one of the machines described as a 'small Aviatik' in the communiqué.

The account by Lt Tudor-Hart, a 22 Sqn observer, of how he managed to defend and land his aircraft after the pilot was killed, is a testimony to his own courage and determination and to the inherent stability of the F.E.2b.

The B.E.2d, mentioned on 1 November, was a development of the B.E.2c. Another variant, the B.E.2e, which had a different wing structure, had also been introduced during the summer. These two versions, which offered only a marginal improvement in performance, formed the equipment of new squadrons sent to France in 1916, and also replaced the B.E.2cs in the existing units.

The pyrotechnic missiles reported by 6 Sqn on 2 November were a regular feature of the defences of observation balloon sites and were popularly known as 'flaming onions'.

COMMUNIQUÉ NO. 60

The following is an extract from a letter dated 25th July 1916, written by Lt W. O. Tudor-Hart, 22 Sqn, who, with Capt Webb, was reported missing on July 1st:

> I was with Capt Webb and we went about 4 or 5 miles over the German lines in his machine on 1st July at 11 a.m. We saw eight German machines approaching from south-west—they were higher than us, and we flew towards them to attack. Two passed over our heads together about 300 yards or so apart, and I opened fire on one. They both replied together. I gave the signal to Webb to turn so that I could fire at the other machine behind us, but he put the machine's head down. I turned to see what was the matter, and he pointed to his abdomen and collapsed over the 'joy stick'. He died in a few seconds I think, but his last thought was to save his machine.
>
> The machine at once began turning towards the German side, and I had to get back to my machine-gun to fire at a machine diving at us. This happened again and again, but my fire would always prevent them finishing the

dive. Other machines fired from above all the time. I had only time to get the machine pointing towards our lines when I had to get back to the gun. I never got a chance to pull Webb out of the pilot's seat, so had to steer with my hand over the windscreen. I didn't expect to get off alive, but tried to put up as good a fight as possible, and tried all the time to keep her towards our lines, but having to man the gun so often made it impossible to make progress, but the erratic course the machine flew probably saved it.

At last, still being fired at, I got right down near the ground and proceeded to make a landing, as it was all I could do. I saw a lot of men with rifles, and realised that I might get shot before I could set fire to the machine, so I, at the last minute, put her nose down in order to crash.

One wing tip hit first, the whole machine was destroyed, I was hurled out and escaped with a bruised and paralysed side and broken ankle and rib. All right now, but the ankle, I was very kindly treated, and the German pilots acted like sportsmen and gentlemen. . . .

October 28th, 29th and 30th

A spell of unfavourable weather considerably hampered aerial activities.

Some artillery work was successfully accomplished, and on each day many active hostile batteries were located, engaged and silenced, pits being destroyed and ammunition exploded.

On the 29th, the 13th Siege Battery (9.2-inch howitzers) with observation by Capt Walser and Lt Bird of 4 Sqn, obtained 6 O.K.s and 16 Ys on a 4-gun camouflaged battery. All the pits were destroyed and one lot of ammunition blew up. The same battery destroyed one pit and damaged two others in another battery position.

On the 28th October, six Halberstadts and small Aviatiks attacked Lt A. G. Knight and Lt McKay, 24 Sqn, in the vicinity of Pozieres. During the fight the enemy were reinforced by six more machines. At the end of about five minutes of strenuous fighting two of the German machines collided. Bits were seen to fall off, and one of the hostile aeroplanes glided away to the east, apparently under control, but was lost to sight. The fight continued for about another 15 minutes, when all the enemy machines withdrew, and the De Havillands returned undamaged.

It seems probable that this is the fight in which Capt Boelcke was killed. He is reported in the German wireless press as having been killed as the result of a collision in the air on this date.

At 4.15 p.m. on the 29th, a hostile machine was seen to fall in flames over Ligny.

Casualties (*October 28th*)*:* **Sqn 29,** *2 Lt W. A. Niven, killed;* **8,** *2 Lt V. Bayley, wounded;* **21,** *2 Lt M. Sharpe, missing;* (*October 29th*)*: 8824 2 AM C. F. Heatley* (*wireless operator*)*, killed.*

October 31st

Artillery of the IInd Army in co-operation with aeroplanes of 42 Sqn, obtained 4 O.K.s and 10 Ys on a gun position, destroying a pit. On the front of the IVth Army, 59 batteries were located. Fifteen were engaged with aeroplane observation and 18 direct hits obtained. The 12th Heavy Battery, with observation by 2 Lt Coward and Lt Johnstone, 9 Sqn, obtained 6 O.K.s, 21 Ys and 11 Zs on an active battery, causing two explosions and one fire. Lt Macdonald and Lt Freed, 9 Sqn, registered three O.K.s and 14 Ys for the 31st Heavy Battery on an active hostile battery position.

Aeroplanes of the 5th Brigade co-operated in several successful shoots. Capt A. A. Walser and Lt C. B. Bird, 4 Sqn, located and reported by zone call 14 active batteries, five of which were silenced. Observing for the 13th Siege Battery, they engaged an hitherto unshelled 4-gun battery near Miraumont. Two pits were entirely destroyed and a third was damaged. In the course of the day 169 active batteries were reported by zone call. Many were engaged and silenced. A fire started in one battery position and caused ammunition to explode for an hour.

An L.V.G. attacked by Lt T. S. Green and Sgt D. R. Baxter, 3 Sqn, was driven down in a nose dive and seen to land. Its destruction is not confirmed.

Casualties: Sqn 9, *7600 2 AM E. Josling, wounded;* **70,** *2 Lt C. E. Ward, wounded; Lt G. H. Nicholson and Lt T. M. Johns, missing.*

November 1st

High wind with low clouds and occasional showers, which considerably interfered with aerial operations.

Artillery co-operation continued with some successes. An anti-aircraft battery on the 2nd Brigade front was engaged and silenced. On the front of the 4th and 5th Brigades many active batteries were engaged and silenced.

2 Lt Cave and Lt Duke, 4 Sqn, while on artillery observation, saw a hostile machine diving on to a B.E.2d. The B.E.2d was brought down and fell near Courcelette. 2 Lt Cave, and Lt Duke attacked and brought down the hostile machine, which they saw skim over the trees south of Miraumont and stall and side-slip near Beau-Regard dove-cote.

About 7.15 a.m. 13 Kite Balloon was attacked with machine-gun fire by two hostile machines, when at a height of about 2,600 feet. The balloon was hauled down without damage.

A raid carried out by 6 Sqn against an ammunition dump near Gheluvelt at 4.45 p.m. Results were unobserved owing to darkness.

2 Lt Franklin and Lt Jones, 16 Sqn, observing a party of infantry entering Givenchy, dived to 800 feet and fired a drum into them. The party was broken up and great confusion caused. Lt Jones was wounded by machine-gun fire. Capt Philpott and Lt Carden, 12 Sqn, descended to 600 feet, and fired into the German trenches.

Casualties: Sqn 29, *2 Lt F. P. Kane, killed;* **40,** *Capt G. D. Hill, wounded;* **16,** *Lt C. N. Jones, wounded;* **7,** *15355 2 AM P. Brindle, wounded;* **34,** *7912 2 AM T. Alexander and 12391 2 AM W. G. Foreman, wounded;* **9,** *2 Lt S. W. Mann and 2 Lt A. E. Wynn, missing.*

November 2nd

Reconnaissances were carried out by the 1st, 2nd and 5th Brigades.

The weather was unfavourable for observation. Fifty-four targets were successfully engaged with aeroplane observation and 31 with kite balloon observation.

Lt J. Shepherd and 2 Lt G. F. Bishop, 1 Sqn, attacked a Roland Scout over Messines. The hostile machine caught fire and crashed in a field near Warneton.

2 Lt Joyce, 60 Sqn, emerging from a cloud in the course of a combat, found himself almost on the top of three German balloons. He fired a burst into one of them, and a stream of smoke issued from the balloon. 2 Lt Joyce's machine was badly damaged by flaming balls from an anti-aircraft battery. About a dozen balls appeared to be attached to one streamer.

A German machine attacked by Capt Andrews, 24 Sqn, fell out of control, and later in the day a wrecked machine was seen on the ground in the same locality.

Sgt Bromley and 2 Lt Wood, 7 Sqn, were brought down in a combat in the air, the machine falling west of the lines.

Several minor attacks were carried out by the 1st and 5th Brigades. 6 Sqn again attacked the ammunition dump near Givenchy, obtaining two direct hits with 112-pound bombs.

Casualties: Sqn 7, *1312 Sgt C. Bromley, killed;* **32,** *2 Lt R. H. Wallace, wounded;* **7,** *2 Lt G. H. Wood, wounded.*

November 3rd

A very strong wind at 6,000 feet greatly handicapped aerial operations.

One hundred and twenty targets were engaged with aeroplane and kite balloon observation, many direct hits being obtained on emplacements and batteries were silenced. A considerable amount of wire cutting and trench registration was successfully accomplished.

The 65th Siege Battery (12-inch howitzers), with observation by Lt Gabell and Lt Pemberton, 5 Sqn, demolished all four pits in one hostile battery, and damaged three pits in other batteries. Lt Long and Lt O'Hanlon, 4 Sqn, sent zone call for an infantry target. 60-pounder shrapnel caused many casualties. They also informed 17th Divisional Artillery of a party of men working on a strong point. Shrapnel fire was turned on and the party moved. The artillery was switched to the new point, and many casualties were caused in the working party.

A mill on the River Ancre and Baillescourt Farm were practically destroyed by a 15-inch howitzer (R.M.A.) with observation by Capt Mackay and 2 Lt Buckeridge, 4 Sqn.

There was considerable hostile aerial activity on the fronts of the IIIrd, IVth and Vth Armies.

Lt J. M. J. Spencer, 60 Sqn, attacked four hostile machines near Ayette. One of the enemy's machines fell out of control, and the Nieuport was also brought down and fell into the German lines. Lt Pashley, 24 Sqn, drove down a machine apparently out of control, but it could not be followed to the ground. There were many other indecisive combats.

The 1st Brigade carried out a series of minor raids by day and by night. Billets at Fromelles were attacked by 42 Sqn. Six bombs hit the huts.

2 Lt Jameson, 42 Sqn, attacked Potterie Farm and Trois Tilleuls Farm with 40-pound phosphorous bombs. All the bombs exploded, and the light caused by the explosions was so dazzling that 2 Lt Jameson was temporarily unable to see his instruments and lost his bearings. The phosphorus spread over a very large area, and continued to burn for about ten minutes after reaching the ground.

15 Section's kite balloon broke adrift at 1.50 p.m. 2 Lt Bevan, the only occupant, threw out all maps and papers, and descended safely in a parachute near Elverdinghe.

13 Kite Balloon Section's ground position was shelled. No damage was caused.

Casualties: Sqn 11, *2 Lt H. H. Turk, killed; 2 Lt J. Allen, killed;* **60,** *Lt J. M. J. Spencer, missing;* **22,** *2 Lt W. E. Knowlden, missing; 2 Lt B. W. A. Ordish, missing; Capt A. J. M. Pemberton, missing; 2 Lt L. C. L. Cook, missing; Capt A. T. Lord Lucas, missing; Lt A. Anderson, missing;* **18,** *24130 Sgt C. G. Baldwin, missing; and 2 Lt G. A. Bentham, missing.*

November 4th

Low clouds and ground mist made observation difficult ⇜ Aeroplane observers dealt with 46 targets ⇜ There was no hostile activity and no fighting took place.

Douai Railway Station was attacked by the 1st Brigade with 58 bombs. Observation of results was hampered by cloud. The 2nd Brigade dropped 16 bombs on a headquarters in a farm south of Houthulst Forest.

5 – 12 November, 1916

To assist the hard-pressed Royal Flying Corps, 8 Sqn of the Royal Naval Air Service had been detached to the Somme front on 27 October and was now in action.

'Naval Eight' as the squadron was popularly known, initially flew mixed equipment—one flight each of Nieuport Scouts, Sopwith 1½-Strutters and Sopwith Pups. The Pup had been used by the R.N.A.S. in the Dunkirk area since September. It had a much better climb and speed than the existing British Scouts flown by the R.F.C. and retained superb manoeuvrability at high altitudes. As a flying machine it was a match for the new German Scouts, but it suffered the disadvantage of being armed with only a single synchronised machine-gun.

The air battle which developed during the bombing of an ammunition dump at Vraucourt on 9 November was the biggest fought up to that time. The heavy British losses—two B.E.2cs, two D.H.2s and one F.E.2b which crashed in 'no-mans'-land'—were inflicted mainly by Jasta 2's Albatroses. Von Richthofen shot down one of the B.E.s.

Roland Scouts reported in this communiqué are likely to have been Albatroses.

F.E.2bs of 18 Sqn flew some successful night interdiction sorties against railway targets on 11 November.

COMMUNIQUÉ NO. 61

November 5th

In spite of an exceptionally strong wind and unfavourable weather, some useful artillery work was carried out by machines of the 3rd, 4th and 5th Brigades. Capt E. Johnston and Lt Rickards, 5 Sqn, worked for 3 hours and 10 minutes with the 152nd Siege Battery, recording several O.K.s on a trench target.

Casualty: Sqn 45, *2 Lt H. T. Birdsall, wounded.*

November 6th

Wind, clouds and showers throughout the day ⌔ *Fifty-seven targets were dealt with by aeroplane observers* ⌔ *There was no hostile aerial activity.*

Casualty: Sqn 9, *15816 2 AM A. Maude, wireless operator, wounded.*

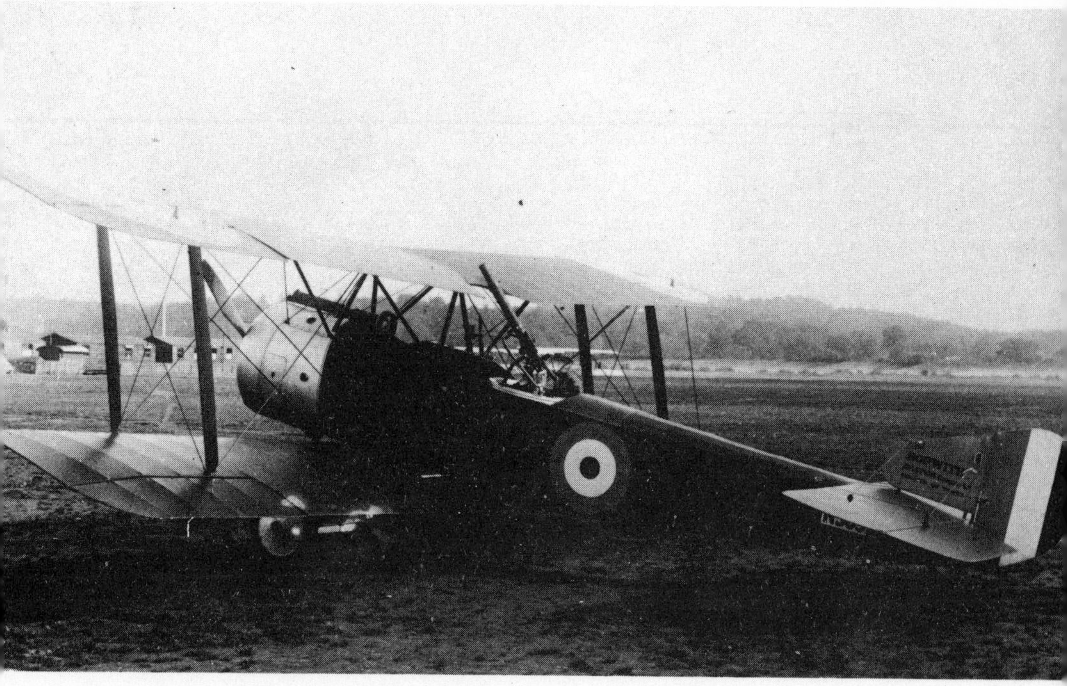

Above: Sopwith 1½ Strutter
Below: Gotha G II

Above: Halberstadt D II
Below: F.E.8

November 7th
Unfavourable flying weather ⌔ Nothing to Report.

November 8th
Weather conditions were again unfavourable for all aerial operations.

Aeroplane observers of the 4th and 5th Brigades dealt with 47 targets. Lt Edwards and Lt Power, 5 Sqn, observing for the 166th Siege Battery, reported all the 4 gun pits of a battery to be destroyed. Three rounds fell into the pits and 5 others on the edges of them.

During a patrol, Capt Parker and Lt Harvey, 8 Sqn, had 3 encounters. In the course of one the German was engaged at very close range, and the observer was hit and seen to fall forward.

Casualties: Sqn 45, *2 Lt H. G. P. Lowe, killed; 2 Lt W. Jordan, killed;* **2,** *2 Lt G. K. Palmer, wounded.*

November 9th
A bright clear day resulted in exceptional activity on the part of hostile aircraft. His aeroplanes actively co-operated with his artillery, on several occasions, our artillery and photographic machines were interfered with, and bombing expeditions, reconnaissances, and patrols were constantly engaged throughout the day over the enemy's country.

One hundred and sixty-seven targets were dealt with by aeroplane observers, and 36 by kite balloon observers. Heavy artillery of the Ist Army co-operating with machines of the 1st Brigade obtained 17 O.K.s on hostile batteries, and on the IInd Army front observers recorded 18 direct hits on hostile gun positions. On the front of the 4th Brigade, 27 batteries were engaged with aeroplane observation; 5 of them were silenced. Twenty-three direct hits were obtained, and 11 pits were damaged. In co-operation with machines of the 5th Brigade, artillery destroyed 2 pits, damaged 13 others, damaged trenches and exploded ammunition.

Lt A. A. Patterson and Lt H. M. Yeatman, 34 Sqn, were attacked by a German machine over Le Sars. The hostile machine dived at them from behind, and Lt Patterson, apparently already hit, kept straight on. The first burst of fire from the hostile machine considerably damaged the B.E. which got into a spin. Lt Yeatman took control and landed the machine on a French aerodrome. Lt Patterson died of his wounds.

Sgt Darvell, 40 Sqn, encountered 3 hostile machines over Souchez, 1 of which he appears to have driven down out of control. Observers at the 61st Anti-Aircraft battery report that the machine fell in a vertical nose dive and appeared to crash.

Six F.E.s of 25 Sqn, while on offensive patrol, attacked a hostile formation consisting of 6 Roland Scouts and 2 Fokker biplanes. The F.E.s attacked at right angles, splitting up the German formation into separate units. One Fokker biplane was driven down by 2 Lt Leith and descended in a spinning nose dive, emitting a stream of smoke. The hostile formation scattered and refused combat. Finally Capt Tedder got within 150 yards of a Roland Scout which he drove down apparently out of control. A piece of metal was seen to fly out from the Roland engine followed by a stream of smoke.

During a combat between an offensive patrol of 24 Sqn and several German machines, Lt Knight drove down two. One was lost to sight, the other went down in a steep spiral with engine full on. Later on 2 machines were seen on their noses over Le Transloy, in which neighbourhood the fight took place.

Flt Sub-Lt Galbraith, R.N.A.S. Squadron, dived from 17,000 feet and opened fire at a range of 50 yards at a hostile machine which had crossed our lines. The observer of the hostile machine was seen to fall over his gun. Later Lt Galbraith attacked a second machine and again the observer was hit and disappeared into the fuselage. Both the hostile machines broke off the engagements and flew east. Flt Sub-Lt Simpson and Flt Sub-Lt Compston, R.N.A.S. Squadron engaged the leader of 2 hostile machines which they encountered near Bapaume. The German nose dived and disappeared into the clouds with, it is believed, his observer killed.

A bombing raid of the 3rd Brigade consisting of 16 bombing machines and an escort of 14, was attacked on its way to Vraucourt by at least 30 Germans, chiefly fast scouts. The enemy attacked from the front, and our scouts dived and got to close quarters with them. As the fight progressed the escort got gradually below the bombing machines. Meanwhile the enemy was reinforced and the bombers were attacked from both sides. Numerous individual fights ensued. Capt Davey and Lt Harrow-Bunn, 11 Sqn, dived to the assistance of 2 B.E.s, each of which was engaged by 2 or 3 hostile machines. The F.E., however, arrived too late to be of assistance, and both the B.E.s were lost. Two De Havillands, which are also missing, were seen low down and very hard pressed by several hostile machines over Adinfer. Capt Davey and Lt Harrow-Bunn, being separated from the remainder of the formation were exposed to many hostile attacks, and with a failing engine, had some difficulty in regaining our lines. Cpl Ward, observer 11 Sqn, was killed. His pilot, Lt Cowie, was wounded and narrowly escaped capture, his machine falling close to our front line trenches. Lt Bell-Irving, 60 Sqn, was wounded but managed to land safely in our lines. Lt T. Hayes, 12 Sqn, in one of the bombing machines, was also wounded. In such close and continuous fighting it was impossible to accurately gauge the enemy's losses. There seems little doubt that 3 of his machines were destroyed, and others suffered considerable damage.

In addition to the above fight, offensive patrols and reconnaissances of the 3rd Brigade were engaged in 26 combats. Lt Brearley and Lt Hallam, 29 Sqn, returning to our lines with an offensive patrol saw a formation of 7 hostile machines in the vicinity of Arras and attacked them. The remainder of the patrol did not see the enemy. Lt Brearley closed with the nearest German and manoeuvred into a favourable position, but found his gun was partially jammed and would only fire occasional bursts. He turned away to rectify this, but finding it impossible he decided to return and was attacked from behind, his machine suffering extensive damage. When at about 500 feet Lt Brearley was wounded in the chest. He just managed to clear the German front line trench and effected a descent in no man's land where the whole machine collapsed. The wreckage was subjected to heavy rifle and machine gun fire, but Lt Brearley managed to roll into a shell hole, where he remained for 4 or 5 hours until dark. He then crawled towards our trenches, but got hung up in the wire, from which he was rescued by the infantry. Lt Brearley stated that he last saw Lt Hallam, who is missing, fighting extremely well.

A hostile kite balloon is reported to have been brought down in flames by one of our aeroplanes over Hulluch. This is believed to have been done by Capt Mapplebeck of 40 Sqn, who is missing.

Don Station was attacked by the 1st Brigade. Heavy bombs hit two groups of houses, a factory near the station, an engine, and the railway yard. Hutments and dumps were attacked by 1, 6 and 42 Sqns in the 2nd Brigade. The 3rd Brigade attacked an ammunition dump at Vraucourt, where 72 bombs were dropped. Several bombs were seen to burst near the objective, but observation of results was difficult owing to the interference of hostile machines. The Martinsydes of 27 Sqn bombed Arleux railway station with success. The majority of bombs fell on the objective.

Two hostile aeroplanes attempted an attack on 10 Section's Kite Balloon. Effective barrage by our anti-aircraft guns frustrated the attempt.

Casualties: Sqn 34, *2 Lt A. A. Patterson, killed;* **11,** *Cpl C. G. S. Ward, killed;* **12,** *Lt T. Hayes, wounded;* **60,** *Lt A. D. Bell-Irving, wounded;* **11,** *2 Lt J. D. Cowie, wounded; Lt G. E. Goolden, wounded;* **29,** *2 Lt N.*

Brearley, wounded; 2 Lt H. A. Hallam, missing; **18,** *Capt G. H. Norman, wounded;* **40,** *2 Lt H. F. Evans, missing; Capt T. Mapplebeck, missing;* **29,** *Capt A. C. Bolton, missing; 2 Lt I. Curlewis, missing;* **12,** *2 Lt J. G. Cameron, missing; and Lt G. F. Knight, missing.*

November 10th

One hundred and twenty-six targets were dealt with by aeroplane observers and 24 by kite balloon sections. Many hostile batteries were successfully engaged and several gun pits destroyed. On the IVth Army front 18 direct hits were obtained on battery positions and 20 on trenches. A working party was engaged and scattered by the zone call.

On the front of the Vth Army damage was done to trenches and wire. Four gun pits were destroyed and 12 damaged, and one lot of ammunition was burned.

An offensive patrol of 24 Sqn, engaged two low flying hostile aeroplanes which were working close to the line over Le Transloy. The patrol dived to the attack, but only Lt McKay and Lt Wood got within range. Lt McKay got in several good bursts at close range and saw his enemy go down in a steep spiral, but owing to his gun jamming he turned off and did not see the German hit the ground. Lt Wood engaged the second machine and drove it down low over Le Transloy. An observer of 3 Sqn reports that one of these machines crashed.

Capt I. H. D. Henderson, 19 Sqn, in a Spad attacked a hostile machine in the vicinity of Bapaume. The German opened fire with Capt Henderson about 1,000 feet above him. The Spad dived and came up below the tail of the hostile machine, and Capt Henderson, closing to about 150 yards, fired about 50 rounds in bursts. The German machine caught fire and fell in flames near Gueudecourt.

Capt A. M. Vaucour and Lt R. D. Elliott, 70 Sqn, whilst alone on patrol saw 6 hostile biplanes and drove down one of them with a column of smoke coming out from the fuselage, but apparently under control. A patrol of 70 Sqn encountered 5 hostile machines, probably Halberstadters, over Ytres. One of the Sopwiths, after being heavily engaged, was seen to collapse in the air and fell on fire.

While on offensive patrol at about 9 a.m. Lt Shirtcliffe, 25 Sqn, observed a formation of hostile machines leaving Douai aerodrome. He flew over them at a height of 11,000 feet and when the formation was at 2,000 feet, he dropped a phosphorus bomb timed to burst 9,000 feet after release. It burst well over the German machines, one of which dived to the ground and crashed.

The destruction of a hostile machine which was attacked by a patrol of 24 Sqn on the 9th instant is confirmed.

During the day a machine was seen to fall in flames near Flers and another was seen to crash between Bertincourt and Ytres.

A machine which landed near Barastre was fired on by Lts Coward and Morris, 9 Sqn, after it had landed.

Pilots of the R.N.A.S. Squadron had several combats. Flt Sub-Lt Grange drove off a two-seater near Sailly, after hitting the hostile observer who disappeared into the fuselage and ceased firing. Flt Sub-Lt Galbraith, R.N.A.S. Squadron, engaged the rear machine of a formation of 5 Germans. The hostile machine went down in a spinning nose dive, apparently out of control.

An offensive patrol of 32 Sqn encountered a German patrol over Bihucourt. During the fight, which lasted about 10 minutes, the pilot of one of the hostile machines was apparently hit. He turned towards our lines and appeared to be out of control. The observer, however, appears to have taken control of the machine, as it turned east and dived away.

Valenciennes aerodrome was attacked by 27 Sqn. Forty-four bombs were dropped. One bomb hit a hangar and the others fell near by. One bomb fell among 5 aeroplanes which were seen on the aerodrome. 1, 6 and 42 Sqns attacked hutments on the Second Army front.

On the night of the 9th/10th November the following attacks were carried out: 1st Brigade: Henin Lietard was attacked with 34 bombs which fell on and around the station. The 2nd Brigade dropped 17 bombs on hutments at Houthem. Douai aerodrome was attacked by the 3rd Brigade and bombs were seen to burst among the sheds. Eight 20-pound bombs were dropped on a train at Vitry and 2 bombs at a searchlight, causing it to be extinguished. 2 Lt Tremlett and Sgt Twist, 18 Sqn, dropped bombs on Velu and Lebucquiere.

Capt Callaghan and Sgt Ankers dropped bombs on a lit-up aerodrome at Villers. As soon as the first bombs were dropped, all lights on the aerodrome were extinguished and a German machine was seen to leave the ground. At a height of 2,500 feet the pilot apparently decided to return. The bombing machine immediately opened fire, using ordinary ammunition, at a range of about 300 yards, and the German machine was not seen again. After waiting for about five minutes more bombs were dropped; two fell on the landing ground and one on a hangar.

Lt Campbell and 1 AM Watts, 18 Sqn, dropped bombs on an aerodrome near Buissy, the lights of which were immediately extinguished, and a party from the ground opened machine-gun fire on them. On their way home they observed four trains in Queant station, and descended to 300 feet and opened fire.

2 Lt Reed, 19 Sqn, dropped 8 bombs on Arleux station and sidings; 4 of the bombs exploded on a train moving south, and the remaining

four exploded in the station. 2 Lt Reed, before returning, fired about 20 rounds from his machine-gun into the train.

A night patrol was carried out by 8 Sqn. Several drums of ammunition were fired into the trenches from a low altitude.

Casualties: Sqn 70, *2 Lt C. E. McCrae, killed;* **25,** *2 Lt E. S. P. Hynes, killed; 2 Lt C. H. Bidmead, killed;* **20,** *6640 1 AM H. Alexander, wounded;* **70,** *2 Lt M. Allport, missing; and Lt T. M. Bennet, missing.*

November 11th

Thick mist and low clouds throughout the day.

Night of the 10th/11th instant: the 1st Brigade dropped bombs on Pont à Vendin, Meurchin and Berclau; three machines of 6 Sqn dropped 20-pound and phosphorus bombs on a searchlight, which was extinguished, and on a railway junction; 42 Sqn dropped 10 bombs on Perenchies; and Capt Murray, 13 Sqn, made two attacks on Douai aerodrome. Three phosphorus bombs were dropped on each occasion, and fires appear to have broken out in the sheds.

Capt S. F. Heard and Capt J. L. Head; 18 Sqn, set out to bomb lit-up aerodromes. None being visible they returned to Velu, where they found two trains in the station. Bombs were dropped from 2,000 feet. One burst on the train near the engine and others fell on the tracks near the train. More bombs were dropped on the station, causing two small explosions. A searchlight from the east of Velu then became active and they were subjected to fairly accurate fire. On the way home they fired at transport on the road, the lights of which were immediately extinguished and the transport came to a halt.

Lt P. C. Campbell and 1 AM O. Watts, 18 Sqn, report as follows:

> Crossed the line by following the railway from Albert to Arras to Achiet-le-Grand and then west. Identified Ervillers by bend in road; also Behagnies and Sapignies. A train was going north along the St Leger—Boyelles railway. We came down to 2,000 feet, but did not bomb it as I thought it might be empty. (10.45 p.m.). I then followed railway until I saw three balloon sheds. Dropped one 20-pound Hales and two incendiary bombs. They missed the sheds, but hit a shed in the town. The bombs were dropped from 2,000 feet. (10.55 p.m.). I then saw a train coming west, just west of Ecoust. I caught up the train from behind. It was a short one composed of about four closed and three open trucks. The latter were full of boxes. We were 150 feet above it, and I dropped the one single bomb remaining on right side, but it fell behind the train. The other four fell on the second closed truck behind the locomotive. The explosion knocked back my observer, who was leaning forward, and made my machine sway. We then circled round and emptied two drums into the train, which had stopped. The light on the tail of the train was still lit, also the headlights, Then we went west again and climbed to about 3,000 feet. We saw another train coming from Boyelles to St Leger. We came down to the north side of the train and turned to follow it. My observer opened fire at it at about 200 yards range when we were about 200 feet

up. He got about two shots into the centre of the train. The next few shots were just low; the next ten or so went over; the remainder hit the train, including the front of it about the engine, which put on speed. I crossed the line and gave my observer time to change the drum, and then turned to the left and flew over the train again, going down to 100 feet. My observer got the range and emptied all the second drum into the front carriages and engine, which stopped and gave off clouds of steam. We then went south-west and saw that the train had caught alight in front. These two drums were entirely full of tracers (Buckingham) which were fired without a jamb or stoppage. When about a quarter of a mile west of Ervillers two star rockets were fired at us while we were 1,000 feet off the ground. The first passed just behind my tail at my height and the second just over me. I then turned west and came down, and the next one went over me about 500 feet or so. I then turned north for a minute or so and then west. No more rockets were fired.

Capt J. C. Callaghan and Sgt B. Ankers, 18 Sqn, crossed the lines at 10.40 p.m. with the intention of bombing aerodromes. When over Achiet-le-Grand they saw a machine flying at about 1,000 feet and attempted to follow. Finding no aerodromes lit up they decided to go to Cambrai. They were subjected to heavy, but inaccurate anti-aircraft fire over Havrincourt and Cambrai. Seeing no activity at Cambrai they went over to Valenciennes. All lights in Denain were extinguished on their approach. The station at Valenciennes was lit up and Mons which could be seen in the distance was well illuminated. There appeared to be about 4 trains in Valenciennes stations and 6 bombs were dropped there. The bombs burst on the station and a fire broke out and burned brightly for several minutes. On their way home 2 searchlights attempted to pick them up, so they dived at them and fired 2 drums and 1 of the lights was extinguished. Capt Baker, 18 Sqn, dropped bombs on Velu and 4 on what appeared to be a dump on the railway.

Capt Allen, Lt Orlebar and Lt Buck, 19 Sqn, dropped 24 bombs on Havrincourt château. All the bombs appeared to fall near the mark.

2 Le Reid and 1 AM A. M. Alexander, 20 Sqn, were attacked over Menin. 1 AM Alexander was wounded in the right arm early in the fight, but continued to fire his gun, using his left hand. Eventually, when attacked by a second hostile machine, the Lewis gun was shot, and the observer was again hit in the side.

2 Lt J. Duncan, 21 Sqn, fired about 40 rounds at a single seater-scout over Le Transloy. He was then attacked from above by two more Germans and had both his petrol tanks punctured and his machine gun put out of action. He landed safely on an advanced French aerodrome, where French eye-witnesses of the combat state that one of Lt Duncan's opponents had fallen out of control.

Casualties: Sqn 9, *8893 2 AM W. Buckley, wireless operator, killed; and 12325 AM H. Naphtall, wireless operator, wounded.*

12 – 19 November, 1916

The Somme battle ended on 18 November and despite the introduction of the new German fighters, aircraft losses on both sides were surprisingly even.

The R.F.C. in effect lost 363 aircraft—190 shot down and a further 173 which struggled back in such damaged condition as to require complete rebuilding. Aircrew killed, wounded and missing totalled 499. Germany lost 359 aircraft over the same period. The R.F.C. losses showed a sharp rise after the formation of the German Jagdstaffeln—of which 25 were in being by early November.

During the period of the battle R.F.C. aircraft flew more than 2,000 artillery-spotting sorties and dropped nearly 300 tons of bombs.

On 16 November the first specimen of an Albatros DI Scout fell into British hands virtually undamaged. Ironically it was forced down by one of the much maligned B.E.2 variants. This aircraft was later tested in England and was still being flown at Turnberry in the summer of 1918.

References in this communiqué to prolonged spells of machine-gun firing unbroken by stoppages suggest that the R.F.C. squadrons had been experiencing troubles in this direction.

COMMUNIQUÉ NO. 62

November 12th

Unfavourable weather & Nothing to report.

Casualty: 12 Kite Balloon Section; *15788 1 AM T. H. E. Sawyer, wounded.*

November 13th

On the fronts of the 3rd, 4th and 5th Brigades no flying was possible on account of the weather.

Sixty-eight bombs were dropped by the 1st Brigade. Provin aerodrome and station were attacked. A dump at the station was set on fire, and bombs fell close to aeroplane hangars. Becelaere was attacked by 6 Sqn, 8 bombs falling on billets and starting a fire.

Casualty: Sqn 40, *524 Sgt F. E. Darvell, wounded.*

November 14th

Low clouds and mist made observation very difficult throughout the day. Forty targets were successfully dealt with, with aeroplane observation and 15 with kite balloon observation.

On the front of the Vth Army 157 active batteries were reported by zone call. Most of these were engaged, and many were silenced.

Capt Hudson and 2 Lt Laird, 15 Sqn, brought artillery fire to bear, and fired with their Lewis guns, on 2 parties of hostile infantry in trenches.

November 15th

Low clouds and mist continued to hinder aerial observation ~ Co-operation with artillery was practically impossible throughout the day.

2 Lt R. B. Wainwright and Sgt S. Birch, 20 Sqn, engaged a hostile machine over Gheluvelt. The hostile machine was last seen in a nose dive with its propeller stopped. During the engagement, Sgt Birch was slightly wounded in the arm.

On the night of the 14th/15th twelve 112-pound bombs were dropped by the 1st Brigade at Sallaumines. 6 Sqn dropped bombs on Coucou aerodrome, and on the railway and a train near Menin, at about 3 a.m. on the night of the 14th/15th. This was in retaliation for the hostile bombing of Abeele aerodrome, where no damage was done.

Ten pilots of 18 Sqn carried out a series of successful bombing raids on the night of the 14th/15th instant. Stations, sidings, trains, sheds and searchlights were attacked with bombs, and several of the pilots used their guns against targets. Five bombs were dropped on a moving train near Velu station. Two of the bombs hit the train, which stopped and extinguished all lights.

November 16th

Ninety-eight targets were dealt with by aeroplane observers. Visibility for kite balloons was bad throughout the day, and only one target was registered. On the 4th Brigade front 14 batteries were engaged, of which two were silenced. Many direct hits were recorded on emplacements and trenches.

On the Vth Army front the enemy's infantry in Munich, Pys and Frankfort trenches were engaged by zone call. Casualties were inflicted on a party working at a dump near Miraumont. Several dugouts and trenches were blown up, and others were damaged by enfilade fire. In all, on this front there were 20 shoots on gun positions. A 6-gun battery position was completely destroyed, seven other gun pits were demolished, 19 were damaged, and four large and several minor ammunition explosions were caused. Fifty-one active batteries were reported by zone call, and many of them were silenced by our artillery fire. The 13th Siege Battery with observation by Capt Walser, 4 Sqn, destroyed two gun pits in one position, and all the pits in another 4-gun battery position. In the latter case, all 4 pits were set on fire and finally blew up.

Capt Mackay and Lt Buckeridge observed 100 rounds for the 76th Siege Battery. Five direct hits on a hostile battery caused an explosion of ammunition.

2 Lt C. H. C. Woolven and 2 Lt C. H. Marchant, 25 Sqn, after dropping bombs on Somain, saw an F.E. engaged with a formation of Roland Scouts, and turned to assist. The Germans, reinforced by a second formation from below, attacked 2 Lt Woolven's machine. 2 Lt Marchant continually firing two or three shots at each of the hostile machines to keep them off, drove down one with damaged engine, and another after tracer bullets had entered the pilot's side. Later on, while 2 Lt Marchant was firing over the top plane, he saw one of the German machines fall like a stone in a cloud of smoke. During the fight 2 Lt Marchant fired $1\frac{1}{2}$ double drums and 2 single drums without a jam.

Lt E. L. Benbow, 40 Sqn, attacked an Albatros two-seater near Provin. After firing 15 to 20 rounds at close range, the hostile machine fell like a dead leaf and struck the ground near Annoeullin.

Capt R. S. Maxwell and 2 Lt W. T. Gilson, 20 Sqn, had encounters with 3 hostile machines, all of which they drove off. During the fighting between 600 and 700 rounds of ammunition were fired without jamming.

An offensive patrol of 24 Sqn encountered 3 hostile aeroplanes over Beaulencourt. Lt Pashley opened fire at one machine at 100 yards range. The engine stopped, and the machine did a complete turn and dived east. It was not seen to hit the ground. Capt Long and Lts Begbie, Evans and Begg engaged the other two machines. One of these was brought down and fell into Delville Wood. Capt Long closed with the third, and fired half a drum at close range. The hostile machine returned one burst of fire, doing considerable damage, and then went down emitting large clouds of smoke. Capt Long fired the remainder of his drum at 40 yards range, and the German fell and crashed near the trench lines.

2 Lt V. H. Baker, 41 Sqn, dived at and fired one drum of Buckingham tracer ammunition at a hostile balloon. The balloon was lowered when attacked, but was shortly afterwards put up again.

2 Lt J. W. Francis and Lt F. R. C. Cobbold, 20 Sqn, were attacked by 3 hostile machines between Ypres and Dickebusch. One of the German machines appeared to be hit and dived steeply towards his own lines. Meanwhile, the two other hostile machines heavily engaged the F.E., the controls of which were shot away. 2 Lt Francis turned towards

Poperinghe, and was followed to 6,500 feet by one of the Germans. The F.E. eventually landed and was completely wrecked near Abeele.

Capt Parker and 2 Lt Hervey, 8 Sqn, attacked an Albatros Scout coming from the direction of Puisieux. After a long encounter at close range, the German was forced to land near Pommier. Capt Parker landed alongside him. The machine is very slightly damaged.

An offensive patrol of 60 Sqn engaged a formation of eight German machines over Gommecourt. The hostile formation was dispersed and driven off after a hard fight. The patrol was now attacked from above by a second German formation. The attack was beaten off, but one of our Scouts was seen descending apparently out of control, closely pursued by a hostile machine.

Flt Sub-Lt Goble, R.N.A.S. Sqn, dived on to and fired 25 rounds at a hostile machine over Gommecourt. He got within ten yards of the German, and he had to bank steeply to avoid a collision. The German machine fell sideways, and disappeared out of control. Owing to the presence of more of the enemy, Flt Sub-Lt Goble was unable to watch it to the ground.

An offensive patrol of 32 Sqn dived on to a hostile machine over Grandcourt. The observer ceased firing, and the machine commenced to fall out of control. When last seen, it was 1,000 feet over Bois Loupart. It was undoubtedly badly damaged, and the observer either killed or wounded. Lt Hunt and Capt Jones, of the same patrol, drove down one German machine out of control.

A hostile machine attacked by Flt Sub-Lt Galbraith, R.N.A.S. Sqn, at a range of 15 to 20 yards, was driven down out of control.

On the night of the 15th/16th successful bombing raids were carried out by 18 Sqn. A train was hit at Achiet-le-Grand, and an explosion followed. The railway at Ervillers, sheds near Velu station and transport were also attacked, and machine-guns were used against the trains and transport.

Somain Junction was attacked by day by the 1st Brigade. Eight 112-pound bombs burst on the railway lines, and others hit the station buildings, sidings and a truck. Other bombs were dropped on the station and its vicinity, and a large fire was started. Dumps and a sugar factory were attacked by the 2nd Brigade. The sugar factory was hit, and damage was done to the permanent way. A dump at Courcelles was attacked by the 3rd Brigade. A number of bombs were seen to hit the objective.

Hutments and an ammunition dump in Logeast Wood were also attacked. Observation was difficult, but the majority of the bombs were observed to burst in the wood. Six Martinsydes of 27 Sqn attacked Hirson Station. Bombs were released from a height of 1,000 feet and were seen to hit the sidings. Six coaches were blown off the railway line, and two buildings in the station were destroyed. Other rolling stock was damaged.

Capt Pender and 2 Lt Barker, 15 Sqn, engaged large numbers of infantry in trenches with Lewis gun fire, and reported their position to the artillery by zone call. Lt Acland and Capt Moore, 15 Sqn, opened fire with their Lewis guns on two trenches thickly occupied by the enemy, in one case dispersing them into dug-outs.

Casualties: Sqn 60, *2 Lt H. E. Martin, killed;* **4,** *Lt J. A. G. Brewis, wounded;* **9,** *Lt J. V. Barry, wounded;* **5,** *2 Lt H. B. Rickards, wounded;* **25,** *2 Lt W. W. Fitzgerald, wounded;* **7,** *2 Lt D. A. MacNeill, missing; 2 Lt R. G. R. Allen, missing;* **60,** *Lt D. H. Bacon, missing;* **70,** *Sgt R. S. Evans, missing; and 2 Lt L. F. Struben, missing.*

November 17th

One hundred and thirty-three targets were successfully dealt with by aeroplane observers and 8 with kite balloon observation. On the front of the Ist Army 2 anti-aircraft batteries were successfully engaged and many O.K.s were recorded on trench and other targets by Siege and Field Artillery. On the 2nd and 3rd Brigade fronts artillery with aeroplane observation successfully engaged trench targets, an anti-aircraft and several other hostile batteries. Aeroplanes of the 4th and 5th Brigades co-operated successfully with artillery in counter-battery work. Several pits were destroyed, others were damaged, and ammunition was exploded in many instances.

A patrol of 5 machines of 25 Sqn encountered 8 Rolands and Fokker Scouts over Douai. Three of our machines for various reasons were forced to return to our lines, and for a quarter of an hour Lt Dunlop and Capt Chadwick with their observers maintained a stiff fight, at the end of which only 3 of the hostile machines remained on the scene of the action. The others were driven away and one crashed near Vitry.

An offensive patrol of 29 Sqn, consisting of 8 machines, attacked three of the enemy, one of whom was driven down out of control. During the encounter two of our machines collided while diving at one of the Germans, both the machines falling in hostile territory.

Flt Sub-Lt Trapp, R.N.A.S., drove down a hostile machine out of control near Bertincourt. Being attacked by other hostile aeroplanes, he was unable to see it crash. Flt Sub-Lt Goble, R.N.A.S., drove down a German machine which landed in a field near Bapaume, crashed into a fence and was wrecked.

2 Lt Mare-Montembault, 32 Sqn, attacked and drove down a hostile machine completely out of control. It was seen falling within a few feet of the ground by 15 A.A. Battery. A second hostile machine was forced to land in a field near Bucquoy.

The following raids were carried out on the night of the 16th/17th. 2nd Brigade: Reckem Aerodrome was attacked by 6 Sqn. Four incendiary bombs appeared to demolish a small shed, and a 20-pound bomb hit one of the bigger sheds. Coucou Aerodrome was also attacked by 6 Sqn. A 112-pound bomb hit one of the sheds. Lille Station was attacked by 42 Sqn, and a fire was started. 3rd Brigade: Dumps at Logeast and Biaches were attacked. Several bombs burst around the latter objective and a motor lorry appeared to be hit.

Carvin was attacked by day by the 1st Brigade. Bombs hit the station, railway buildings and houses in the vicinity, doing considerable damage. Provin aerodrome and other places of minor importance were also attacked. Minor bombing raids were carried out by the 2nd and 5th Brigades.

Over 500 photographs were taken during the day.

The balloon of 5 Section was up throughout the night of the 16th/17th, reporting many flashes. 11 Section's balloon broke away early in the morning and drifted north. The observer, 2 Lt Rowbotham, was unhurt and the balloon was eventually wrecked in a tree.

Casualties: Sqn 15, *5385 1 AM A. Allardice, killed;* **3,** *2 Lt R. V. Tivy, wounded;* **18,** *Lt A. V. Shewell, wounded,* **5,** *Lt R. Goudie, wounded;* **22,** *2 Lt M. R. Helliwell, wounded; and 5243 Pte F. D. Cox, wounded;* **24,** *2 Lt W. C. Crawford, missing;* **29,** *2 Lt W. S. F. Saundby, missing; and 2 Capt S. E. Cowan, missing.*

November 18th

No flying.

The following report has been received from an Agent:

> Douai: during the night of October 10th/11th, Allied aeroplanes dropped bombs on the station, which was considerably damaged. A large number of troops were in the station, waiting to entrain. About 100 of them were killed, also a large number of horses. Hangars on the aviation grounds were struck by bombs.

This raid was carried out by aeroplanes of the 3rd Brigade.

19–26 November, 1916

On 23 November an F.E.2d formation of 25 Sqn, led by Capt A. W. Tedder (see Communiqué No. 40) won a notable victory against a superior force of enemy scouts.

Naval Eight Squadron had a very successful week. Flt Sub-Lt R. A. Little, who destroyed an enemy aircraft on 23 November, was credited with 47 victories at the time of his death in action in 1918.

The 18 Sqn F.E.2b (Lts G. Hall and G. Doughty) lost on 20 November was another of von Richthofen's victims.

COMMUNIQUÉ NO. 63

November 19th

In spite of low clouds and showers some useful artillery work was carried out by the 4th and 5th Brigades. Thirty-four targets were dealt with by aeroplane observers.

Artillery of the IVth Army, co-operating with aeroplane of the 4th Brigade, silenced 6 hostile batteries. On the front of the 5th Brigade, artillery with aeroplanes observation inflicted heavy casualties on bodies of infantry. A large number of hostile batteries, which were reported by zone call, were silenced. One gun pit was destroyed, 3 damaged, and 3 ammunition pits were blown up. Trenches were also much damaged.

Some successful contact patrols were carried out by the 5th Brigade. In several instances, casualties were inflicted on the enemy's infantry with machine gun fire from the aeroplanes.

November 20th

The weather was again unfavourable for much aerial work.

On the Vth Army front 1 gun pit was destroyed, 11 others damaged, and 3 ammunition pits blew up. Fifty-eight active hostile batteries were reported by zone call, several were successfully engaged, and a large explosion of ammunition was caused.

The following information was obtained from prisoners of the 57th Field Artillery Regiment:

Artillery losses: They state that losses in personnel varied; they had been heavy in the case of some units; on the other hand the loss in material had been extremely heavy throughout all units.

A large number of guns and howitzers had been put out of action by direct hits, and they ascribed this to the accurate work of our air observation. Gun crews often had to retire and leave their guns for hours at a time. A large number of ammunition dumps had also been blown up recently.

A number of guns have become unserviceable through wear; this especially applies to the 77 mm. field gun. The wear of the latter gun was in excess of the capacity of the *Ersatz Abteilungen* to replace them.

It was due to this fact that the field gun *Abteilungen* from F. A. Regiments on the Verdun front had been transferred to the Somme. In some cases single guns or pairs of guns and howitzers from batteries on other fronts had been brought here. An N.C.O. stated, however, that even these expedients had been unable to keep pace with the wastage incurred.

Casualties: Sqn 15, *2 Lt J. C. Lees, missing; Lt H. T. Clarke, missing;* **18,** *2 Lt G. Hall, missing; and 2 Lt G. Doughty, missing.*

November 21st

A thick mist which lasted all day made aerial work practically impossible, but a little reconnaissance, bombing, and artillery work was carried out.

On the night of the 20th/21st, successful bombing attacks were carried out by the 1st and 5th Brigades. 1st Brigade: 20-pound and incendiary bombs were dropped on billets in Annay, Pont-à-Vendin and Avion. Houses in each place were hit. 5th Brigade: Six machines of 18 Sqn dropped bombs on the railway stations at Achiet-le-Grand and Velu, and near Cambrai. At Cambrai 5 searchlights were directed on to 1 of our machines, which attacked and put out 2 of the lights with machine-gun fire.

Capt F. C. Baker and Lt J. A. Hollis, 18 Sqn, saw a number of lorries on a road. Three bombs were dropped from a height of 500 feet, but missed the transport. The machine then turned and flew over the transport again, and succeeded in dropping 3 bombs into the middle of it. Turning again, the observer fired 1 drum of tracer ammunition at the lorries from a height of 150 feet. The F.E. was fired at by a machine gun using tracer bullets.

November 22nd

A thick mist until late in the forenoon rendered observation difficult.

During the day 38 targets were dealt with by aeroplane obervations, and several successful shoots on trenches and gun positions were carried out.

Hostile Aircraft

Capt Davey and Lt Harrow-Bunn, 11 Sqn, while getting their height in the vicinity of Arras, saw an L.V.G. above them. A burst of fire caused a large column of smoke to issue from the hostile machine, which started to glide towards the lines, closely pursued by the F.E. After Lt Harrow-Bunn had fired two-and-a-quarter double drums, the German lost control and crashed on our side of the lines near Arras. The pilot and observer of the German machine were both killed.

2 Lt Tolhurst and Cpl Johnson, 22 Sqn, drove down a hostile machine out of control near Beugnatre.

Capt Andrews, 24 Sqn, destroyed a hostile machine, which crashed on our side of the lines near Les Boeufs. Another German machine attacked by Lt Pashley, 24 Sqn, was destroyed and fell in our lines east of Eaucourt–l'Abbaye.

Pont-á-Vendin was attacked by the 1st Brigade with forty-eight 20-pound bombs. The railway line and surrounding houses were hit and considerably damaged.

Casualties: Sqn 70, *Lt G. L. Colomb, killed;* **15,** *2 Lt P. McL. Haarer, killed; 2 Lt A. C. Laird, killed;* **70,** *2 Lt T. R. Gilby, wounded;* **3,** *2 Lt E. P. Roberts, wounded; and Capt G. L. Watson, wounded;* **32,** *Lt R. Corbett, missing.*

November 23rd

Successful reconnaissances were carried out by all Brigades. A special reconnaissance was carried out by 2 Lt Smith, 42 Sqn, at a height of 600 feet, for the purpose of reporting as to whether the pavé had been removed from the Lille–Armentiéres road.

One hundred and twenty-eight targets were dealt with by aeroplane observers, and 35 by kite balloons. On the 4th Brigade front 23 direct hits were obtained on batteries, and 21 on trench targets. Eight emplacements were destroyed or damaged, and one explosion was caused. On the 5th Brigade front a bridge over the River Ancre was damaged by fire from a 6-inch Howitzer.

Flt Sgt Halstead and Capt Walser, 4 Sqn, engaged three hostile batteries with the 13th Siege Battery. One battery position was practically destroyed, and in the others, one pit was destroyed, two were damaged, and one lot of ammunition exploded.

2 Lt Richardson and 2 Lt Cotton, 7 Sqn, sent zone call for infantry assembling in the trenches. Effective fire was brought to bear, and, in addition, machine-gun fire was opened on the infantry from 2,000 feet.

Returning from a bombing raid against Brebieres village and station, two offensive patrols of 25 Sqn were heavily engaged with about twenty hostile Scouts. The rear patrol, under Capt Tedder, was attacked by eight

Above: Albatros D I
Below: Sopwith Pup

Above: Albatros C VII
Below: R.E.8

Scouts, who dived at the three highest machines. Lt Morris was hit in the arm at once, and having his aileron control cut at the same time, he planed back to the lines and landed safely near Arras. Sgt Matheson's radiator was hit, and he was also forced to return to the lines and landed safely. The second patrol, under Capt Chadwick, turned to assist Capt Tedder, and a general mêlée ensued, the eight German Scouts being reinforced by about twelve more. At this period of the fight, 2 Lt Moller was hit in the back, but continued fighting until his radiator was hit and his engine seized up. He landed safely near St Eloi. Towards the end of the fight, two De Havillands of 29 Sqn came up and one of them damaged and drove down one of the enemy. Lt Knight, 29 Sqn, reports seeing four hostile machines driven down in a damaged condition. One of these was shot down by Sgt Horrocks and 2 Lt Woollven, and was seen to crash early in the fight. Another was driven down by Sgt Brown and Capt Chadwick, 25 Sqn, and yet another, engaged by Sgt Green and Cpl Bower, 25 Sqn, at close range, went down in a spinning and uncontrolled nose dive. 2 Lt Johnson and Lt Heald drove down another. After fifteen minutes' close fighting the hostile Scouts drew off and the F.E.s returned towards the lines in formation. When near the lines they faced about and prepared to attack the Germans. One or two of the latter dived past the F.E.s firing, but there was no close fighting, and at 4 p.m., Capt Tedder dismissed the formation. Capt Tedder with the two De Havillands remained east of the lines until every hostile machine had gone away.

Hostile aircraft activity on the front of the Vth Army was rather above normal. Nineteen combats took place, mostly in the vicinity of Bapaume.

Flt Sub Lt Little, R.N.A.S., in a Sopwith Scout, drove down a hostile machine in flames. Its destruction is confirmed by Flt Sub Lt Simpson, R.N.A.S. Flt Sub Lt Corbett, R.N.A.S., and Flt Sub Lt Mackenzie, R.N.A.S., whilst escorting a photographic reconnaissance attacked two German machines, both of which they drove down apparently out of control. Flt Sub Lt Galbraith, R.N.A.S., attacked the rear machine of a formation of six Germans. After he had fired about sixty rounds, the left wing of the hostile machine folded up and the German fell out of control.

2 Lt Baines and 2 Lt Fordred, 23 Sqn, were attacked from behind by a single-seater Scout. As the machine passed very close to them, 2 Lt Fordred opened fire and the German fell vertically and crashed near Beugnatre.

An offensive patrol of 32 Sqn, observed two hostile single-seater Scouts attacking a B.E.2c north of Pys. The patrol attacked and one of the Germans, at which Lt Hunt opened fire at close range, fell out of control and with the centre section on fire. The destruction of this machine is confirmed by the 3rd Battery, R.M.A.

A hostile machine attacked by Lt Crichton and 2 Lt Fyfe, 23 Sqn, was driven down near Bancourt. It was not seen to crash.

2 Sqn dropped bombs on Meurchin on the night of the 22nd/23rd instant. Brebieres village and station were attacked by the 1st Brigade.

Casualties: Sqn 29, *Lt N. Hargreaves, killed;* **23,** *2 Lt E. G. Whelon, wounded;* **12,** Kite Balloon Section: *Lt W. E. Hazleton, wounded;* **25,** *Lt A. P. Morris; and 2 Lt F. S. Moller, wounded;* **11,** *Lt A. L. Harrow-Bunn, wounded;* **3,** *2 Lt R. B. Dormer, wounded;* **12 Kite Balloon Section**: *22838 2 AM S. A. Gough; G21271 2 AM A. Carmichael; and 1557 2 AM Lovesay, wounded.*

November 24th

Low clouds and mist, with occasional rain ~ Very little successful flying was accomplished.

During the clear intervals 13 targets were engaged with aeroplane observation and four with balloon observation. Activities of hostile aircraft were normal. Lt Jowett and 2 Lt Hughes, 4 Sqn, were attacked by two machines when returning from a photographic reconnaissance. Their induction pipe was shot through, and they were forced to land near Martinpuich.

Casualties: Sqn 34, *2 Lt B. H. M. Jones, wounded;* **12 Kite Balloon Section**: *16859 2 AM D. W. North, wounded;* **21,** *2 Lt B. N. Blayney, missing.*

November 25th

Nothing to report.

23 November – 2 December, 1916

The briefly-reported combat of 23 November during which Maj L. G. Hawker, V.C., CO of 24 Sqn, was killed culminated in a protracted duel between the British pilot and von Richthofen.

At this time Hawker was credited with nine combat victories and von Richthofen with ten. Hawker was a highly-skilled pilot, flying the more manoeuvrable, but slower aircraft. For minutes the two machines twisted, circled and climbed, avoiding each other's fire. Running short of fuel over enemy territory, Hawker eventually had to break for the British lines, and started to weave his way back, flying at only 150 feet. With the faster aircraft and double the fire power, von Richthofen seized his opportunity, and a bullet from one of his short bursts shot Hawker through the head when he was a mere 50 yards from safety.

COMMUNIQUÉ NO. 64

November 23rd*

On November 23rd, a defensive patrol of 24 Sqn, consisting of Maj Hawker, Capt Andrews, and Lt Saundby, engaged two hostile machines near Bapaume and drove them east. They then saw two strong hostile patrols approaching high up. The patrol was about to retire when Maj Hawker dived and continued the pursuit of the first hostile machines. The De Havillands were at once attacked by the two strong hostile patrols, one of the enemy's machines diving on to the tail of Maj Hawker's De Havilland. This machine was driven off by Capt Andrews, who was then attacked in the rear and having his engine damaged was forced to break off the combat. Lt Saundby drove off one hostile machine which was attacking Capt Andrews and then engaged a second and drove it down out of control. Maj Hawker was last seen engaging a hostile machine at about 3,000 feet.

Casualties: Sqn 24, *2 Lt H. B. Begg and Major L. G. Hawker, V.C., D.S.O., missing;* **RNAS,** *Flt Sub Lt W. H. Hope, missing.*

* The original text has an explanatory note stating that the following two paragraphs were omitted in error from Communiqué No. 63.

November 26th
Very little flying owing to bad weather.

Casualties: Sqn 41, *2 Lt G. S. Deane, missing;* **29,** *2 Lt W. B. Clarke, missing.*

November 27th
Forty-seven targets were engaged with aeroplane observation, and four with kite balloon observation.

2 Lt V. Castle and 1 AM O'Lieff, 1 Sqn, after firing five drums of ammunition at a hostile machine, drove it down out of control. The destruction of this machine is confirmed by escaped Russian prisoners of war.

Flt Sub Lt Goble, R.N.A.S., whilst on offensive patrol, observed a single hostile two-seater machine flying below him. He suspected it as a decoy, and looking behind saw four hostile Scouts. He commenced to dive at the single machine, but after going down about 300 feet he flattened out and opened fire at the rearmost of the four Scouts as they dived past him. The hostile machine went down in flames.

Seclin Station was attacked by the 1st Brigade. A factory was hit and apparently destroyed, and a number of bombs fell on the sidings and on the permanent way near the station. Other damage was done to a château and a dump. The 2nd Brigade dropped bombs on a dump, information of which had been obtained from escaped Russian prisoners of war. A large explosion was caused. St Leger Station was attacked by the 3rd Brigade.

Casualties: Sqn 18, *2073 1 AM O. Watts, killed;* **18,** *Lt F. A. George, wounded;* **60,** *Capt G. A. Parker, missing;* **9,** *Lt J. T. Hanning and Lt V. A. Strauss, missing.*

November 28th, 29th and 30th, December 1st and 2nd
Practically no flying on account of fog.

3 – 10 December, 1916

Bad weather drastically curtailed flying and there was little to report.

The vertical dive technique employed against a 25 Sqn patrol on 4 December was a characteristic of the Halberstadt Scouts. They were of exceptionally strong construction and virtually immune from the structural failures reputed to afflict various other types when flown in this manner.

COMMUNIQUÉ NO. 65

December 3rd
Fog ~ No service flying.

December 4th
Twenty-three targets were successfully engaged with aeroplane observation, and two by kite balloons.

On the IVth Army front twelve hostile batteries were successfully engaged, sixteen direct hits being recorded. The 75th Siege Battery, with observation by Lt Lowcock, 34 Sqn, obtained seven direct hits and several Ys and Zs.

The 1st R.M.A. 15-inch howitzer destroyed the only occupied emplacement in a hostile battery. In another four-gun battery position two pits were destroyed, and a third was badly damaged, probably destroyed. A large explosion of ammunition was caused behind the battery. Aeroplane observation for this battery was by Capt Walser and Lt Bird, who, in the same flight and under indifferent weather conditions, reported other active batteries by zone call, and completed a useful reconnaissance of a number of gun positions.

Lt Young, 4 Sqn, observing for the 80th Siege Battery, located 150 infantry in Miraumont, and reported them by zone call. Accurate fire was brought to bear in about eight minutes, and the infantry were dispersed with casualties. Fire was also brought to bear on a second party of infantry, but results were unobserved.

Capt D. O. Mulholland and Lt E. L. Benbow, 40 Sqn, when on patrol, saw three hostile aeroplanes manoeuvring for position to attack a B.E.2c. Capt Mulholland attacked and destroyed one of the German machines. Lt Benbow got to within 50 feet of a second and fired twenty rounds. The hostile machine turned over and fell to earth in a slow spinning nose dive.

A patrol of 25 Sqn, led by Lt Chadwick, was returning to the lines after dropping bombs on Pont-á-Vendin. The formation, which was well closed up, was approached by four Halberstadter Scouts and one large two-seater machine. Two of the hostile Scouts remained high up, the large machine 1,000 feet above the formation, and the others dived vertically and attacked. 2 Lt Johnson, who was in the middle of the formation, was apparently hit at once, as the F.E. dived straight to the ground and was seen burning in the Bois de Farbus. The other Scout was attacked by Lt Dodson, who drove it down, forcing it to land near Sallaumines. The remaining hostile machines drew off, and the F.E.s continued their patrol.

On the 4th Brigade front aeroplanes were driven down apparently out of control by 2 Lt Clement and 2 Lt Campbell, 22 Sqn, and Capt Duffus and 2 Lt McEntee, 22 Sqn.

Hostile aerial activity on the Vth Army front was considerably above normal, but was confined to the German side of the line. The Vth Army reconnaissance carried out by 23 Sqn, and a bombing raid carried out by the same squadron, were repeatedly attacked.

Flt Sub Lt Little, R.N.A.S., engaged and drove down a hostile machine, which was last seen going down out of control. He forced a second to land in a ploughed field, and drove down a third, which also made a forced landing.

2 Lt Crompton and Flt Sgt Halstead were brought down in our lines as a result of an aerial combat. The pilot was killed and the observer wounded.

Pont-á-Vendin and other places of minor importance were attacked by the 1st Brigade. The results were mostly unobserved owing to mist. 1 Sqn dropped twenty-eight 20-pound bombs on a dump, and 6 Sqn attacked a bomb factory with six 112-pound bombs, obtaining one hit. A successful raid was carried out by the 3rd Brigade against a station and dump at Biache; fifteen 112-pound bombs were seen to burst all round the objectives. 23 Sqn attacked Beugnatre Aerodrome with forty-two 20-pound bombs. The formation was heavily attacked by hostile aircraft, and results were difficult to observe. An explosion was observed to take place on the aerodrome, and several bombs were seen to burst near the sheds. Some bombs fell very near an observation balloon, which was rapidly hauled down.

December 5th to 9th (inclusive)

No service flying took place owing to unfavourable weather.

Casualties (*December 4th*): **Sqn 4,** *31017 2 AM C. W. Newton, killed; 2 Lt H. D. Crompton, killed;* **R.N.A.S.** *Sub Lt Hon. A. Corbett, killed;* **16,** *2 Lt C. F. Woolley Dod, wounded;* **4,** *2 Lt P. J. Long, wounded;* **25,** *Capt A. Higson Smith, wounded; 9279 Cpl A. O. Bower, wounded;* **23,** *2 Lt J. C. Griffiths, wounded;* **4,** *856 Flt Sgt G. W. Halstead, wounded;* **25,** *2 Lt D. S. Johnson and Lt I. Heald, R.N.V.R., missing;* (*December 5th*) **22** Balloon Section: *32125 2 AM R. G. Hughes, died of wounds;* (*December 6th*) **12,** *Capt L. O. Crowther, killed;* **1,** *Capt T. A. Tillard, killed;* **12,** *2 Lt A. B. Fanstone, wounded;* **1,** *Lt D. M. Murdoch, wounded.*

10 – 17 December, 1916

Flying was again restricted by bad weather.

Lt K. L. Caldwell, 60 Sqn, a New Zealander, ended the war with a victory score of 25. During World War II he reached the rank of Air Commodore in the Royal New Zealand Air Force.

Damage to the propeller by objects flying backwards out of the nacelle —as suffered by an F.E.8 on 11 December—was a fairly frequent hazard with pusher aircraft.

COMMUNIQUÉ NO. 66

December 10th

No work was possible on the fronts of the 1st, 2nd or 3rd Brigades.

Capt Mackay, 4 Sqn, completed a successful artillery patrol in low clouds and frequent drizzle. He located and reported by zone call six active hostile batteries, one of which was silenced. A party of 30 infantry were located and dispersed by accurate gun fire opened within six minutes.

Three machines of 2 Sqn, during the night of the 9th/10th, carried out bombing raids. One returned owing to low clouds. One dropped two 112-pound bombs on Salome and Billy respectively, wrecking houses. The third pilot, 2 Lt Wadleigh, lost his way in the low clouds, but eventually came within sight of the sea where the sky was clear. He recognised that he was over Ostend, and dropped two 112-pound bombs, observing the bursts on factories near the canal. He subsequently landed at Dunkirk.

Casualty: R.N.A.S.: *Flt Sub Lt S. V. Trapp, killed.*

December 11th

Thirty-three targets were dealt with by aeroplane observers. Many shoots were interfered with, owing to mist. Seventeen hostile batteries were successfully engaged.

The 1st Brigade had eight indecisive combats. An F.E.8, attacked by two hostile machines, had its petrol tank shot through, and on the return journey to the lines, an ammunition drum flew out of the pocket and hit the propeller. The hostile machines were eventually driven off by a B.E.2e.

A reconnaissance of 11 Sqn encountered a formation of German machines, variously estimated at from 15 to 20. Many combats ensued, and the enemy were eventually dispersed.

An offensive patrol of 60 Sqn, consisting of Lts Caldwell, Daly, Whitehead, Weedon and Meintjes, and led by Capt Grenfell, dived at an Albatros over Dainville. All our machines opened fire, and the German was at once forced to land. Capt Grenfell, who followed the German to the ground, was unfortunately injured on landing. The pilot of the German machine was injured in the foot. Before surrendering, his observer set fire to the machine, but was severely injured in the process, owing to an explosion occurring.

An Albatros, brought down by A.A. fire, fell near our front line trenches near Beaurains. The pilot was killed; the observer was captured.

A hostile machine, attacked by Capt Long and Lt Pashley, 24 Sqn, and Capt Duffus and 2 Lt G. O. McEntee, 22 Sqn, fell in Bapaume and burst into flames. Flt Lt Goble, R.N.A.S., attacked and drove down a German machine east of Bucquoy. Its destruction is not verified.

2 Lt G. W. Dampier and 2 Lt H. C. Barr, 10 Sqn, while on escort to a photographic patrol, were attacked and brought down in our lines. The pilot and observer were killed.

The dumps and railway sidings east and north-east of Mory were attacked by six machines of 23 Sqn. Nineteen bombs were actually seen to hit the dumps, from which large clouds of red and black smoke issued. Lt B. P. G. Hunt, 32 Sqn, who was part of the escort, failed to return. His machine was seen to make a forced-landing, apparently due to engine trouble, in the German lines.

Casualties: Sqn 10, *2 Lt G. W. Dampier and 2 Lt H. C. Barr, killed;* **2,** *2 Lt R. B. Davies, wounded;* **60,** *Capt E. O. Grenfell and 2 Lt E. J. L. W. Gilchrist, wounded;* **4,** *2 Lt S. Willmett, wounded;* **32,** *Lt B. P. G. Hunt, missing.*

December 12th–15th

Very little flying was possible, owing to unfavourable weather ~ There is nothing to report.

December 16th

Twelve targets were successfully dealt with by aeroplane observers. A thick ground mist considerably hindered observation.

The 153rd Siege Battery, with observation by Lt Pemberton, 5 Sqn, caused two explosions in a battery on the south-west edge of Biez Wood. The 16th Heavy Battery and the 113th Heavy Battery, with observation by Lt Clarke, 5 Sqn, registered two hostile batteries. In the first case explosions were seen in two pits.

The enemy's aircraft were fairly active on his own side of the line. On the IInd Army front six indecisive combats took place. In one of these the observer in the hostile machine appears to have been shot. A machine of 12 Sqn, engaged in photography, was attacked near Agny, and brought down. The observer, Lt Murray, was killed, and the pilot, 2 Lt Thomson, slightly wounded. An officer of Y 12 Trench Mortar Battery reports having seen the combat, and states that the hostile machine appeared to be driven down damaged.

A hostile machine, attacked by Capt Knight, 29 Sqn, is reported by anti-aircraft observers as having been brought down, apparently out of control.

There were 9 other indecisive combats on the IIIrd Army front.

6 Sqn dropped four 112-pound bombs on hutments at Holle Bosch. One hut was completely demolished, and another bomb fell amongst the huts. 20 Sqn dropped one 336-pound bomb on hutments at Becelaere. The result was unobserved.

Casualties: Sqn 12, *Lt H. G. Murray, killed; 2 Lt Thomson, wounded;* **16,** *Lt J. P. Greenwood, wounded.*

17–23 December, 1916

This was another period of limited flying activity due to the bad weather.

Capt T. Leigh-Mallory, 5 Sqn, commanded 12 Group, Fighter Command, during the Battle of Britain, 1940. As Air Chief Marshal Sir Trafford Leigh-Mallory, he was killed in a flying accident towards the end of World War II.

Capt A. G. Knight, 29 Sqn, was shot down and killed by von Richthofen on 20 December during a battle in which four other D.H.2s were forced down, in the British lines, by Jasta 2's Albatroses.

COMMUNIQUÉ NO. 67

December 17th, 18th, 19th
No flying ~ *Nothing to report.*

Casualties: Sqn 3, *11378 1 AM A. Rogers, killed;* **3,** *7768 2 AM R. Oxley, wounded.*

December 20th
Successful reconnaissances were carried out by all Brigades.

Eighty-five targets were successfully engaged with aeroplane observation.

A hostile anti-aircraft battery was hit by heavy artillery of the Ist Army, and Siege artillery obtained 9 direct hits on 3 gun pits, causing an explosion of ammunition. Nine direct hits were obtained on other targets. With aeroplane observation by the 2nd Brigade, artillery obtained 2 direct hits on trench mortar emplacements. Artillery of the IIIrd Army, working with aeroplanes of the 3rd Brigade, secured 3 direct hits on hostile batteries. Artillery co-operating with aeroplanes of the 4th Brigade, obtained 13 direct hits on hostile batteries and trenches.

The 152nd Siege Battery, with observation by Capt Leigh-Mallory and 2 Lt Parker, 5 Sqn, either destroyed or badly damaged 3 pits of a gun battery. 2 Lt Arnold and 2 Lt Clarke, 5 Sqn, observed for the 47th Siege Battery. Seven explosions were caused in a hostile battery position. 2 Lt Mayo and Lt Pemberton, 5 Sqn, observed for the 153rd Siege Battery, an explosion and the destruction of 1 pit in a hostile battery resulting.

The 153rd Siege Battery, with observation by Capt Johnson and Cpl Wilson, 5 Sqn, destroyed 1 pit and damaged 2 others in a hostile battery.

Lt E. L. Benbow, 40 Sqn, engaged an Albatros south of Lens. He dived at it and opened fire at a range of about 70 feet under its tail. The hostile machine was destroyed.

Twenty-six combats took place on the front of the IIIrd Army.

A patrol of 11 Sqn was very heavily engaged by 9 Albatros Scouts. A reconnaissance of 11 Sqn attacked 4 hostile machines near Monchy, 1 of which was driven down out of control by Capt Quested and Lt Lutyens.

On the front of the IVth Army, 1 hostile machine was driven down damaged.

2 Lt Pateman and 2 Lt Macaulay, 15 Sqn, engaged and drove down a Fokker biplane near Beaumont Hamel.

Flt Lt Hervey, Flt Sub Lt Soar, Flt Sub Lt Todd, and Flt Sub Lt Little, all of the R.N.A.S. Sqn, had encounters with, and drove off, hostile machines.

The dump at the Sugar Factory north-west of Vraucourt was successfully attacked by machines of 23 Sqn. Many direct hits were observed and several explosions caused. Large clouds of smoke were seen to issue from the Factory. Our machines drove off repeated attacks by hostile aircraft, and all returned safely.

Seven hundred and forty-one photographs were taken during the day.

Capt Leask and 2 Lt Adkin, 16 Sqn, carried out a successful contact patrol in connection with an infantry attack made by the Ist Army.

Casualties: Sqn 11, *Lt W. O. Boger, wounded;* **29,** *2 Lt W. K. M. Britton, wounded;* **18,** *2 Lt L. G. D'Arcy and 2 Lt R. C. Whiteside, missing; Lt C. H. Windrum and Lt J. A. Hollis, missing; Lt R. Smith and Lt N. Fiske, missing;* **29,** *Capt A. G. Knight, missing.*

December 21st

Six targets were engaged with aeroplane observation. The 72nd Siege Battery with observation by 2 Lt D. W. Davis and 2 Lt W. M. V. Cotton, 7 Sqn, damaged one gun pit and obtained 4 direct hits on the position. This machine failed to return.

Casualties: Sqn 15, *Lt H. Brereton, killed; 2 Lt J. P. Morkham, wounded;* **34,** *Lt H. M. Yeatman, wounded;* **7,** *Lt D. W. Davis and 2 Lt W. M. V. Cotton, missing.*

December 22nd

In spite of low clouds, strong wind, and rain, thirteen targets were engaged with aeroplane observation, and an explosion of ammunition was caused by artillery of the Vth Army.

December 23rd

Nothing to report.

24–31 December, 1916

The last few days of the year saw a general improvement in the weather and a limited resumption of routine operations, but 1916 ended on a quiet note.

The Royal Flying Corps now had 38 active squadrons in France, comprising some 700 aircraft. Half the squadrons were employed on artillery-spotting and bombing duties and the other half were fighter-reconnaissance and fighting Scout units. Of the latter, five were flying the obsolescent D.H.2 and F.E.8 and only two—60 (Nieuports) and 8 R.N.A.S. (Sopwith Pups) were really effective against the German Albatros and Halberstadt machines. The British squadrons had a fighting strength of 18 aircraft. The first R.F.C. Sopwith Pup squadron (54) arrived in France on 25 December but was not yet operational.

Germany had 33 Jagdstaffeln, flying a mixture of Fokker biplanes, Halberstadts and the Albatros DI/DII, though it is doubtful whether these were yet up to their full establishment of 14 aircraft per squadron. It is not known how many Albatros Scouts were in service at the end of the year, but the figure was probably somewhere between 150 and 200.

General Trenchard, G.O.C., Royal Flying Corps, was fully aware of the growing enemy challenge and had already made several forceful pleas to the War Office for bigger supplies of improved British fighters.

COMMUNIQUÉ NO. 68

December 24th

Forty targets were successfully engaged with aeroplane observation.

Four direct hits were obtained by Heavy Artillery, co-operating with aeroplanes of the 1st Brigade, and Siege Artillery obtained 20 direct hits on 5 gun pits, and 2 direct hits on trench targets. Three direct hits were also obtained on trench targets by Field Artillery.

With aeroplane observation by the 2nd Brigade, artillery successfully engaged 8 hostile batteries; 28 direct hits were obtained on hostile batteries and trench targets. One explosion of ammunition was caused. Artillery co-operating with aeroplanes of the 3rd Brigade secured 2 direct hits on enemy targets. Artillery of the IVth Army, co-operating with aeroplanes of the 4th Brigade, successfully engaged 2 hostile batteries

During the day some successful photographic work was accomplished, and bombs were dropped on places of military importance by machines of the 1st, 2nd and 5th Brigades.

Casualties: Sqn 1, *Cpl G. Dinnage, killed;* **23,** *Lt W. B. Kellogg and 2 Lt T. B. Jones, wounded.*

December 25th

On the day of the 25th no flying was possible.

On the night of the 24th/25th, bombs were dropped on Pont-á-Vendin, Douvrin, and Cite St Theodore by machines of the 1st Brigade. Four bombs were seen to explode in Pont-á-Vendin.

Vaulx-Vraucourt was attacked by aeroplanes of the 5th Brigade. One house was set on fire. Machine-gun fire was opened into the villages of Vaulx-Vraucourt and Grevillers.

December 26th

Co-operating with aeroplanes of the 1st Brigade, Siege Artillery obtained 12 direct hits on hostile batteries, and caused an explosion of ammunition. One direct hit was obtained on another target. Three direct hits were secured by Field Artillery on 2 targets.

Artillery of the IInd Army successfully engaged 2 hostile batteries with aeroplane observation. One gun pit was hit, and 2 explosions of ammunition caused. Eight direct hits were obtained on enemy targets by artillery co-operating with aeroplanes of the 3rd Brigade. Artillery of the IVth Army, co-operating with aeroplanes of the 4th Brigade, successfully engaged 11 hostile batteries, obtaining 21 direct hits. Five emplacements were damaged, and 2 explosions caused. A working party was engaged and dispersed under zone call.

Some successful artillery work was accomplished with aeroplane observation by the 5th Brigade.

A hostile machine engaged by Capt Long and Lt Sedgwick, both of 24 Sqn, was driven down in a damaged condition.

2 Lt Zink and 2 Lt Mayhew, 18 Sqn, engaged a hostile machine near Velu. The German aeroplane broke off the combat and dived vertically. 2 Lt Macdonald and 2 Lt Smith, 18 Sqn, engaged and drove down a hostile machine out of control. A German aeroplane attacked by 2 Lt Lewis and 2 Lt Royffe, 18 Sqn, was driven down out of control near Velu.

Flt Sub Lt Compston, R.N.A.S. Sqn, engaged several Albatros Scouts, one of which he drove down out of control, and the rest broke off the combat. A German machine engaged by Flt Cmdr Huskisson, R.N.A.S. Sqn, near Ypres, was hit and fell in a series of stalls and appeared to be absolutely out of control. Flt Lt Croft, R.N.A.S. Sqn, engaged two hostile machines near Bapaume, one of which fell apparently out of control.

Lt R. W. P. Hall and 2 Lt E. F. W. Smith, 9 Sqn, on a B.E.2e, were attacked from behind by a Halberstadt. The B.E.2e opened fire with the rear gun. When within about 90 feet range the German pilot was hit, and the machine dived to earth and crashed.

Places of military importance behind the German lines were attacked by aeroplanes of the 1st, 2nd and 5th Brigades. A number of bombs dropped by machines of the 5th Brigade were seen to burst in Vaulx-Vraucourt.

Casualties: Sqn 46, *Capt J. W. W. Nason and Lt C. A. F. Brown, killed;* **18,** *2 Lt G. A. Masters, wounded;* **5,** *2 Lt W. H. Hubbard, wounded;* **24,** *2 Lt E. Lewis, missing;* **5,** *2 Lt F. N. Insoll and 2 Lt H. E. Arnold, missing.*

December 27th

Eighty-six targets were successfully engaged with aeroplane observation.

Artillery of the Ist Army, with aeroplane observation, obtained 12 direct hits on battery and other positions. Two direct hits on enemy targets were obtained by Field Artillery.

Co-operating with aeroplanes of the 2nd Brigade, artillery successfully engaged 9 hostile batteries. Four gun pits were hit, and 2 explosions of ammunition caused.

Artillery of the IIIrd Army, with aeroplane observers, obtained 14 direct hits on hostile batteries. One explosion of ammunition was caused. In co-operation with aeroplanes of the 4th Brigade, artillery successfully engaged 20 targets, and caused 2 explosions of ammunition. With observation by aeroplanes of the 5th Brigade, artillery obtained 8 direct hits on gun positions; 3 gun pits were damaged, and an explosion of ammunition was caused.

During the day, 2 Lt R. B. Wainwright and 2 Lt H. R. Wilkinson, 20 Sqn, engaged and drove down 2 hostile machines, both of which are believed to have been badly damaged. The presence of other German aeroplanes prevented the fate of the 2 enemy machines being ascertained. 2 Lt J. Blackwood and 2 Lt F. H. Bronskill, 20 Sqn, engaged 2 Halberstadt biplanes, 1 of which was destroyed near Zonnebeke, and the other driven off.

Twenty-one combats took place on the front of the IIIrd Army.

Two German aeroplanes were brought down and seen to crash by 11 Sqn. One of these was destroyed by Capt Quested and 2 Lt Dicksee. A third hostile machine was forced to land in a field.

An offensive patrol of 29 Sqn encountered a formation of hostile machines over Adinfer Wood, and drove one down out of control.

A German machine engaged by 2 Lt J. V. Aspinall and 2 Lt J. M. R. Miller, 22 Sqn, was driven down and landed in a field west of Ruyaulcourt.

Capt S. H. Long, 24 Sqn, engaged and drove down a German machine out of control.

A German aeroplane which was attacked by 2 Lt Copeland and Sgt Weare, 7 Sqn, was driven down out of control between Pys and Miraumont.

Seven hundred and thirty-seven photographs were taken during the day.

Bombs were dropped by machines of the 1st and 5th Brigades on places of military importance.

Casualties: Sqn 9, *2 Lt E. F. W. Smith, killed;* **5,** *Lt C. W. H. Parker, killed;* **9,** *2 Lt R. P. C. Freemantle, wounded;* **2,** *Capt J. R. Gould, wounded;* **5,** *2 Lt E. F. Jones, wounded;* **11,** *2 Lt H. J. H. Dicksee, wounded.*

December 28th

Twenty-eight targets were dealt with by aeroplane observers. In co-operation with aeroplanes of the 1st Brigade, Heavy Artillery obtained 3 direct hits on gun pits. Siege Artillery obtained 9 direct hits on gun pits, four of which were destroyed and two badly damaged. A trench target was also hit. Four hostile batteries were successfully engaged by artillery co-operating with aeroplanes of the 2nd Brigade. Two gun pits were hit, and 2 explosions of ammunition caused.

Artillery of the IVth Army, co-operating with aeroplanes of the 4th Brigade, obtained several direct hits on 3 trench points. With observation by aeroplanes of the 5th Brigade, artillery successfully engaged 6 hostile batteries, and obtained 8 direct hits on gun positions. Four gun pits were damaged, and an explosion of ammunition caused.

Auchy and Lievin were attacked by machines of the 1st Brigade. In both places buildings were hit. Bombs were dropped on Miraumont, and a dump in Rossignol Wood by aeroplanes of the 5th Brigade.

Casualties: 14 Balloon Company: *22177 1 AM L. V. Bulmer, wounded; 24208 A/Cpl J. Chappell, wounded; 46641 2 AM L. Hadley, wounded; 40941 2 AM J. Newman, wounded;* **Sqn 27,** *Capt H. Spanner, missing.*

December 29th
No flying ∽ Nothing to report.

December 30th
Very little work was done owing to bad weather.

Artillery of the Second Army, with aeroplane observation, engaged three hostile batteries. Two gun pits were hit.

Bombs were dropped on trenches and places of military importance by machines of the 1st Brigade. One bomb dropped in Cite de l'Abattoir was seen to burst on a house.

Index of Names